Power in Projects,
Programs and Portfolios

Project management is nowadays considered as a competitive strength for an organization and has therefore become increasingly important. The book *'Power in Projects, Programs and Portfolios'* describes the project management as a holistic management discipline, differing from the traditional view of regarding it purely as a project management tool. Based on their many years' hands on practice, the authors have succeeded in giving a comprehensive telling of project management's history, framework, planning, leadership and communication in a straightforward and easy to adopt manner. This book could be a valuable inspiration and instruction for both fresh and experienced project managers as well as for the different levels of line managers who have direct or indirect influence on project management in their organization.

Fei Chen, Vice President, Haldor Topsøe A/S

Fei Chen has more than 20 years of experience in innovation management and general management from different industries, such as biotech, food, medical device and water treatment. She has a broad educational background: MSc. From Zhejiang University, China, Ph.D. from the Technical University of Denmark, Copenhagen and Stanford Executive Program, Stanford Graduate School of Business.

Just about the worst affliction an organisation running projects can suffer from is viewing project management as a one-size-fits-all approach to managing projects. In *Power in Projects, Programs and Portfolios*, Olsson and Attrup prescribe the antidote – a holistic view.

Unlike most texts on project and program management, this book systematically walks you through the different project types and with those differences place different demands on the project manager in terms of objective setting, stakeholder management and communication, planning, organisation, leadership and governance.

Olsson and Attrup's book offers a refreshing and holistic perspective and is a must-read for anyone involved in project design, execution and governance. It is one of those books that once read will become one of the key references that you will return to repeatedly.

Søren Porskrog, Program Manager, Damco International (a Maersk-company)

Søren Porskrog has more than 15 years of experience in Innovation & Strategy Execution. He has been Project Director and external Program Manager at companies like Novo Nordisk, Nordea, Siemens and several Maersk companies. He has been a research fellow at Cranfield University's International Centre for Program Management and has a broad educational background: MBA, Henley Business School, Executive Development Program, Stanford University and several Graduate Diplomas from Copenhagen Business School.

John Ryding Olsson and Mette Lindegaard Attrup

Power in Projects, Programs and Portfolios

Achieve project excellence and create change with strategic impact

DJØF Publishing Copenhagen
2015

John Ryding Olsson and Mette Lindegaard Attrup
Power in Projects, Programs and Portfolios
Achieve project excellence and create change with strategic impact

First edition 2015

© 2015 Worldwide rights owned by DJØF Publishing, Copenhagen, Denmark.

All rights reserved.
No part of this publication may be reproduced,
stored in a retrieval system, or transmitted in any
form or by any means – electronic, mechanical,
photocopying, recording or otherwise – without
the prior written permission of the Publisher.

Illustrations: Yogi
English translation by Jenifer Lloyd
Cover designed by Bo Helsted

Printed and bound in Great Britain by
Marston Book Services Ltd, Oxfordshire

ISBN 978-87-574-3409-5

Sold and distributed in Scandinavia by:
DJØF Publishing
Copenhagen, Denmark
Email: forlag@djoef.dk
www.djoef-forlag.dk

Sold and distributed in North America by:
International Specialized Book Services (ISBS)
Portland, USA
Email: orders@isbs.com
www.isbs.com

Sold in all other countries by:
The Oxford Publicity Partnership Ltd
Towcester, UK
Email: djof@oppuk.co.uk
www.oppuk.co.uk

Distributed in all other countries by:
Marston Book Services
Abingdon, Oxon, UK
Email: trade.orders@marston.co.uk
www.marston.co.uk

Contents

Introduction 7
About the authors 13
Structure of the book 14
Overview of tools 19

Chapter 1. History of the Project 23
1.1. The history of the project – from stick to carrot 24
1.2. The project as an organizational method 30
1.3. The project as a management technique 37
1.4. Can line management be a temporary work form? 43

Chapter 2. The Project Work Form 49
2.1. Features of the project 50
2.2. Project types 57
2.3. The projects in the organization 77
2.4. Reflections on the project work form 84

Chapter 3. What is the objective of the project? 89
3.1. Where are we going, what is our aim? 90
3.2. The objective, project cycle and uncertainty 98
3.3. Development of the objective 102
3.4. Reflections on objective-setting 114

Chapter 4. Who will use the results? 117
On managing the project stakeholders 117
4.1. Special interests at stake 118
4.2. Reflections on stakeholder management 143

Chapter 5. The Project Plan 147
5.1. The principles behind a good project plan 148
5.2. Planning the project within the team 167
5.3. Project types and planning methods 176
5.4. Planning in an uncertain world 184
5.5. Risk analysis 195
5.6. Reflections on planning 204

Chapter 6. Project organization 209
6.1. Roles within the project organization 210
6.2. Reflections on organizing the individual project 224

Chapter 7. The Project Manager as Captain 227
About active steering and follow-up 227
7.1. The project plan as a steering tool 228
7.2. Follow-up in the project 230
7.3. Steering the project 243
7.4. Meeting facilitation 252
7.5. Reflections on project follow-up and steering 262

Chapter 8. Communication and change 265
8.1. Projects often suffer when it comes to communication 266
8.2. Common mistakes in project communication – if there is any
    communication at all 275
8.3. Targeted communication throughout the entire project 277
8.4. Project branding 287
8.5. Communication that supports change 296
8.6. Reflections on project communication 313

Chapter 9. Leading the Team 317
9.1. From management to leadership 318
9.2. Forming the project team 322
9.3. Motivation and feedback 340
9.4. Coaching or, rather, a coaching management style 348
9.5. Conflict management 357
9.6. Reflections on team leadership 372

Chapter 10. Project Governance. Management of multiple projects 377
10.1. Project governance 379
10.2 Portfolio overview 382
10.3 Well-defined roles and distribution of responsibility 387
10.4 Solid basis for decision-making – prioritizing projects 402
10.5. Common language – project model, methodology and KPIs 411
10.6. Development of the organization toward Project Excellence 425
10.7. Reflections on project governance and the project work form ... 434

International Bibliography 437
Index 441

Introduction

Power in Projects, Programs and Portfolios is the best-selling project management book Denmark, and we have decided to launch the book internationally. The book is dealing with both classic project management disciplines, but also looks in depth at areas such as change management, change communication, benefit tracking, program management and portfolio management. The book represents the Scandinavian way of leadership in project management.

Project management, today, is a leadership profession primarily aimed at managing and creating change. Change that is both in line with the organization's strategy and has a significant impact on the organization and the world in which it operates. Recent years have seen a pronounced increase in the need for professional management of projects and the project portfolio as a whole, as success with projects becomes evermore vital for the development and survival of organizations. It's no longer enough for projects to 'just' produce a set of deliverables. They are expected to make a genuine difference within the organization and in the world. Consequently, project management is not just about project managers, it's about how senior management manages the portfolio.

It takes power – strength, drive and energy – within the individual project as well as within the organization's programs and entire project portfolio. And it places new demands on both the project manager and senior management.

Today's project management extends beyond individual management tools. The challenge for project managers is to both manage and communicate – via personal presence and by employing effective project management tools.

Power in Projects, Programs and Portfolios takes up this challenge. This book pays equal consideration to project management and tools while integrating both aspects. We know that tools won't produce results without a good craftsman to wield them. While a good craftsman knows that it takes the right tools to achieve the best results. Our aim with this book is therefore not only to highlight the management tasks in projects, but also to show how to use tools in the execution of these management tasks.

We also wanted to write a book that covers senior management's involvement in the management of the entire portfolio of projects. The individual project should underpin the overall strategy and policy priorities. This book explores how this correlation can be established by breaking down the strategy into programs and projects, and how the value of the portfolio as a whole can be managed. We also describe the new trends of breaking projects down into smaller projects that are coordinated more closely by means of a professional program management team – an approach that requires more project managers and greater involvement by senior management in the management of the portfolio.

This book employs a liberal definition of project work that comprises the new project types seen in both the private and public sectors as well as the overall management issues concerning program and portfolio management.

With *Power in Projects, Programs and Portfolios*, we have taken a more holistic approach to project work and project management, which is informed by four specific trends:

1. More and more projects involve a high degree of change management. This increases demand for project management skills that extend beyond the traditional administrative and management tools.
2. The spread of the project as a concept to new sectors and subsequent development of new project types, e.g. in the public sector.
3. Interest in projects has 'climbed' to the top tiers of management. Project work has evolved from a work form to a management technique.
4. Sweeping demands for change make it necessary to break down the organization's strategy into programs and projects, with change taking place via the projects.

The project manager used to be primarily a technician – the highly organized expert who knew all about Gantt charts, activity-based network planning, successive calculation and the like. Today, we are seeing a shift toward viewing the project manager as someone who can motivate, communicate, operate in the political game and resolve conflicts.

Increased demand for management skills

We are also seeing a corresponding increase in the complexity of the projects, as both society and organizations become more complex and dynamic. Projects represent change and change requires management. Being able to administer and handle the technical aspects is no longer enough. When we talk to project managers and their superiors, they all say the same thing: when a project fails or runs into problems, it is rarely due to technical or planning issues. Instead, it is the human and organizational aspects, such as a lack of motivation among the project team, insufficient understanding of and support for the project among management and lack of acceptance of the outcome among the users. The project manager needs to get out of the office and concentrate on motivating the team, handling stakeholders and calling attention to his or her project internally and externally. This doesn't mean that traditional project management tools are superfluous, but rather that they should be used as integral and active elements in the management of projects.

We also increasingly meet an interest in project manager certification, as both project managers, who participate in our many courses and workshops, and organizations seeking to make project management a career path want to be able to document their skills. The problem for many firms is that the talented, heavy-hitting project managers disappear into line management, as that is where the prestige is – measured by titles and fringe benefits like office windows and company cars. However, we find that this somewhat antiquated assessment of job prestige is changing; in the future, professional and personal challenges will be valued higher. One day, project management and line management may no longer be two separate career paths, but rather two management techniques that managers in development-oriented firms must master.

Spread of the project as a concept and new project types

There is also a need to refine the project management literature to match the many different project types that exist today. Much project management literature is still characterized by having been written for building and construction projects, where it is possible to predict, control and manage many elements. Today, the project as a concept has spread to many other sectors and now comprises quite a few project types that are less predictable and oriented more toward stakeholder management. Examples of this are projects in political organizations, projects aiming to create organizational change and many IT projects.

One reason for the spread of the project as a concept is a change in the language used. Whereas in the past government agencies would appoint a working group or a committee, now they appoint a project team.

However, the use of projects is also about embracing the advantages of organizing development tasks and other specialized tasks into projects.

Interest in projects has climbed the organizational ladder

Once the exception in many firms, projects have now become the standard. This is due to, among other things, a significant increase in the rate of change in both public and private-sector organizations.

As a result, the people who manage or work on projects are not the only ones interested in project work. The organization's ability to execute projects has also caught the eye of the people upstairs as a means of executing change, having a genuine impact and realizing the strategy.

An increasing share of the resources in an organization are now devoted to projects. Areas such as portfolio management and program management are therefore becoming significant fields of activity for senior and executive management.

Upper management's interest in projects also means a growing understanding of the fact that it is not enough just to gear the individual project manager to handle the challenges. Without the right organizational framework within which to develop, he or she will only have limited scope of action. This book is therefore also relevant as an element in the process of helping an organization achieve excellence in project execution.

With this book, we want to inspire everyone who works hard every day to execute projects and make organizations more project oriented. We have attempted to combine tools for project management with the management perspective and use both aspects as a basis for concrete and useful advice that can be put into practice on a daily basis.

Acknowledgements

The ideas presented in this book are a concentration of experiences, discussions and concepts contributed by clients and colleagues at Implement Consulting Group P/S. Over the years, Implement Consulting Group P/S has helped gear many private and public-sector organizations to be more project oriented and thus to excel at development. During the process, we have boosted the skills of many thousands of project managers and senior managers. Much of the inspiration for this book comes from experiences and stories we have collected while working with our innovative clients.

In particular, we would like to thank the following people, who have contributed with inspiration and invaluable criticism: Niels Ahrengot, Henriette Divert Andersen, Claus Sehested, Michael Kræmmer, Michael Ehlers, Mikkel Lau, Henrik Bachmann, Herik Sonnenberg and Søren Dahlgren Bergsøe.

Our special thanks also go to Marianne Thastrup, who has so skillfully helped with the adaptation of the manuscript; and to Ida Præstegaard for adapting the toolbox.

About the authors

John Ryding Olsson holds a BSc and BCom. Since 1996, he has been a partner at the Scandinavian consultancy firm Implement Consulting Group P/S, where he helps make organizations and firms more project oriented. He started his career in 1977 as project manager and later manager of R&D at Medimatic A/S. In 1986, he became managing director and later co-owner of Dansensor System A/S (now PBI Dansensor A/S). Throughout the 1990s, he worked as a consultant in project management and management of new product development at the Danish Technological Institute and Sant + Bendix, then part of PricewaterhouseCoopers. He has been chair of the new product development association Dansk Forening for Produktudvikling and member of the board of the Danish Project Management Association. Currently, he is an assessor for the International Project Management Association and one of the four Lead Assessors in Denmark who have contributed to the development of the system. He is the co-author of several books on project management and new product development.
https://dk.linkedin.com/in/johnrydingolsson

Mette Lindegaard Attrup holds a master's degree in Danish and rhetoric and is Executive Assistant and Communication Partner at Novo Nordisk A/S. From 2002 to 2007, Mette was a management consultant at Implement Consulting Group P/S, and prior to that a project manager at Advice Kommunikations- og ledelsesrådgivning A/S. These positions provided Mette with in-depth experience in strategy implementation, change processes and project management. Since 2000, Mette has been a guest lecturer and supervisor at the University of Copenhagen, where she teaches change communication and organizational theory. Mette has contributed to, among other publications, a Danish anthology on Appreciative Inquiry.

Structure of the book

Our focus in *Power in Projects, Programs and Portfolios* has been to inspire practitioners and students to take a more holistic and management-oriented approach to projects. The book seeks to inspire, present new perspectives and encourage a desire to work with projects, as well as being a practical guide with concrete tools that you can use in your work with projects.

Toolbox in electronic format
A key element of the book is the link to a powerful toolbox on the website of this book. In addition to the tools introduced here, it gives you some additional tools. The aim of the link is two-fold: First, it's easier to carry with you than a heavy book. Second, it presents the tools in electronic format, ready for use directly on your PC. At the beginning of each chapter, there is a reference to the relevant tools.

One case story to illustrate theories and tools
We also show you how the theories and tools introduced in each chapter can be used in practice, i.e. how to orchestrate project management as a project manager and thus conduct yourself as a leader. We do this by means of a single case story that runs through the entire book. The case is about the introduction of improved customer service in a firm with departments in several countries. The case and the people are fictitious, but based on experiences from our own projects as well as projects where we have coached the project managers. We use this project as a case because provides an excellent demonstration of the complexities that make up so many projects. It has aspects of IT, organizational and procedural changes, while also touching on existing professional divides, procedures and cultures. While we have done our best, it is, of course, impossible to illustrate all the complexities of such a project in the brief fragments of the case story as presented here.

You may wonder why implementation has not been given its own chapter in the book. This is not because the implementation phase has been left out, quite the contrary. After all, at Implement Consulting Group P/S, we have a name to live up to. Instead, we want to emphasize implementation, not as an independent final phase in a project, but rather as an action that runs continuously throughout the entire project and is woven into every activity. We want to promote the incorporation of implementation in the organization of projects with steering committees, reference groups and project teams – and in the preparation of stakeholder and risk analysis and the communication plan. In every single part of the project, we want to assess the best way of incorporating implementation to produce the necessary knowledge, quality and ownership among stakeholders, thus ensuring the success of the project.

Implementation – not a separate phase

The book's chapters are organized as follows:

Contents of each chapter

Chapter 1 on the *History of the Project* presents an overview of the last 3,500 years in projects: from construction projects, like the pyramids and the Colosseum, to today's many different types of projects, including organizational change projects, IT projects and policy projects in national or local government. This chapter also discusses the evolution of the project as a concept from its emergence in the 1950s until today. We explore how the project has developed from initially being viewed as a work form, then as an organizational method, until now, where a sharp focus on development and consequently on projects has transformed it into a management technique. Finally, we consider the future of project work: are projects just a transitory phenomenon?

History of the Project

In Chapter 2, *The Project Work Form*, we provide some insight into which tasks are most suited to projects and which are best performed within the operations organization. Not everything can be a project. We also give an overview of six different types of projects. The aim is to develop the language we use in connection with projects, as the various types of projects pre-

The Project Work Form

15

sent different challenges and require different management techniques. The six project types are: 1) Engineering and construction projects; 2) Product development projects; 3) Research and technology development projects; 4) System and IT projects; 5) Organizational change projects; and 6) Analyses and basis for decision-making. Finally, this chapter provides an overview of various designs for organizations that need to handle both development and operations.

What is the project objective? In chapter 3, *What is the objective of the project?*, we describe how the overall objective can be defined by the project purpose, project deliverables and success criteria. How to define a clear objective despite – or even because of – the turbulence in the world. Objectives are a key management tool for the project manager, for instance when negotiating contracts and reconciling expectations, providing direction and focus, and promoting motivation and participation among stakeholders. Setting objectives is also elaborated upon in relation to the six project types introduced in Chapter 2.

Who will use the results? Chapter 4, *Who will use the results?*, presents ways to handle the project stakeholders. Special emphasis is placed on the management task in relation to the stakeholders. The message here is that the project manager needs to get out of the office in order to handle the stakeholders. This chapter introduces a concrete method of identifying and prioritizing stakeholders and determining how to deal with them. Further, it describes how to segment stakeholders into manageable, homogenous groups, thus improving your chances of handling them appropriately.

The Project Plan Chapter 5 deals with *The Project Plan*. This chapter covers the challenge of designing a plan in such a way that enables full control over the project – but without losing project flexibility or the project manager being lulled into thinking he or she has now calculated the future of the project. We present the principles behind good planning with special focus on using the project plan in a management context. The planning methods vary depending on the type of project and how predictable and manageable it is; an area that is also covered in this chapter. Finally, at the end of the chapter, we provide some insight into estimating time consumption and briefly introduce the concepts of risk analysis and risk management.

Chapter 6, *Project Organization*, deals with the challenges associated with creating the right organization for each individual project. That is, ensuring an optimal framework for the project through conscious decisions regarding the composition of the steering committee, project team or reference groups. The chapter also discusses the distribution of responsibilities among the individual players within the project organization. Finally, focus is aimed at the project manager's duty to clarify expectations and define roles upwards in the steering committee and outwards to the hearing committees.

Project Organization

In Chapter 7, *The Project Manager as Captain*, we take a closer look at the project manager's responsibilities for keeping the project on the right track and following up on the work carried out within the project. We look at how the plan can be utilized actively in the management process and how the project manager can establish a foundation and a structure that increases the likelihood of agreed deadlines, quality requirements etc. being met by the project participants. We also discuss the project manager's responsibility for monitoring the planned deliverables. Finally, we cover meeting management, as projects are organized around many different meetings, for instance with the steering committee and project team. Competent meeting management is therefore a vital discipline for the project manager.

The Project Manager as Captain

In Chapter 8, *Communication and Change*, we take a look at communication within the project and its importance in the implementation of change. This chapter focuses on the formal communication in the project, such as information material about the project, dialog meetings and communication to management, as well as the informal communication, like rumors, receptions and talk around the water cooler. Three areas of communication are addressed: targeted and strategic planning of communication to the stakeholders; branding of

Communication and Change

the project to stakeholders; and using communication to underpin change.

Leading the Team Chapter 9, *Leading the Team*, spotlights the project manager as a leader. Many of the disciplines and tools introduced in this chapter are just as important for line managers with personnel responsibilities. However, significant differences between the project manager's job and that of the line manager are also discussed here. This chapter focuses on team and project start-up, because in projects as in so many things in life, well begun is half done. This chapter introduces tools and methods for a number of the 'softer' project management disciplines, such as conflict management, coaching, team motivation and team development.

Project Governance Chapter 10, on *Project Governance*, looks beyond the individual project to consider the project-oriented organization and the challenges of making room for both operations and development. This chapter is particularly relevant for managers with responsibility for the entire project portfolio of an organization, department or office and for program managers heading up multiple projects. However, this chapter should also be read by project managers, as it enables a more qualified dialog between project managers and management. In this chapter, we introduce the concept of Project Excellence and outline the work streams an organization can follow to boost project orientation. We also cover the principles of LEAN project management and topics such as impact measurement (benefit tracking) in projects, programs and the portfolio as a whole.

Overview of tools

These practical tools can be found on the link – www.djoef-forlag.dk/da/boeger/p/power-in-project – ready for you to use in practice.

2.1   Assessment of Project Complexity

3.1   Objective Breakdown Structure (OBS)
3.2   Impact Case and Benefit Tracking

4.1   Stakeholder Analysis

5.1   Milestone Plan
5.2   Activity Descriptions
5.3   Milestone Descriptions
5.4   Gantt Chart
5.5   Three-point Estimation and Successive Calculation
5.6   Risk Analysis
5.7   Financial Follow-up

6.1   Distribution of Responsibilities
6.2   Project Anchoring
6.3   The Resource Contract

7.1   Project Journal
7.2   Minutes of Meetings
7.3   Project Review

8.1   The Communication Plan
8.2   Resistance to Change Mapping

9.1   Project Team Recruitment
9.2   The Team Constitution
9.3   Evaluation and Feedback
9.4   Planning Workshop

Overview of tools

10.1 Project List
10.2 Portfolio Overview
10.3 Project KPIs
10.4 Health Check or Risk Level Check
10.5 Strategic Fit of Project
10.6 Project Auditing
10.7 Project Management Models, Project Models
10.8 Project Descriptions, Project Contract
10.9 Idea Description

History of the Project
– From hierarchy to team

Project management is a matter of direction
– not walking in step

CHAPTER 1

History of the Project

In this first chapter, we describe the history of the project from the first construction projects 3,500 years ago to modern IT and dot-com projects.

Challenges

Is it possible to continue to think in terms of the projects, which range in type from classic engineering, and construction projects through R&D to organizational change and policy development projects?

How will the project develop as a concept in the future, once the volume of projects becomes so overwhelming that concepts like portfolio management and program management become everyday managerial tasks?

This chapter outlines the evolution of the project work form, the underlying trends and the methods developed by means of projects. It also provides insights into the development trends that have influenced the project work form, resulting in the creation of six project types:

Benefits

- Building and construction projects
- Research and technology development projects
- R&D projects
- IT and systems development projects
- Organizational change projects
- Policy development projects

The development of the project is presented in three stages, from Noah's Ark to the present day.

Focus

The project work form
The project developed as a concept in the late 1950s and early 1960s, where several project types emerged.

The project as an organizational method

From 1960 until the 1970s, we saw the advent of theories on group dynamics, resulting in the creation of the basic unit of the project – the project group or team In the 1980s, the traditional organizations came under pressure and the demand for integration and interdisciplinary processes produced many organizational changes. These changes were implemented in the form of projects. This is the period when organizational change projects became an everyday occurrence.

In the 1990s, demand for continuous change increased. Short lead times and parallel processes became buzzwords within management and project work. The methods and theories behind change management emerged and new organizational and behavioral skills were developed and expanded via projects.

The project as a management technique

The volume of projects within many organizations has now grown so great that top management is developing an interest in portfolio management – that is, the management of vast numbers of projects. The project is becoming so widespread an approach that a significant share of an organizations overall resources work in projects. And since the turn of the millennium, organizations and firms have systematically broken down strategies into programs and projects.

1.1. The history of the project – from stick to carrot

The word project

What does the word project mean? And where does it come from?

In dictionaries, we see a 'project' is something that is contemplated, devised or planned. It can also be a major undertaking. Further, the verb 'to project' means to throw, cast or set forth, for instance to project an image on a wall. The words 'projectile', 'projector' and 'projection' are all members of the same family with an element of setting forth an image, an idea, a material – moving it from one place to another. Projection was a primary goal of alchemy, where the 'powder of projection' could be used to alter a substance. While yet another meaning of the verb 'to project' is to stick out, as in 'the jetty projects out into the bay', while the 'center of projection' is the focal point.

Thus, planning or executing a project is the process of creating an image that sticks out – a new image. It is the process of projecting this image onto a new place – from the mind or a sheet of paper onto reality – and altering reality toward the focal point.

1.1.1. From Egypt, through Rome to modern day

We might think we live in the age of the project, but in fact, people have worked in projects for thousands of years. The first descriptions of projects date back 3,500 years. In Genesis 6, there is a description of the successful project called 'Noah's Ark'. Noah was given a detailed project description: The ark must be 300 cubits long, 50 cubits wide and 30 cubits high. The roof must project upward no more than 1 cubit ... etc.

The hierarchy across 3,500 years

Just as in modern project management theory, the objective, deliverables and success criteria were clearly defined. The project fit into top management's overall strategy. When the Ark was ready, it started to rain – the timing was spot on and the project was a success.

The Tower of Babel, however, was a different story. The objective was clear, but did not mesh with management's wishes: 'The people would assert themselves!' The deliverables were not described, and when management did not support the project, the project participants began speaking in different tongues – rendering cooperation impossible. There is no reference to technical problems; the project failed due to cooperation problems.

The oldest projects took place within the building and construction sector, such as the building of the pyramids in Egypt and later the Roman temples, aqueducts, bridges, roads and structures like the Colosseum. These projects were carried out within a very hierarchical organizational structure. We can read about the hierarchy in Exodus 18, where Moses receives advice from Jethro, his father-in-law, on how to organize the work to be done.

Moses was worn out, and when his father-in-law saw all the work that needed to be done, he said: 'Why do you sit alone ... and all the people stand about you from morning until evening?

... You shall select out of all the people able men ... who hate dishonest gain ... you shall place these over them as leaders of thousands, of hundreds, of fifties and of tens. ... If you do this thing ... then you will be able to endure, and all these people also will go to their place in peace.' Interestingly, Jethro describes delegation as a way to make the life of the leader easier and make the people happier. At the same time, he defines the 'span of control' as being ten people. (You could say Jethro was one of the first management consultants 3,500 years ago.)

1.1.2. Rulers and slaves

Vertical division of labor

At that time, there was no difference between projects, the army and other jobs – the hierarchy was applied across the board. The basic principle of the hierarchy is division of labor. In the beginning, the division of labor was first and foremost vertical – the difference between the ruler and his subjects. Certain people did the thinking, planning and coordination, while others did the work. This division of labor represented knowledge/power and hands/feet. Management was simply giving orders, and the motivation was literally the stick. The carrot as a management tool didn't arrive until much later. The 'employees' were slaves or soldiers, who were wise to obey.

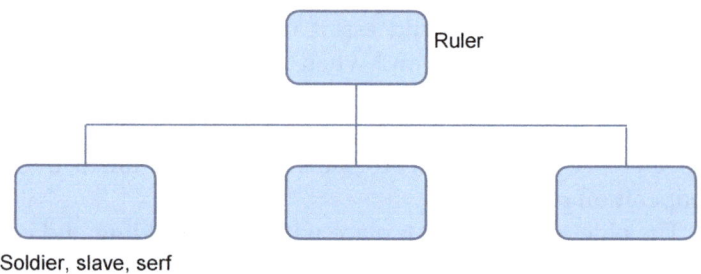

Figure 1.1. Vertical division of labor based on power – management was practiced by giving orders.

1.1.3. Professional divides

Horizontal division of labor

There were many homogenous groups in the hierarchy that dragged stones to the pyramids. However, in the preceding two centuries, the horizontal division of labor also grew in importance. Specialization became part of the hierarchy's strength. Within the construction sector, the professions of carpentry, masonry and plumbing developed. The superiors were selected on the basis of their professional insight, while the subordinates were no longer slaves, but craftsmen.

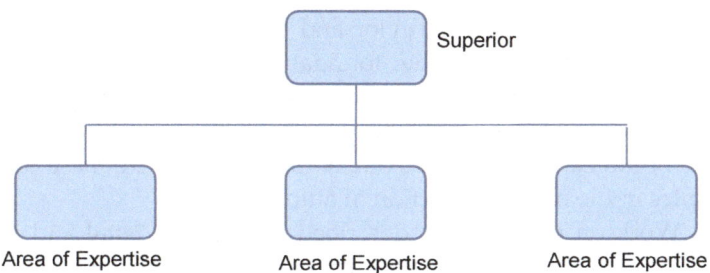

Figure 1.2. Horizontal division of labor based on specialization.

1.1.4. Rule-based management and delegation

Management within the state was divided into economics, law, the army etc. Especially within central administration, the hierarchy developed into rule-based management, marking the advent of bureaucracy. The individual's place was no longer a question of personal power, but of the right to enforce a set of rules. It was an efficient way to ensure uniform management, even with delegation. The individual's function became impersonal and controlled by the set of rules. **Bureaucracy**

Bureaucracy's strength is a stable world with few changes. It was therefore at this time that the first divisions emerged into projects and other types of assignments. Projects were still conducted within the hierarchy, but the construction sites were not as strongly governed by rules as many other organizations were at this time. A differentiation was beginning to form between the operating environment and projects.

In as early as 1697, Daniel Defoe, the author of Robinson Crusoe, called the 1600s 'the Projecting Age' in 'An Essay Upon Projects'.

He proclaimed that England needed more projects in order to develop the country, calling projects a way to create change, growth and improvements. Defoe also discussed the role of the project managers as planners and 'projectors'.

1.1.5. Industrialization in the 1900s – standardization, specialization and mass production

Taylor, Ford and Lenin

In the beginning of the 19th century, the differentiation developed between project work and work on the line, in production and in operations. Taylor and the principles of scientific management formed the foundation for industrialization, which was built on the comprehensive specialization and standardization of products, processes and activities within the organization. Ford was one of the first to utilize these principles in the mass production of automobiles.

Work on the line was described in extreme detail and immortalized in the famous Chaplin film about working on the assembly line, where the employees perform the same repetitive movement all day long. In Russia, this management form was implemented on a societal level after the revolution. Lenin was deeply fascinated by Taylor and Ford, and he created a society governed by rules based on a level of specialization and standardization the likes of which the world had never seen before. There were three types of supermarkets, built according to the same three building plans and all containing the exact same 125 products. There were bread shops selling two types of light bread and one type of dark bread and specialized dairies selling only milk. The names of the dairies were Dairy no. 23, Dairy no. 24 and so forth.

This large-scale specialization and standardization created problems across the organizations. In 1937, Luther Gulick described the idea behind the matrix organization. However, many years would pass before any real action was taken to change the interdisciplinary processes within the organizations. The 1930s also saw the advent of the first bar chart, which has since become a standard planning tool in projects.

The advent of the project as a concept

In contrast to standardized operations, projects were carried out when there was a need to develop new products or build new factories. They were one-off assignments for the purpose of developing new products or establishing production capacity. Projects were still carried out within a relatively hierar-

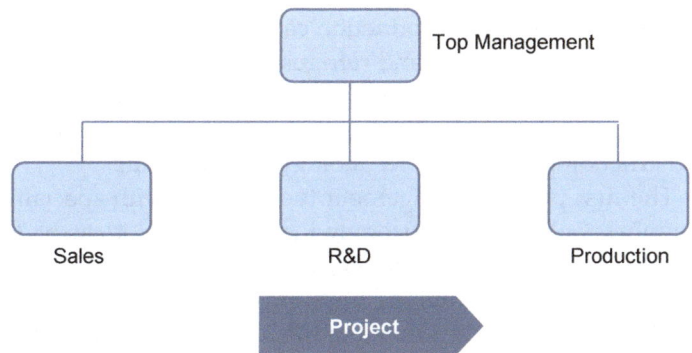

Figure 1.3. Projects were executed as a sequential process in the development department or by a construction company.

chical structure, and often by specialist departments, like the development department.

Despite the fact that construction projects had been carried out for 4,000 years, it was not until the 1950s that the concept of the project arose as a well-defined work form with a special structure, methodology and tools. This may be because the project work form differed so greatly from the line, which had by this time become even more standardized and controlled by rules. Classic project management theory stems from the late 1950s and early 1960s. From this point on, development of the project work form really picked up speed.

According to legend, when the Soviet Union sent Yuri Gagarin into orbit around the Earth, the US fell behind in the space race. This compelled John F. Kennedy to proclaim the vision: 'Man on the moon in this decade!'

To achieve this, NASA needed to work in an entirely new way. This led to the development of network planning, where the planning of activities took dependencies into account and it was possible to define the critical path throughout the project.

1.1.6. The project as a way to solve technical problems and acquire more products to meet demand

Society's main purpose at this time was to acquire products to meet demand. Firms had relatively few competitors and markets were growing. If a firm had an idea for a new product, there was a market for it.

1950 to mid-1960

Demand exceeded production capacity, and new products, like the radio, television and refrigerator, were quickly disseminated. The limiting factor was the development and manufacturing of the products. The main project types were therefore construction projects and technology development.

The first project management theory dealt with specialized planning tools and was strongly inspired by the ideas of Taylor and operational analysis on breaking projects down into sub-activities and estimating time and resource consumption.

This period saw the advent of the basic planning mindset as represented by PERT: Program Evaluation and Review Technique, developed in the US in 1958 for the Polaris Program, and CPM: Critical Path Method, developed by the DuPont chemical company in the US for managing plant construction projects.

For many years, these methods made up the essence of project management, forming the basis for classic project management theory on critical junctions, critical activities, critical paths, various types of slack, earliest start time, latest start time, etc.

1.2. The project as an organizational method

1.2.1. New needs, motivation and the team

1960 to mid-1970

In the western world, product capacity and demand were in balance, and the marketing activities of firms increased in importance as more suppliers of the same products joined the market. Technological development alone was no longer enough to win over customers, and R&D projects began to take form as a way to combine technological possibilities with market needs.

By this time, the project work form was influenced by three factors:

- Increasing interest in the project's 'customers'
- New theories on motivation
- The establishment of the theoretical framework known as group dynamics.

The advent of the R&D project

R&D projects were still carried out as a linear technical and rational process. However, it became clear that demand was not limitless. Interest therefore shifted from a highly technology-driven process towards more needs-driven R&D. As a consequence, projects began to include activities such as needs assessment, where the market became the source of ideas. Interest in the users and the project stakeholders grew. And we saw the first R&D projects that were not pure technology development.

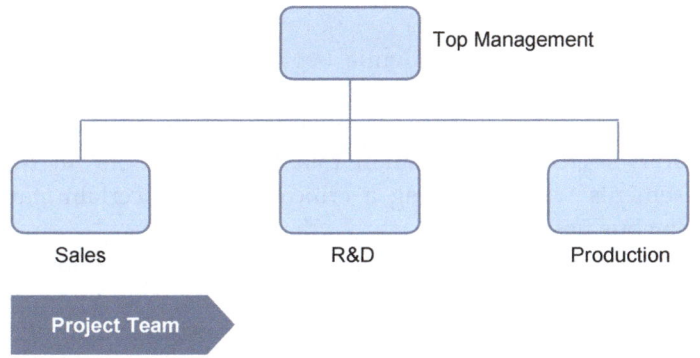

Figure 1.4. R&D projects resulted in a growing interest in the customers' needs.

Team development and motivation

The theories on group development and group dynamics produced a conceptual framework for the basic unit of the project – the project team. A need developed within firms to improve productivity and theories on motivation and working in groups emerged. Firms began experimenting with autonomous groups and the theories on group dynamics and development became widespread.

R. Meredith Belbin studied roles within teams and gathered his findings in book form in 1983.

With the establishment of an entire conceptual framework for the project team, the project developed as the basic working unit. According to the theories of motivation, what motivates us is not the authority of the boss, but rather responsibility, appreciation, achieving results, influence, etc. These management theories were built on the tools project managers had at their disposal. Whereas the project work form had traditionally focused on tools and structures, projects had now evolved into an organizational method. This evolution meshed well with the Baby Boomer's values of community, solidarity, commitment, optimism, idealism and experimentation.

Computer science: not yet IT and still relegated to the basement

Computers, however, were still only found in the basement, where they were the responsibility of creative computer operators, engineers with an interest in electronics and mathematicians. The focus was on linguistics and tools rather than workflow.

Slowly, however, academia began to awaken to the concepts of workflow, quality and efficiency in the development process. This can probably be attributed to the business community's growing realization that the 'calculators' in these basements were becoming a critical factor in certain stand-alone business processes.

The project as a concept was as yet immature and not clearly defined. However, people were beginning to apply process terminology to systems development, thus supplementing the strong focus on mathematics/algorithms with a growing focus on the workflow in systems development.

Tom de Marco and Yourdon, considered the Taylor and Ford of computer science, launched their ideas about 'structured design' focusing on the workflow.

Engineering projects refine the planning process

The methods of working within engineering and construction projects didn't change much during this period. However, the planning methods were still being refined, and in 1978 Steen Lichtenberg, a Danish professor of project and construction management, published *Projektplanlægning – i en foranderlig verden* (Project Planning – In a Changing World), setting out the principles of successive planning and budgeting.

1.2.2. We have the products we need – time for organizational change and to introduce IT

The 1980s

This period was troubled by stagnating demand, price competition and inflation. For the first time in history, production capacity exceeded demand in the western world. Forced to focus on rationalization, firms began working with strategy

1.2. The project as an organizational method

development and customer orientation. The buzzwords were strategic management, quality assurance, service management and total quality management (TQM).

Customer and service orientation led to a mindset that spanned the line organization, especially outward toward the customers. In R&D projects, a link was established between the technical functions and the marketing function, resulting in some of the R&D functions no longer reporting to the technical director but rather to the sales and marketing director.

By this time, a significant dynamic had developed in the new product programs of firms. Booz-Allen & Hamilton studied the revenue shares of new products.

In 1982, new products represented 33% of a company's revenue and 22% of their profit. However, due to the high volume of products on the market, firms began differentiating their products by means of immaterial goods or services, such as customer service, design and lead times. With this trend, the product was no longer just a technical core service, but a series of supplementary services offered by the organization.

Now, R&D also comprised the development of service packages and customer support.

Concurrent engineering with parallel and interdisciplinary processes

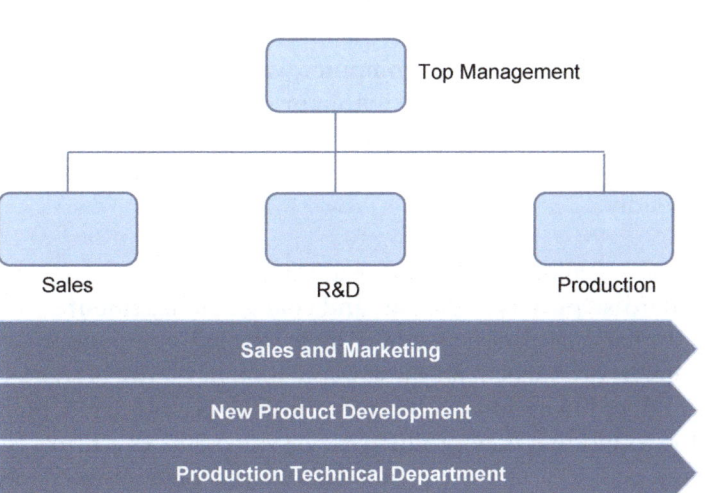

Figure 1.5. In Concurrent Engineering, the project is carried out in parallel by staff from Sales, R&D and Production.

33

The mid-1980s saw the advent of the concept of Concurrent Engineering. The principle was that in addition to developers, the project team should also comprise representatives from sales and production.

Organizational change as a project

Firms began to implement a range of organizational change projects, such as the introduction of quality assurance, TQM projects and the introduction of service management. The legendary Scandinavian Airlines CEO, Jan Carlzon, proclaimed it was time to 'flatten the pyramids'. Internal organizational and change projects became an everyday occurrence. Organizational change projects became just as common as R&D projects.

IT projects

IT development also began to take on the form of projects as computers moved from the domain of the operators into the business community in general. It was now possible for computers to support entire processes and not just individual operations and calculations.

Programming languages like Pascal and PL/1 were developed which, unlike the earliest languages, COBOL and FORTRAN, made it possible to increase the division of labor.

Systems development became an independent discipline and training came into focus. The business community was developing a taste for user-friendliness and user influence.

In 1984, the personal computer was launched, making huge volumes of data available within projects. Computer programs were written to manage time, resources and costs within projects. And the programs became simpler and more user-friendly.

1.2.3. Projects with short lead times

The 1990s **Interdisciplinary processes and change management**

Internationalization resulted in increasing competition from foreign products. And these many foreign products shortened product life cycles significantly. In 1992, Booz-Allen & Hamilton found that new products represented 50% of a firm's revenue and 40% of their profit. This placed high demands on a firm's ability to respond. Time meant everything.

1.2. The project as an organizational method

Lead times in R&D projects were reduced by half in many firms by grouping project teams together.

Short lead times and parallel processes

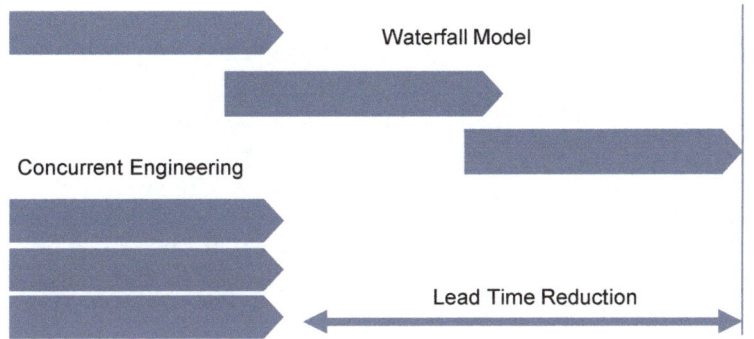

Figure 1.6. The principles of Concurrent Engineering were applied to other project types, reducing lead times by means of parallel processes.

Interdisciplinary processes came into focus and new management concepts emerged: time-based management, business process reengineering, process owner and team orientation. Project orientation and project management became widespread management techniques.

The latest buzzwords were interdisciplinary processes and short lead times.

Countless internal change projects were implemented in order to build up and redesign the interdisciplinary processes. The concept of change management was introduced by, among others, John Kotter, with organizational change projects now being implemented based on a new conceptual and theoretical framework. Stakeholder involvement and reducing resistance to change were now added to the project manager's responsibilities.

Change management

Even though IT projects tended to entail comprehensive organizational change, they were often carried out simply as technology development projects. In the 1990s, numerous IT projects were implemented for the purpose of integrating a firm's various functions. Enterprise resource planning projects, like SAP, were often a combination of IT and organizational change projects where interdisciplinary processes were introduced.

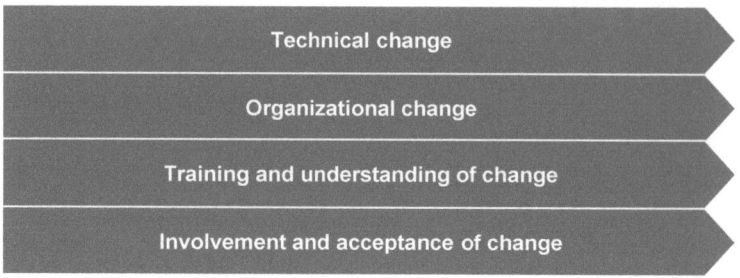

Figure 1.7. Organizational change projects were carried out as parallel processes with several work streams to ensure acceptance and understanding of the change.

From computer science to IT In the world of IT, the project as a concept was beginning to be taken seriously, gaining both visibility and respect. The academic, scientific and business communities all took an interest in IT projects.

Developments in technology presented new opportunities for the division of labor within the systems development process. PCs could be connected to microcomputers and client/server development technology emerged along with a new set of standards.

Large-scale IT projects The IT operations department ceased to be a powerful force – the age of the IT project had arrived. Management firms opened their eyes to the IT market in the 1990s. Riding the wave of SAP and ERP, they doubled and tripled in size.

Fast dot-com projects The dot-com boom gave birth to new work forms within the systems development process.

In fact, the dot-coms represented the first serious challenge to the classic project world. Shirking highly structured methods, like the waterfall chart, dot-comers were driven by commitment, spontaneous business sense and communicative insight (as well as large amounts of Coca-Cola and pizza).

They worked with hard time boxes, rejecting tried and tested methods, like requirements specifications, testing and certain general project management tools. Concepts and principles like 'extreme programming' gained traction.

The 1990s was also the decade when the public sector embraced the project work form – at least in Denmark and many parts of Europe. Municipalities, agencies and ministries were facing an ever-changing world. Many assignments, like district planning, policy development and internal change initiatives, were well-suited for project work.

Policy development conducted as projects

With the introduction of the project work form in the public sector and the growing popularity of change management techniques, project work was no longer viewed solely as a rational process. Many projects required the handling of various types of stakeholders and a political approach based on tools like compromise, negotiation, power and influence. These trends were also a reflection of such Generation X values as pragmatism, informal relations and self-reliance.

By this time, the project work form was no longer a matter of planning and management, but rather a creative process towards a vision that wasn't always clear from the outset. The classic project management theory concept of 'accuracy' (achieving the planned result) was called into question.

When accuracy isn't the ultimate goal for project management

The 1990s produced books on project management in more loosely organized systems.

In contrast to the classic virtues of realistic objectives and accuracy, the mantra became: 'Set ambitious objectives, but keep sanctions fair.'

1.3. The project as a management technique

1.3.1. The learning organization and value-based management

A multitude of products, services and technologies are engulfing us at break-neck speed from all over the world, resulting in a continuous flow of change. According to organizational

From the year 2000 to modern day

theorist Ralph D. Stacey, a more dynamic organizational development is beginning to take form.

Entirely new organizational forms are emerging in response to globalization and the many changes that are taking place. Many people work in networks built around agreements between individuals. And often these networks cross both organizational boundaries and national borders.

In international projects, many people work within virtual project organization where the participants are spread out all over the world and often only know each other through communication by email. This is one of the major challenges for the traditional project teams of the 1970s. The individual project participant must be able to manage him or herself to achieve the set objectives. On the path toward this objective, decisions must be made based on the project participant's competences and the organization's values.

All the while, the high pace places demands on learning and development. The concept of the learning organization has been known since the last half of the 1990s and this project work form is often used in connection with competence-building. The small generations from the 1980s demand assignments that is both challenging and boost personal development. They are comfortable with the project work form from the educational system, where children are learning to work in projects from as early as the 1st grade.

This increases the pressure on the classic manager – and the stick is no longer a viable management technique, as it is just as antiquated as the pyramids themselves.

The future   Even in projects that don't have learning as a direct objective, a project manager is expected to be a coach for the project participants. The project manager role has evolved from the planner and administrator of the 1960s to today's figurehead, politician, coach and inspirational leader. The project manager is now the culture bearer and culture creator, representing and challenging the organization's values and attitudes.

The project as a work form differs drastically from the traditional hierarchy of the 1960s. Now it is used by all types of organizations for R&D, the implementation of change and the introduction of new methods and systems. Further, many services and deliverables are carried out via the project model.

1.3.2. Portfolio management and the Zap Generation

In the near future, we face two key challenges:

1. The **project volume** within the organization or individual firm is increasing, requiring overall management of the entire range of projects. Having talented project managers is no longer enough. The entire organization, and especially top management, must be project oriented. One of the biggest challenges for top management will be to practice intelligent portfolio management – that is, management of the entire armada of projects.

Projects used to make up only a small share of the work conducted within an organization. Today, however, it's not unusual for projects to occupy 20-30% of an organization's total resources. Interest in systematic prioritization of the entire project portfolio is therefore increasing.

Increasing project volume

The firms and organizations that conduct a great many projects have already begun gathering projects into programs and introducing tools and methods for portfolio management, such as project offices, project management models, project lists, methods of prioritization, resource allocation, systematic competence development, etc.

Portfolio management, when there are many projects

Project management deals with the management of individual projects and is viewed as a discipline for the project manager. However, with the growing volume of projects, this is not enough. Portfolio management and program management deal with the overall management of multiple projects and is a discipline for top management. The project work form is moving into the top tiers of management. And as the volume of projects rises, we also see a growing number of project-like ad hoc tasks that can't be naturally performed on the line.

At the same time, today's project manager may be a dying breed. Since projects represent an increasing share of an organization's activities, it no longer makes sense to differentiate between line management and project management as career

Chapter 1. History of the Project

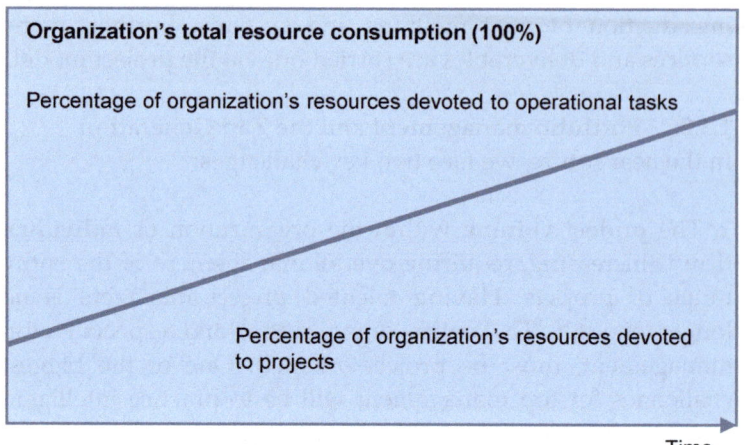

Figure 1.8. The spread of the project work form has led to a growing share of organizations' resources being devoted to projects. The question is, how long will this trend continue?

paths. The leader of the future will need to be competent in both disciplines – and will need to know when to employ each management technique.

2. The **Zap Generation** represents a significant share of the participants in current and future projects. Also called the Y Generation, the @ Generation, the Me Generation and the Project Generation, this is the generation born in the period 1972 to 1980.

They just want to have fun

One would expect a generation known as the Project Generation to be very well-equipped for participating in projects. However, the management of these project participants represents a serious challenge.

This generation is often accused of being disloyal and willful. They stay in the same job for an average of two years, whereas Generation X tends to stay for five years and the Baby Boomers for ten years.

Many in this generation thrive on fixed-term project positions, calling themselves free agents or freelancers. This presents a challenge for employers who have an understandable interest in retaining the best workers – or at least retaining them until the project is completed – as free agents are constantly on the lookout for new and potentially better situations. However, this vilified, nomadic zap culture may turn out to be a necessity for surviving the project environments of the future, in the same way as the attitudes of the Baby Boomers regarding authority and solidarity played an important role in the development of flatter organizations and working in groups and teams.

Perhaps a zap culture is a necessity for surviving in an organization where projects start up and end suddenly at the whim of changing priorities. You need to be fully committed to a new project even though you joined up at the halfway mark, and so forth. If you are unable to enjoy a movie simply because you missed the first half or if you can't follow three movies at once then you may not have a chance in the turbulent working environment of the future.

The management challenges are massive. Until now, the most important elements of a project have been the project team and management of that team. However, the project participants of the future no longer have solidarity as a key value. Instead, they think in terms of 'me', differences and 'giving it all you've got'. This doesn't mean that the Zap Generation lacks the skills to work in teams; they are simply teams of individuals.

The future project participants are committed, but want to 'brand' themselves within the team and the firm. What retains and motivates them is personal development, interesting assignments and having fun. The future participants are independent and expect to be given responsibility and to be allowed to plan their own work. And they get a thrill from doing what others think is impossible.

At the same time, the future project participants require a clear sense of meaningfulness from the firm, that is, what we as a firm contribute to the world. The meaningfulness of the individual projects also needs to be clear: How is the project meaningful in relation to the firm's overall strategy? What difference does it make? The project participant of the future develops his or her brand and identity via the project's and the firm's identity. Firms therefore need to be more deliberately communicative and their portfolio management needs to be more consistent.

The Swedish project management veteran, Torbjörn Wenell, describes the four principles of project management in the future:

- **Freedom:** The individual must be able to assume responsibility; the goal is to set the employee's competences and creativity free.
- **Simplicity:** Projects must be carried out by means of simple models and overall milestone plans. The goal is not complex systems.
- **Small and short:** Divide projects up into smaller subprojects that can be finished quickly.
- **Trust and team:** Delegate and exploit the dynamics of the project team.

This trend is already visible, with project-oriented organizations devoting more energy to defining project programs. We are now seeing a shift from large-scale, complex projects toward dividing assignments up into smaller, more manageable projects that are then closely coordinated within a program. Agile project management and Scrum are being introduced, with projects being broken down into sprints. Top management is taking active part in program management. Chapter 10 explores this trend and defines the concepts within portfolio management: programs, projects and ad hoc tasks. Many organizations are developing new management structures, comprising a project committee, steering committees, a project office and a program manager.

The program mindset was originally developed under US Defense Secretary McNamara in the early 1970s when he couldn't achieve the desired effect from development in the navy, army and air force. He therefore set out to coordinate the development initiatives in the various armed forces so that they supported a common objective. The program mindset has been gaining traction since 2000 with the growing volume of projects and the many ad hoc tasks that top management can't cope with.

1.4. Can line management be a temporary work form?

Chapter 1 provides an overview of the history of the project from the earliest engineering and construction projects 3,500 years ago to the multitude of project types in modern organizations.

100 years with projects

For the first several thousands of years, there was no difference between project management and all other types of management. It wasn't until bureaucracy and industrialization defined the operating environment that projects were considered separately as fixed-term development and one-off assignments.

Separating the project from the operating environment

In the beginning of the last century, the engineering and construction project was the only project in use. These projects had a highly hierarchical structure, almost resembling order production. The project wasn't defined as a work form in its own right until the technology development projects and construction projects of the 1950s.

The project work form

In the 1960s, the technology development projects grew more customer-oriented, ultimately becoming R&D projects. Throughout the 1970s, the project work form grew to also comprise needs assessment, stakeholder analysis, group dynamics and theories of motivation. At this point, the project had evolved into an organizational method with the team as the key element.

The project as an organizational method

In the late 1970s and early 1980s, the IT industry began to adopt the project work form. During that same period, the project also began to be used to manage organizational change, giving rise to the organizational development project.

In extension of the organizational development project, the 1990s saw the advent of change management methodology. The entire public sector developed an interest in the project work form, and policy development activities were defined as projects.

In the 1990s, it became increasingly difficult to apply the methods and principles of classic project management to the

43

two new project types: organizational change and policy development. Concepts like specific objectives, detailed plans and accuracy were called into question. Meanwhile, the IT sector, which didn't adopt the project work form until the late 1970s, began questioning the waterfall chart during the dot-com boom.

The project as a management technique

From the 1960s up to the 1990s, the volume of projects increased markedly within most organizations.

In the beginning of this period, projects were executed by the development department. But then organizations began using continuous projects to develop services, change procedures and introduce new IT solutions, while in many municipalities, agencies and ministries, the development of policy and proposals was carried out in the form of projects. We are now approaching the far right side of Figure 1.8 where a significant share of an organization's resources are devoted to projects.

Portfolio management

For this reason, many firms and organizations developed and introduced methods of portfolio management and program management throughout the 1990s. Project management developed into a management technique, not solely for project managers, but also for top and middle management.

For thousands of years, management and project management were executed within in the same hierarchical structure. It wasn't until bureaucracy and industrialization defined the operating environment that projects were considered separately as development-oriented one-off assignments. The question is whether the world has become so turbulent that the multitude of one-off assignments within the operational environment is beginning to resemble project work. Perhaps we will wind up back where we started, with no difference between line management and project management. Projects have become the dominant management form and method of organizing work and tasks.

In the early years after 2000, the concept of **Project Governance** emerged. Project Governance covers the overall management of projects within an organization. Management of the many projects has become a multi-tiered management task, just like line management. Project Governance covers four basic management areas:

1.4. Can line management be a temporary work form?

- Overall portfolio overview
- Transparency and solid basis for decision-making
- Clear distribution of roles and responsibilities into portfolio, programs and projects
- Common language in the form of the project model and described project processes

Line management is evolving into project management

In firms and organizations that have mastered portfolio management, there is a growing tendency to divide projects up into smaller sub-projects that can be finished quickly. As Torbjörn Wenell says: 'Small and short'. Coherence is ensured by the program management, which contextualizes the individual project within the corporate strategy and vision – thus making it meaningful in a zap culture.

We call projects transitory – perhaps it was only in the 1900s that project management differed from line management. The project as a work form may be transitory in several ways. In the future, operations might well comprise many project-like tasks, with line management evolving into portfolio management. So perhaps operations is the transitory phenomenon!

The LEAN mindset, regardless of whether it's production-oriented or administrative, is one way to build on continuous change in line management. LEAN generates many small changes or ad hoc tasks that are not directly operational, but are too small to be considered actual projects. It can be quite helpful to organize these many ad hoc tasks into programs.

Within the world of projects, the early 2000s saw the advent of the concept of **LEAN project management**. The principal of LEAN project management is, of course, to create rhythm and tact in the project portfolio. Rhythm and tact are well-known concepts in production (line management).

And so the two work forms are approaching each other.

Chapter 1. History of the Project

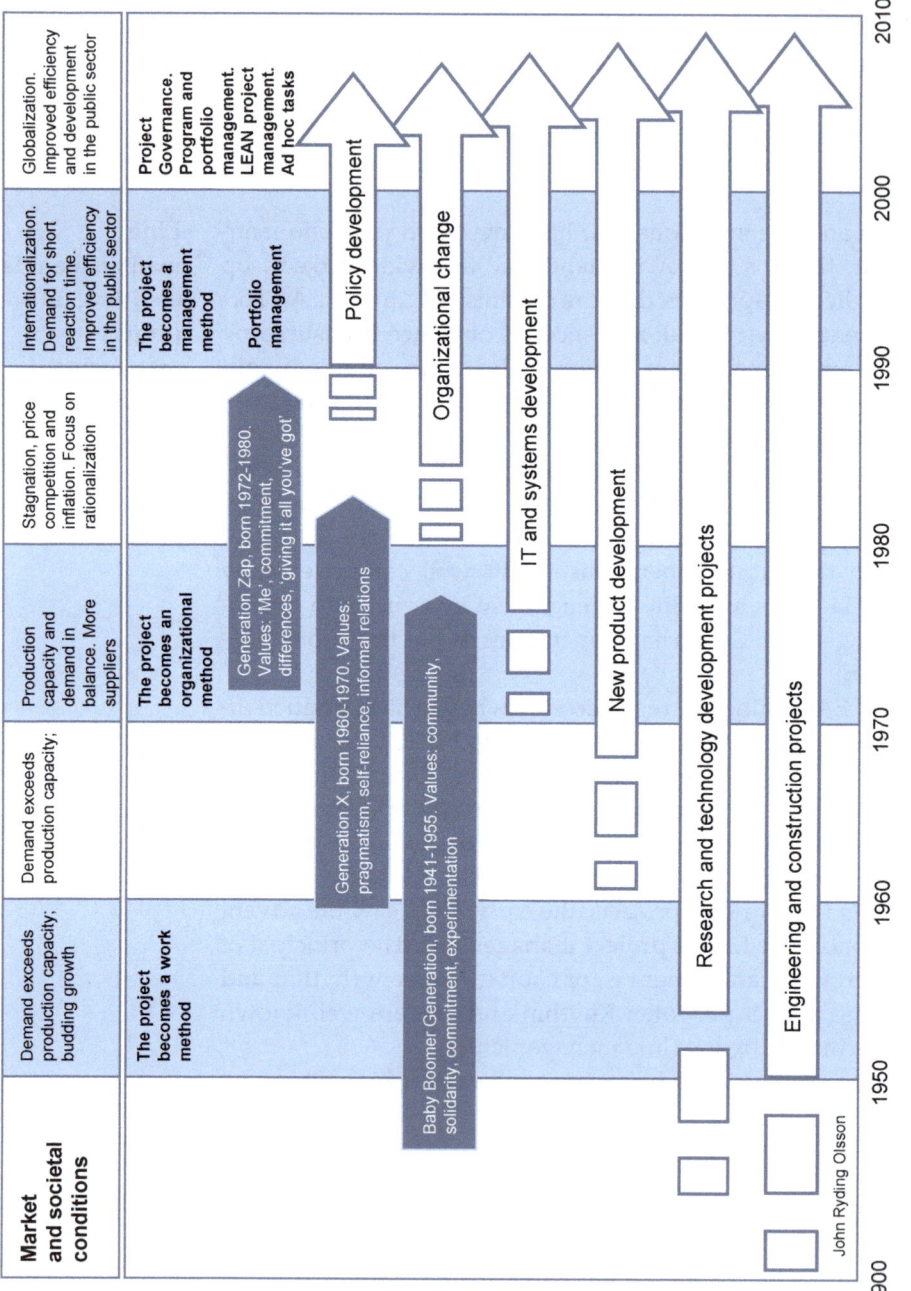

Figure 1.9 Summary of the evolution of the project work form from the year 1900 to 2010.

The Project Work Form
Task, team and direction

Development can be achieved when different people work together

CHAPTER 2

The Project Work Form

Is the task a project?   **Challenges**
The project work form is gaining in popularity, but not everything is suitable for project work. The trick is to select those tasks that would benefit from being carried out as projects.

There are many types of projects, each with their own approach, organization and management style. It is therefore important to recognize the characteristics of the project in question and take them as your basis for choosing the right approach.

Projects are carried out within a variety of organizational frameworks, each of which has a different impact on the project manager's options and management style.

This chapter provides answers to the following questions: **Benefits**
What is the fundamental difference between an operational task and a task that is suitable for project work?

No two projects are the same. However, there are some typical project archetypes requiring different management approaches to be successful. This chapter presents the various archetypes and explains what their differences mean for the management of each project type.

The aim is to give you an understanding of projects and their differences, in order to enable you to choose the appropriate strategy before execution of your project.

Basic principles   **Focus**
This chapter describes the basic elements of the project work form. You will be given an introduction to which tasks are suited to project work as well as to the fundamental features of the project. The six types of projects are:

- Engineering and construction projects
- Research and technology development projects
- R&D projects
- IT and systems development projects
- Organizational change projects
- Policy development projects

We also present three fundamental methods of organizing projects, along with the advantages and disadvantages of each method. Finally, we take a look at management skills when working in projects, with reference to the chapters where the various elements are presented in more detail. The correlation between the strategy and the process of breaking down the strategy into programs and projects is described in Chapter 10. In this chapter, we start with the project.

Tool Tool 2.1 Assessing the project's complexity

2.1. Features of the project

2.1.1. When is an assignment a project?

Working in projects has become trendy. It seems like every firm and organization wants to work in projects. 'We should be doing it, too!'

Tasks and projects In reality, though, not all tasks are suitable for project work. The method should always be adapted to the assignment. This means the organization of the assignment, the procedures and the employees involved should all be chosen based on the nature of the assignment.

The key therefore is understanding which tasks are most suited for project work and which tasks are best performed within the line organization.

The operating environment is structured to be able to perform recurrent activities. The various tasks have often been distributed among specialized units, which each perform their own sub-tasks. Because the tasks are recurrent, there are generally established workflows, procedures and methods that must be adhered to.

2.1. Features of the project

Projects are often an option when a task doesn't fit into the existing line organization, for instance because it can't be executed by one department alone or because it involves changing the existing operating environment. It can also be a task the organization is carrying out for the very first time.

In contrast, we saw in Chapter 1 how operational tasks within many organizations are beginning to resemble projects. Many 'operational tasks' are of a one-off nature that set out to address one-time problems or that are more developmental in nature. Examples include a new senior citizen policy in local government, a new type of marketing campaign for a retail chain and so on.

It is therefore becoming increasingly difficult to define projects in relation to a static operating environment, as such environments are not always static. There are also many ad hoc tasks that are performed by individuals over a few days. These aren't really suitable for project work, because the methodological framework of the project work form is too comprehensive and bureaucratic in nature.

Rather than focusing on the opposite of recurrent operational tasks and small ad hoc tasks, we have chosen to focus on what characterizes the tasks that are best suited for project work.

Task that are suitable for project work tend to have the following features:

Recurrent operational tasks and small ad hoc tasks

Suitable for project work

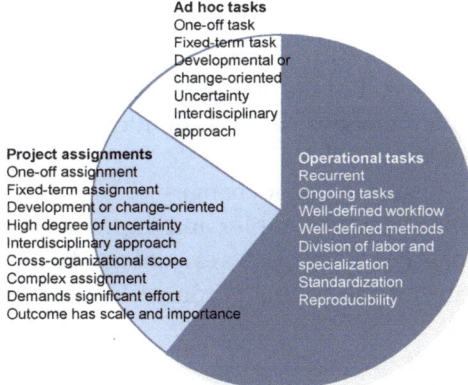

Figure 2.1. Division of tasks into operational tasks, ad hoc tasks and projects. Projects and ad hoc tasks have many common features, but differ in size and complexity.

51

Change and development	**Development and changing the current situation** The project is appropriate as a work form for one-off assignments that create change and are developmental in nature. Examples include changes to production, changes to the organizational structure, the introduction of a new IT system, development of a new product or new technology, building a new headquarters, developing a policy statement, and so forth.
Boundary-crossing tasks	**Tasks requiring an interdisciplinary or cross-organizational approach** One feature of the project is that the existing professional divides or departmental structure can't cope with the task, which must be executed across the existing organization or in collaboration with other firms and/or organizations.
Large and complex assignments	**Tasks that is complicated and comprehensive in scale** These are tasks that can't be carried out by a single individual, but require contributions from many different people over an extended period of time. The complexity can comprise many sub-systems, multiple areas of expertise and unknown solutions. The complexity has several dimensions. The International Project Management Association (IPMA) certification program describes project complexity based on the following dimensions:

A project is more complex when:
- It is very important to the organization
- There are many political conflicts of interest
- There are many stakeholders
- The project results in major changes
- The outcome is highly complex and unpredictable
- The solutions and technologies are unknown
- The structure of the results is comprehensive and complicated
- The schedule is very tight
- The project is labor-intensive
- The necessary participant competences are both professionally and culturally highly diverse

- The project organization comprises many units across several organizations, spanning vast geographical distances and different time zones

Source: IPMA Competencies in Project Management. NCB National Competence Baseline for Scandinavia. 2009.

Tasks that is important to the organization | Important tasks
The outcome of these tasks is vital to the firm, society or multiple stakeholders. They are the object of cross-organizational interest because the outcome affects many people – often over an extended period of time. These projects often have major financial consequences. An employee who is implementing a change to his or her own procedures, for example, is not carrying out a project, even though the activity involves the development of something new.

Individual assignments that haven't been tried before – or only rarely | One-off assignments
Tasks that are not routine are perfect as projects. They might be one-off assignments or assignments that are rarely carried out. For instance, the annual conference for a trade union or the annual budget round in an international corporation can easily be carried out as a project.

A task doesn't necessarily have to meet the above criteria to make it appropriate for project work. However, the more of the above elements it encompasses, the more suitable it is for the project work form.

Based on the above, project assignments generally have the characteristics described in more detail below.

2.1.2. Projects are characterized by uncertainty

The main feature of a project assignment is that it is more uncertain than tasks within line organization. This is because the task is being carried out for the first time and often involves development or changes that are not daily jobs. | **Significant degree of uncertainty**

These tasks tend to be interdisciplinary, meaning that no individual person can keep tabs on every little aspect of the entire assignment. This uncertainty applies to both the objective and the funding. In the beginning, it can be difficult to say exactly what the ultimate objective is – determining deliverables is generally part of the project.

As long as the objective is unknown, it is difficult to plan the approach and methods, which makes it difficult to calculate how long the project will take and how much it will ultimately cost.

Nevertheless, the results of the project are expected to be on time and on budget. A key aspect of project management is therefore coping with this uncertainty.

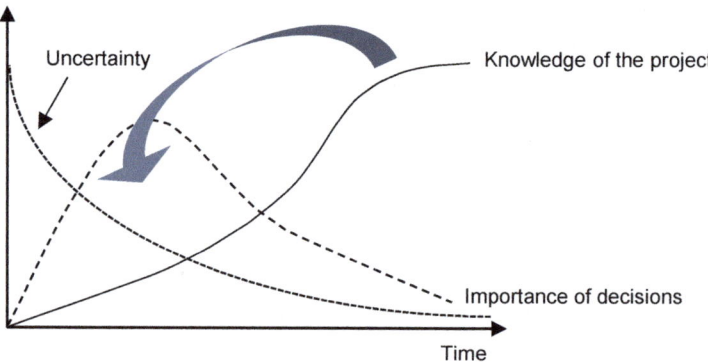

Figure 2.2. Project uncertainty decreases over time as knowledge about the subject in question increases and the project participants understand more about the project.

Defining the assignment and approach

Objective, framework and approach must be planned each time

Because no two projects are the same, the objective, framework and approach must be planned every single time. The project manager and the project team are expected to plan the approach and choose which methods to use.

For some employees participating in project work for the first time, this can come as a surprise. They may experience project work as chaotic and directionless, feeling that there is a lack of leadership! Of course, this may actually be the case. However, it's more likely that they need to define the objective and plan the approach themselves – who else is going to do it?

2.1. Features of the project

This interdisciplinarity is a key feature of projects. However, one consequence is that the manager and top management don't always know how the task should be carried out – which is why they have appointed a project team.

Consequently, it's the project team's job to flesh out the objectives and the details of the project plan.

Herein lies the difference between a project assignment and an operational task. In the operating environment, workflow, procedures and methods are well described and tested.

Temporary organization

A project is transitory. Consequently, the project team is transitory. This is one of the project manager's key challenges. Within the line organization, everybody knows each other, all the employees have the same background and staff turnover is relatively low.

A project comprises a team of employees with different professional backgrounds who are expected to start up quickly – often on a task that is neither well-known nor well-defined. This requires a huge effort by the team to be able work well together quickly.

Toward the end of the project, it can be difficult to maintain the necessary high level of commitment as some of the participants may have already moved on to other exciting new projects. Getting everything finished on time is therefore often a challenge.

During the course of the project, the project participants generally report to a manager in the line organization as well. This makes the project manager a 'temporary' manager for the project participants, seriously affecting the project manager's authority, as the participants are well-aware that the line manager is permanent, while the project manager is temporary. It is therefore easy to imagine who they would 'listen to' should conflicting interests arise between the project manager and the participants' immediate superiors.

Projects are transitory

Handling conflicts of managerial authority and stakeholders

Because a project is a temporary organization, conflicts of managerial authority may arise between the project manager and the participants' superiors on the line.

The project is part of its surroundings

55

This is probably the most common type of conflict between the project and its surroundings.

A typical situation in projects is when the agreed resources are not made available because an urgent task has arisen in the line organization.

A project produces change, which means that many people within the organization have a vested interest in the project's outcome. All stakeholders will attempt to influence the project to their advantage. The problem for the project team is that these stakeholders are in disagreement and may even have conflicting interests.

Some want to expand the project, others want to change its course and still others would rather see the project shelved. Handling these stakeholders presents a huge challenge for the project manager. As a rule, it's impossible to satisfy everyone, so informed choices must be made.

Task management	**Focusing on the task and the big picture rather than on specialization**

In line management, the manager's job is to build up the department and develop the employees, methods and workflows. The manager is not involved in the execution of the individual task, but solely responsible for personnel management. The line manager enables the department to execute the tasks.

In projects, the individual tasks are the primary focus. The project manager's job is to head up the project – manage the tasks. The project manager achieves results with the help of the project team. However, in order for the project to succeed in the short term, the participants need to possess the necessary competences. Generally, it's not possible to develop these competences during the project period.

A firm's organizational structure is often based on areas of specialization with separate departments for finance, sales, production, legal, property, environmental issues, etc. The project brings together various specialists to execute a specific assignment. A key element of project management is to ensure the close integration of competences in order to carry out a unique assignment.

The right resources and work integration   **The battle for**
Executing projects requires resources, not just in the form of   **resources**
qualified participants, but also in terms of materials, equipment, workspace, etc. The fact that projects are transitory and wrought with uncertainty complicates the resource issue even further.

First, it is often difficult to predict the scope of resources the assignment will require. There is rarely anybody within the organization who knows all the qualifications of all the participants. Consequently, the selection of participants tends to be based on the opinions of managers without a full understanding of the content of the project or the specific expertise of the participants.

The success of a project depends on the individual giving his or her very best, even doing the impossible if necessary. It's not a 9-to-5 job and often an extraordinary effort is required to achieve the milestones. Generally, there are significant differences between how each individual performs in such situations. Consider the physical abilities of humans for a moment. The world champion may run twice or three times as fast as the average runner. The world champion may jump three times higher than the rest of us. However, the differences between the various project participants can actually be 100 fold. What one person can do may simply be impossible for another person. This is where we find huge differences in the competences at our disposal for a given project.

2.2. Project types

2.2.1. Refining the language

The Eskimos have many words for snow. They have refined   **There are**
their language to reflect the fact that they use snow in many   **several types of**
different contexts and that snow isn't just snow...   **projects**

In much the same way, the daily language used in connection with project work needs to be refined in order to promote a more qualified dialog. The language we use in connection with projects seems not to have kept pace with the development of new project types. Depending on the type of project, there are significant differences in the demands placed on the project manager and where the project takes place.

Six project types

For our purposes, we will focus on six project types, as illustrated in Figure 2.3.

- Engineering and construction projects
- Research and technology development projects
- R&D projects
- IT and systems development projects
- Organizational change projects
- Policy development projects

The five basic elements of the project

The Danish project management duo, Hans Mikkelsen and Jens O. Riis, describe the characteristics of projects based on five basic elements:

- **The assignment:** The underlying needs. The project purpose and deliverables.
- **The approach:** What is the project structure and primary course of action? How are management and communication to be conducted?
- **The surroundings:** The conditions to which the project is subject, e.g., surrounding systems, regulations, norms and physical surroundings.
- **The stakeholders:** Everyone who has a stake in the project or the project's outcome.
- **The resources:** People, knowledge, expertise, equipment, materials and funding.

The first two basic elements indicate the type of project: What is the task to be carried out and how are you to go about it? Briner *et al.* divide projects up based on two dimensions – uncertainty in terms of objective and means:

- How specific is the project?
- How structured is the approach?

Highly specific projects have precise, clear and concrete deliverables from project start-up. In **less specific projects**, it isn't possible at the project start-up phase to define exactly which deliverables the project will produce, as a number of possibilities must be explored first.

Highly structured projects have a clear-cut structure and well-defined roles, as well as standards for project execution and project tools. **Less structured projects** don't have a clear and formal organization, nor can they make use of standards within project execution; rather, they work things out along the way.

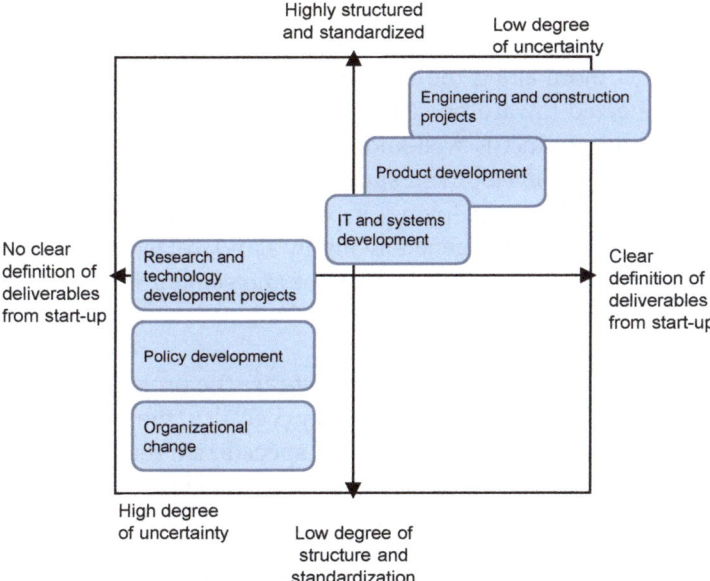

Figure 2.3. Project types are classified based on two axes: The degree to which it is possible to specify deliverables from project start and how structured and standardized the project is. Inspired by Briner et al. 1996. The placement indicates the 'typical' project; there are also differences within the individual project types. This figure further suggests that some IT *projects are just as highly structured as R&D projects*.

2.2.2. Engineering and construction projects

As we pointed out in Chapter 1, the oldest examples of projects are found within the building and construction sector. This is the oldest type of project and oddly enough, it is the one project type in use today that has evolved the least in the last 50 years. In fact, there is growing criticism of the construction sector's lack of productivity.

Standardized product for one customer

The assignment

The construction of buildings, roads and bridges – along with military projects – pioneered the use of the project work form. Examples of engineering and building projects include bridges and tunnels, building and repairing railroad lines, building houses, factories and production plants, and technical installations.

To the customer, this is a one-off assignment, but to the supplier it is more along the lines of contract manufacturing. The task is geared toward one customer and often a matter of logistics, as the product is well-known and comprises standardized elements. The development stage is usually referred to as planning and consists of copying or compiling already known elements. The product is generally highly standardized and subject to compliance with norms, regulations and standards.

Project management is logistics

The approach

Engineering and construction projects are the project type with the highest degree of bureaucracy because the production process has been standardized and specialized, thus making it possible to handle complex assignments quickly and efficiently. For construction companies, projects make up their operational environment.

Governed by contracts, norms, regulations, collective agreements

A key feature of this type of project is that there are standards for how procedures and activities are to be carried out, such as bidding, activity planning, risk assessment, site meetings and time estimation. For instance, the various trades may be governed by collective agreements concluded with trade unions that dictate, say, what a carpenter earns per square foot of roof installed. The organization is also predetermined to include the various trades, like electricians, plumbers, masons, carpenters, etc. However, in recent years we have seen more and more multi-trade consortia and contractors who can provide several trades at once, such as electrical, plumbing and ventilation.

Compared to the other project types, engineering and construction projects have the lowest degree of uncertainty, as the projects comprise many repetitive elements and the organization can utilize its significant experience gained from previous projects. This isn't to say that there are never any surprises in this type of project. Each project is still unique. There are huge differences between erecting an apartment building, a high-tech production plant, a concert hall with high architectural and acoustic demands and wind turbines in the mountains of Kyrgyzstan.

The surroundings
Strict regulation in the form of norms and environmental and safety regulations. The solutions are generally subject to approval by the local authorities and must comply with district plans and servitudes.

The stakeholders
The project has many stakeholders, including the project owner, consultants, investors and users. Within projects, there are many subcontractors, each with their own business-related interests. Suboptimization of professional interests is widespread. However, new modes of collaboration like partnering have developed, which seek to minimize clashes of interests.

The resources
The organization tends to be clear-cut and well-defined. Engineering and construction projects have a full-time project manager and a number of full-time sub-project managers. The team is made up of experienced specialists who generally allocate 100% of their time and have clear and well-defined roles by virtue of their areas of specialization. The clear-cut organization is underpinned in several areas of the engineering and construction sector by the fact that project management is defined as a career path. There are often several levels of project managers, senior project managers, executive project managers, foremen and shift bosses.

Problems can arise with resource utilization due to very sharp professional divides, collective agreements and demand from other projects.

Chapter 2. The Project Work Form

High degree of uncertainty and project complexity

Megascale engineering projects

A special type of engineering and construction project with high uncertainty is the so-called megascale project. This term covers large-scale infrastructure projects, such new roads, railroads and bridges, with price tags in the tens of billions. One example is the Fehmarn Belt Fixed Link between Denmark and Germany or the tunnel between England and France. A key feature of megaprojects is extremely high project complexity, which most often resemble programs. They tend to run for many years and have an abundance of stakeholders on all levels, including politicians, citizens and the press. These projects therefore have some of the same qualities as change projects that are politically initiated.

What's characteristic for these megaprojects is an extremely high degree of uncertainty regarding costs and benefits. Bent Flyvbjerg *et al.* illustrate in *Megaprojects and Risk*[1] how the prognostic benefits often fall 50-100% off the mark and the costs are generally underestimated. Many megaprojects end up overshooting the budget by 100-200%.

Blurred lines between project types

Engineering and construction projects rarely have a clear-cut project type. They frequently overlap with other project types, such as IT and systems development projects or organizational change projects. One example is the renovation of the head office of a public authority. It would initially appear to be a straightforward engineering project. However, as the work with the architects and contractors progresses, the project may evolve into a comprehensive organizational change project. With innumerable and persistent stakeholders, there may be a protracted debate about the pluses and minuses of open-plan or standard closed offices, the physical and psychological working environment and the future of the organization.

---

1. *Megaprojects and Risk. An Anatomy of Ambition.* Bent Flyvbjerg *et al.*, Cambridge University Press, 2003.

2.2.3. R&D projects
The assignment

R&D projects seek to generate business. The project outcome must therefore cater to two needs. The sales department must be able to sell the product for the highest possible price, while production and distribution must be carried out at the lowest possible cost. While engineering projects deliver to only one client, R&D projects must satisfy many customers and customer segments. Consequently, this type of project includes a range of marketing activities, technical and testing activities, and production-oriented tasks.

Developing a business

The challenge is not only to create a technical product or service, but also to develop the immaterial goods and services, like customer service, user training, installation, image and potential market positions. Consequently, R&D projects tend to include elements of organizational change.

Attracting more customers

Typical examples of R&D projects include the launch of a new wind turbine by Vestas or Siemens Wind Power, the development of a compressor by Danfoss, LEGO's warriors, Apple's iPad and Novo Nordisk's insulin pen. R&D also includes projects like the introduction of a new customer service program by Bank of America, a new citizen service request phone line for a local authority and an insurance company offering online customer service outside standard opening hours.

The approach

In contrast to engineering and construction projects, R&D projects often have a very long objective formulation phase, which may be followed by comprehensive testing.

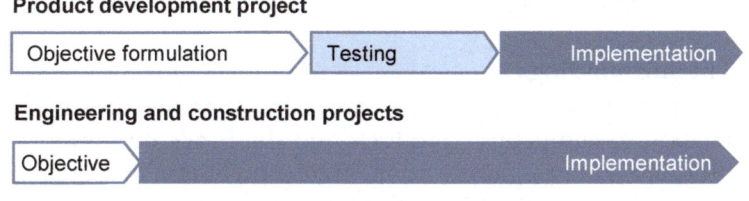

Long objective formulation phase

Figure 2.4. In R&D projects, the business, product and production concepts need to be fleshed out and tested before execution. It's not uncommon for this phase to span half of the total length of the project.

63

The outcome of an R&D project targets many potential customers. Consequently, needs assessment methods, customer analysis and concept development are key activities. It's important to ensure that the future product can be sold in the intended volume and at the intended price.

Parallel processes, sales, development and production

An R&D project comprises parallel processes in which the project team executes activities within sales, marketing, production preparation and service, concurrently with the development of the actual product. The project is divided up into phases called stage gates, a term coined by Robert G. Cooper.

Gate models

After each phase, there is a decision point (a gate) that must be passed through. At each decision point, an assessment is made to determine whether the 'business' behind the project is still interesting. In principle, each gate marks a GO/NO GO decision. This contrasts markedly with engineering projects, where the transition to a new phase is more along the lines of follow-up.

Known technology

R&D projects can pass through several phases before the ultimate objective is fully defined. This rarely happens before the following has been verified: the concept has been tested on the market; the prototype has been performance tested; any new technology has been tested. In principle, all product development builds on known technology. If a project requires new technology, it will be developed concurrently as a separate technology development project. Many people are under the impression that R&D is inherently high in uncertainty. However, this is frequently due to the marketing activities having been skipped and the technological development not having been carried out separately.

The surroundings

The product needs to be positioned in different segments in relation to competitive products and the firm's own product program. Due to globalization, high competition and technological progress, the lifespan of new products is growing ever shorter.

There are many national and international normative requirements and safety regulations that must be complied with.

It is also necessary to consider such aspects as the sales concept, sales channels and distribution.

The stakeholders
This type of product is to be sold to potential customers. Consequently, advanced methods are used for target group segmentation, needs assessment and clarification, customer and user analysis and concept testing. There are often customers on several levels, such as subsidiaries, wholesalers, retailers, sales representatives, customers and users.

Internally, there are a variety of stakeholders, from sales, production and service to the parent company and subsidiaries. Stakeholder involvement can be problematic from a competition point of view. R&D projects are often 'top secret' and customer testing needs to be conducted with the greatest of care.

The 'top secret' project

The resources
Specialists in the R&D department are often allocated to the project full time. However, there may be competition from other projects or ad hoc troubleshooting tasks, while specialist teams can cause bottlenecking.

Involvement from sales and production is often problematic as well, because these project participants are not normally 100% attached to the project.

2.2.4. IT and systems development

It is debatable whether IT and systems development represents a separate project type. It's possible to consider software development R&D development, while the supply of systems can be considered a technical engineering project. However, if an IT system results in significant changes to the organization, it will also have elements of an organizational change project.

We have chosen, here, to designate the systems development project as a separate project type, because of the special conditions associated with it.

Chapter 2. The Project Work Form

Young project culture
- The IT sector is extremely young, from both a professional and project-oriented point of view. As a result, we don't find the same project culture as in R&D and engineering projects.

Close customer collaboration
- Systems development often takes place in close collaboration with the customer in a shared learning process – something which is not found in engineering and R&D projects.

Iterative process
- IT and systems development projects are highly iterative and there is resistance to strictly defined phases and waterfall charts.

Adjusting the system onsite

The assignment
A typical project assignment is the development or changing of an administrative or technical system with a combination of technical, administrative and organizational issues. This type of project covers a variety of IT issues with databases, networks and data distribution. The assignment is often to adapt the supplier's 'standard system' to the customer's specific needs.

This kind of project is carried out in close collaboration with the customer. A learning process is often involved, where the system is adapted to the customer's procedures, needs and current systems. Typical examples of this type of project are: adaption of ERP or SAP systems to meet the needs of a specific customer; development of a specialized record-keeping system for a local authority or hospital; and integration of a hospital's electronic patient medical records and medication management systems.

The approach
The projects are organized in manageable sub-elements, but orchestrated situationally. The work form is not as structured as for engineering projects or stage gate models. This may be due to the fact that the IT community was relatively slow to adopt the project work form. Today, it's considered a matter of course that all aspects of IT are organized into projects. But that wasn't the case far into the 1970s.

One reason for the late introduction of the project as a work form is that the IT world managed for several decades to maintain an aura of innovation. A self-image of an innovative and creative process with a touch of the artistic was achieved, where IT wizards were critical workers no to be bothered by structures and management theories. Traces of this attitude are still found in today's IT projects.

Because the system has to be adapted to the customer's procedures, the objective and project description can be developed and fleshed out along the way. This, however, requires methods for illustrating the system and testing the users' acceptance of the solution proposal.

A central project team is vital, but the many stakeholders need to be continuously involved throughout the process. Results-based management can be difficult, as the work takes the form of a learning process for the customer and the systems supplier. Often, the customer is unable to express clearly what they want before seeing the options. Similarly, it can be difficult to present the various options before the customer's problem has been clarified.

The flow in an IT project (software development) is different from projects where physical units are developed (hardware development). Figure 2.5 illustrates the difference. In most hardware projects, there is a production period spanning from the moment the design is ready until there is a testable prototype. In many projects, this phase can last several months, for example if it's necessary to produce an 80-meter-

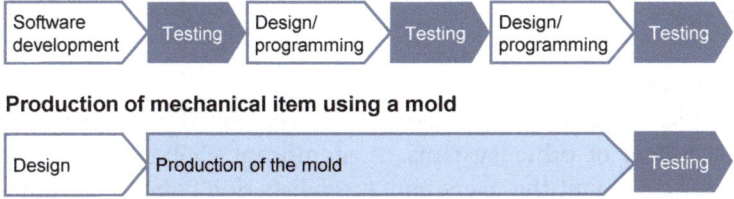

Figure 2.5. This is an illustration of the work forms associated with hardware and software design. Hardware design often has long production times from design to testing, measured in weeks or months. Software has very short cycle times from design to testing, making it possible to work much more iteratively in IT projects.

long mold before casting a new fiberglass blade for a wind turbine. For this reason, a great deal of time and energy is devoted to making sure the design is correct before proceeding to the next step in the process.

Short cycle time In software design, the computer code can be tested immediately after writing the program, and there is no production time afterward – the finished program can simply be copied. With the fiberglass mold example, once the mold has been approved, it still takes time to produce the first test blade.

In software design, it's possible to make some suggestions and allow the customer to assess them – and even make minor adjustments. The cycle time is extremely short. For that reason, the product lifetime of software also tends to be short, often necessitating the use of new solutions during the course of the project without the opportunity to execute a concurrent technology project, which is otherwise considered good practice in new product development.

Project management generally takes place by means of action lists, where problems are added as they arise. The problems are then categorized and labeled as either 'can wait', 'ongoing', or 'solved' and 'tested'.

The surroundings
This project type requires coordination with the customer's other, sometimes older, systems.

Often, the customer wants to use existing systems and is unwilling to make changes across the board. This is the adaptation of a standard solution, which is already found in the market and which the systems are expected to be able 'to interact with'.

The stakeholders
Typical stakeholders are users, management, IT specialists and suppliers of other systems. A significant challenge in these projects is that the users and specialists don't speak the same language.

The resources
Specialists often work as consultants on several projects at once, which can cause bottlenecking. The users tend to lack time, expertise and insight. The superusers are often given training too late in the project, ultimately straining the overall user training and making implementation problematic. The resources on the business side are a part of the operation, and they don't have the necessary time for the project.

2.2.5. Research and technology development projects
The assignment
The task is to solve a well-defined problem, to prove or disprove a hypothesis. The purpose of the project is to establish clarification, generate knowledge, gain new understanding or find explanations for correlations.

Examples of research and technology projects include investigating a technology's yield under specific conditions, determining whether a new method can solve the problem in a satisfactory manner and new pharmaceutical research. The task is characterized by uncertainty about the outcome and whether it is even useable. The outcome can be a rejection of the hypothesis.

Proving or disproving a hypothesis

The approach
The project description will be fleshed out gradually as newly gained understanding makes it possible and necessary. This approach builds on the testing schedule and methods that are relevant within the discipline in question.

It will often be necessary to alter the approach during the course of the project. The choice of method has a significant influence on the quality of the outcome. Choosing the wrong approach can produce invalid results.

Development departments often conduct this type of project as a preliminary project to an R&D project, for example testing how a new type of plastic can be processed or bonded to other materials before deciding to use it in the next R&D project.

If you don't find out whether this type of plastic can be bonded, you risk not completing the R&D project on time – and in R&D projects, this is often tantamount to failure.

Ongoing adjustment of the project description and approach

Quality above deadline Research and technology projects are carried out by means of key milestones and reviews with the participation of specialists. The project team is often smaller, with the project manager serving as the principal specialist. Quality is prioritized above deadlines. However, it can be a very good idea to think in terms of time boxing. There is always room for improvement in knowledge development, for we never finish developing new knowledge.

The surroundings
Depending on the problem, there may be many interfaces. Delimiting the task can have a direct influence on the quality of the solution.

Within the pharmaceutical industry, for instance, projects are highly formalized due to the large range of statutory requirements that must be complied with to achieve approval of results and products.

The stakeholders
In some projects, communication to the surroundings will be hindered by demands for confidentiality due to the desire to patent the results. However, as in all development activities, it's a good idea to contact specialists who can contribute with their expertise.

The resources
The possibilities depend on the specialist knowledge available and the network of contacts the individual employees have at their disposal. What is new knowledge to the firm or organization is often known knowledge in the outside world. So finding the right collaborative partners is key. Access to the right equipment can also be critical for the outcome.

2.2.6. Organizational change projects

Uncertainty about the objective and the approach **The assignment**
The organizational change project covers everything from development and implementation of a new corporate strategy, the introduction of value-based leadership in a local authority and competence-building within an organization, to the introduction of the project work form in a government ministry,

increasing customer focus in a retail chain and improving quality in production – and the list goes on. The task is developmental in nature and the organization will most likely have only limited experience with the problem. It will often be a one-off assignment.

Organizational change projects are characterized by deliverables that are rarely clearly defined from project start-up, just as the desired impact can also be unknown. In some cases, the desired impact is taken as the point of departure: 'We need to reduce response times in the service department,' but how to go about it isn't clear at the start of the project. The objective formulation phase is often a political process involving a number of stakeholders, who are all crucial to the success of the undertaking. What the project owner and other stakeholders actually expect from the project is negotiated and renegotiated throughout the course of the project. See Chapters 3 and 4 for a more detailed presentation of this process.

The approach
This type of project is characterized by a low degree of structure and standardization, as the 'raw materials' in the project are the people who need to change their behavior, which is dictated to a great extent by the context within which they work. It is therefore difficult to create standardized 'recipes' for how to go about changing behavior. The project description and approach are fleshed out on an ongoing basis; far into the implementation phase, there will be changes to the deliverables and required outcome.

In this type of project, work streams covering information, stakeholder consultation, training and education are of great importance. It's vital that everyone can see the urgent need for change, the common vision and what the changes mean for the individual. **Information, communication and training**

A significant challenge in this type of project is the turbulent surroundings in which it takes place and the fact that top management seems to lose interest as time passes. The burning platform is often the hottest at project launch. But after a time, many project managers find that the platform becomes tepid at best.²

Thus, the project manager needs to be able to clarify and communicate the purpose and explain why the project is necessary. The project manager needs to retain top management's support of the changes for the duration of the project.

Disagreement on objective and approach

Organizational change projects are about getting people to change their behavior. Top management and the project manager are key to achieving broad commitment across the organization.

The surroundings are the projects

The surroundings

The project's limits can be extremely difficult to define, as the project deals with the organization in which it is being implemented. Changes in one area will often have consequences in many other areas.

Many conflicting interests

The stakeholders

The individual employees and managers will often have both a professional and personal interest in the project. Production managers may be able to see the business advantages of outsourcing to subcontractors; however, they may not like the idea of making reductions to their 'own department'.

There will be many conflicting views on what the problem is and on what the best solution is. There may be a lack of understanding of the situation accompanied by a great deal of resistance and a this-is-how-we-have-always-done-things attitude.

---

2. According to Christensen and Kreiner, contextual uncertainty in projects is the difference between the knowledge and terms upon which we base the design and plan of a project and the knowledge and terms that form the basis for assessment of the project. The more turbulent the surroundings, the longer the project will take and the greater the risk of very high contextual uncertainty.

The resources
The organization's internal qualifications are often sparse when it comes to the issue in question. Further, this project type tends to have project managers and participants who also perform tasks within the line organization concurrently with the project work. This can be problematic when it comes to freeing up resources.

It can be useful to seek help from the outside for this type of project. Training activities will often be comprehensive, and there just isn't enough time.

No experience, nobody has time, everyone has an opinion

2.2.7. Policy development projects
The task
This type of project is often found in politically governed organizations, such as ministries, municipalities, agencies and NGOs. However, it can also be found in private-sector firms. The task is to prepare a basis for decision-making, analyses, reports or policy development. One example is a survey of refugees' opportunities for finding jobs in the European Union, which is to form the basis of a political proposal from the European Commission and European Parliament.

This type of project has many of the same characteristics as organizational change projects, including that it's often undesirable – or even impossible – to specify the deliverables from the outset. There is an overall purpose, but the official objective may include other agendas that can't be explicitly expressed. For instance, during collective agreement negotiations with the trade unions, it may not be possible to clearly communicate the strategy or which results would be considered acceptable.

Hidden agendas

The purpose can't be communicated

The approach
At times, it may seem to project managers within political organizations as though the actual success criterion for a project is simply to enable the minister to say: 'We've appointed a committee to look into the matter'. What the outcome of the project eventually turns out to be is often of very little interest later, as the press and the public have very short memories.

The process of defining the purpose and deliverables can thus be subject to several agendas, making it necessary to utilize a different rationale for objective-setting than in, say, R&D projects. This means the project manager must possess political flair and be a brilliant stakeholder manager. Success criteria are very difficult to set, as they tend to fall completely outside the influence of the project.

The purpose of the project may actually be to stop a different bill – rather than to get the result of the project, in the form of draft legislation, passed.

When the hierarchy is part of the project

This type of project is also organized differently from other project types. Such projects are, in many areas, still subject to the chain of command found in line management, which means, among other things, that the project manager often doesn't have access to the project owner/steering committee, because he or she reports to the office manager or another immediate superior in the traditional hierarchy. This also means that there are fairly strict standards for the written deliverables, such as memorandums and reports.

Such projects tend to be executed with a very small project team that serves as secretariat for several reference groups and hearing committees. The project manager's personal clout and political flair are vital in this regard. In this type of project, the organizational legitimacy of the deliverables is often more important than the quality objectives themselves.

Politics is daily life for project managers in public and private-sector organizations

Political games in connection with projects aren't limited only to state, regional and municipal organizations – they occur in all types of organizations. Project managers everywhere know all too well the hidden agendas and power struggles that make political flair one of the project manager's most important management skills.

Disagreement on the steering committee, and they're proud of it

The surroundings

The boundaries of the project surroundings can be extremely difficult to define. One feature is that the steering committee or top management have based their decisions on different interests and make it a point to call attention to these divergent points of view.

2.2. Project types

Basic element	Engineering and construction project	Product development	IT and systems development	Technology development	Organizational change	Policy development
The assignment	Well-defined product objective from start-up. Standardized tasks for one customer. Experience from similar projects.	Product objective developed in early phases. Product for many customers with sales concept and production concept.	Ongoing development of product objective in collaboration with customer. Development-oriented deliverable for one customer.	Project objective is described as hypotheses to be tested. Project objective changes with new understanding.	One-time assignment. Uncertainty about objective and process at start-up. Project objective clarified in a process between project owner and stakeholders.	Achieving compromise. Hidden agendas. Objective can't always be communicated. Product objective developed in a political process between stakeholders.
The approach	Fixed and structured approach divided into phases. Hierarchical structure with established professional boundaries. Many subcontractors. Management based on contracts and milestones.	Integrated parallel process. Management based on project model with phases, gates and standard work streams. Development of requirements specification. Management based on requirements specification and milestones.	Management based on purpose, deliverables and key milestones. Close collaboration with customer. Iterative process. Short cycle time. Use of action lists.	Ongoing adjustment of project description and approach. Quality over deadline. Management based on key milestones.	Situation-based process structure, with emphasis on information, communication and training. Establishment of a governing coalition is crucial.	Politically appointed steering committee. Approach chosen based on possible alliances. High degree of consultation of stakeholders.
The surroundings	Requirement of adaptation to systems, norms and rules.	Position in the market. Technological development. Bound by existing production and sales channels.	Coordination with customer's other systems.	Delimitation has strong influence on outcome, as expertise can be found in the surroundings.	The surroundings are the project. Can be difficult to delimit. Working conditions can be stipulated in collective agreement.	Disagreement among steering committee members and they're proud of it. Many systems and political interfaces.
The stakeholders	Multiple business interests and authorities.	Multiple in-house interests. Customers and authorities.	Stakeholders speak different languages. Specialists and users.	Marked use of stakeholders.	Conflicting views of the problem and solution. Resistance and lack of understanding and acceptance.	Conflicting interests that change with the wind. Power struggles and political games.
The resources	Specialists, professionals. Competition between several projects.	In-house specialization. People can cause bottlenecking.	Limited user knowledge. Need for training.	Governed by personal interests and professional ambitions.	Nobody has experience, nobody has time, everybody has an opinion.	Interest-oriented process.

Figure 2.6. Characteristics of various project types.

The press can have just as strong an influence as the steering committee, and timing in relation to the public debate is critical.

In ministries, it is often the case that as long as the minister is happy, it doesn't really matter what all the other stakeholders and parliament think.

Conflicting interests

The stakeholders

There are many stakeholders with conflicting interests. Interest tends to follow the public debate and change with the wind.

There are all varieties of political games and power struggles. Alliances are formed and broken as new opportunities arise. For this reason, the order of a project's decision-making process is of no consequence – the recipe is: 'How can we get the thing passed'.

Interest-oriented process

The resources

Both hearing committees (reference groups) and project teams can comprise participants with highly conflicting interests. In projects where several organizations need to work together, the process is very stakeholder-oriented. However, the project manager doesn't have direct managerial authority over all the participants on the project team.

Some participants are there to keep abreast of developments or to steer the project in a specific direction rather than to make a contribution. Often times, the participants can't contribute until they have received approval from their 'support base'.

Individual 'consultations' with the support base is a common method.

In this type of project, resources are more than just expertise; the acceptance of supporters is equally important.

The characteristics of the various project types are listed in Figure 2.6.

2.3. The projects in the organization

2.3.1. The insurmountable silos

For years, we have seen a tendency in most larger organizations to organize according to area of specialization. In this type of organizational structure, operational tasks generally follow the easiest path through the organization. Operational tasks are characterized by the fact that they are known and therefore can be easily placed with the individual who is deemed to be the most competent for the job. At the same time, that person can seek assistance from an entire department of specialists, which can support the performance of the task.

In the last 20 or so years, most organizations have seen an increase in the number of projects. Typical for these projects is that they can't all be placed in just one silo, because it's not possible to limit them to a specific unit within the organization. According to their nature, they should be executed as cross-organizational assignments. However, this can be a challenge for the organization, as cross-organizational coordination tends to be difficult in practice.

Projects typically live on the edge of the line management for a while, often growing more and more anemic before top

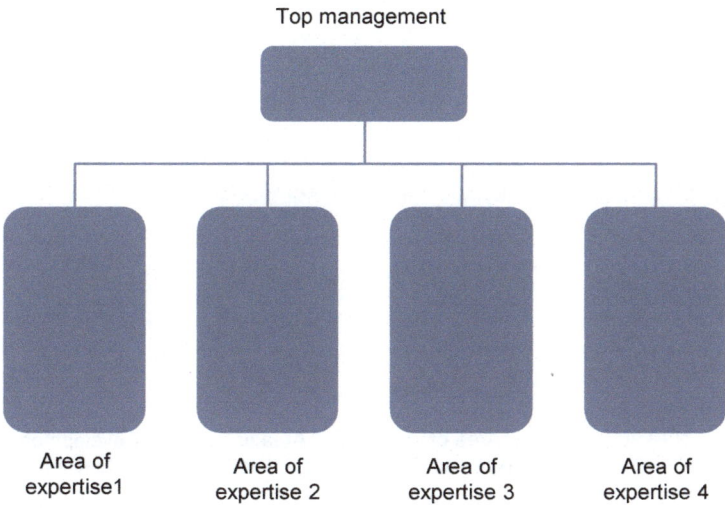

Figure 2.7. The ordinary silo-based organization as we know and love it.

management steps in and reorganizes things to achieve a more project-oriented approach. Reorganization is generally not worthwhile if projects make up more than 10-15 percent of the business and are furthermore vital for the business in the relatively short term. In the following, we will focus on the project conditions in the silo-based line organization.

2.3.2. Three typical organizational designs

When top management makes the decision to reorganize, a purely political process is triggered. There are typically a number of middle managers who stand to lose power, as their responsibilities are delegated to others. There are of course innumerable ways to design an organization to both cope with the schizophrenia and continue to be oriented toward growth and operations. There are generally three basic structures, which can be used as templates. The three templates place different demands on the project manager.

We need a project department

We'll just create a new silo – the elitist model
In the elitist model, the organization is still divided up according to specialization – this means the silos that are already in place can be retained. Development in the form of project exe-

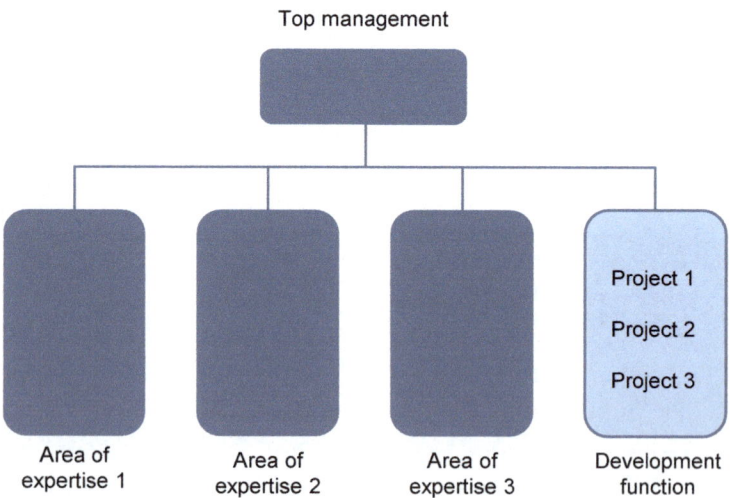

Figure 2.8. The manufacturing company with a development department – a classic since the 1960s.

cution is simply a new silo with the 'autonomy' to carry out the vast majority of the development work within the organization. The project managers are recruited directly into the development department, where they typically sit for the duration of their employment in the organization. This type of organization is often found in large technology-based firms.

Advantages:
- It's possible to focus long-term and intensively on the individual project
- Maintaining a highly 'realistic' perspective isn't crucial
- Appeals to true 'developers'
- Ideal for genuine development projects, which require innovative thinking

Disadvantages:
- Risk of tunnel vision
- Risk of prima-donna behavior among developers
- Risk of an A and B distinction within the organization, where developers are regarded with envy
- Risk of developing unusable solutions
- Risk of over-specialization among developers
- Inflexible and at times expensive if the number of developers is overdimensioned

The integrated model
The integrated model arises when an ad hoc project unit is appointed with the project managers who are only affiliated for a limited period of time. The project managers are then moved somewhere within the line organization – usually after 6 months to a year. This gives the project managers a perfect opportunity to utilize the expertise and the network they bring with them from the line organization. The projects thus benefit from floating on the edge of the line organization. This is the best organizational design for the execution of operational optimization projects.

Chapter 2. The Project Work Form

Projects are necessary, but operations is our livelihood

Manufacturing or service companies tend to choose this type of organization – firms where the main focus is still operations and where development is simply a way to optimize an already well-functioning line organization.

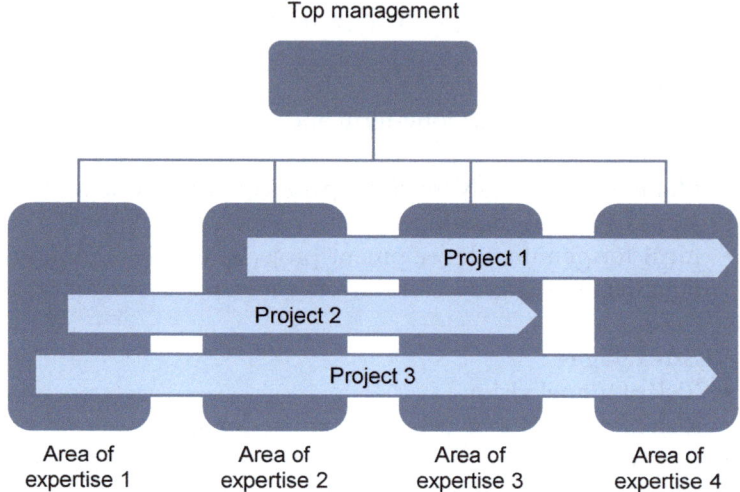

Figure 2.9. The integrated model, as we know it from many manufacturing or service companies, ministries, agencies and municipalities since the early 1990s.

Advantages:
- Close correlation between operational demands and the opportunity for development
- Ideal for operational optimization projects
- Good opportunity for variation in work tasks over time for the individual employee
- Flexible and 'cheap', as there is a sizeable group of potential project staff who can be brought together to execute a project

Disadvantages:
- The projects tend to seek to improve already existing solutions – projects without discontinuous innovation.

- If the project staff aren't moved physically from their operational units, there will be the same challenges as in the old bureaucratic organization
- Inexperienced project managers and lack of project competence

The project-oriented organization
In project-oriented firms, the central unit within the organization is the individual project. The number of projects and their type constantly change, depending on what the customers demand in terms of specializations and resources. This means that the organization is governed at all times by the current project portfolio. At the same time, there is only one underlying, virtual division between specializations or competences. Consequently, the individual must be able to execute self-management in a network of agreements with colleagues and project managers.

This structure is generally preferred by smaller, knowledge-based organizations, such as ad agencies, consulting firms and development departments in large technology-based compa-

When operations is one big project portfolio

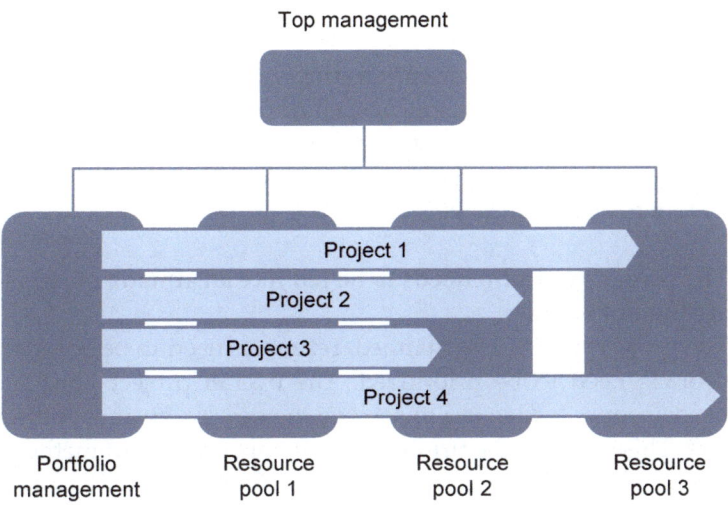

Figure 2.10. The project-oriented organization. Typically seen in consulting firms and ad agencies.

81

nies. Ministries and agencies tend to develop in this direction as well, with their ongoing project portfolio of draft legislation and policy development projects. This type of organization generally pops up when the volume of resources devoted to projects exceeds the resources devoted to operational tasks, or in organizations where the line environment is one big project portfolio.

Advantages:
- Flexible in the transition to a new project portfolio
- Geared toward optimization of the individual project
- No disruptive operational focus
- Ideal solution for (external) customer projects

Disadvantages:
- Driven solely by the project requirements that arise in the individual project
- Knowledge transfer from project to project occurs at random
- There are no operational tasks to 'fall back on' for the individual – it is often a fairly competitive environment
- There is a tough Darwinist selection process – it's obvious which project staff are passed up. Employees tend to focus on personal branding

Management of project work in the organization
In all three types of organizational design, it isn't enough for the project manager to manage the individual project. Project work needs to be managed on several levels within the organization to ensure success.

Someone needs to lead the entire fleet

The project portfolio needs to be led like an armada of ships setting out to sea
The projects need to be manned, resources need to be secured, projects need to be prioritized. The overall project portfolio needs proper leadership to achieve the desired business objective. This is where the firm's project competences and methods are developed.

Portfolio management is conducted by the top management within the organization and on a lower level within the

2.3. The projects in the organization

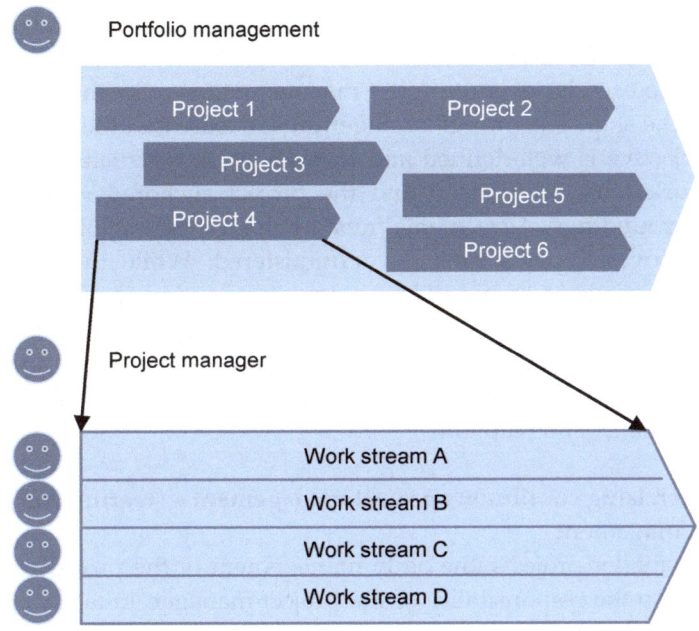

Figure 2.11. Management of the project-oriented structure requires management on several organizational levels: portfolio management, project management and management of work streams and sub-projects.

program management. Portfolio management is covered in Chapter 10, where the concepts of portfolio management, program management, project management model, project committee, etc. are presented.

The project manager as the captain of the ship – leadership   Leadership
The project manager's job is to plan and establish the project and execute the overall project management. This is where the project manager displays leadership.
Establishing the project consists of concluding agreements with the steering committee on objective formulation, resource allocation and the overall schedule planning. It's important that the project manager is actively involved in the process of appointing the team, i.e. who should be part of the project and how it should be organized. This is covered in Chapters 3, 4

and 5, which deal with the project's objective, stakeholders and organization.

To exercise overall project management is to be the captain of the ship. The project manager must ensure that the project's objective is well-defined and that the work is structured. The work must be planned and the project anchored within its surroundings. Agreements must be made with suppliers, and the overall plans must be administered. While the project manager isn't responsible for actual execution, he or she is responsible for making sure the work gets done. This element of the project manager role is described in Chapters 6, 7 and 8, which cover the milestone plan, communication and the project manager as captain.

Steering and management

Exercising continuous project management – steering and management

In smaller projects, the daily management of the project team is also the responsibility of the project manager. In larger projects, the daily management will generally be delegated to people with responsibility for the individual work streams, often referred to as sub-projects.

This is a steering and management task. Detailed processes must be planned, activities specified, and there must be follow-up on quality, time and resources.

The basis for cooperation and motivation must be developed, and the ongoing communication promoted. The participant's competences must be boosted by means of sparring and coaching.

This aspect of the project manager role is explored in Chapter 9 on leadership, team building and methods.

2.4. Reflections on the project work form

How does your project look?

The project assignment
- Is your assignment a project or simply an ad hoc task?
- Which project features are characteristic for your assignment?
- How complex is your project?

2.4. Reflections on the project work form

- What makes your project complex, and what impact does this have on your choice of approach?
- How uncertain is your project – what is the root cause of the uncertainty?

- Which project type is your project – what impact does this have on your choice of approach?
- Does your project combine elements of several project types?
- What characterizes your project's five basic project elements: assignment, approach, surroundings, stakeholders and resources?

Project type

- Which organizational structure is your project subject to? What are the advantages and disadvantages on a day-to-day basis?
- What would it mean for your project if it were to be conducted within an elitist or integrated model?
- How does your project organization differ from the project-oriented organization?

The organization

- How does your project feature in the overall portfolio?
- What correlations are there to other projects?
- What have you done to establish the right project team?
- How is your project organized?
- What does your daily project management consist of?

Top management

What is the objective of the project
– where are we going?
Begin with the ending

Once you have established the objective, you have something to navigate by!

CHAPTER 3

What is the objective of the project?

Is the objective clear, realistic and accepted?   Challenges
One of the biggest challenges with projects is describing a clear objective that also has the support of the most important stakeholders. The clearer the objective is defined, the more apparent it becomes that the stakeholders disagree. It's easy to agree as long as the objective is weakly formulated and everyone can twist it to suit their own interests. In situations where the conflicts of interests are overwhelming, the whole process can get very political and it may be necessary to avoid coming across too strong.

The objective needs to be clear and realistic. However, in a turbulent environment and an ever-changing world, we may have a clear objective, but only until we define a new clear objective. And yet, making too many changes to the objective can have a demotivating effect on the project participants. The challenge is to define a clear objective among disagreeing stakeholders that is relevant in a changing world.

This chapter provides answers to the following questions: Benefits
- How is objective-setting used as a management tool?
- How can the objective be broken down into the project purpose, deliverables and success criteria?
- How is the project's objective breakdown structure developed?
- What is a SMART objective?

Objective-setting and management   Focus
This chapter focuses on using objective-setting as a management tool within such areas as:

- Negotiating contracts and reconciling expectations
- Providing direction, coordination and focus
- Promoting motivation and commitment
- Establishing a common objective and team building
- Promoting learning and experience building

This chapter also examines the objective breakdown structure (OBS) as a useful, creative tool for formulating the problem and clarifying the individual goals and their mutual coherence within the overall objective.

Tools Tool 3.1 Objective Breakdown Structure (OBS)
Tool 3.2 Impact Case and Benefit Tracking

3.1. Where are we going, what is our aim?

3.1.1. We begin with the ending

Why talk about objective-setting?

In Chapter 1, we learned that projects are about creating an image of a desired future. It is a process of projecting this image onto a new place – from the mind or a sheet of paper onto reality – and altering reality toward the focal point.

In Stephen Covey's *The Seven Habits of Highly Effective People*, he writes that when we want to achieve something, we need to 'begin with the ending in mind' – to begin with a vision of where we want to end up. We have to set an objective.

You can't start leading until you have established the objective

The word *leadership* comes from the Anglo-Saxon word *laed*, which means path or road. This word comes from the verb *laeden*, which means to travel or embark on a journey.

Leadership is finding a path

The Anglo-Saxons adapted the word to various situations. For instance, *laed* was the term for a ship's heading. The leader was the person who showed the way. On land, the leader would take the lead and find the path. At sea, the leader was the ship's mate or the person responsible for navigation.

The concept of leadership is also closely related to finding a path and setting a course to reach a goal. It's impossible to imagine leading a project without an objective. If you don't know where you're going, how can you navigate?

For leadership purposes, we operate with three types of objectives.

Project purpose, deliverables and success criteria

The project purpose or vision tells us where we're going and why the project is interesting. It provides meaning – the impact we want to achieve.

The deliverables, or project outputs as they are often called, tell us what we have delivered at the end of the project. What we can plan to execute. They are what we carry out with the resources we're allocated – the project's output.

The success criteria describe the impact we wish to achieve with the project. This is how we measure whether we have achieved the purpose and made the desired difference. The project's outcome – the specific measurable impact.

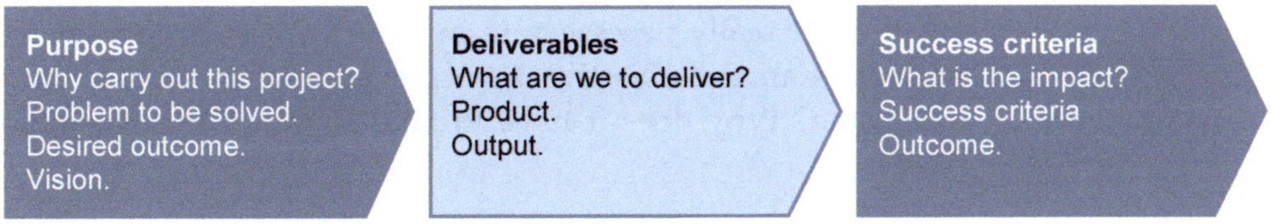

Purpose
Why carry out this project?
Problem to be solved.
Desired outcome.
Vision.

Deliverables
What are we to deliver?
Product.
Output.

Success criteria
What is the impact?
Success criteria
Outcome.

Figure 3.1. The three elements of the objective that show us why the project is necessary, what we need to deliver and what the desired outcome of the project is.

In addition to defining the direction of the project, the objective also influences key management areas:

- Reconciliation of expectations and contract negotiation
- Direction, coordination and focus
- Motivation and commitment
- Common objective and team building
- Learning and experience building

3.1.2. Reconciliation of expectations and contract negotiation

Decision makers within an organization initiate projects in order to make a difference and have an impact. This work needs to be carried out by 'someone'. Describing the project's future impact and deliverables makes it possible to conclude an agreement between those who want the project carried out (the project owner or steering committee) and those who are to carry out the project work (the project team).

Three specific questions are of interest to both parties:

- What is the project team expected to deliver?
- What resources will be allocated by the steering committee?
- What is the timeframe for deliverables?

A specification of the objective will therefore quickly give rise to discussions between the two parties. Are these the deliverables we need to achieve the objective? Does it have to cost so much? Is it really necessary to operate with such limited resources? Can the objective be achieved within such a short timeframe? Why does it have to take so long? The more de-

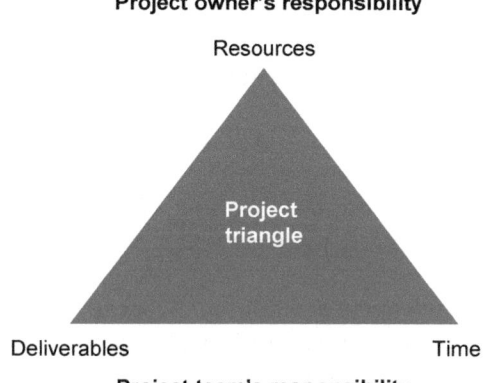

Figure 3.2. The agreement between the project owner (steering committee) and the project team is built on three cornerstones. The project team undertakes to deliver the agreed results at the planned time and with the agreed resources, while the project owner undertakes to allocate the necessary resources. It is interesting how the three cornerstones correspond with the organization's overall strategy.

tailed the deliverables, the louder the discussions. This adjustment of expectations is a necessary process, and it's impossible to carry out without defining the objective.

Use the agreed project triangle
In *Project Leadership*, Colin Hastings describes the six elements of the project manager's role as leader. He calls one of these elements 'looking upwards' – this is how the project manager relates to the steering committee. In this context, objective clarification is a vital management tool for the steering committee as well as the project manager. Both parties need to agree on the right combination of deliverables, resources and deadlines. Since it's perfectly normal for the project requirements to change during the process, it is important to know the point of departure. A sharply defined objective is literally worth its weight in gold when the project changes begin pouring in.

In relation to the project's other stakeholders, it is also important that the objective is clearly communicated and accepted. The objective must be attractive to the most important stakeholders; otherwise, you will lose their support for the project. Choosing the right objective to minimize resistance can get very 'political'. Hastings calls this process of managing stakeholders 'looking outwards'. Much of the project manager's time is spent on this process of reconciling expectations, which need to be adjusted constantly as the stakeholders gain more and more insight into the many aspects of the project.

> **Use the agreed project triangle**

One of the biggest reasons projects fail is a lack of clear, attractive and specific deliverables. 'We thought we were in agreement, but when we realized what the project was actually about, everything looked different!'

This is why it's crucial that the objective is defined precisely enough that it can be used both as a guide and as a basis for negotiations.

The project triangle is the 'contract' between the steering committee and the project. As soon as there are changes, the contract must be renegotiated. The area of the triangle indicates the agreed risk level. For instance, if we change the resources and choose not to use the most experienced experts or

> **Changes entail renegotiating the project triangle**

Chapter 3. What is the objective of the project?

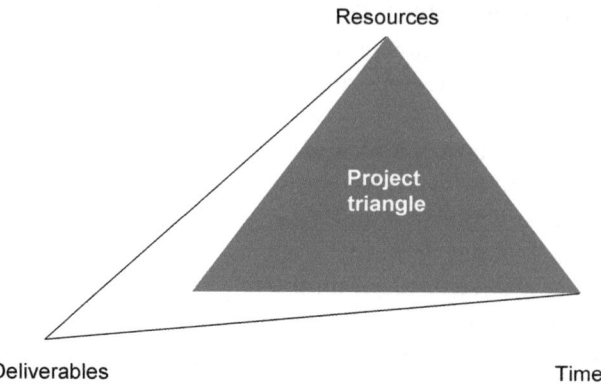

Figure 3.3. When you pull on one corner of the project triangle, the angle changes in at least one other corner – often in both of them. It's not possible to change the deliverables without influencing the resource consumption or timeframe. The same applies to the other two corners.

the right equipment, then we also change the level of risk. The shape of the triangle indicates the project's overall business case. If the deliverables are delayed, we won't achieve the same impact at the agreed time. This weakens the business case.

Direction, coordination and focus
One of the most important reasons for having a clear objective is that we need a something to guide us. With that said, it is also understood that the world is bound to change after the project has been defined. It's therefore necessary to continuously assess whether the objective is still relevant or the 'right' one in light of the current situation. Søren Christensen and Kristian Kreiner show in their book, *Projektledelse i løst koblede systemer* (Project management in loosely organized systems), that it's impossible to define the objective at the beginning of a project, as we don't have enough knowledge at that time. However, this does not mean that objective-setting is impossible or that it's useless to formulate an objective based on what is known so far. A turbulent world doesn't mean that the objective loses its meaning. On the contrary, you need to have a well-define objective at all times. You just have to be prepared

to adjust the objective to ensure that it remains up to date and relevant. The objective can and will change.

It is a mistake to conclude that it's not necessary to define the objective in an ever-changing world. Take for instance a captain steering a ship to safe harbor. A course has been set, but he can't know everything about weather, current and wind conditions. If a storm or thick fog develops, it can be difficult to stay on course, but that doesn't make the course any less important. In just such difficult situations, it is vital that we know where we should be in relation to where we are.

Objective-setting is also important in a turbulent world

The problem arises if we set the objective in stone without considering that conditions can change during the course of the project. One of the project manager's (the captain's) jobs is, therefore, to constantly look ahead and assess whether we can reach land before we run out of supplies and fuel. If there are problems, the project needs to change its heading and put into port elsewhere or take on more resources.

3.1.3. Motivation and participation

The objective describes the level of ambition and the obligations the project team has assumed. We are all affected by what the world expects of us. This is why the objective can be very motivating if it is set properly.

A well-formulated project purpose makes the project team's work meaningful. The team can accept that the chosen future is worth working hard – even extremely hard – to achieve.

Well-defined deliverables clearly show what the team is expected to deliver. Most people are motivated by knowing exactly what is expected of them.

A positive and logical link between the project purpose and the deliverables releases a great deal of energy and passion. There is a correlation between what we have chosen to deliver and the difference we want to make in the world – this has a motivating effect on all parties.

The American psychologist Frederick Herzberg is recognized for his theory on what motivates employees to make an extra effort. According to his findings, the most important motivational factor is being able to see the results of your work – in a project, this can be the deliverables you have achieved.

The next factor is recognition for our work – that is, regular feedback on the results we achieve. The third factor is the nature of the work – is it challenging, can I use my competences, is it stimulating?

The fourth factor is responsibility, for instance for deliverables and milestones during the course of the project.

We are highly motivated by what people expect of us

Objective-setting can therefore be used actively to motivate the project team:

- If the project participants are encouraged to help define the objective and specify the deliverables within their areas of expertise, they assume shared responsibility for the project.
- If the objective can be divided up into smaller sub-objectives, we can document the results and give the project participants recognition for their work.
- If the objective is challenging, then it will stimulate personal and professional development.

The latter has been the subject of much debate in recent years. Classic project management theory emphasizes accuracy and objective achievement.

However, if people are motivated by aspects such as challenging and stimulating objectives, a dilemma can arise between a realistic objective and a motivating objective.

Christensen and Kreiner discuss this issue in their book. If a realistic objective is required, then the objective will generally be set too low out of fear of not being able to achieve the objective, thus ensuring that the objective is realistic.

Make demands, but be fair and give praise

Often, it is therefore better to set very ambitious objectives and then accept that we may only achieve 80 percent, rather than aiming for a lower 'realistic' objective. The final outcome may turn out better if we accept the uncertainty and concentrate on motivation. Christensen and Kreiner provide 10 unorthodox project management tips, including:

- Make unreasonable demands, be insistent, but keep sanctions fair.
- Share the project successes with the participants – chances are you'll have to rely on each other again!

In leadership, there is great truth to this approach to objective-setting. Make demands, be fair and give praise.

Common objective and team building
Another element of the project manager's role, as described by Colin Hastings as 'looking downwards', aims to maximize the team's performance. A crucial element in this context is team building. In management literature, a team is often described as a group of people with a common objective. A central aspect of the definition of a team, then, is that the group has a common objective or works toward a common goal.

If you consider the activities carried out under the guise of 'team building', one of the first things you will work with is achieving a common objective. Then you will move on to achieving a distribution of responsibilities that both reflects the individual's contribution or competences and is based on the deliverables.

No objective; no team – just a random group of people

Thus, the project team's clarification of the project purpose is more than just a practical arrangement for achieving the right objective of high quality. It's also a fundamental team-building activity that promotes acceptance of the assignment and commitment among the team members.

3.1.4. Learning and experience building
Projects are fraught with uncertainty because our knowledge about the problem in question is limited in the beginning. We grow wiser as the project progresses.

This learning is a vital aspect of project work and requires that you wonder why things are progressing differently than expected. This reflection, which makes learning possible, requires that you know where you were originally heading. If the project team has no idea how the project ought to have progressed, how can they wonder why things are going differently? Objective-setting is thus not only a matter of being able to lead, but also of being able to reflect on the progress of the project and learn in the process.

If we need to drive 100 miles in a car and have calculated that it will take about 5 gallons of gas, then you know that there is a problem if you have used up 3 gallons after just 50 miles (especially if there are only 2 gallons left in the tank). If we don't know that there are 100 miles to travel and 5 gallons in the tank, then it's difficult to pay attention to the gas consumption before the car stops running. And when it stops running, there can be any number of reasons why it won't start, and we may have wasted our chance to do something about it.

According to Hastings, part of the role of project manager is to constantly look back and assess whether the deliverables are being delivered as planned. Deviations are a source of learning and experience so the course can be re-established or adjusted.

3.2. The objective, project cycle and uncertainty

3.2.1. Objective-setting requires knowledge

Objectives can't be set without careful analysis

At the beginning of a project, the degree of uncertainty is very high and relatively little is actually known. It is therefore impractical to set objectives too early before the necessary insights have been gained.

For this reason, objective-setting is carried out over several steps throughout the initial phase(s), as illustrated in Figure 3.4 below.

The objective is realized at different junctures

The steering committee or project owner will often have formulated the purpose of the project – a problem to be solved or a vision to be achieved. The project owner may have also defined some success criteria for the project. Based on an analysis of the project, the project team will be able to define the deliverables that fulfill the project purpose and success criteria.

In other cases, the project owner is not as certain, and only the purpose is known. It is consequently the project team's job to determine both the deliverables and the success criteria.

3.2. The objective, project cycle and uncertainty

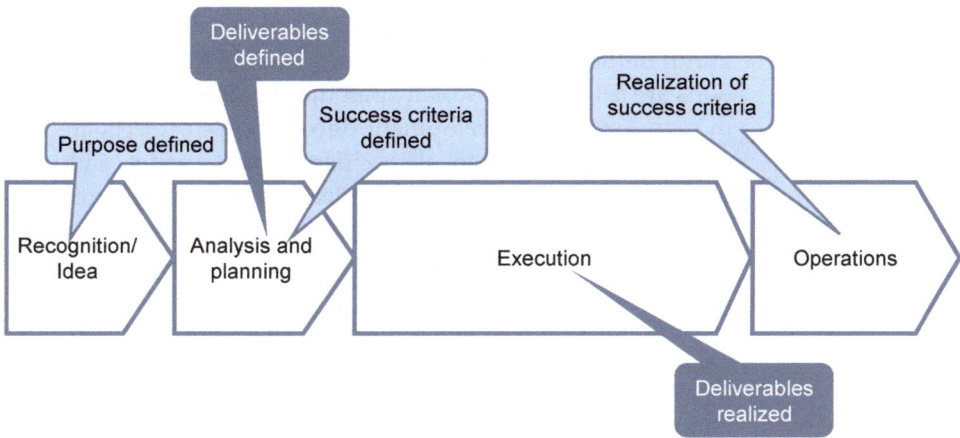

Figure 3.4. Objective-setting takes place in steps as the level of knowledge increases and the degree of uncertainty decreases. First, the purpose and desired impact are established. Then the deliverables are determined. The entire objective consists of three elements: the purpose, deliverables and success criteria.

Everything is discussed with the project owner prior to the implementation phase. This iterative process is often carried out in several 'loops'.

Sometimes it isn't possible to set a deadline for defining the objective before a draft plan has been drawn up – and a plan can't be developed without knowing what the deliverables are. It often isn't until both the objective and the plan have been drawn up that it's possible to say with any degree of certainty when the success criteria can be fulfilled, etc.

3.2.2. Objective-setting phase depends on the project type
The objective-setting phase varies according to project type.

Engineering and construction projects tend to be characterized by this phase being completed before the project team has actually been formed. It may therefore seem like the objective is stated in the contract. Sometimes these objectives are stated as functional specifications, and the actual detailed description of deliverables and planning represent the first phase of the project.

Development projects are characterized by a relatively long objective-setting phase, often called a concept development phase. The objective is generally validated by the customer group in the form of a test of concept before the final specifications are set. This phase can span up to half the project period. In many product development departments, projects are executed in accordance to a specified project model with pre-defined phases. For example: idea phase, concept development, design phase, prototyping, trial production and launch.

Often, the objective is not set until the second or third phase.

In organizational change projects, the point of departure is generally the desire for a more or less well-defined improvement, such as shorter lead times, fewer errors or greater flexibility. The employees are often involved in the specific organizational changes and the final solution therefore evolves very late in the course of the project. Even for larger projects, where centralized pilot projects have been carried out before the solution is rolled out to the entire organization, the decentralized solutions will not be identical to the pilot project's solutions. The objective is set early in the project and often resembles a purpose rather than a precise specification of the deliverable – the future organization.

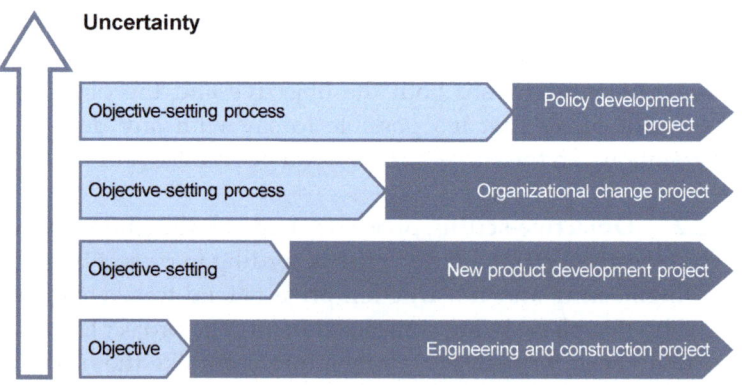

Figure 3.5. Depending on the project type, the objective-setting phase varies in length and content (light-gray arrows). But regardless of project type, it's important to have a well-defined objective. The question is how early in the process this can be achieved.

In policy development projects, the objective is created as a string of compromises in a political process between the stakeholders. The objectives can't always be communicated until very late in the process.

In order to define the objective in detail, it is divided into three elements: the project purpose, deliverables and success criteria. The six project types are executed based on very different points of departure in relation to these three elements.

Engineering and construction projects are basically carried out based on the deliverables. The project purpose is almost imperceptible in the project and the success criteria are extremely specific performance measurements. The success criteria are often derived directly from the deliverables, for instance the insulating property is derived from the number of inches of insulating material, which is a deliverable.

Technological development and research projects are conducted based on the purpose. The purpose is often to prove or disprove a hypothesis. Consequently, the deliverable can be both positive and negative.

In product development projects, deliverables and success criteria are the focus. The purpose is generally limited to market shares and contribution margins, and is often the same for many of the firm's development projects.

IT and systems development projects are managed on the basis of the deliverables. These tend to be adjusted during the course of the project, while the success criteria are used to test the technology.

Organizational change projects are executed based on the purpose and success criteria. The deliverables are often not known until late in the process. The success criteria are generally not measured after the project has been completed, although it is a very good idea to do so.

Policy development projects are managed based on the purpose. The deliverables are rarely defined in much detail. The success criteria tend to be difficult to measure and often don't provide a realistic picture of the project's political success.

3.3. Development of the objective

3.3.1. Objective-setting: the three elements

Purpose: Why carry out this project?

The project purpose, or vision, tells us where we're going, why the project is interesting and what the project's expected outcome is. The purpose provides meaning.

A good rule of thumb when defining the project purpose is that it should answer the question why. Why are we carrying out this project? For example: 'We are carrying out this project to ensure uniform quality!' The purpose, then, is to ensure uniform quality.

Ask: 'Why should we carry out this project?'
Answer: 'In order to...'

Deliverables: What are we to deliver?

Deliverables, or project outputs as they are often called, tell us what we have delivered at the end of the project. The deliverables say how we will achieve the purpose and what we need to deliver in order to fulfill that purpose. It is the product we hold in our hands at the end of the project when there is nothing left to do.

The deliverables are formulated by asking: 'What do we need to deliver in order to achieve the purpose?' For example: 'To draw up a quality handbook; train every single employee; etc.'

Ask: 'How can we achieve the purpose?'
Answer: 'By delivering...'

Always describe deliverables as a status. Deliverables: Every employee has been trained and the quality handbook has been compiled.

Success criteria: Did it make a difference?

Success criteria describe the impact we wish to achieve with the project. It is how we measure whether we have achieved the purpose and made the desired difference. The question is: 'How do we measure the achievement of the purpose?'

For example: 'By measuring whether the error rate has been reduced to 0.5 percent.'

Ask: 'How can we measure the achievement of the purpose?'
Answer: 'By measuring...'

There will often be certain success criteria that are critical for determining a project's success. A set of critical success criteria is therefore designated.

The purpose, deliverables and success criteria represent the objective breakdown structure (OBS). In terms of the timeframe, they are often defined in the order: purpose, success criteria and deliverables. During the course of the project, they are realized in the reverse order: the project realizes the deliverables, which produces an impact, which can be measured by means of the success criteria, whereby the purpose has been achieved.

3.3.2. The objective breakdown structure – creative objective-setting

When developing and defining the objective, it's a good idea to work with the OBS, which lets you work creatively with the problem formulation and objective-setting. The purpose, objective and means are often subject to discussion. Technically, there's no difference, it is solely their placement in the OBS that determines whether we are dealing with the purpose or the deliverables. There are fundamental differences between the OBS: Objective Breakdown Structure and the WBS: Work Breakdown Structure. The OBS focuses on the result you want to achieve, while the WBS focuses on the activities that need to be carried out, the work packages. In this book, our focus is on the OBS; however, WBS development is carried out according to the same principles.

It's a good idea for the project team to spend time developing the OBS hierarchy. Working in-depth with objective definition increases your understanding and provides a holistic view of the project. There is a tendency to focus on the immediate solutions and to settle on known solutions too early in the process. However, there are generally many alternative solutions that can fulfill the same purpose.

To illustrate the objective-setting process, we will use a case story which we will return to throughout the book.

Chapter 3. What is the objective of the project?

Case: Happier Customers!

Creative objective-setting, step by step

The purpose of the project is often formulated by management or the project owner. Now, it's the project team's job to define how to achieve that purpose. In some cases, several sub-projects have been defined, which combined should fulfill the common purpose. Consequently, it will be the project team's job to define the project deliverables in relation to the other projects for the benefit of the project as a whole and avoid major overlaps or duplicated work. The OBS can be used in both situations.

The project: Happier Customers!

A company that produces machinery for the plastics industry is under pressure to lower their prices and therefore wants to be more competitive in relation to the competition. Thus, the overall and long-term strategic goal is to boost the company's competitiveness. Increased competitiveness can be the purpose of several of the company's change projects. One of the many projects that underpins this purpose is the development of the sales processes to make them more efficient and to give customers better assistance and better customized solutions – the company wants to generate fans!

Use of cards for group work

At one of the company's regional sales offices, a project team has been formed, tasked with implementing the new sales and consulting concept. The team comprises participants from sales, marketing, after-sales service and the technology department. It has been decided to host a kick-off seminar to flesh out the project objective. They need a method that is suitable for group work. To ensure that everyone can make a contribution – which is the whole point, after all – the OBS is to be developed on the wall, so everyone can follow the process. The project is headed by the product manager, Lisa, who has chosen to use cards or Post-its for the purpose so they can be stuck to the wall as the various elements are defined. This method also makes it possible to change and move things around during the process.

In this case, the company wants to improve the customer assistance they provide in connection with customizing their equipment to suit the customer's needs and production systems.

3.3. Development of the objective

Step 1 – Defining the purpose

The OBS hierarchy will often be based on the purpose, although this is not a requirement. When a deliverable or a purpose is placed on the wall, it can be moved up or down the hierarchy by asking why and how. The Post-its on the wall might read:

Find the purpose – ask why?

- Better customer assistance
- IT tools for impact assessment of the customer's various suggestions
- Better knowledge-sharing between the tech department and sales staff
- More rational workflows
- Support of employees' daily work procedures

In the Happier Customers project, the purpose is 'increased competitiveness'. Top management has decided that this most likely involves developing rational workflows and supporting employees' daily work procedures. Another key area might be to improve the quality of the company's customer assistance to give customers better solutions. To break down the purpose, Lisa asks the project team: 'How can we achieve the purpose: increased competitiveness?' The answer is: 'By optimizing resource utilization and increasing the quality of our customer assistance.' Consequently, the project outcome is twofold: 'Better resource utilization and better customer service'.

The team breaks down the OBS hierarchy by asking: 'Why do we need to utilize our resources better?' The answer is: 'To

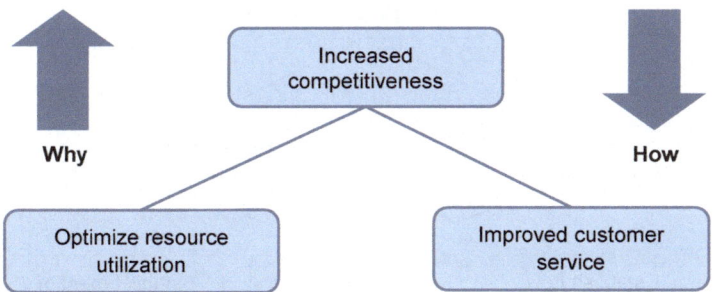

Figure 3.6. The principle of the OBS. You move up the hierarchy by asking why and down by asking how.

105

Chapter 3. What is the objective of the project?

be more competitive.' 'Why do we need to improve our customer service?' The answer is: 'To be more competitive.'

Step 2 – Ask: 'How can we achieve the purpose?'

Find the deliverables – ask how?

Draw up the OBS by asking 'How?' As the team continues to ask questions, the deliverables get fleshed out in more and more detail. Due to time constraints, Lisa now decides to divide the kick-off seminar into two groups. One group is to continue working on 'optimizing resource utilization', while the other group is to discuss how 'customer service can be improved'.

The group working on resource utilization asks: 'How can we ensure the optimization of our resource utilization?' The possibilities include introducing new workflows, working more flexibly and introducing an IT system that supports the work of the sales staff. This would make it possible to capture data directly from the customer and in the tech department or from the sales departments in other regions or countries.

How can we give our customers better service and assistance? Possible initiatives might include closer contact and knowledge-sharing between the tech department and the sales function. This may also require new workflows and training of the sales staff.

In this way, the OBS can be fleshed out and we achieve more insight into possible deliverables and how they relate to the purpose. An important outcome of using the OBS hierarchy is the creativity that can be achieved in the solution pro-

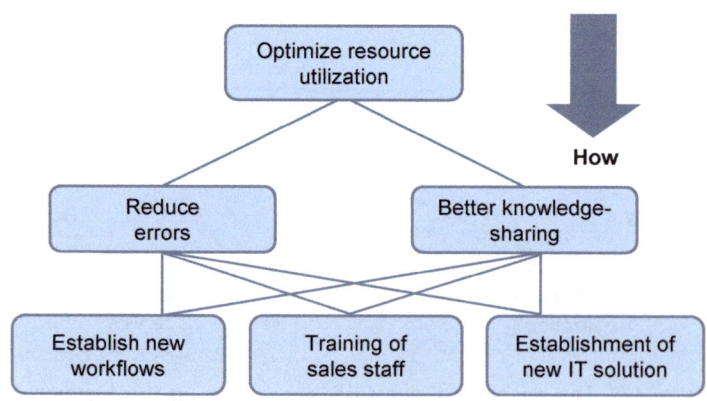

Figure 3.7. The OBS is fleshed out by asking how.

3.3. Development of the objective

posals. It's important to avoid settling for the 'the first and best solution' – this is where the OBS can be very useful.

Step 3 – Move up and down in the hierarchy a couple of times to assess whether the problem is defined at the right abstraction level

Move up in the hierarchy by asking why. It is important to move up and down in the hierarchy several times. Only then will you have achieved the holistic view that can form the basis for a good project.

Why do we need new workflows or a new IT solution? In order to ensure better knowledge-sharing between the sales staff and tech department and thereby reduce the number of errors in our customer assistance.

Why do we need to train our sales staff? To ensure that we can use our new IT system and can benefit from the knowledge-sharing it enables.

We need to provide them with training in our technical solutions and products in order to reduce the number of errors in their customer assistance.

The purpose is formulated by asking: Why do the various results need to be delivered?

The OBS establishes coherence in the project and the most important deliverables are clearly revealed as the results that support most of the sub-purposes. Another key characteristic of the OBS is that the purpose is fleshed out in detail, which makes it possible to use it to chart the future course of the project. Unfortunately, the purpose is often formulated in such general terms that it can't be used in this way. If you continue to ask why, however, you end up with: 'Why are we here – what is the meaning of life?' While this is useful information, it can be difficult to navigate by.

When the two groups meet again at the kick-off seminar, they can now work together to prepare the entire OBS, as seen in Figure 3.8.

One group is in the process of asking how they determined that 'error reduction' can be achieved by 'creating new workflows', 'establishing a new IT system' and 'training the sales staff'. The other group has just suggested that they need 'a new organization and to define new roles'. This supports 'er-

Change abstraction level – move up and down in the hierarchy

Chapter 3. What is the objective of the project?

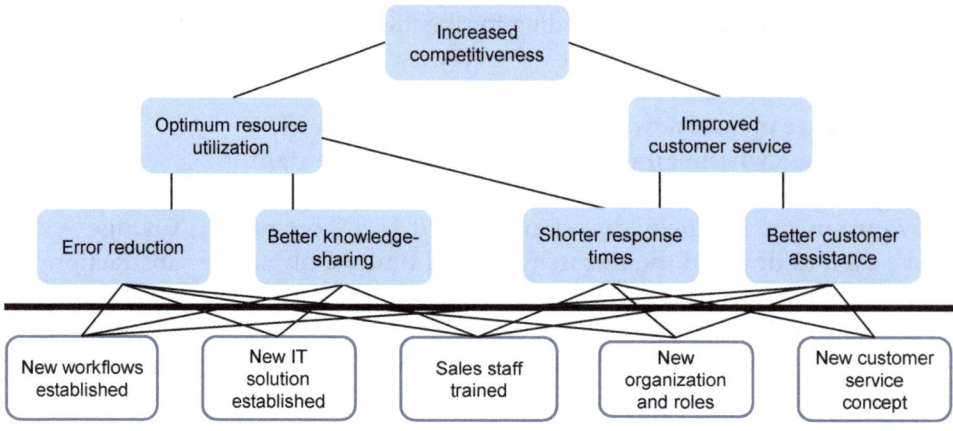

Figure 3.8. The final OBS showing the purposes above the line (the blue boxes) and the deliverables below the line.

ror reduction', as an organizational structure consisting of inappropriate transfers of responsibility gives rise to misunderstandings and information not reaching the right people. By working with the OBS, it is possible to define the correlations within the project.

What do we want to achieve? – the purpose
What do we need to deliver? – the deliverables

Step 4 – Keep the purpose and deliverables separate

Draw a line in the sand

Keep the purpose and deliverables separate

The question now is what are the project purpose and deliverables?

There is a practical reason for keeping the purpose and deliverables completely separate. The separation of the purpose from the deliverables defines where the project ends – when the project team's work is done!

Lisa's project team now embarks on a lengthy discussion of what the purpose of the project is. Top management has voiced the strategic objective of 'increased competitiveness'. But that can't be achieved by the project team with this project alone. The purpose has been further broken down into the sub-purposes of 'optimizing resource utilization' and 'providing better customer service' within the sales regions where the project team operates. And there is still some debate as to whether this definition is too broad. As one project participant

108

says: 'If we want to increase our competitiveness, it will require many initiatives that are not part of our project'. They therefore decide to define the purpose in even more detail in the third level of the OBS, coming up with the following description.

Purpose: This project is being carried out in order to:
- Reduce errors in our individual customized solutions
- Improve knowledge-sharing between sales and the tech department
- Reduce reaction times in connection with customer queries
- Provide better assistance to the customers who require customized solutions

The purpose and deliverables can be separated by drawing a line in the sand that defines when the project is complete. In other words: What you hold in your hands when the project is over becomes the deliverables; while the impact of the deliverables becomes the purpose. See Figure 3.8.

The project team therefore concludes that the project comprises five important deliverables, as illustrated directly below the line in Figure 3.8. In other words: The project team has achieved the purpose (above the line) by delivering the following deliverables (below the line):

Deliverables:
- New workflows established
- New IT solution established
- Sales staff trained in the new IT system and customer service concept
- New organization and roles established
- New customer service concept developed and tested

Lisa now suggests that the team break off into five groups of two to flesh out the deliverables. The project participants working with workflows come from both sales and the tech department. Those looking at the new IT system are from IT, and so forth. When the team gathers again, the deliverables have been defined in even more detail.

The pair from the IT department can ask: 'How do we establish a new IT system?' in order to define their deliverables. And by specifying the system requirements, they can determine the hardware required as well as the service organization needed to maintain the system in the operational phase. They can climb the breakdown system again by asking: 'Why do we need new hardware?' 'In order to implement a new IT system.' 'Why do we need a new IT system?' 'Reasons include reducing errors and improving knowledge-sharing between departments.'

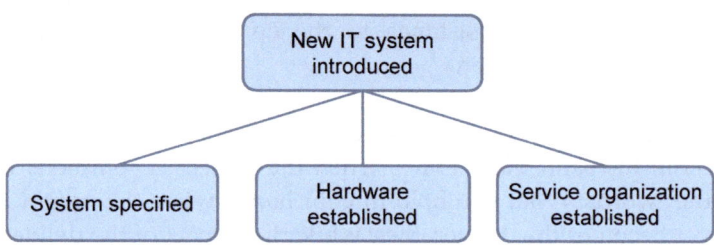

Figure 3.9. The deliverables can be fleshed out by asking how. This will produce a number of sub-deliverables.

Success criteria

Find the success criteria just above the line

Where are the success criteria in the OBS? The aim of the success criteria is to make the purpose measurable. Figure 3.10 illustrates how the success criteria can be 'measured'. To ensure that the success criteria don't fall too far outside the scope of the project, it's important to define the criteria as close to the project deliverables as possible – these are the white smileys. The light blue smileys are also relevant; however there is a greater risk that other factors will influence these criteria in a different direction than that in which the project is moving. Care must be taken when using success criteria that fall so far outside the scope of the project as the dark smileys in the diagram.

There is also a temporal dimension. The success criteria just above the line – the white smileys – can be measured as soon as the project ends. The light blue smileys can be measured in the medium term, while the dark smileys can only be measured in the long term.

3.3. Development of the objective

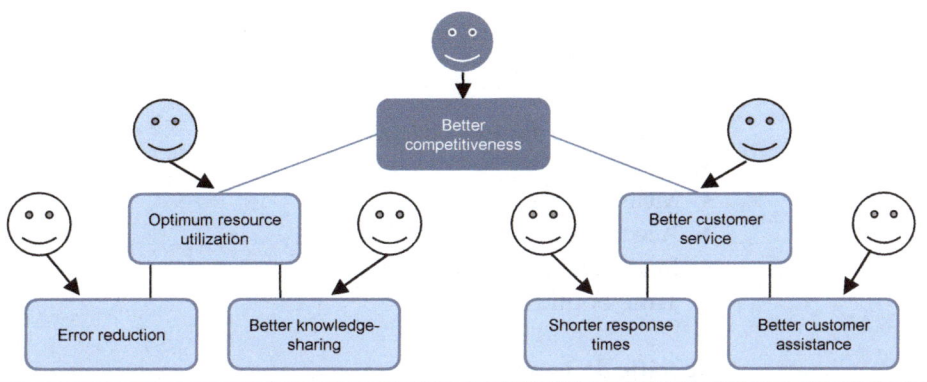

Figure 3.10. This figure indicates how the success criteria can be 'measured'. The success criteria must not fall too far outside the scope of the project. The success criteria should be defined for the sub-purposes just above the line, as close to the project deliverables as possible.

In the Happier Customers project, the project team has defined the following success criteria:

Purpose	Success criteria
Error reduction	Reduce the error rate by 15% by May 5th
Shorter response times	Reduce response times by 50% by May 5th
Improved knowledge-sharing	In the average tender material, 90% is reused solution elements and sections from past tenders, 6 month after project completion
Improved customer guidance	70% of customers asked are satisfied or very satisfied and give a rating of 4.5 on a scale of 1-5, 1 year after project completion

3.3.3. Good deliverables and success criteria are SMART

It's important that the individual deliverables are as sharply defined as possible to ensure focus and avoid too much discussion about whether or not they've been achieved. Good deliverables and success criteria should therefore meet the following criteria.

The objective should be SMART:
- Specific
- Measureable
- Accepted
- Realistic (but also ambitious)
- Time-bound

Specific deliverables
The deliverables should be highly specific so that they can be used for planning. This isn't possible if the deliverables are too loosely defined. If you can't formulate highly specific deliverables, then it's impossible to make them measurable. Not all deliverables can be made 100% measureable, but with practice they can all be highly specific.

Deliverables are measurable
Galileo said, 'Measure what is measurable, and make measurable what is not so.' Deliverables that can't be measured are not really deliverables. It's important to remember that we define deliverables because we want to be able to follow up on the progress of the project. The lowest degree of measurability, therefore, is that it's possible to determine whether or not the deliverable has been delivered.

Deliverables should be accepted – and attractive
The deliverables must be accepted by the steering committee, the project team and the most important stakeholders, otherwise the project will be hindered from the outset.

It is vital for the project team's motivation that their deliverables have been accepted; otherwise, it's difficult for them to maintain the necessary commitment to delivering the product.

Deliverables should be realistic and ambitious
The question of what is realistic is always the object of debate. Is a realist a pessimistic optimist or an optimistic pessimist? This is an extremely important balancing act in the objective-

setting process, as you also need to ensure commitment and accuracy.

Let's put it this way, deliverables should be realistic enough that the project team can see a possible solution. The project team should not be resistant from the outset because the deliverables are unachievable under the given conditions.

On the other hand, the deliverables should be ambitious enough that there is a risk of failure if the project team doesn't make an effort. This type of ambitious objective promotes commitment and creative solutions. A great deal of psychology lies in stringing the bow correctly without the string breaking.

Figure 3.11. Objectives should be realistic and ambitious.

Deliverables are time-bound – they have set deadlines
A common comment is: 'We made our delivery, just six months late.' Deliverables are fixed in time, and if they can't be realized by the deadline, the quality of the deliverable may not be up to par. Furthermore, it's important to bear in mind that when sub-deliverables are late, this can significantly change the overall objective of the project! The business case changes because the expected savings or earnings are delayed.

3.4. Reflections on objective-setting

Think about your own project or a project you are involved in:
- Is the objective broken down into a project purpose, deliverables and success criteria?
- What is the purpose and can it be broken down further using the OBS?
- Is there coherence between the deliverables and the purpose as evident in the OBS?
- What is needed for the objective to be SMART?
- Try to compose an OBS for your project and break it down into purpose and deliverables.
- What do you need to be able to describe the entire project triangle?
- What extra deliverables have you been pressured into including in your negotiations with the steering committee? Have you allocated extra time or resources to cover the extra work?
- Name five ways you will use your deliverables to motivate your project participants.
- How will you use the purpose and deliverables for team building during the course of the project?
- How will you carry out your project's objective-setting process?
- How will you ensure that all the stakeholders clearly understand the project purpose?
- How will you ensure that the project objective is in line with the firm's objectives and standards?
- Are you enthusiastic about the project's chances of success? What might give you cause for concern?
- What can you do to ensure that the budget is approved by the project owner?
- What documentation is required in order to be able to measure the success criteria?
- Are the project's financial and commercial advantages clear to the project owner?
- How will you present the deliverables and purpose to the most important stakeholders?

Who will use the results?
Think in terms of win-win

The stakeholders are the final judges of whether your project is a success!

CHAPTER 4

Who will use the results?

On managing the project stakeholders

No stakeholders, no project – and no project without stakeholders   **The challenges**

Projects are only successful if the most important stakeholders are satisfied. An important aspect of project management, therefore, is the ability to manage stakeholders and secure their support for the project. And dealing with stakeholders with different, and possibly even conflicting, interests doesn't make that job any easier.

One of the biggest challenges for the project manager – and for the entire team – is to map the project's 'stakeholder landscape' and decide how to deal with and monitor the important stakeholders. When working with the project stakeholders, the project manager needs to concentrate on forming relations and communicating about the project.

Chapter 4 presents the basic principles behind mapping and managing the project stakeholders, providing methods for: **Benefits**

- Stakeholder identification – who are they?
- Stakeholder prioritization – who are the most important stakeholders?
- Understanding stakeholders – what is their agenda?
- Developing strategies for managing stakeholders – what do we do?

This chapter focuses on the project manager's actions in the competent management of stakeholders and presents specific methods for analyzing the project's stakeholder landscape. The chapter takes a closer look at: **Focus**

- The project stakeholders – who are they?
- The project manager as a network builder
- Stakeholder analysis – when and how?
- Stakeholder segmentation
- Stakeholder analysis in the *Happier Customers* project

Tools Tool 4.1 Stakeholder Analysis

4.1. Special interests at stake

The project stakeholders are the people or groups that influence and are influenced by the execution of the project or by its results. They can include customers, employees, financial backers, authorities and NGOs – just to name a few.

Who can help – and who is a potential enemy?

With some stakeholders, their interests and the project's interests are pretty much the same, and it is therefore possible to obtain the stakeholders' backing for and assistance with the project. Other stakeholders, however, may have interests that conflict with those of the project. They can therefore be expected to resist the project or to try to influence it in a different direction than planned.

As the project manager, you will meet innumerable stakeholders, all of whom will want something different from the project. Most stakeholders – whether they are in favor of the project, against it or somewhere in-between – will seek to use the project to their own advantage. Even in the cases where everyone supports the project, they will see the project from different angles. For example, everyone may want the new product, but to the people in production, it's important that the product can be manufactured with the existing equipment and that there are only a limited number of variations. The service department, on the other hand, wants the product to be modular to make it easy to forward spare parts later. Meanwhile, sales wants a range of variations and great-looking design to satisfy customers. And so forth. Everyone wants the product – but which product?

Exercising good project management therefore means identifying the many stakeholders, finding out what they want

4.1. Special interests at stake

and, especially, deciding how they can be managed. Ultimately, it's the project stakeholders who determine whether the purpose, deliverables and success criteria are appropriate and relevant.

Stakeholder analysis provides important inspiration for several other elements in the planning of the project as well.

Stakeholder analysis contributes to:

Setting the objective: Are the purpose, deliverables and success criteria attractive to and accepted by the most important stakeholders?

Planning the project structure: Are there aspects that need to be clarified with specific stakeholders before it makes sense to take the next step? How should the decision-making process be designed? What decisions need to be made first and who should be involved?

Risk analysis: Which stakeholders represent a risk? Can we prevent possible conflicts of interest?

Organization: Which stakeholders should be involved when?

As the number of stakeholders seeking to exercise their influence grows, the complexity of the project increases, and it is important that the project team is aware of the waters they need to navigate in the project.

Wenell puts it this way:

Can't we just be left alone to work?

'I think we could actually do a very good job managing the individual project if everyone would just leave us alone.'

Wenell 2001

That world, as we know, is but a fantasy – and after a while, it would probably grow boring for most project managers anyway, because project management is about dealing with the unknown – problems as well as happy surprises.

By cutting yourself off from contact with the stakeholders, however, you run the risk of solving problems that nobody has or producing results that nobody will use.

With that said, many project managers have undoubtedly toyed with the tempting notion that if they could just follow their well-laid plan without interference and interruptions by the stakeholders, then everything would be perfect.

4.1.1. Networking competence

Relations need to be established and maintained

The more experienced a project manager is, the greater the focus on stakeholder management and on building and maintaining relations within and outside the organization.

In many firms, the ability to establish and maintain a relevant network is one of the skills the project managers are evaluated on.[1] When a project manager needs to drive a complex project through the system, it is a simple necessity that the manager is respected and has contacts within the organization. This requires a large and relevant network as well as the support of both the formal and the informal organization.

A large company with many projects once studied the characteristics of the project management of their successes and failures. One of the most notable differences was revealed when they interviewed the project participants about the project manager's behavior. The managers of the projects that were **less successful** were generally described as leaders who were very organized and always to be found in their offices if they were needed. The **successful projects**, on the other hand, had managers that were hard to get hold of, meetings were canceled and nobody really knew quite what the manager spent his or her time on.

Project managers need to get out of the office

This came as a surprise to the top management. But after further analysis, it was revealed that the managers of the successful projects spent a great deal of time networking. They simply cleared the way for the project within the organization, making sure that their team was left in peace to do their work.

Another study came to a similar conclusion, showing that a major difference between a good project manager and an average project manager is the ability to network. According to Briner *et al.*, the good project manager continuously keeps

---

1. Assessments can be formalized in annual 360-degree evaluations, i.e. feedback where the project manager and his or her superior, employees and possibly also customers, evaluate the project manager's performance in relation to a pre-defined set of competence areas. The evaluation is generally used for employee appraisal interviews to call attention to the project manager's strengths and weaknesses as well as to map future competence development.

everyone – team members, management and customers – informed.

They don't succumb to 'mushroom management'[2], because everyone expects the worst. They know that good and bad news are equally important (Briner 1996). As Briner points out, a good network should be combined with high personal credibility and respect. This credibility is boosted by the project manager also being willing to communicate when there is bad news or simply no news at all. If you only share the success stories, you risk damaging your credibility if others have a different view of the project. And low credibility is disastrous, regardless of whether you're a politician, leader or project manager.

Small talk is rarely a waste of time
The good project manager therefore devotes time to developing and maintaining relations and is both known and recognized within the organization and among the relevant external stakeholders.

To the people around the project manager, including his or her superior, network building is often viewed as a waste of time. Furthermore, many project managers already have fully-booked calendars and don't feel they have the time to chitchat in the cafeteria, grab a beer after work or have an extended phone conversation with an acquaintance. As a project manager, you obviously have to communicate with the people who are involved in the project, but it can seem difficult to find the time for all the other informal communication – especially because it's often a long-term investment with no visible benefit in the here and now.

An unfortunate side effect of dropping the informal contact is that many project managers miss out on vital information and important chances to sow the necessary seeds that might come in handy later in this or a future project. Relations need to be developed before they can be used, however. You need

---

2. Mushroom management is like mushroom cultivation, the employees are kept in the dark (uninformed) and buried in dung (bad assignments).

to accumulate some goodwill before you can draw on a relation.

Successful project managers understand and utilize both formal and informal channels to obtain information and ease a decision's passage through the system. According to Briner *et al.*, the project manager is actually expected to bypass the normal chain of command and traverse professional and organizational boundaries within the organization (Briner 1990).

Win-win – a sustainable philosophy
A sustainable network isn't just something you use; you have to give to it without expecting anything in return right away. Networks are built on what Tor Nørretranders in *The Generous Man* calls the 'gift economy'. This is the principle of reciprocity and the belief that gifts will always come back to you.

It's a good idea to think about whether your 'networking account' is currently in the black or the red.

In *The Seven Habits of Highly Effective People*, Covey writes that the basic principle for all human interaction is win-win. People tend to make agreements and find solutions that benefit both parties in order to feel satisfied with the agreement and obligated to follow through. Win-win is not a negotiation technique, Covey points out, but a fundamental attitude toward how we interact with others (Covey 1998).

David Maister, author of *The Trusted Advisor* (Free Press, 2000), talks about building relationships in terms that are almost like a mathematical equation. The trust you receive from others can be considered a fraction, where the numerator is the sum of reliability, competence and intimacy and the denominator is the total selfishness demonstrated.

Think in terms of win-win and earn 'respect points' that can be cashed in later

As a project manager, you need to constantly make deals and form and cultivate relations with the project stakeholders. Project managers who leave in their wake a string of aggrieved partners, colleagues and project team members rarely have their job for long. Much more enduring are the project managers who base their actions on a win-win philosophy where personal success is not achieved at the expense of the success of others. Instead, they believe there is enough success to go around.

Let's take a closer look at the stakeholder groups we typically find in projects.

4.1.2. Who are the project stakeholders?

Stakeholders can be identified by asking: Who will come into contact with the project? Who will affect and be affected by the project? Remember to think in terms of both the **project's** lifetime, i.e. throughout the various phases of the project, and the **product's** lifetime, i.e. who will use the project's results.

Some of the most common project stakeholders are illustrated in figure 4.1.

The stakeholders looking downward

The project team and the project manager are central stakeholders, as their efforts are clearly of vital importance to the project. While this may seem obvious, we see time and again project managers who don't have a clear idea of what their project participants each want to get out of the project, and sometimes they don't even know what they can actually contribute to the project. The argument for not spending time clarifying the individual project participant's interests and strengths in relation to the project is often: 'But the participants have been told to participate in the project by their superior and, besides, they get paid for doing what their job requires.' We don't disagree with this – but we do question whether these project managers are practicing the kind of leadership that produces results by bringing out the best in the project participants. In the chapter on leading the team, we will examine more closely the various managerial tasks associated with project management. This includes how the project manager reconciles expectations with the individual participants and creates the motivation and commitment that is a key success factor in the vast majority of projects.

For the organization as a whole, it is relevant to examine who is actually running the strategically important development projects, as well as how these people are selected and motivated. As a member of the top management in an organization with a large share of heavy projects, the selection process for project managers should be just as well-considered as the selection process of line managers.

Chapter 4. Who will use the results?

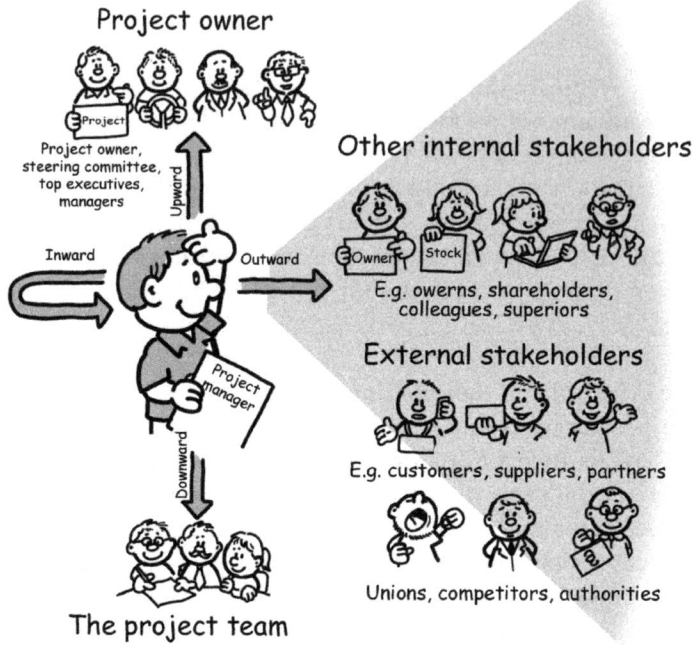

Figure 4.1. Examples of stakeholders from the project manager's point of view looking upward, downward, outward and inward.

In addition to the project manager and the project team, it is also reasonable to consider the families of the project manager and team members as central stakeholders (c.f. Wenell 2001). Many project managers feel burnt out after several years of heavy work pressure, overtime and constant demands to meet deadlines and targets. One of the most common arguments people give for changing to a job in the line organization as manager or employee is that they felt they were neglecting their family.

This fact presumably costs companies many good project managers every year. Luckily, more and more companies are addressing this issue and making efforts to improve conditions for their heavy-hitting project managers and team members, for instance in relation to workload. This ought to make the work-life balance more sustainable for both project participants and managers.

What can you do as a project manager if you want to take the families of the project participants seriously as stakeholders? Here are a couple of examples: When composing the team, make sure to communicate clearly and honestly about the expectations regarding overtime, workload and flexibility in relation to the individual's private life. During the course of the project, make sure people understand that working hours and workload are legitimate topics for discussion. Some firms invite families to open-house events, which is particularly appropriate for engineering and construction projects – a reception for a rule simplification project just isn't all that interesting.

The stakeholders looking upward
Looking up, we have the people who finance the project. Often, this also includes the project owner, i.e. the person who 'commissioned' the project (see Chapter 5 on organization).

The project owner's role is to be the organizational spearhead for the project. The project owner needs to use his or her visible support and formal power to pave the way for the project and the project manager. However, not all project managers are aware of this particular role, just as they and other projects are in a constant struggle for the project owner's attention.

It is therefore a good idea for project managers to promote their project on a regular basis to the stakeholders upwards in the organization, as they are constantly competing with the firm's other projects for resources and attention.

At project start-up, it's important that you, as the project manager, already have a good understanding of what the project owner expects from you: Why did they pick you specifically to head up this project? What do they expect from you? And vice versa: What do you, as the project manager, expect from the project owner? And what do you expect from the outcome of the project? Many firms now conduct formal job interviews for project managers and participants in which they draw up performance contracts, bonus agreements and agreements on   **Are the project owner's expectations of the project manager clear?**

other incentives, such as training, promotion and new challenges – provided the agreed objectives are met.

The stakeholders looking outward
Looking outward, we have the firm's internal and external stakeholders. The external stakeholders include customers, suppliers, partners, NGOs, authorities, competitors, the general public and the press. The internal stakeholders are typically line managers, managers of other projects in the firm (perhaps the scope of your own project touches on these projects), other employees and managers, union representatives, safety committee and liaison committees.

The stakeholders who take over the project's results are often called the end users, for example the users who will be using the new IT system or the colleagues who will be working according to the new quality management program. It makes sense to refer to and consider the end users as customers. The group may even include 'real' customers, such as wholesalers, retail, customers and users. The word customer symbolizes a different relationship and reminds the project manager and team why the project and the entire project team were originally established.

The end users should be considered and treated like customers with the freedom to choose

In projects aimed outside the firm, it is often a very good idea to measure customer satisfaction.[3] To many project managers, it can feel 'fake' to consider colleagues and managers they are close to as their customers. However, it is a mistake to think that because their customers are often **required** to accept the product (for example a new building or a new management policy), then they have no choice. It is true that many stakeholders can rarely choose not to take over the product – for example it would be unwise for a middle manager to say no to a management policy that has been approved and accepted by top management. However, the middle manager does have

---

3. Robert G. Cooper points to satisfaction among the project's customers as the most important success factor in most projects. The next most important success factor is delivering products that meet the agreed objective and specifications.

the freedom to choose how he or she uses it, for instance by criticizing the policy or simply ignoring it.

Customers can therefore take over the project with very different attitudes and many projects have failed because the customer's acceptance was taken for granted.

Thinking of the end users as customers calls attention to the end users as conscious consumers, because they have a choice when it comes to taking over and using the project's results.

4.1.3. Stakeholder analysis – when and how?

We have covered the importance of established relations in project management and which stakeholder groups you will find when you look downward, upward and outward from the project.

Now we will look at how the project team can use the stakeholder analysis to plan how to manage the most important stakeholders.

How should the stakeholder analysis be used?

The stakeholder analysis is the foundation that gives the project team the best prerequisites for managing the often quite complex assortment of stakeholders. After all, the project's stakeholders determine whether the project is a success or a failure.

As the project team, it is therefore important that you have a detailed understanding of who populates the project's world and who holds influence, and then develop a strategy for what you can do specifically in relation to each stakeholder – as a team or individually.

In projects that involve people having to change their behavior, a vital part of stakeholder management is predicting, preventing and addressing any resistance to change.

When should the stakeholder analysis be carried out?

The stakeholder analysis is one of the first analyses to be carried out, because the information that comes from the stakeholder analysis will be used for, among other things:

- Developing and refining the objective. The purpose, deliverables and success criteria are key elements of the contract

– psychological and/or legal – you enter into with a number of the central stakeholders.
- Organizing the project, including composition of the steering committee, hearing committees and working groups.
- Planning the right approach for the project, such as decision-making processes and scheduling.
- Planning the implementation strategy.
- Planning the communication strategy.
- Preparing the risk analysis.

The objective, stakeholder analysis and organization of the project all crisscross and influence each other. The purpose, deliverables and success criteria you define influence how the stakeholders relate to the project. And the stakeholders you prioritize influence the definition of the purpose, deliverables and success criteria. Finally, the composition of the steering committee, project team and any hearing committees influences both the objective formulation and the attitudes and behavior of the stakeholders – and vice versa. Some projects are formulated for the sole purpose of satisfying central stakeholders. For instance an educational institution, which initiates a project called 'More research projects in collaboration with the private sector' just to put an end to criticism that the institution is too self-contained and not oriented enough toward the outside world. Or a ministry that launches a project because a case has sparked debate in the press. By initiating the project, they can rightfully claim that 'we are already looking into how things can be changed' (and then hope that the case is forgotten before the project is complete). Product development projects are adjusted so that specific target groups (market segments) will find the products more attractive than competing products.

Stakeholder analysis is a highly organic process. As with objective-setting, stakeholder analysis is a process that must be repeated and qualified regularly as the project progresses, because stakeholders will often change their position during the course of the project. What might seem, during the analysis phase, like harmless deskwork for a particular stakeholder, can suddenly become very relevant to that stakeholder at a later point. Or a team that was once very committed can suddenly develop other, more pressing interests. It is therefore important to monitor the stakeholders for the duration of the project.

Who should conduct the analysis?
It's important that the project manager doesn't carry out the stakeholder analysis alone, but in conjunction with the project team. There are two main reasons for this:

1. The project team often comprises people from several disciplines and different areas within the organization, so together they possess significant insight into the entire organization and various stakeholders' attitudes toward the project. Using the entire team as well as the project owner to compile the stakeholder analysis should therefore make it possible to reveal the most important stakeholders.
2. As representatives of the project, the project team is continuously in contact with the stakeholders. Obviously, the entire team needs to be acquainted with the stakeholder analysis and the strategies for managing the stakeholders.

The stakeholder analysis often contains quite inflammatory material and the discussions the project team has during the analysis process require both honesty and confidentiality – at least in cases where the project team has created a climate in which it is okay to have such discussions. For instance, the stakeholder analysis is when you discuss how the long-standing conflict between Vice President A and Vice President B might affect the project. Or how the union representative's affair (an official secret) with Manager L, whose department is being shut down, might affect the project. And so on.

It's generally unwise to publicize the entire content of the stakeholder analysis

As a project team, you therefore need to take great care what you write down and distribute to, say, the steering committee and project owner.

How is the analysis conducted?
A stakeholder analysis generally consists of four steps:

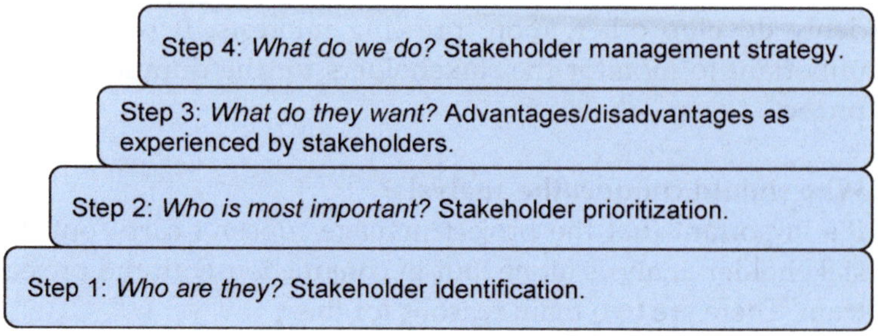

Step 4: *What do we do?* Stakeholder management strategy.

Step 3: *What do they want?* Advantages/disadvantages as experienced by stakeholders.

Step 2: *Who is most important?* Stakeholder prioritization.

Step 1: *Who are they?* Stakeholder identification.

Figure 4.2. The four steps of the stakeholder analysis

Step 1
Step 1 of the stakeholder analysis is mapping the landscape, i.e. identifying **who** the project's stakeholders are. In many project types, the stakeholders are identified by simple methods like brainstorming. Other projects have a longer identification process. For example, developing and launching a new product can require comprehensive customer analysis.

When the project team works on identifying the stakeholders, they need to think in broad strokes to include every single person and group that might potentially have an effect or be affected – both during the course of the project and in relation to the project's product/result.

Step 2
The purpose of step 2 is to select and prioritize the most important stakeholders. In short, this is useful when determining where to concentrate the project team's energy when managing stakeholders.

When prioritizing the stakeholders, the project team can simply assess who is the first, second and third priority.

However, it can be a good idea to clarify the criteria upon which the prioritization should be based. One method is to prioritize based on the following criteria:

- **Influence:** What power and influence does the stakeholder have to affect the project?
- **Participation:** How important is the stakeholder's participation for the success of the project and/or the product/result?

4.1. Special interests at stake

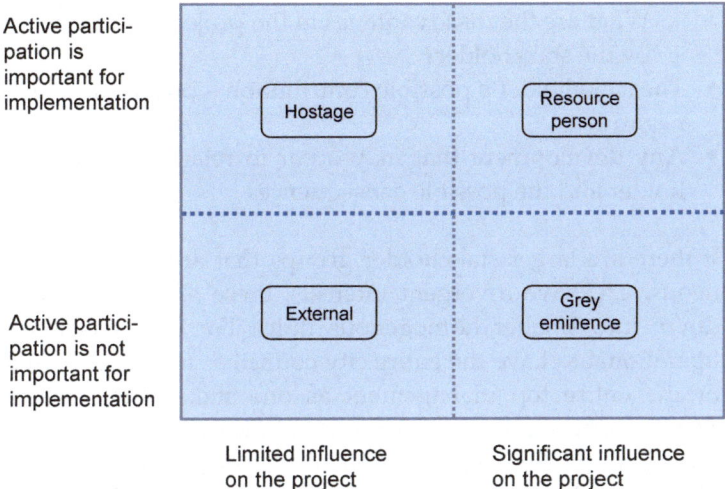

Figure 4.3. Stakeholders can be grouped into four categories based on an assessment of how much influence they have on the project and how important their participation is for the success of the project.

The stakeholders are then placed in a matrix according to these criteria and we get the following categories:

The influence/participation matrix focuses the project team's attention on where it is most expedient to concentrate their energy and also contributes to the organization of the project. You can read more about the influence/participation matrix in the toolbox.

Step 3

The purpose of step 3 is to obtain more information on how the most important stakeholders relate to the project and what you can expect them to contribute – in the form of either support or resistance.

Typically, you want to describe:

- The stakeholder's interest in the project; the stakeholder's motive and objective
- To identify conflicting or common interests you want to ask:
  - What are the advantages as experienced by the stakeholder?

131

- What are the disadvantages in the project as experienced by the stakeholder?
- The stakeholder's possible contribution – positive as well as negative
- Any development that may occur in relation to the stakeholder and the possible consequences

If there are larger stakeholder groups that are very heterogeneous, e.g. have divergent interests, these should be broken down into smaller homogenous units. For example, it isn't operational to have the entire city council as a one stakeholder or the entire top management as one stakeholder, because there can be many different and conflicting interests within these groups. Successful stakeholder management requires a detailed understanding of who the individual stakeholder is.

Stephen R. Covey writes:

'Seek first to understand, then to be understood.'

Describing and, where necessary, segmenting your stakeholders tells you what the stakeholders think, experience and feel – you *seek to understand*. This lets you put yourself in your stakeholders' shoes and have a dialog with them in order to see the project's consequences the way *they* see them. Only then can you *seek to be understood* by targeting your communication as much as possible at them.

We will cover the process of segmentation in more detail in the following pages.

Step 4
Now you have identified the stakeholders, selected those you will concentrate on and described what characterizes them. The final step is to develop a strategy for stakeholder management. The project team needs to determine: **what** needs to be done and **when** in relation to the prioritized stakeholders.

This generally entails communication and participation initiatives, and stakeholder management needs to be included as part of the project plan, because poor stakeholder management is one of the main reasons for project failure. The project team should therefore be organized during this process, defining milestones, identifying persons of responsibility and establishing follow-up/evaluation routines for communication to and involvement of stakeholders.

In step 4, we also look at the other elements of the project plan to see if they need fine-tuning. Examples are:
- What are the consequences of the stakeholder analysis for the **objective and project scope**? Have you overlooked the needs of important stakeholders and should they be addressed by adjusting the objective? Are the stakeholders so resistant that you should abandon the project entirely? For some projects, it's wise to start with the stakeholder analysis before trying to formulate the objective, as the stakeholders can have a decisive influence on the purpose, deliverables and success criteria.

- What are the consequences for the **project plan**? What approach do you choose out of consideration for the most important stakeholders and to ensure the quality of the project?
- What does it mean for the **organization** of the project? Are the right people included on the project team and the steering committee? What is the optimum composition of the hearing committees and similar groups?
- How should the **communication** be planned to ensure the right stakeholders are involved and informed at the right times?

The toolbox contains more information on the four steps of the stakeholder analysis and the different methods that can be used. The case at the end of the chapter also illustrates how the four steps of the stakeholder analysis can be carried out in practice, including examples of which initiatives the project team launches based on their stakeholder analysis.

The following is a brief introduction to using segmentation as a tool in the stakeholder analysis process.

4.1.4. Stakeholder segmentation

Segmentation is the foundation of a targeted dialog

Segmentation is used when you want to break down large heterogeneous stakeholder groups, like 'employees' or 'customers', into manageable units to obtain more specific information about their attitudes and behavior.

We segment stakeholders in order to target the dialog with the project's stakeholders. In other words, segmentation provides answers to the following questions:

- What characterizes this stakeholder group?
- How can we reach them?

What is segmentation?

Segmentation comes from marketing, where there is a strong tradition for breaking down consumers into well-defined, manageable units in order to target advertisements and other communication.

For example, *Sports Illustrated* readers represent a segment that is attractive to Tag Heuer, malt whisky and sports cars. The ads often feature beautiful, scantily clad women and little or no reference to price or the actual qualities of the product. In contrast, *Women's World* features fashion and make-up ads targeting an entirely different segment and communicating in a completely different style.

Segmenting requires extra time early in the project. But if you work with large, complex stakeholder groups, it's worth the effort, as the more you know about your stakeholders, the better you can target your dialog with them. If you work with groups that are too heterogeneous, i.e. too dissimilar, in your stakeholder management, you risk shooting at random and you'll be lucky if you manage to influence anyone at all.

Groups that are too heterogeneous are found in projects where the 'employees' are viewed as a single group or 'office staff' are considered a single group. This is not competent stakeholder management, because 'office staff' covers everyone from 23-year-old Ashley, who just wants her paycheck and doesn't care for change, to 59-year-old Nancy, who finds the project's new ideas exciting and throws herself wholeheartedly into the process. Ashley and Nancy should not be managed as stakeholders in the same way. Nancy and others with the same attitude should perhaps be involved as resource people so that they can, via their behavior, help the Ashleys understand why the project is necessary and useful.

The parameters of segmentation
In theory, you can segment according to any personal characteristic. You can have a Coca-Cola-drinking segment, a BMW-driving segment, a *New York Times*-reading segment, etc. The usefulness of the segmentation, however, depends entirely on your choice of relevant parameters for categorizing the stakeholders.

When you segment the project stakeholders into groups, it may be relevant to use **demographic data**. Demographic data is information about employment, education, geographic placement and nationality, for example whether the stakeholder group works in the firm's subsidiaries in Germany, France or Poland, or whether the stakeholder group is academics, sales people or unskilled workers.

It can also be relevant to segment stakeholders according to the **behavior** they display. If the objective of the project is to develop a new smoking policy, it would be relevant to break employees down into 'non-smokers', 'heavy smokers' and 'smokers'. If the project objective is improved customer service, the customers might be segmented into 'customers who complain' vs. 'satisfied customers'.

In some contexts, it may be interesting to base segments on how you can establish **contact** with the stakeholders, such as colleagues who use the intranet daily, managers who attend monthly meetings and employees who read the company newsletter.

One last example of parameters you can base segmentation on is the attitudes of the stakeholders. For instance, you can segment a stakeholder group based on how much they 'support the idea'. This would give the following segmentation:

- Those who are already convinced (i.e. the people who already agree with the project's messages and/or consider it relevant to them).
- Those who may be in agreement/convinced of the project's messages (often the largest and most interesting group).

Which stakeholders should you focus your energy on?

- Those who disagree or are uninterested (those who disagree are often the loudest group).

Source: Jørgen Poulsen, 1996

It's worth noting that as a project manager you may find yourself spending the most time and energy on the stakeholders who are most against the project and make the most noise – people whom you may not even be able to convince, no matter how hard you try. This can really tap the energy of the project manager and the entire team.

It also steals time, making it difficult to cultivate the stakeholders who are already convinced, but whose support may not be a matter of course. For instance, groups who may be onboard, but are not being given enough attention.

A project manager's job is therefore to ensure that the project team regularly reflects on whether the team is prioritizing its time and energy appropriately in relation to the stakeholders. Are you remembering to cultivate the ones who are already onboard? Where is your time best spent to achieve the greatest impact?

When segmenting stakeholders, there are four useful questions the project team can ask to test the relevance of the segments:

- Are the segments meaningful? There is no reason to break the stakeholders down into groups that have no influence or importance.
- Is the segment homogeneous with regard to their interests in the project?
- Can you actually find and reach them?
- Will managing the segments make any difference? If not, there is no reason to break them down further.

How much energy to devote to stakeholder segmentation is always a judgment call from project to project. However, experience shows that the subsequent handling of and communication with the stakeholders won't be effective until you have a clear understanding of the groups you are communicating with – until you know their wishes in relation to the project in question and target your communication accordingly.

Stakeholder management in the six project types

The scope of stakeholder management in the project varies depending on the type of project.

The six project types

In **policy development projects**, like political reports and bases for decision-making, stakeholder management often represents 90 percent of the effort in the project. From project start-up, you have to constantly consider how to deal with the most important stakeholders. The passing of new legislation, for example, depends largely on how successfully you involve the right parties (political parties, NGOs, etc.) at the right time so that they can be heard and made to feel they have an influence on the process, either formally or informally. Employees in political systems are often highly trained in stakeholder management. Seen from the outside, projects in political systems can therefore appear to be unnecessarily lengthy and complex, because everything must be put out to consultation, discussed in committees and officially approved – often by a long list of people. It is important to emphasize that some of the deliverables in this type of project take the form of support and acceptance from specific stakeholders. Stakeholder management should preferably be a well-defined element in the project plan, often as an independent work stream. The milestones in a project of this type are often the achievement of legitimacy from a dominant stakeholder group.

Organizational change projects have many of the same characteristics as policy development projects. These projects also require involvement and establishing a sense of ownership among important stakeholders who can approve and provide acceptance of the project's solutions. When planning the project approach, the deciding factor is often consideration for the stakeholders. Is a quality improvement project to be carried out by means of a bottom-up process, where employees and managers at all levels are to be involved in how quality can be improved? Or is it to be a top-down process, where the management, possibly in collaboration with a small in-house working group or team of external consultants, analyzes how quality can be improved and only one person decides on the appropriate solution? The chosen approach often influences how easy or difficult it will be to implement the solutions among the employees.

IT and systems development projects also focus a great deal on stakeholders, especially the end users. Often the end users are involved from project start-up, helping to assess the needs for the final system.

In **research and technology projects**, obtaining information via networking is crucial. For instance, the project manager needs to design a project to appeal to the best researchers in the area in order to attract their contributions to the project. Managing stakeholders during the project and at the end of the project appears to play a less dominant role in many environments. For example, who are the project's customers and users? Who must approve the project's progress and milestones?

However, there is a growing trend of universities and other research institutions collaborating with and being financed by private-sector companies and foundations, which places new demands on the researchers' communication of the project's ongoing status and end results.

As we learned in Chapter 1, **product development projects** focus on potential customers. The projects are often launched with the aim of identifying a need among customers which would then be met by developing a product. In the opposite case – that is, when the idea for the product comes first – the stakeholder perspective is taken up very quickly: How do potential customers respond to the idea? Is there a market for the product and what are the reactions to the product? There are often many adjustments to be made along the way, based on the findings of customer and market testing. An important task is market segmentation to find the right target group for the product or service.

In **engineering and building projects**, the stakeholder perspective is generally less dominant. This is where you find the most visible stakeholder groups – the subsuppliers to the project, such as plumbers, carpenters, masons, electricians, etc. The management of these stakeholders, called supplier management, is a crucial discipline to master in engineering and construction projects. In some projects, the neighbors and other elements of the public will be important stakeholders. Examples include building a new prison, a larger bridge or a new freeway. However, the responsibility rarely rests with the supplier. Instead, it's the responsibility of the project owner, which in the examples above would be found in the political system.

Stakeholder analysis in the *Happier Customers* project
The project manager, Lisa, and the project team have just carried out the stakeholder analysis. Her considerations prior to working with the stakeholder analysis are how to ensure an open and trusting environment for the team so they can discuss the stakeholders honestly. The project team comprises sales consultants and marketing staff, engineers from the tech department, service staff, IT experts, etc. If they each see themselves as representatives of a specialist group, there is a risk that they will end up at each other's throats instead of having an open dialog about the stakeholders and which threats or resources they represent.

Lisa therefore spends time explaining why the stakeholder analysis is necessary, going into detail on the method she would like them to follow. She emphasizes that much of the information in the stakeholder analysis is for the project team's eyes only, and that it is initially based on their subjective assessment, but that they may, of course, expand that basis with, say, interview studies or questionnaire surveys, if they lack information on the important stakeholders.

The project team is supportive of the idea and Lisa guides them through the following steps in the stakeholder analysis:

Step 1: Identifying the stakeholders
The project team identifies the stakeholders by asking:

'Who is affected by and has an opinion about the project and its results?'

Here, the project team brainstorms by writing all the stakeholders they can think of on cards or post-its – one stakeholder per card/post-it. Everyone on the team writes and posts their ideas on the wall. This enables them to follow each other's ideas and ensures a dynamic and rapid process. During step 1, nobody may comment on the relevance of the individual stakeholders.

The project team ends up with a large number of stakeholders on the wall, and it's clear that they are dealing with a complex project, not least because of the many stakeholders.

Step 2: Categorizing the stakeholders
The project manager chooses to have the team obtain an overview of the many stakeholders by assessing how important the stakeholders' active participation is for the project's success and how much influence and power they have on the project. She divides the wall into two dimensions and the project team proceeds to break down the individual stakeholders into the four categories.

It takes time, but gives rise to a number of important discussions about the individual stakeholders as well as what the project purpose, deliverables and success criteria will mean to the various stakeholders. For example, they discuss:

- What does the introduction of the new IT system mean for the planning of the sales staff's work and their freedom to act?
- What impact does the project have on workflows and professional boundaries?
- Do the product managers and sales manager have the power to stop the project?

Following is a list of the stakeholders the team identifies and categorizes in the matrix on the wall.

Step 3: The advantages and disadvantages as experienced by the stakeholders
Now that the project stakeholders have been identified and categorized, the next step is for the project team to assess:

- What are the advantages and disadvantages of the project as experienced by the stakeholders?
- And how can they contribute to the project – in both a positive and a negative way?

The project team quickly realizes that they need to break down some of the stakeholders into smaller segments, because a

4.1. Special interests at stake

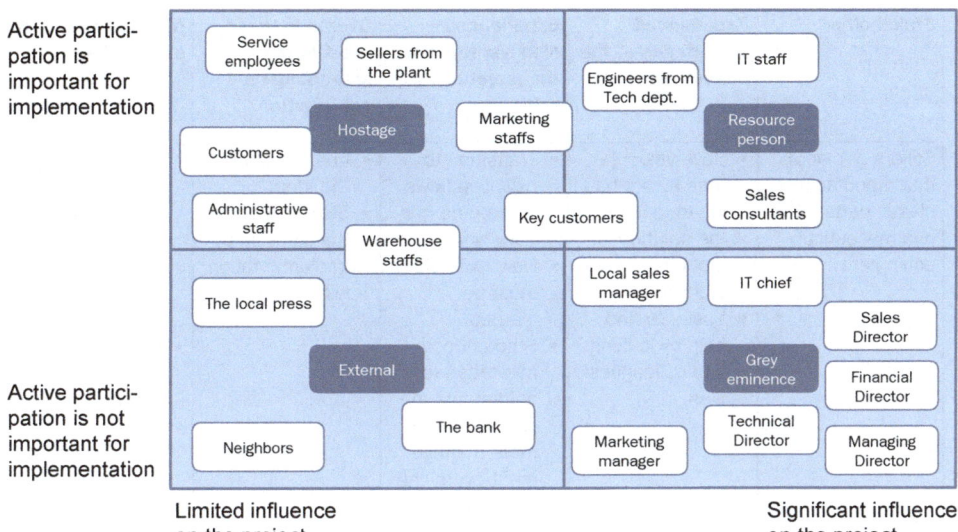

Figure 4.4. A selection of stakeholders in the Happier Customers project.

segment like 'sales staff' covers too many different groups. The team agrees to segment the sales staff based on area of specialization and the type of customers served.

The project team also assesses whether other stakeholder groups should be segmented and if so, which criteria it is relevant to base the segmentation on.

It is sometimes a good idea for the project manager to delegate this task to a couple of the project participants, who can then present a proposal for smaller and more homogeneous stakeholder groups at the next meeting.

After the stakeholders have been broken down into relatively homogeneous segments, the team discusses the advantages and disadvantages they think the stakeholders might experience during and after the project. They use the following template to give the process structure and ensure that all important information is collected.

Chapter 4. Who will use the results?

Stakeholder	Experienced advantages of the project results	Experienced disadvantages of the project results	Overall assessment of the stakeholder's contribution/ position	Management of the stakeholder
Sellers of plants that manufacture plastic parts for pharmaceutical equipment.	• Save valuable time by not having to look for the solution proposal in the archives. • Easier to find help by looking into colleagues' files.	• Transition to new workflows takes time in a busy workday. • New technology must be learned. • Stricter documentation requirements in future, making more management oversight possible.	• Positive about the idea. • Skeptical about the extra time implementation will require.	• Comprehensive training in new systems and workflows. • Representative on hearing committee or similar. • Continuous communication about project. • Thorough introduction to IT system prior to implementation.
Engineers from Tech dept.	• Aren't bothered as much by sales staff, as they will be able to find the solution proposal themselves in the system.	• Significant work pressure during new system rollout. • Concerned that sales staff may take over some of the tasks engineers are currently responsible for. • Some powers of decision will be moved from engineers to sales staff.	• Concerned about long-term consequences for their specialist group. • Concerned that some of the savings will come from reductions in engineer staff.	• Make future work fields of activity visible to engineers. • Continuous involvement throughout project.
Etc.				
Etc.				
Etc.				

Step 4: Stakeholder management strategy, incl. monitoring
The project team now discusses how they will handle the individual stakeholder groups in the various project phases. They use the last column on the template to make note of important ideas from their discussions.

The project has a large number of stakeholders who are important for the project's success. The team therefore chooses to establish special work streams in the project plan where they concentrate on managing the most important stakeholder groups and make the agreed initiatives an integral part of the project plan.

The project team agrees that throughout the project period Lucy should bring up the stakeholder analysis at their project team meetings so that the entire team can assess the impact of the initiatives they launch. They will also assess whether new stakeholders have come to light and whether any stakeholders have 'changed positions', for instance if the external stakeholders suddenly play a critical role or if any stakeholders' attitudes have changed from positive to negative.

4.2. Reflections on stakeholder management

How does your project look?
- Who are the most important stakeholders in this project? Are they segmented into manageable, homogeneous groups?
- What makes the purpose and deliverables attractive to the most important stakeholders? Have the success criteria been approved by the stakeholders?
- To what extent is there agreement on the project's objective among the stakeholders?
- Who agrees/disagrees that the chosen approach for the project is appropriate and accepted?
- To what extent have the influential stakeholders accepted the project's decision-making process?
- To what extent does the organization ensure that the right people are involved?
- Have the stakeholders had the opportunity to contribute early in the project?
- How is the project's communication strategy targeted toward the most important stakeholders?
- How have the complete deliverables and purpose been presented to the most important stakeholders?

- Which stakeholders understand the most/least about the project and possess the ability to use its deliverables?
- Which stakeholders have/haven't assumed ownership of important project actions?
- What has been done to prevent possible conflicts of interest?
- Do the stakeholders understand the project's limitations (what the scope of the project does NOT include)? And have they accepted them?

The Project Plan

If there's a difference between the plan and reality – it's best to stick to reality!

The plan shows the path – but the project participants have to travel it

CHAPTER 5

The Project Plan

How do we plan projects when the uncertainty is high, we don't entirely know what we're supposed to do and it's very difficult to estimate the time consumption for the activities we do know? Even though the planning process seems difficult, we need to understand that the project plan is the only management tool that can give us some idea of where we should be at a given time. Carrying out projects without a plan is like steering a ship without a heading and nautical charts. It requires an extraordinary degree of luck.

Challenges

In Chapter 3, we learned that *a leader* is a person who shows the way. The concept of leadership is closely related to finding the way. If we want to lead, we must have the opportunity to stake out the route. Some management books claim that planning is impossible because planning builds on the assumption of predictability, and projects are per definition unpredictable.

This attitude stems from a misunderstanding of what a plan actually is. A plan is not a prophecy about the future, but an objective – something to aim for. The challenge, therefore, is to develop a plan that lets us manage the project, but also gives us a sense of having calculated the future of the project.

Chapter 5 describes the requirements and challenges that come with drawing up a good plan, presents the principles behind good project planning and explains how to use the plan.

Benefits

This chapter provides insight into:

- Structuring and using the plan
- Organizing the plan so it can be used to follow up on results, resources and finances

- Using the plan to ensure a steady pace and intensity
- Why the plan should be drawn up by the project team
- Project types and various planning types
- Estimation of uncertain activities
- Risk analysis and management

Focus This chapter focuses on the principles within planning and how the various project types differ. The principles of estimation and risk analysis are also introduced. A detailed description of the methods can be found in the toolbox.

Finally, this chapter looks at the managerial approach to planning, explaining how plans can be used for project management, as a means of communication and in negotiation situations.

Tools
Tool 5.1   Milestone Plan
Tool 5.2   Activity Descriptions
Tool 5.3   Milestone Descriptions
Tool 5.4   Gantt Chart
Tool 5.5   Three-point Estimation and Successive Calculation
Tool 5.6   Risk Analysis
Tool 5.7   Financial Follow-up

5.1.   The principles behind a good project plan

5.1.1.   Why draw up a plan?

Is planning worthwhile? Why should we draw up a plan when projects are uncertain and the surroundings turbulent? The plan comprises the landmarks we note on the navigational charts before setting sail. However, at that time, we don't know anything about the current and wind conditions. Obviously, it's difficult to predict the voyage if the winds constantly change and a storm develops. But no captain would ever claim that the nautical charts and compass become less important, the more unpredictable the weather is! In calm weather, we can use the charts to calculate the optimum route. In a storm, the calculations don't hold, but a nautical chart is still our only chance of reaching land alive!

In dynamic projects with a high degree of uncertainty, the plan is the means we have for ensuring that we are moving in the right direction. If nothing else, we can at least determine: 'We aren't where we should be' or 'The landscape doesn't look like what we expected', which is a very important property of a plan. The plan doesn't need to be 'right' to be an excellent management tool. Being able to ascertain that we haven't at this time achieved what we thought was possible is a giant step in itself, compared to if we hadn't given the route any consideration at all. Without the project plan, we can't see if things are running off course and it's difficult to learn from the process.

What are the requirements of a good plan?
Basically, a good plan should provide an overview and enable a structured approach, thereby providing an understanding of the correlations within the project. The plan itself isn't necessarily the most important concern. What matters more is how the planning process provides insights into the correlations within the project. Consequently, planning isn't an individual task for the project manager, but a process to be carried out together with the people who know the different areas of specialization and who are responsible for executing the plan.

Using the plan

The plan expresses the strategy of the approach that has been chosen for executing the project. Thus, the planning process is very much a strategic process with the aim of ensuring optimal project execution – to enable us to see alternative ways of achieving the objectives and choosing the approach. For example, whether you need to focus on the pace of the project work, optimum resource utilization, ensuring results achievement or attaining stakeholder acceptance of the results, etc.

Good planning is a prerequisite for management and follow-up, but you need to draw up a plan in order to use it as a guide! Many plans have a design that makes it impossible to use for follow-up, even though that's the whole point of the project plan. It should be possible to carry out follow-up on several levels. The program manager needs to be able to obtain an overview of multiple projects, the project manager needs to be able to follow up on the project and the participants need a plan to guide their work.

Chapter 5. The Project Plan

The plan is also a means of communicating to management, stakeholders and project participants to keep them informed of what the future brings, the current status, critical elements, etc. This plan should address the various communication needs of these groups. What are the results we are to achieve and when? Who needs to do what and when? How will I be involved? When is the steering committee to be involved next? And so on.

Who will use the plan?

The various groups have different requirements for the plan.

The project team and the project manager
The plan will be used by the project's workforce to coordinate the daily work. Consequently, the plan needs to be detailed enough to ensure that each participant knows exactly what they are supposed to do and when – i.e. the 'results' that the individual is to deliver. This includes who they are to receive deliverables from and who is to receive their deliverables.

At the same time, the participants need to be able to see how their work affects and correlates with other project participants and the overall objectives. Thus, the participants need to plan on different levels.

The stakeholders
The people who will ultimately accept the project's results need to know who among the project team to ask about various topics. The stakeholders will also be interested in when they can influence various decisions and when new knowledge and reports will be available. When will they be informed or have their say? When is their last chance to raise objections – when is it too late?

The steering committee and program management
The project's decision-makers will use the plan as a follow-up and coordination tool on a general level – to form the basis for overall decision-making regarding resource allocation in relation to the project and other assignments within the organization.

This means that the plan presented by the project manager to top management should not be too detailed, but rather should focus on critical elements requiring decisions on an overall level. The plan should be structured so that the project can be compared with other projects in the portfolio or program.

5.1.2. There are 10 overriding requirements for good project plans

A good plan meets the following requirements:

10 requirements for the plan

1. It is prepared by the project participants to ensure high quality and acceptance.
2. It establishes a common understanding and acceptance of the approach.
3. It demonstrates correlation between the end deliverables and the path to achieving them.
4. It clearly indicates the correlation between the deliverables and the individual's work and responsibilities.
5. It can be used for follow-up and management on several levels as well as for program and portfolio management.
6. It is broken down into levels so everything you need can fit onto a single sheet of paper.
7. It is resilient to uncertainties, thus reducing the need for constant adjustment.
8. It sets the pace and intensity of the project.
9. It shows when major risks and decisions need to be clarified.
10. It has only one critical path.

To ensure that the plan meets these requirements, it's a good idea to develop the plan according to the following principles.

Structure of the plan, including work streams, milestones, phases, decision points and role distribution

The following is a brief description of the principles behind the plan structure. These principles also indicate the most important steps in the planning process.

From objectives to plan and the individual's role

Chapter 5. The Project Plan

Step 1 Breaking the project down into work streams
Step 2 Defining milestones within the individual work streams
Step 3 Defining dependencies between the work streams
Step 4 Breaking the plan down into phases
Step 5 Scheduling the most important decision point meetings
Step 6 Defining activities
Step 7 Estimating the time consumption of the activities
Step 8 Risk analysis and adjustment of the plan

From objectives to plan

The project planning begins with the objective breakdown structure – the OBS

The only parameter that is known when project planning starts is the objectives. The objectives, and thus the deliverables, therefore form the starting point for the planning process.

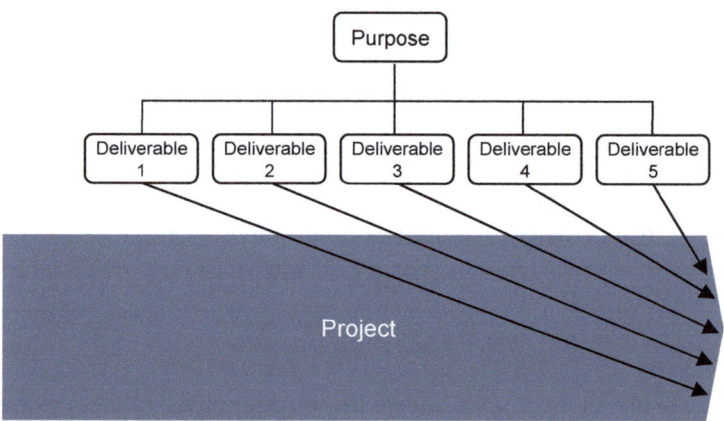

Figure 5.1. The project and its objectives. The objectives must be achieved by the end of the project. This means all the deliverables have been delivered.

The deliverables describe the desired output at the end of the project.

It is therefore an excellent point of departure for the planning process.

5.1.3. Step 1: Breaking the project down into work streams

The first step in the planning process is to assess how the project can be broken down into a set of sub-tasks with a view to achieving the objectives. These sub-tasks are called 'work streams'. Work streams can often be defined based on the project deliverables. In some cases, the project can be broken down into work streams corresponding to the individual deliverables. In other cases, it may be more useful to group two deliverables together into one work stream.

Defining work streams based on the deliverables

Figure 5.2. Step 1 in the planning process: breaking the project down into work streams. If we tip the OBS 90 degrees, we can break the project down into the work streams that lead to the various deliverables.

A work stream is the series of activities that leads up to one or more project deliverables. Work streams are also sometimes called results paths. Some management books refer to a Work Breakdown Structure, or WBS, where the structure resembles a hierarchy corresponding to the Objective Breakdown Structure (OBS). The work streams are part of this structure. Within the individual work streams, the work can be broken down into work packages or main activities that follow each other over time.

Work streams are results paths

The advantage of breaking the plan down into work streams is that it provides a good structure for the project. Work streams are often used as a basis for organizing the project. A work stream can be an area of responsibility for a sub-project manager. It often makes sense to break down contract work, budgets and documentation into work streams in this way. For example, on a construction project, there will be masonry, carpentry, plumbing, electricity, etc. An organizational change project, however, might be broken down into new organizational structure, new workflows, IT system, user training, and so on.

It's a good idea to identify the work streams based on:
- Physical sub-systems, e.g. engine, body work, interior and electrical system.
- Problems, e.g. user needs analysis, technical testing of principle.
- Geography, e.g. implementation at corporate offices in London, Paris, Düsseldorf and Rome.
- Systems, e.g. software for invoicing, sales management, bookkeeping and production management.
- Organizational elements, e.g. training of steering committee members, project managers, project participants and line managers.
- Processes, e.g. welding, molding and assembly methods.

Work streams are used to focus on key areas or key problems in the project. For this reason, work streams can also be defined based on critical focus areas that are not derived directly from the objectives. The implementation of a critical new technology can be defined as a work stream in order to call special attention the uncertain elements of the project.

In a systems development project, changes and additions to the specification can be treated as a separate work stream. In larger organizational change projects, information and stakeholder management will often be a separate work stream. The same applies to user and staff training.

In larger projects requiring a great deal of coordination, project management can represent a work stream in which project management, coordination meetings and consultations are planned.

This can help make the project management more proactive rather than just reacting to the steady stream of problems and crises.

5.1.4. Step 2: Defining milestones within the individual work streams

After establishing the work streams, the next step is to determine how we get from the starting point to the final deliverables within the individual work streams. Which sub-results need to be achieved along the path to the deliverables?

Milestones along the path to the objective

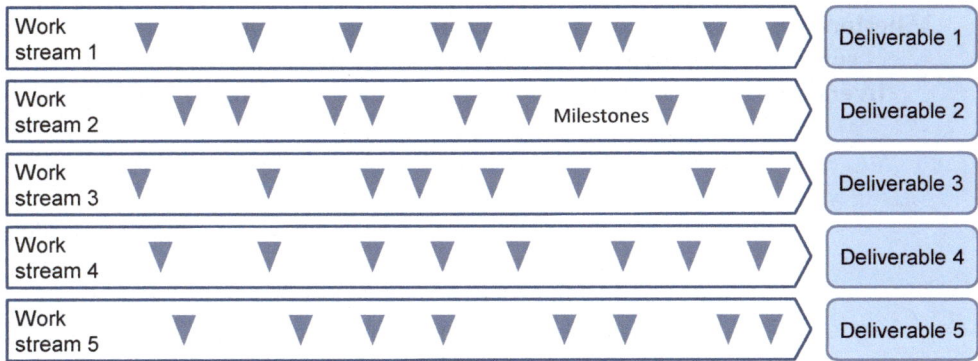

Figure 5.3. Step 2 in the planning process: Defining the milestones within the individual work streams. The milestones in a work stream result in the end deliverable, for instance deliverable 2 in work stream 2.

This is actually the process of breaking the OBS down further by continuing to ask how something should be done or what needs to be delivered to achieve the end deliverables. There are two schools of thought on this topic: either we can start from the deliverables and work backward or we can start from the beginning and move to the right toward the deliverables.

It is often a matter of individual taste, as both approaches can yield useful results. However, with projects that are highly standardized and which have been tried before, it appears to be easiest to start at the beginning and work toward the deliverables. The reason being that everyone knows 'how we usually do things'.

On projects that are starting from scratch, it may be easiest to begin with what is to be delivered and work backward from there. In these cases, you may want to ask: 'In order to achieve a deliverable, what needs to be completed immediately pre-

Chapter 5. The Project Plan

ceding that deliverable?' 'To achieve that, what do we have to do immediately before that?' And so on.

Why use milestones?

Milestones are sub-results (sub-deliverables) to be achieved by a specific deadline. There are several reasons why we prefer milestones to activities as the basis for the overall plan.

Milestones as sub-deliverables

The first reason is that the basic principle of management by objectives is to start by thinking about what we have to achieve before discussing how we can achieve it. The opposite is absurd if we don't know what the end deliverable is. We therefore have to define the milestone before we can talk about the activities.

The second reason why milestones are much more resilient to change than activities is simply because we tend to change the activities in order to achieve a milestone. For instance, we can achieve the milestone '2 miles outside the city' with the help of a variety of activities. We can take the bus, a taxi, ride a bike or we can choose to walk. There are almost always a variety of possible activities for achieving a milestone. Within a project, we often find ourselves in a situation where we change the activities in order to achieve the milestone. If we had planned to take the bus, but didn't make it on time, then we have to change to a new activity and, say, take a cab to achieve the milestone on time.

Milestones are resilient to change

Take another example. Say we've planned a training program with the first milestone being: 'training needs mapped' and the second milestone being: 'training material prepared'. In this plan, we don't actually know which activities need to be carried out prior to the milestone until we have achieved milestone 1. The training needs have to be identified before we can decide which activities need to be carried out in order to draw up the training material. But regardless of which needs might come with milestone 1, we know that some training material needs to be created to achieve milestone 2. Thus, milestone plans are much more resilient than activity plans because we change the activities as our understanding of the project increases in order to achieve the milestones.

If we start by trying to draw up an activity plan for such a project, we will discover that it will need endless changes, which will lead us to conclude that it's impossible to plan uncertain projects. However, this is simply because we are trying to use activities rather than milestones. Projects where long-term activity planning does work tend to be highly predictable, such as construction projects. In fact, one could say that this type of project bears a strong resemblance to contract manufacturing and is in fact not generally one-off in nature, a characteristic that is otherwise part of our definition of a project.

The third reason is that we can use milestones for follow-up, which as we know is an important property of a plan. It's interesting to note that the most commonly used planning principle is the Gantt chart based on activities. But this particular tool is impossible to use for follow-up. Let's look at en example.

Management according to the milestones

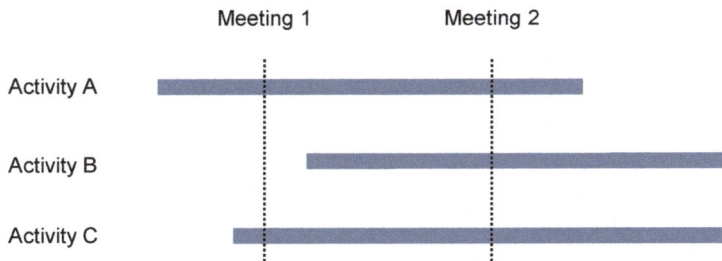

Figure 5.4. Gantt chart or bar chart indicating three activities and times for two meetings.

In Figure 5.4, we see three activities – activities A, B and C. At some point a project team meeting takes place to follow up on the progress of the project. How far along should activities A and C be at the time of meeting 1? Activity A should be well underway and activity C should have just started, but how far should they have come? It's impossible to tell. At meeting 2, we have the same problem. We can't see how far along activities A, B and C should be at the time of the meeting. For this reason, we can't follow up and assess whether we're on track.

Follow-up in the middle of activities often takes the form of a brief chat about how things are going and whether we think we can make the deadline. Follow-up is about knowing two things. Where we should be and where we actually are. Some might object that we can simply break down activity A into sub-activities and require that one of the sub-activities must be completed by meeting 1. This would enable us to determine whether the sub-activity has been completed. This is true, of course. The sub-activity's deliverable would be available prior to the meeting, and we would be able to determine whether we have achieved the planned sub-deliverable. But this is because a sub-deliverable is a milestone. The completion of an activity results in a sub-deliverable, which we can follow up on. Have we achieved the expected result? Have we achieved the milestone?

What are milestones?
A milestone is a result (a sub-deliverable) by a specified deadline. The result may be a report, a decision, a completed analysis, a clarification, an approval, a well-functioning test result, a new design, a user acceptance, etc. Regardless of the milestone, the result is always a status.

5.1.5. Step 3: Defining dependencies between the work streams

After defining the milestones within the work streams, they need to be organized in the proper order within a timeframe. It's not enough to place them one after the other within the individual work streams. There are often dependencies across the work streams, i.e. a milestone in one work stream may depend on the results of a milestone in another work stream.

This is an important part of the planning process, because work streams are also used to delegate responsibility to various project participants or sub-teams. Generally, the dependencies across the work streams (and across the areas of responsibility) are what cause problems. For this reason, it's a good idea to highlight the milestones that provide 'input' to another area of responsibility and set fixed deadlines for them. These milestones may not be changed without mutual agreement with the people responsible for the work streams they affect.

5.1. The principles behind a good project plan

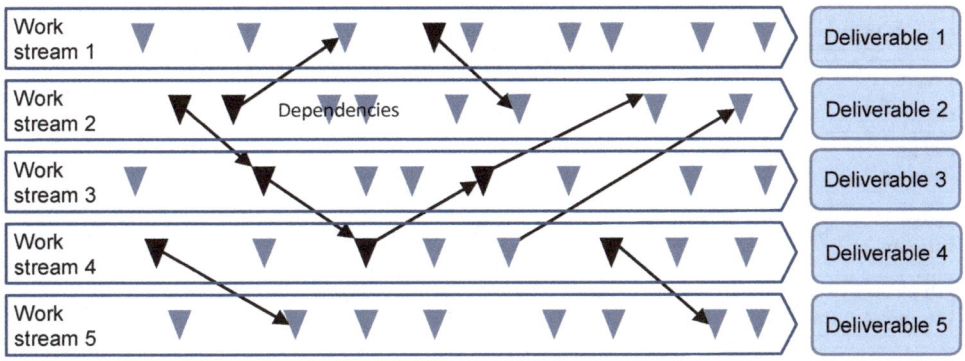

Figure 5.5. Step 3 in the planning process: defining the dependencies between the work streams. Organizing the milestones in the proper order within a timeframe. The black milestones depend on the timeframe for another work stream, and the deadline may therefore not be changed without coordinating it with the other work streams.

If there are many criss-crossing dependencies between two work streams, it is probably worth considering whether these two areas of responsibility are so closely related that they should be grouped as one work stream. It's pretty much impossible to manage individual work streams if everything is dependent on another work stream.

The daily follow-up is carried out by the person responsible for the work stream. The project manager should instead concentrate on the 'black milestones', which create dependencies across the project.

Focus on the milestones that provide input to other work streams

5.1.6. Step 4: Breaking the plan down into phases

After the dependencies have been mapped and the milestones organized in the proper order, it's possible to observe when the content in the project changes. Looking at the individual milestones, we often see a series of milestones dealing with analysis results. Then come the milestones dealing with proposals or solution design. These are followed by testing of the various proposals and finally we have the actual implementation.

The point of breaking the project down into phases is to divide it up into relevant sub-sections based on time. One reason for doing this is that projects are uncertain. Breaking

159

Chapter 5. The Project Plan

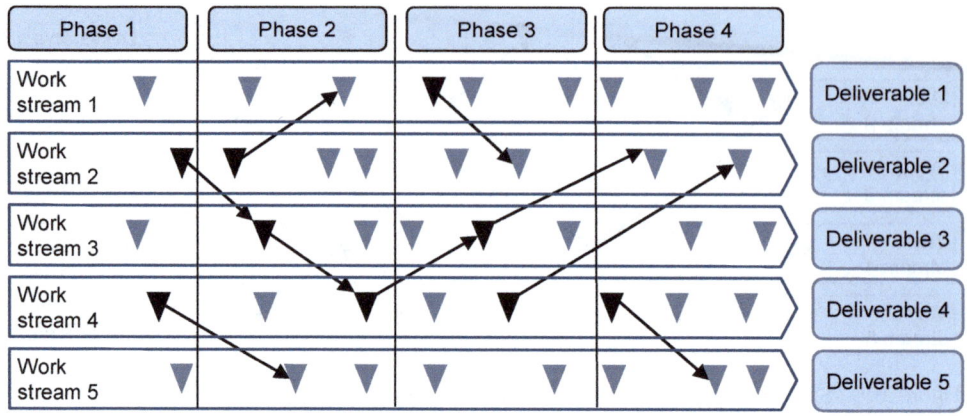

Figure 5.6. Step 4 in the planning process: Breaking down the project plan into phases.

the process up into steps makes it possible to initiate the costly activities gradually over time as the degree of uncertainty decreases and the level of knowledge increases.

Projects change phases as the nature of the assignment changes. Generally, projects begin with an analysis phase, where the uncertainty is high because the problem and possible solutions have not yet been fully explored. Analysis isn't very costly, and once the analysis has been conducted and we have a better understanding of the problem, the uncertainty falls and the level of knowledge increases. Now begins the design phase.

With the completion of the design phase, the level of knowledge increases further. Now we have specific design proposals, which means that the subsequent implementation phase can be initiated on a sounder basis. The degree of uncertainty has been reduced even further.

The point of phases is for the preceding work to be completed and thus ensure a more robust status before proceeding to the next phase. In the transition to the next phase, the nature of the project changes. This generally also entails a change in the management tasks for the project manager.

In the beginning, the primary focus is generally on problem clarification and achieving a consensus about the problem. The design phase concentrates on working creatively with many alternative solutions before deciding on the final design.

Once the design has been adopted, it's time to delegate within the individual work streams. During the implementation phase, the project manager acts as consultant and sparring partner for the sub-project managers. In the final phase, everything should fall into place. This is where project management often focuses on deadlines and coordination between the work streams. There is generally a fair amount of crisis management in the final phase.

The phases are also introduced to make it possible for management to follow the project on an overall level, for example in portfolio management and program management, as explained in Chapter 10. It's important to bear in mind that the phase transitions can take place at different times within the various work streams. It's not always realistic for all the work streams to progress to the next phase on the same date and at the same steering committee meeting.

5.1.7. Step 5: Determining the most important decision point meetings

After each phase, it's necessary to decide how the project should proceed.

Part of the planning process is to define which critical decisions the steering committee is to be involved in. There may be many important decisions, but as a minimum, the steering committee should be involved in the transitions to new phases. Because of the high degree of uncertainty in projects, it's important for management to approve a project's transition to the next phase.

At each phase transition, the steering committee must decide on or approve the following:

- Has the project realized the expected result at the present time? And is this result good enough to build on?
- Has the project's uncertainty been reduced enough to progress to the next phase?
- Are the revised plan and budget for the next phase and the rest of the project acceptable?
- Is the revised risk assessment for the rest of the project acceptable?
- Is it still relevant to implement the project?

Chapter 5. The Project Plan

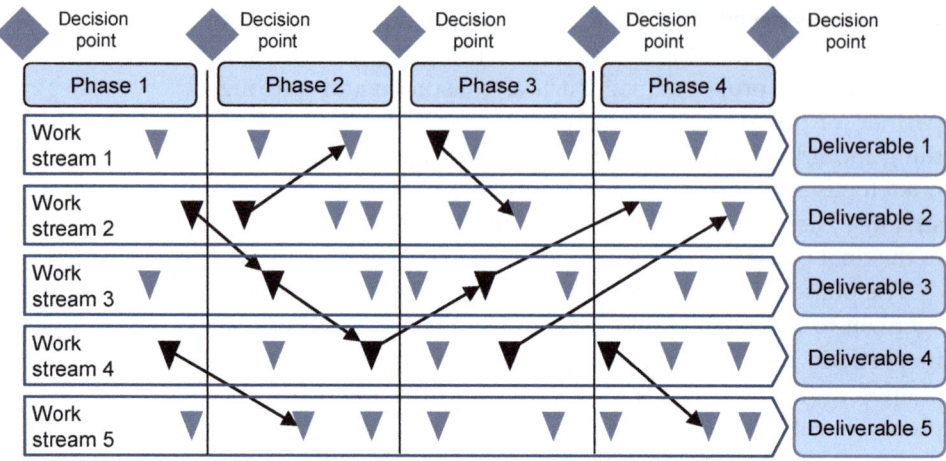

Figure 5.7. Step 5 in the planning process: Making important decisions over the course of the project. The steering committee is involved in the project at the decision points.

However, it may also be necessary to include decision meetings mid-phase. There are two points of view when it comes to planning decision points. The project manager needs to secure support at critical junctures in the project so that the project team doesn't have to work without the support of management for too long. This helps prevent the need to repeat work. At the same time, the steering committee needs to ensure that they have enough control over the project. The length of the intervals between the decisions indicate how short or long a line the project manager has been given.

The aim is for the project team to be able to work independently between the decision point meetings. Meanwhile, management can exert control over the project at the decision meetings.

The length of the intervals between the decisions indicates the degree of delegation

There is, of course, a fine line between not enough meetings, with the associated risk of a lack of reconciliation of expectations between management and the project manager, and so many decision meetings that the project manager is reduced to a mere 'errand boy'.

It's crucial that the decision point meetings are noted in the plan with dates so management knows when they are ex-

5.1. The principles behind a good project plan

pected to make the important decisions. This is to avoid the project team having to wait on decisions by management. It can be difficult to keep up the motivation of a team that has worked weekends to get the material ready – and is then forced to wait on the decision.

When the steering committee has approved the plan, they also accept the degree of delegation to the project manager.

5.1.8.   Step 6: Defining activities

The last step in the planning process is defining the activities that fall prior to the individual milestones. It is rarely possible to define the activities in detail for the entire project. This is why planning is usually carried out on several levels.

For instance, you may have a general activity plan for the entire project and a more detailed plan for the next phase or for the individual work streams.

Activity planning is based on milestones. The milestones are the sub-deliverables, which are the result of the activities. The activities are what require resources. We define activities by assessing what needs to be carried out in order to achieve the milestone in question. The activities fall prior to the milestone within the timeframe and must be completed in order to achieve the milestone.

It is important to plan the activities in such a way that there is only one critical path through the project. The critical path is defined as the chain of activities that can't be delayed without delaying the entire project. Figure 5.8 is an illustration of a plan with one critical path.

The advantage of this planning principle is that it leaves room **One critical path**

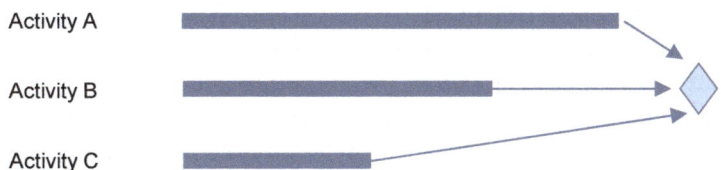

Figure 5.8. Activities prior to the milestone. Only activity A is critical.

163

Chapter 5. The Project Plan

for the project manager to maneuver. Activity B and C can withstand quite a bit of delay without affecting the milestone. This means that the project manager can concentrate on activity A. And if activity A runs into problems, it may be possible reallocate resources from activities B and C to activity A.

Certainty of delay Even though the plan has been drawn up following this sensible approach, activities B and C will often become delayed for the simple reason that they aren't very critical. This can easily result in a plan like Figure 5.9, where the project has become deadlocked.

Figure 5.9. Activities prior to the milestone. All activities are critical. The project will almost certainly be delayed.

If the plan is drawn up as in Figure 5.9, the milestone will almost certainly be delayed. The likelihood that just one of the three activities is delayed is very strong. There isn't much the project manager can do about such delays because all the activities are critical. Reallocating resources from one activity to another just isn't an option.

The plan's elements and levels
Going back to the 10 fundamental planning requirements from 5.1.2, we can see how they are built into the plan and we find the following correlations.

We break the plan down into work streams because the aim of the plan is to show the correlations between deliverables and the path to achieving them. There should also be a correlation between the deliverables and the individual's work and responsibilities. Later, we will look at how to use work

164

streams to organize projects and achieve a clear distribution of responsibilities.

We use milestones because we need to be to use the plan for follow-up and management on several levels, including program and portfolio management. Milestones are useful to this end because they describe the sub-deliverables that must be achieved by specific deadlines. At the same time, they are much more robust than activities, which can change as we gain greater insight into the project. The aim is for the plan to be resilient to known uncertainties and thus reduce the need for constant adjustment.

We break the plan down into phases and decision points because this gives an indication of when significant risks and decisions need to be clarified, for example to ensure that costly decisions aren't made until the degree of uncertainty has been reduced.

We define the activities in more and more detail as our knowledge of the assignment grows. The activities are planned in such a way that there is only one critical path through the project.

The following are the basic elements of good project planning
- Work streams based on the objective's deliverables
- Milestones describing sub-deliverables within the individual work streams
- Dependencies between milestones
- Breakdown into phases with decision points
- Activities describing the work that needs to be carried out

Basic elements of project planning

Breakdown into levels
At first, a 16-page project plan, complete with arrows and lines, may look very professional. However, the aim of the plan is to provide an overview, communicate the current status of the project, and serve as a basis for follow-up.

This means that the person using the plan should be able to find all the information he or she needs on a single sheet of paper. To achieve this, the plan needs to be broken down into levels. Typical levels might include:

Management level
This is the master project plan used by the project managers, steering committee, program management and top management. The plan corresponds to Figure 5.7 and provides a general overview of the project without going into detail.

The master project plan comprises:
- Work streams
- Primary milestones
- Primary activities
- Phases and decision points

Project management and steering group level
A detailed plan for the next or current phase of the project can be drawn up based on the master project plan. This plan can be broken down even further into one plan for each work stream in the current phase. The aim of the plan is to facilitate management and coordination of the work.

The project phase plan comprises:
- Work streams
- Milestones for the phase
- Essential dependencies
- Activities for the phase

Sub-project manager and project team level
Within the individual work streams, the work will be carried out in accordance with task lists and minutes of meetings, in addition to the project plan itself. This is where the final details are planned and coordinated. The actual working plan is developed on this level. What is to be done on Wednesday afternoon? The master project plan isn't dynamic enough to include this type of information.

Working plans consist of:
- Task and issue lists
- Project journals
- Minutes of meetings

Planning your own work
Finally, the individual needs to plan their own work. This is generally where the entire planning process can fall to pieces. Drawing up a project plan is one thing, but how do we ensure that it trickles down to the individual team member's calendar?

From project plan to personal plan

Here are a few tips:

- Only use project participants who are allocated to the project full-time, and have them sit together.
- If that's not possible, introduce a project workday on one or two specified days each week, where everybody sits together.
- If that's not possible, then work together when major elements have to be delivered. Use workshops.
- Draw up resource contracts with the participants and their superiors.
- Agree on which results each participant is expected to deliver – not which activities.
- Plan the individual's work jointly with the project participants.
- Use a common electronic calendar system.

The project plan should be formulated to ensure high quality as well as acceptance and ownership among the project team members. The plan should also establish a common understanding and acceptance of the approach among the project team.

Planning the project within the team

5.2. Planning the project within the team

5.2.1. Let the team do the planning – this facilitates quality and ownership

The project plan should be formulated to ensure high quality as well as acceptance and ownership among the project team members. The plan should also establish a common understanding and acceptance of the approach among the project team.

Chapter 5. The Project Plan

The project team creates quality

Quality within the plan

It is vital that the plan is prepared by the project team so that the various areas of expertise can contribute to the plan with their knowledge. This is the whole point of appointing a project team in the first place. It is this particular combination of qualifications that can get the job done.

The quality of a plan improves when it is drawn up by the experts who understand the problem. The right people can work in more detail and know what the content should be and where the uncertainties lie. This is the primary argument for allowing the project team to participate in the planning process.

A very simple rule of thumb is that if the project participants can't break the plan down into activities of one week in duration, then they don't know enough about the subject.

The project team creates ownership

Ownership of the plan

It's not enough for the plan to 'be' right. The individual also needs to feel a sense of obligation to the plan. The plan needs to 'feel' right. This can only be achieved by the individual being involved in the planning process and being allowed to contribute with his or her specialist insight and knowledge. An individual who has participated in the development of the plan, listened to the concerns of the others, listened to why it's important that the deliverables to others in the project aren't delayed and listened to what each member considers critical, has an entirely different relationship to the plan. It is *our* plan, and we all have a stake in it.

A planning workshop saves time

Planning Workshop

A planning workshop or kick-off seminar, as it is sometimes called, can vary in length and content depending on the scope and nature of the project. Two days is probably the most common duration for such a workshop, but some teams choose to spend an entire week on the process. One day may also be sufficient.

The important thing is that the program and duration are properly matched to achieve the necessary quality. The duration depends primarily on how comprehensive the project is

5.2. Planning the project within the team

and how much time the project team needs to get to know each other.

Some may feel it's impossible to spend an entire week on the process, as they're too busy. However, a kick-off seminar doesn't really take extra time. It saves time in the long run – shortening the project start-up phase by several weeks. Once you've tried it, you'll never start up a project again without bringing the entire team together to decide on who does what and when.

Prior to the workshop, it's important to consider the following:

- Who should participate?
- When should the seminar take place?
- How long should it take?
- What are the content and agenda?
- What needs to be prepared – and by whom?
- What planning tools will be needed?
- What will you do to facilitate acceptance and ownership?
- How will you build trust and cohesion among the team?

A typical program looks like this:

Day 1
- The purpose according to management. Have someone from management explain why the project is important.
- Stakeholder analysis. What expectations and requirements are there to the project?
- Purpose and deliverables. Defining the assignment.
- Milestone plan. Begin with the work stream breakdown.
- How can we build trust and cohesion among the team? Often some sort of event in the evening.

Day 2
- Milestone plan, cont. What are the milestones and dependencies?
- Organization. How should we organize the project? How should responsibilities be distributed among the team members?
- The participants' calendars and scheduling meetings.

Conclusion (possibly incl. presentation to management for their feedback and immediate response).

5.2.2. Prepare the plan together in a workshop

It has become fairly commonplace to organize a planning workshop at an early point in the project. The planning workshop is an effective method, because it 'hits two birds with one stone'. It ensures high quality and ownership as well as serving a team-building function and communicating what the project is about and how everything correlates.

If we look at the team-building activities, a planning workshop has the following impact:

Team building is about achieving a clear and common objective
A team is a group that works toward a common objective. For this reason, there is a significant team-building effect in discussing the project and achieving a consensus on what the assignment actually entails. When the team works together to draw up the plan, they are forced to discuss the content and the scope in detail. And the more detailed the discussion, the easier it is to discover if people have different perceptions of the project. This creates a high degree of clarity and produces a common objective.

Everyone needs an overview
In a true collaboration, everyone needs an overview of the assignment. What is the nature of the assignment? Who needs to do the preliminary work, so I can do my part? What do I need to deliver to others? This overview is created for everyone involved as the team works together to draw up the plan. Being able to see how 'my assignment' affects 'the others' assignments' has a highly motivating effect.

Everyone needs to feel useful and important
Another motivating factor that is also part of team building is figuring out what the individual's role is in the project. What is expected of me? Why am I, specifically, involved in this project?

This becomes clear as the project plan unfolds and the various areas of responsibility are defined.

5.2. Planning the project within the team

Everyone needs an appropriate degree of influence
When the team works together to draw up the plan, members have the opportunity to provide their input on areas where they have specific knowledge and experience. In addition to producing a better plan, this sense of responsibility is one of the strongest motivating factors. In the joint planning process, the individual has the opportunity to exert influence in the areas where he or she has something to offer. When it comes time to delegate responsibilities, the individual feels a sense of shared influence in the areas where they have commitments. It is extremely important that the individual participants feel a sense of responsibility for their contribution to the project, as the project manager normally doesn't have the authority to give the participants direct commands.

Team building is also about trust and mutual support
At the planning workshop, the critical areas of the plan will be discussed. Where are the critical areas in my work? What are the consequences for others, if I don't get my part done on time? How difficult is it for those who have to deliver to me? How can I help them to ensure that I receive my sub-deliverables on time? Before issues become problems, the team members can talk about how they can help each other so everyone recognizes the importance of delivering their contribution on time.

A workshop can be a useful method in other areas of the project as well. **Using workshops in other areas**

In addition to the start-up seminar, a 'kick-off meeting' is often held, although it will generally be of a more informative nature. This is where larger groups can be invited to hear about the project. The various types of workshops include:

Pace change: The deadline has been moved up, so the project needs to be completed earlier than planned. The project team meets to draw up a plan that can increase the likelihood that the project can be executed more quickly.

Re-start: The project has been delayed or stopped temporarily. Now it is time to get the ball rolling again and get back on track.

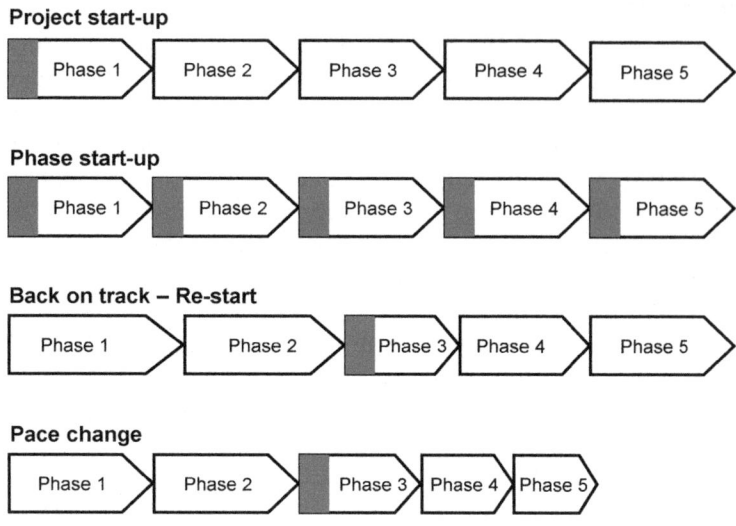

Figure 5.10. Using planning workshops in various areas of the project.

Phase start-up: At the beginning of each phase, it can be a good idea to draw up a detailed plan for that phase. This will ensure enthusiasm, motivation and focus on the critical elements in the phase.

Crisis seminar/troubleshooting seminar: Crises can often be solved by the project team meeting to plan: 'What do we do now?'

Handover to operations: It can be a good idea for the project team and representatives from the line organization to conduct a seminar to plan the handover of the project to operations.

5.2.3. Planning workshop in the *Happier Customers* project

The project manager, Lisa, is ready to draw up the plan for the comprehensive project. She has asked to the project team to specify the objectives. She originally chose to develop the objectives with the help of the project team because she didn't have any experience with IT and the workflows in the various departments. At the same time, she considers it important that the project participants feel a sense of ownership of the objectives, so that they are accepted and are perceived as realistic. She feels it should be possible to do the same with the project plan.

5.2. Planning the project within the team

Figure 3.8 shows the final OBS hierarchy, which the project team settled on, with the purposes indicated above the line and the deliverables below the line. At the project team meeting, Lisa presents her ideas: 'At the last meeting, we decided on the following deliverables:'

- New workflows established
- New IT solution established
- Sales staff trained
- New organization and roles established
- New customer service concept developed

'As you all know, since our last meeting, I have had interviews with some of you to get an idea of what you would prefer to work with and where your strengths lie. I have now drawn up a proposal for how we can divide the project up, and I would like to discuss it with you.'

'I picture grouping the establishment of new workflows and new organization and roles into one work stream called workflows and organization. I feel it's important that this particular team comprises people from sales, tech, marketing and finance. I therefore propose that Erik, who has worked with quality assurance and mapping workflows, be made responsible for this team.'

After some discussion among the project team, it is decided to divide the project up into the following work streams:

- Workflows and organization (Responsible: Erik)
- IT solution (Responsible: Michael, an IT expert)
- Sales training (Responsible: Elizabeth, an experienced salesperson who has worked within several product areas)
- Customer service concept (Responsible: Nick, product manager of a product group with a high degree of customization to customer needs)

Lisa says the group should set aside an entire day for planning the project. She wants Erik, Elizabeth, Nick and Michael to get together before the planning meeting to decide which milestones should be part of the individual work streams. Preparation consists of describing each milestone on individual cards.

Chapter 5. The Project Plan

At the planning meeting, the team can then hang the cards on the wall and discuss their order and any dependencies.

Two weeks later, the team meets to plan the project.

Lisa likes to have things under control, but there should still be room for the various participants to utilize their experience and knowledge. The individual should have the opportunity to influence the plan. Lisa has therefore planned the planning process itself very carefully, while leaving the content up to the participants.

The day begins with Lisa announcing the following agenda:

8:30 am	Welcome, program and participants' expectations
9:00 am	Setting milestones for the individual work streams
12-noon	Lunch
12:45 pm	Dependencies and phase breakdown
3:00 pm	Risk analysis
4:30 pm	What we are to do over the next two weeks?
5:00 pm	Team dinner

Before starting the meeting, Lisa has hung up green poster boards with the four work streams. She has also hung up a

Figure 5.11. Project Manager Lisa informs the team of the day's program, standing in front of the "empty" plan.

5.2. Planning the project within the team

general timeline on which the milestones are to be placed.

Under the next item on the agenda, Erik, Elizabeth, Nick and Michael each place their yellow cards with milestones on the wall as they explain why they have chosen these particular milestones.

There is a lively discussion, and Lisa suggests that they talk about each work stream, one at a time. The project participants working on the customer service concept feel there are some milestones missing in the workflows and organization work stream. The IT staff agree.

They work through the plan in this way, adding new milestones and reformulating others.

The milestones within the individual work streams have now been established. After lunch, Lisa gives a brief introduction to collaboration across the individual work streams. She suggests that everyone mark the milestones in another work stream that are needed as input in their own work stream.

The project participants working with IT have many suggestions for the input they need from the workflow and organization work stream. Other work streams need similar input

Figure 5.12. The project participants discuss the milestones and their placement.

175

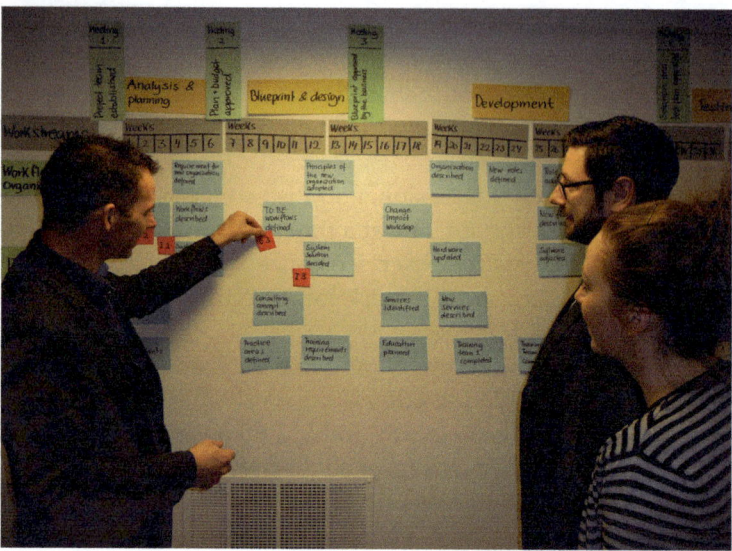

Figure 5.13. Two project participants discuss dependencies between the work streams.

from IT. For example, it's important that the IT system is completed as quickly as possible so that it can be used in the planned sales training. This develops into a lengthy discussion because the IT staff suddenly realize that their deadline isn't actually immediately prior to implementation, but rather prior to training start-up.

Later that afternoon, these critical milestones are incorporated in a risk analysis to give all the project participants an overview of what can go wrong and of the 10 greatest risks in the project.

5.3. Project types and planning methods

The planning methods vary from project type to project type, depending on how predictable the project is and how the project type is managed. The principles are the same for breaking the project down into work streams, milestones, phases, decision points and activities, but the weighting differs.

5.3.1. Engineering and construction projects

Engineering and construction projects are characterized by a low degree of uncertainty. These tend to be projects with a great deal of repetition and generally aren't established until the contract has been signed. This means that the objectives are known from project start-up. This type of project is often strongly regulated by standards and collective agreements and planning is therefore based on 'standard plans' with 'standard times' for the activities.

Detailed activity-based network planning

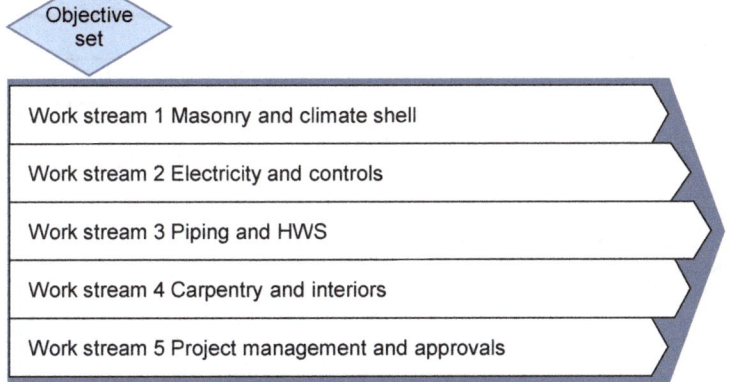

Figure 5.14. An engineering and construction project broken down into work streams by specialization based on discipline or subcontract.

The project is often broken down into work streams that follow the divisions into specialization based on discipline or subcontract. In construction, for instance, the breakdown is very traditional, although we do see more multi-trade consortia and tech contractors that cover several technical areas. In this type of project, the work streams are often legally independent subcontractors.

An important work stream is project management and coordination of the various subcontractors.

Planning is often highly detailed and predictable. This type of project makes use of comprehensive activity planning, which can be estimated with great precision thanks to a significant degree of experience. Due to the low level of uncertainty,

Chapter 5. The Project Plan

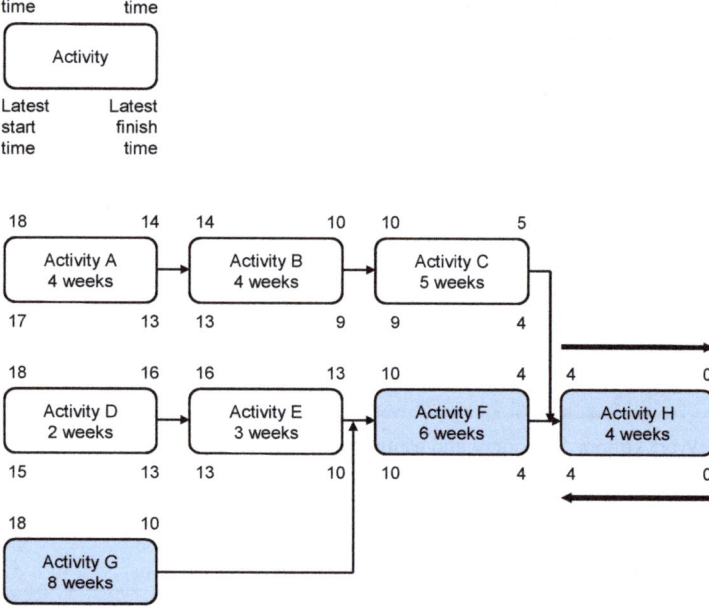

Figure 5.15. Network planning indicating the critical path through activities G, F and H.

it also makes sense to use detailed network planning, where it's possible to calculate critical paths through the project with a reasonable degree of certainty.

The network plan produces a very precise description of the project and its activities, indicating which activities are to be carried out before, others as well as any dependencies between the activities. This makes it possible to calculate the critical path through the project as the series of activities that must not be delayed in any way if the project is to be completed on time.

The timeframe for the individual activities can be calculated with the help of three-point estimation and successive calculation, as covered in section 5.4. After the duration of the activities have been calculated, the latest start times of the activities can be calculated working backward. If activity H must be finished by deadline O, then it must be started at the latest 4 weeks prior to O, as it takes 4 weeks to finish. Working backward, activity F must start 10 weeks prior to the deadline, and activity G 18 weeks prior to the deadline.

When the calculations for all the activities have been worked out moving backward, we have the latest start times. For activity G, it's 18 weeks prior to the deadline, for activity A it's 17 weeks prior and for activity D it's 15 weeks prior. If we imagine that we start activities A, D and G in week 18 prior to the deadline, then we can calculate the earliest start and finish times in the project. This means that activity A can be completed at the earliest 14 weeks prior to the deadline and correspondingly that activity D can be finished at the earliest 16 weeks prior to the deadline. The earliest finish time for activity G is 10 weeks prior to the deadline.

This calculation shows that activities G, F and H have the same earliest and latest finish times. This means they can't tolerate delay. These activities represent the critical path through the project. In contrast, activities A, B and C can tolerate 1 week's delay without delaying the entire project, while activities D and E can tolerate 3 weeks' delay without affecting the project's final deadline.

This type of planning can be carried out using any of the many IT project management tools that are available on the market. However, it is a prerequisite that the content of the project activities aren't subject to continual change and that the uncertainty isn't too great, as this would result in a constantly changing critical path.

5.3.2. R&D projects
R&D projects are much more uncertain than construction projects. The first two or three phases of the project are often spent preparing the specification. And two-thirds of the total length of the project can pass before the objectives have been set.

Milestone planning and detailed phase plans

Stage gate models
R&D projects also have a high degree of repetition and are often carried out according to a standardized stage gate model. The point of these stage gate models is that all projects pass through the same phases, such as the idea generation phase,

Stage gates

Chapter 5. The Project Plan

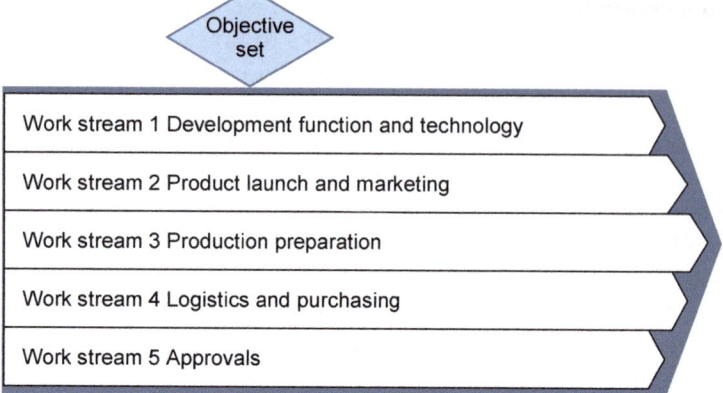

Figure 5.16. Concurrent Engineering is carried out as parallel activities within product, sales/marketing, production preparation, logistics/purchasing.

business case assessment, specification, design, prototyping, 0-series production and launch. In a stage gate model, the decision points between the phases are the gates through which the project must pass.

Changes to the specifications and project execution are often made at these gates. There is therefore a good deal more focus on decisions – GO, WAIT, STOP – at the phase transitions than is the case with construction projects.

For this reason, it is actually not appropriate (and often pointless) to draw up a detailed activity plan for the entire project. The plan often comprises a series of standard milestones that are the same for all projects. Detailed plans are only drawn up for the individual phase up to the next 'gate' (decision point). R&D projects are primarily managed by means of the milestones and the major decisions.

In many R&D projects, the approval process by official bodies in various countries is so time-consuming and resource-demanding that it represents its own work stream. At the same time, it's an activity type that lies beyond the project manager's control and therefore requires extra attention and planning.

5.3.3. Research and technology development projects

This type of project shares certain characteristics with the technical aspects of R&D projects. These types of projects generally have a high degree of uncertainty and can only be planned using important milestones and decision points. Detailed activity planning often takes the form of task lists and testing schedules.

Many of these projects are financed with external funding in the form of grants from foundations, councils and firms in the private sector. Consequently, there is usually an extended application phase, where it is highly uncertain how the project can be realized. Once the funding has been granted, the project can be initiated. There tends to be a high degree of freedom in the implementation of this type of project. However, it is becoming more common for sponsors to require documented results, giving rise to increased professionalization of the implementation phase.

5.3.4. IT and systems development projects

Planning of this project type has a good deal in common with R&D and construction projects. In some system adaptation projects, network planning is used because the activities are highly standardized. In projects with a greater degree of new development, planning is carried out using milestones, as in R&D projects.

Software development, however, is characterized by a great deal of ongoing testing, which affects planning. It is quite common to form work streams for change control so that additions and errors can be handled and planned separately. The detailed plans are often based on 'issue lists', where problems are registered, categorized and marked when completed. (The day-to-day management thus involves making these lists shorter and shorter).

5.3.5. Organizational change projects

Planning of this project type tends to take place according to very generalized milestones, which aren't terribly specific, such as training needs mapped, workflows described, etc. Such projects are often guided by the purpose, which de-

Management based on purpose and general milestones

scribes the desired impact, such as shorter response types, fewer errors, greater flexibility, etc.

Employee involvement is an important part of reducing resistance to change. Consequently, such projects are described in terms of the purpose and general milestones, while the very specific deliverables are defined as the project progresses. This will often be a highly political process, which can result in the elements being planned in an order that doesn't follow the logic of professional knowledge, but rather is dependent on which decisions must be made before the project can proceed to the next decision.

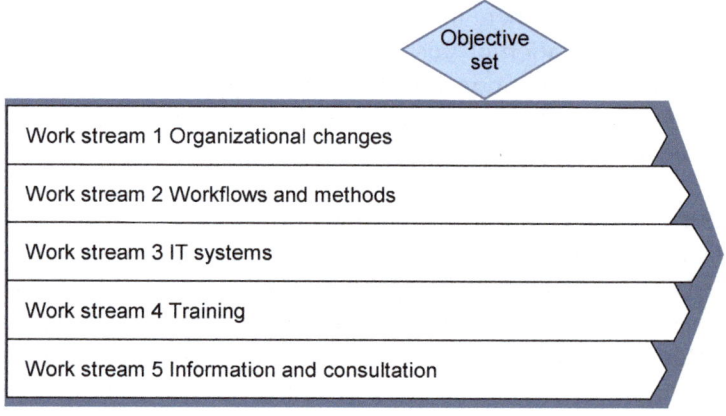

Figure 5.17. Organizational change projects often define deliverables at a very late stage. A good deal of the project period is managed based on the purposes and general milestones.

The work streams, which can often be defined based directly on the project's purpose, may be organizational changes, new workflows and the introduction of administrative (IT) systems. However, it's important in organizational change projects to achieve an understanding of why the change is necessary and of the direction in which the project is moving the organization. For this reason, the plan often consists of two work streams comprising training staff in the new workflows and routines, and an information campaign and consultation period with the various staff groups.

Training is necessary to foster understanding of the new situation and practice the new behavior that is required. It's important that the employees feel comfortable with the new situation, but also with the process toward reaching the new situation.

The information and consultation phase aims to promote acceptance of the purpose of the change and vision toward which the project is moving. These activities must be planned just as carefully as the professional activities for changing workflows.

Generally, these information activities require so many resources that they make up a significant share of the total plan and resource consumption.

Many organizational change projects can be broken down into two phases: development and rollout.

5.3.6. Policy development projects and basis for decision-making

The public sector has embraced the project as a work form, where it has proven useful in many types of assignments, even though some of the project methods need to be adapted to this work form. Common assignments are reports and policy proposals.

It's necessary to adapt the planning process to the political process. Thus, rather than reflecting some sort of professional logic, the plan should follow the order of the political decisions.

Management based on the order of the political decisions

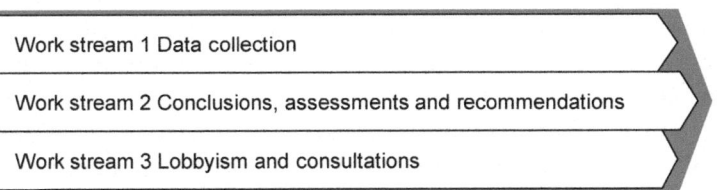

Figure 5.18. Policy development projects often comprise three key work streams: data collection, the report itself and consultations.

Such projects tend to begin with the preparation of a report, which is then presented at political level. However, this process often results in many project teams being told to re-do the report – a rework. If the project is carried out in this way, the plan can be based on a strictly professional logic. This will enable the project to be completed on time, but there is no guarantee that the results will actually be usable.

To achieve a usable result, it's necessary for the project plan to include a series of consultations with the stakeholders. The order of these consultations should be planned so as to gradually reduce the project uncertainty while narrowing the scope of the solution. Choosing the proper order requires in-depth political insight.

This project type is often planned on the basis of important milestones and the order of consultations and decisions. In addition to the report itself, data collection is generally a crucial part of the project and thus represents a separate work stream. It is often necessary to obtain data during the course of the process to support a proposal or neutralize a counter proposal. Data isn't always readily available, but has to be procured. Information, lobbying and consultation are the most important work streams.

5.4. Planning in an uncertain world

5.4.1. Uncertainty

There are two basic types of uncertainty in projects: Uncertainty in the surroundings and uncertainty in the actions we take during a project. Our focus will be on the uncertainties in actions and activities. Uncertainties in the surroundings are more an expression of risks within the project (or opportunities that have arisen).

So far, we have spoken a great deal about milestones, and milestones are definitely a good thing! They have a duration of zero and don't require much effort. Activities, on the other hand, cost us blood, sweat and tears, and can be difficult to predict due to uncertainty.

5.4. Planning in an uncertain world

We find uncertainty on several dimensions:

- How many weeks does it take to complete the work (consumption)?
- When is it possible to be done (duration in the calendar)?
- Is the quality of the result what we expected (quality)?

In the following, we will split the concept of uncertainty into two:

Natural uncertainties and actual risks

- Natural uncertainties, such as traffic jams on a daily commute
- Actual risks, such as engine trouble

Actual risks will be covered later under risk analysis. Here, we will begin by looking at uncertainties that are a natural element of a given activity. For instance, it is completely natural for travel time to work to vary from day to day, depending on the traffic conditions.

As Figure 5.19 illustrates, uncertainty varies depending on the activity. To obtain an overview, we will therefore start out by breaking activities down into four types.

When executing a project, it's important that we can predict which activities involve uncertainty. When we find ourselves in the situation and the delay is a reality, is there something we can do? Can we influence the situation? The project manager's job is to monitor the uncertain activities and prevent their having an impact on the project plan.

Figure 5.19. Milestones with activities. The activities regarding duration and the quality of the result are uncertain. The light blue areas indicate the varying uncertainty of the activities.

It is generally assumed that duration (measured in calendar days and weeks) can be affected by changing the resource allocation. However, allocating more resources won't reduce the duration of all types of activities.

We therefore categorize activities based on their degree of uncertainty and how much it is possible to influence the situation when things begin to falter. An uncertain activity doesn't have to be too serious, provided we can easily fix the damage. Consequently, grouping activities into type based on the degree of uncertainty and our ability to influence the situation (influenceability) calls attention to the uncertain and difficult activities.

Let's start with the activities that are easy to deal with. These activities have a low degree of uncertainty and can easily be fixed in case of delay by allocating more resources. These

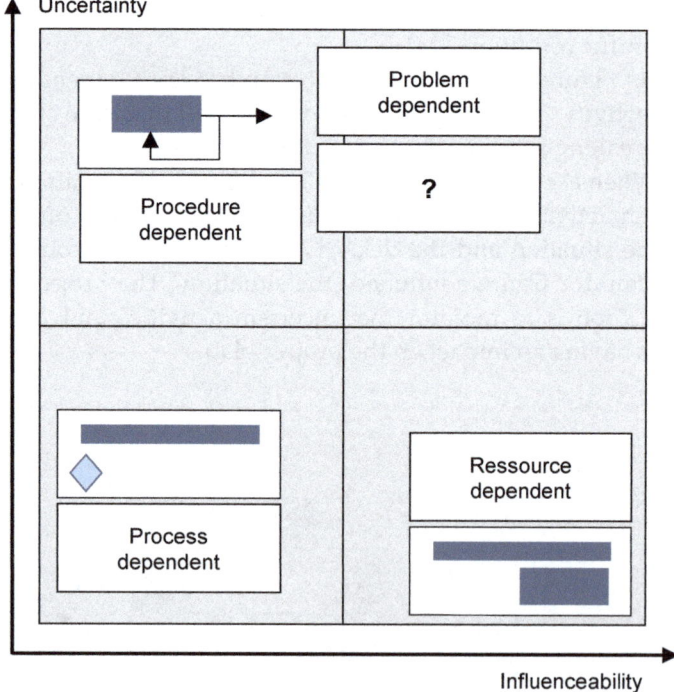

Figure 5.20. Four activity types charted in relation to the activity's degree of uncertainty and possibility of influencing the situation in case of delay.

are called resource-dependent activities, because their duration basically depends on the resource allocation.

5.4.2. Resource-dependent activities

Predictable and influenceable

These are defined as activities where the result is predictable when experienced employees are used. The duration of the activity in calendar time can be cut in half if the number of resources are doubled, as we see in the illustration. There is no guarantee that this correlation is completely linear, but it will be possible to reduce the duration by allocating more resources.

This type of activity includes programming, digging, bricklaying, roofing, questionnaire data entry, construction work, drawing, counting, registration, etc.

However, the absolute duration is influenced by the employees' routines and experience, as well as by the methods and tools used. Another influencing factor is whether the employees are allowed to concentrate on the task and aren't disturbed by telephones and other interruptions.

This type of activity is only resource-dependent as long as it is realistic to add more resources. For instance, if it isn't possible to involve more programmers at the same time, then the duration can't be reduced. The activity then becomes process-dependent and is determined by the time the programming process takes.

5.4.3. Process-dependent activities

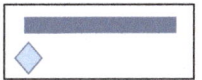

Predictable, but impossible to influence – at the mercy of the process

These are activities where the duration is determined by the process that must be carried out to achieve the desired result.

Process-dependent activities have a low degree of uncertainty with regard to duration and result, as they are solely dependent on the process (provided that the process is under control). Another characteristic of these activities is that we can't speed up process by force. One example of this type of activity is a pregnancy. It takes nine months, and we can't speed up the process by increasing the room temperature or adding more resources. The process takes as long as it takes.

Typical process-determined activities are mechanical processing, hardening of cement, waiting for questionnaires to be returned, training of staff, photocopying, etc.

Because there is nothing we can do once the process has been initiated, it can be relevant to plan with a milestone from the beginning of the process, as depicted in the illustration marking the point where the questionnaires have been sent out or the training process has been commenced.

5.4.4. Procedure-dependent activities

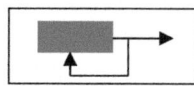

Uncertain and difficult to influence – actually pretty boring

These are the activities where specific procedures must be introduced, for instance steering committee meetings, consultation rounds or testing procedures. These activities are characterized by following pre-defined procedures, and can therefore be speeded up by force. At the same time, there is uncertainty about the result, as the illustration shows.

The uncertainty doesn't have an impact on the duration of the procedure, which is highly predictable and fixed, but solely on the outcome of the procedure. For instance, whether the steering committee will say GO or NO GO; whether the draft proposal will be approved in consultation; whether the test will result in approval or rejection.

Ultimately, a NO GO, non-approval or rejection would require the project team to re-do some of their work – a rework. This takes extra time.

The uncertainty in duration therefore lies in the potential scope of the rework.

Procedure-dependent activities include decisions, consultations, approvals, testing activities, trials and public approvals.

5.4.5. Problem-dependent activities

How long does it take to catch a fish – and which fish?

These activities involve solving a problem or developing new methods and solutions. These are generally innovation-based activities and the uncertainty rests in both the result and the duration. How long will it take and how useful is the result? These activities are not as subject to influence as process-oriented activities, but can be influenced by allocating more resources and using parallel or competing teams. However, there is not the same correlation between resource consumption and result as for resource-dependent activities.

Problem-dependent activities typically include design projects, development tasks, creative processes, achieving consensus among stakeholders, etc. We don't know how long it will take, and we don't know what the quality of the result will be.

The nature of the activities can change depending on the level of experience

Resource-dependent activities are only resource-dependent as long as experienced employees are used. If we use inexperienced employees, we will soon discover that what we thought was predictable in terms of duration and results becomes a problem-dependent activity of an innovative nature. This is because an inexperienced employee has to work by trial and error – subsequently, the activity takes longer and the quality drops.

Inexperienced resources cause problems

If we don't have enough workstations, a resource-dependent activity like data entry suddenly becomes process-dependent. We can't allocate more resources; all we can do is wait for the data entry work to be completed.

Limited resources cause process-dependence

In much the same way, a process-dependent activity can become a procedure-dependent activity if we don't have the process under control. Not specifying a method for conducting the project causes many procedure-dependent activities to resemble testing and trials – thus causing rework. A well-prepared steering committee meeting can be carried out as a process. Without preparation, however, it becomes a procedure-dependent activity where we don't know whether we will receive a GO or NO GO – again, rework.

Lack of a specified method causes uncertainty

The aim of these activity categories is to allow the project manager to spend less time on the certain activities and focus more on the difficult activities, such as problem-dependent activities that are uncertain with regard to both time consumption and result.

The good news is that a good project manager knows this beforehand. And yet, we still hear the 'good' excuse that the project involved new technology so we couldn't know beforehand whether it would work. No, we could not – which is

189

why you need to take precautions! A good project manager knows beforehand what's problematic and what's easy, what's predictable and what's uncertain. When there is uncertainty, we need to take our precautions.

5.4.6. Estimation is the 7th step in the planning process

To estimate comes from the Latin *aestimare* meaning to assess. We need to assess how long specific activities will take, how much they will cost, etc. The question is, how precise can we be when we have already seen how uncertain activities can be? Obviously, some activities are very easy to estimate, while others are difficult due to a very high degree of uncertainty.

Three conditions relating to estimation are of interest from a project management perspective.

First, the project manager needs to have the best possible understanding of how long the activities will take in order to draw up a robust plan. Without a good estimate, it's difficult to negotiate the necessary resource allocation.

Estimation gives the project manager and participants an idea of the degree of uncertainty of the various activities. Where can things go wrong? What are the key focus areas for the project manager?

Finally, if the project participants have contributed to the estimation process, then they are more likely to feel an obligation to stay on schedule. Without estimates, the project plan is nothing more than guesswork.

Estimation or guesstimation

When it comes to uncertain activities, guesstimation is perhaps a more accurate term than estimation. However, there are some guidelines that can increase the value of our estimates.

When estimating time consumption, one of the first steps is to breakdown the activities into a manageable size and then assess the degree of uncertainty of the individual activities. Generally, the more sub-activities we have, the more precise our estimate will be. This is because an uncertain activity often consists of several resource-dependent and process-dependent sub-activities. What's interesting is where we have the uncertain sub-activities.

Another useful tip is to ask experts in the area and carefully select who is to carry out the activities and the work form. Are they experienced? Will their work be interrupted? Can they focus on the work? Etc.

It is also a good idea to quantify the work content of the tasks – such as 20 interviews, 15 drawings, etc. Define the time consumption per unit and then calculate the total.

Describe the degree of difficulty and uncertainty in the activity and then assess how this will impact the project. For activities with a high degree of uncertainty, it is a good idea to assess a best case scenario for how fast the activity can be completed and a worst case scenario for how bad things can go. Guesses can be qualified significantly using three-point estimation in which the mean value M is calculated based on three different guesses.

- G: 'Likely guess', i.e. the most likely estimate.
- O: 'Optimistic guess', i.e. the best-case estimate.
- P: 'Pessimistic guess', i.e. the worst-case guess.

The following formula is often used in popular PC planning tools for estimating the mean value: $M = (O + 3G + P) / 5$

What's interesting about this three-point estimate is that it gives us an idea of the degree of uncertainty of an activity. How great is the difference between the different guesses? The size of the spread is an expression of the activity's uncertainty. The project participants will often know what it takes for an activity to be completed within the optimistic time estimate. They generally also know what can cause the activity to take as long as the pessimistic guess.

It is a good idea to base discussions regarding planning on such information. What is needed to minimize time consumption and what should be avoided to reduce the chances of ending up with the pessimistic guess? This is really what project management is about.

When conducting three-point estimates, the most likely guess isn't necessarily the mean value. The mean value will often fall somewhere between the most likely guess and the pessimistic guess. Thus, the most likely guess is too 'optimistic', which probably matches the experiences of most project managers – things tend to take longer than expected.

We tend to be optimistic in our time estimates

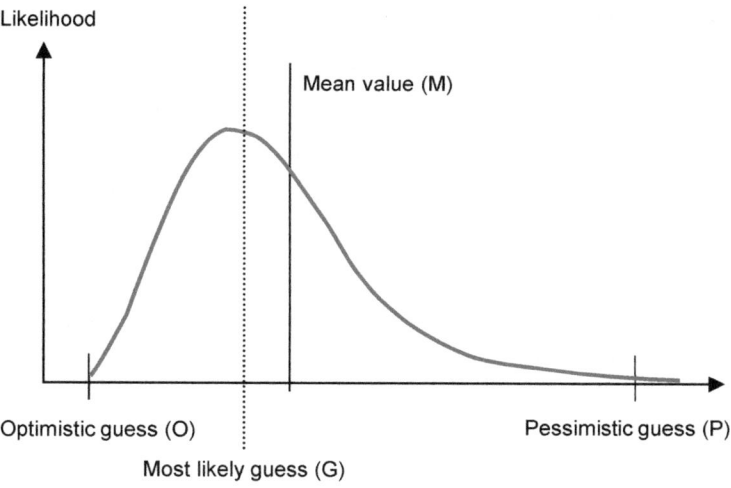

Figure 5.21. Three-point estimation. The mean value of the optimistic, pessimistic and most likely guesses often falls to the right of the most likely guess. Three-point estimation comes from the PERT method.

There are many reasons why the graph looks like this. First, there is the simple explanation that nothing can be done faster than 0 hours. There is a limit to how fast an activity can be completed. Unfortunately, that is not the case at the opposite end. There is almost no limit to how badly things can go wrong. However, it's important to remember that the mean value is an expression of 'only' a 50 percent certainty that the time consumption will be greater than the mean value. (At least with a standard deviation).

Consequently, it is more realistic to indicate the times as intervals. If the plan needs to be more certain, it is necessary to calculate an 'addition' to the mean value. The spread S is an expression of this 'addition', which you must work with to achieve greater certainty that the estimate can contain:

68 percent certainty: Time consumption is max. $M + S$
95 percent certainty: Time consumption is max. $M + 2S$
99 percent certainty: Time consumption is max. $M + 3S$

The spread S is: $S = (P - O) / 5$

The project owner or steering committee will generally not accept simply adding twice the spread to the estimate. It can therefore be difficult to argue in favor of the total time consumption if the calculation isn't more precise. At the same time, the output of the estimation process should correspond to the effort. It will generally not be useful to spend time on highly detailed plans. For this reason, we use successive calculation in cases where greater precision is important.

5.4.7. The principle of successive calculation and planning

Successive calculation builds on the principle that activities with a large spread can be broken down into sub-activities via one or more steps until all spreads are approximately the same size. The smaller sub-activities are more manageable and can be estimated more precisely, because they contain only one type of activity.

Breaking down the uncertain activities and calculating what is important

In Figure 5.22, the activity A has a sizeable spread. This is therefore broken down into activities B and C, where activity C is relatively uncertain and therefore has a large spread. That activity is therefore broken down into D and E, which reveals that D has a sizeable spread and must therefore be broken down again into activities F and G.

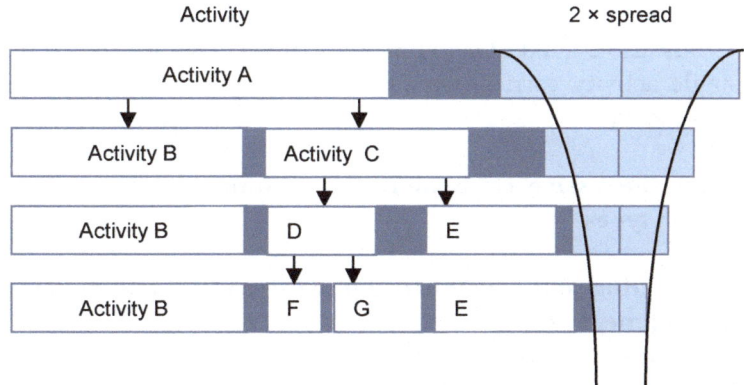

Figure 5.22. Successive calculation. Activities with a wide spread (dark blue) can be broken down until the total spread (light blue) can no longer be reduced or has reached an appropriate level. This principle was developed by Steen Lichtenberg.

The point is to focus on the uncertainty and specify the uncertain activities by breaking them down. A fundamental element of good project management is focusing on what can go wrong – that is, on the uncertainty in the project.

It's not a good idea to break everything down, as this just creates a lot of calculation work while reducing overview.

When activity A is broken down, the mean value of the entire series of activities will increase. The mean value of B+F+G+E is greater than the mean value of A. Basically, it will take longer (the white fields in the figure), but because the activities will be less uncertain, the total spread will be reduced (the gray fields in the figure).

The mean value M of the series of activities is calculated as:

M = M1 + M2 + M3

The total spread S of the series of activities is calculated as:

$$S = \sqrt{S_1^2 + S_2^2 + S_3^2}$$

It's a good idea to continue breaking down the activities until the total spread can no longer be reduced. Any further breakdown will be a waste of time. For some projects, the breakdown process continues until an acceptable degree of uncertainty has been reached, for instance measured as a percentage of the mean.

It is also a good idea to break down the activities so that no single activity carries more than, say, 1 percent of the total uncertainty.

Using successive calculation and planning in the various project types

Engineering and construction projects and IT and systems development projects
These project types are carried out with fairly well-known deliverables using network plans. Successive calculation and planning are widely used. The method is particularly useful in the tender phase because it makes it possible at the rough estimate level to quickly come up with relatively precise estimates.

R&D projects
R&D projects are also relatively deliverable-oriented, especially after the concept development phase. Successive calculation is used to estimate the concept's production costs and to assess the overall time consumption. After the concept development phase, successive planning can produce robust milestone plans, ensuring that the deadlines can be met.

Research projects, organizational change projects and policy development projects
These projects are highly purpose-oriented and the principles of successive calculation generally aren't used. This may seem odd, as these are projects with a very high degree of uncertainty. However, the explanation lies in the fact that it's difficult to even define the activities to be carried out. For instance, what does it take to convince a political adversary or to reach a compromise? These projects are often managed based on deadlines and the results have to be as good as possible under the given conditions.

However, successive calculation can sometimes be useful in planning organizational change projects, for example when the solution needs to be rolled out in a large organization.

5.5. Risk analysis

5.5.1. Risk analysis – step 8 in the planning process
So far, we have reviewed how you can handle natural uncertainty in activities, such as traffic jams on a commute. But how do you come up with plans that are resilient to actual risks, such as engine trouble?

The following is worth remembering:
- The biggest mistakes are made early in the project and discovered late in the project.
- Most errors are made by humans.
- 80 percent of errors can be predicted – and are predicted.
- Predicted risks are not communicated.

Chapter 5. The Project Plan

In our coaching of project managers, we often ask project managers to keep a project log. Looking back over these logbooks, it is interesting how many of the 'big surprises' and problems the project manager was actually warned about early in the project.

Surprises are known well in advance

We are not speaking of just one warning. There are often successive warnings before the arrival of a big 'surprise'. 'I didn't predict that' – no, but just because it wasn't predicted doesn't mean that is was unpredictable.

Risk analysis is an important management tool that should be regularly adjusted by the project team. What are the 10 greatest risks at this time? What do we have to do to prevent them from happening? And how? What do we do if..?

Risk analysis is also a management tool the project manager uses in relation to the steering committee or project owner. The steering committee needs to be informed of the biggest risks and of how the project team intends to deal with these risks. Eliminating risks often requires additional resources, which need to be allocated by the steering committee.

In the following, we define a Risk (R) as the Likelihood (L) that an event will occur with a specific Consequence (C): $R = L \times C$. The risk, then, is a product of the likelihood that something will happen and the consequence of it happening.

Another problem is that we humans are an odd group. What we fear about risk is the consequence. If the consequence is great, then we need to stop it from happening! And when we stop something from happening, we somehow alter the likelihood that it will happen – but that is exactly the consequence we feared! The likelihood may be so small that stopping it from happening may be a waste of resources. It may be better to simply minimize the consequences when it happens. In other cases, we don't consider the risk as very serious, because the consequence is minimal.

But if the likelihood in this case is great, it may pose a serious problem for the project.

$R = L \times C$ (risk, likelihood, consequence)

It may therefore be relevant to reduce either the likelihood or the consequence – and in some cases to plan on reducing both.

Consequently, we conduct risk analysis in order to:
- Prioritize the greatest risks
- Prioritize our efforts
- Obtain insight into the project and the critical elements
- Make the project plan more robust
- And because we think we agree on what the biggest risks are – but we don't!

The basis of risk analysis
When we discuss risks, it is always based on some notion about how the project will be carried out. Risk can only be defined based on an existing plan. If the project needs to be finished in six months, then the risk of delay is greater than if it has a timeframe of one year. If the plan includes the use of new technology, then the risk is greater than with known technology.

Risk analysis is therefore always carried out based on the existing plan. The same project can have completely different risks with a different plan. It is a good idea to conduct the first risk analysis after the first project planning seminar in order to adjust the plan and make it more robust.

Risk analysis can be broken down into two elements: what are the greatest risks and what do we do about them?

5.5.2. What are the greatest risks?
Run through all that can go wrong – preferably at a meeting or workshop with the entire project team. Use checklists, experience and brain storming to assess causes and effects.

To avoid pure guesswork, it is a good idea to define the critical milestones and assess what can go wrong in achieving these milestones. Where are the risks on the critical path through the project?

Once you have a list of everything that can go wrong, the consequence of the individual events needs to be determined. This is done by assessing the individual events on a kind of 'Richter scale', like earthquakes. Small tremors in the project that cause irritation are ranked as 1. Significant ripples and delays requiring a revision of the plan and budget are ranked as 3. Finally, we have serious events that prevent project com-

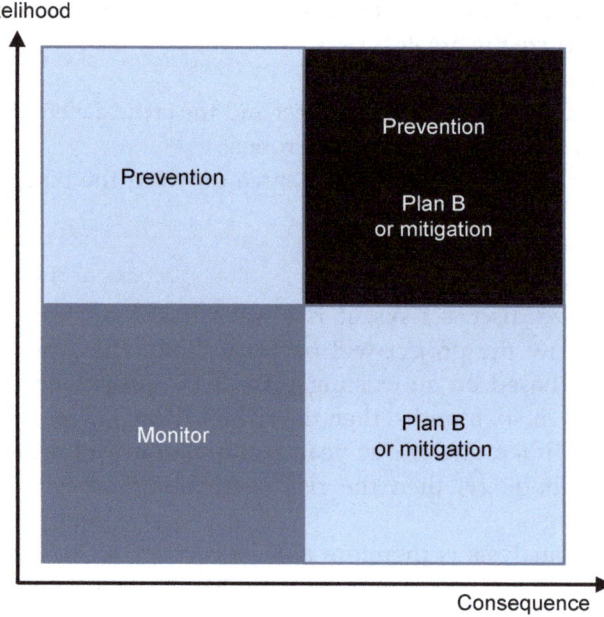

Figure 5.23. Prioritization of risks and the most important strategies for reducing the overall risk and making the plan more robust. The black area illustrates the highest risk and the dark blue area the lowest risk. (Use the Risk Analysis tool in the toolbox).

pletion and ultimately result in the project being shut down altogether. These are ranked as 5.

What can go wrong? What is the likelihood? And how bad can things get?

The likelihood of the individual events occurring is similarly ranked on a scale from 1 to 5, where 1 is a low likelihood and 5 is high likelihood. The individual risks can now be prioritized by calculating a risk ranking (Consequence x Likelihood).

The above figure can be created either by calculating the overall risk ranking for every event or carrying out an analysis on the wall of the project team room. The individual risks can be written on cards or Post-its and the team can discuss their placement. This gives the project team a good idea of the project's risks and their priority.

Once the consequences of a given event have been assessed, it's a good idea to think about the project's business case. A risk is something that reduces the project's business case, such as by increasing costs or reducing the expected impact.

The graphs in the following figures illustrate three typical scenarios for the consequences of risks.

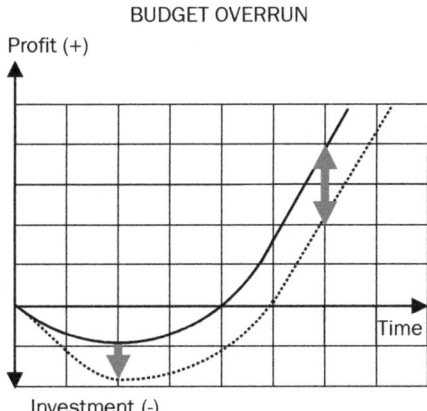

A typical consequence is an increase in the project costs making project completion much more expensive than expected. This is a consequence that is directly reflected in the project follow-up and the project's status reports.

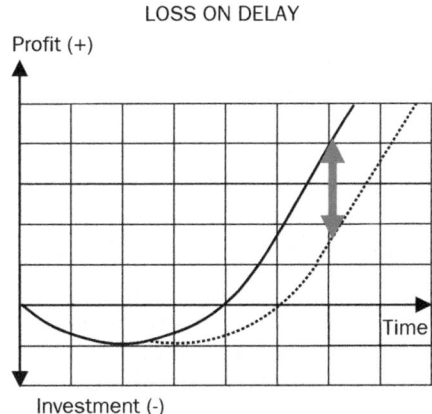

Another typical consequence is that the project becomes delayed. Because all projects are established to achieve an impact, such as cost-savings in operations, increased revenue or new service, any delay will result in loss – even if the delay has not resulted in extra costs during the project period. These losses can be quite extensive and generally aren't directly reflected in the project accounts.

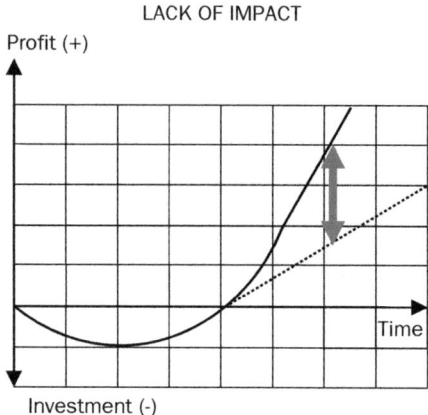

The last consequence is that the impact achieved is not as great as expected, i.e. the increase in earnings or savings was not as steep as expected. A project that has been completed on time and within budget can still have a lower-than-expected impact.

Make sure to consider all three risk types when conducting risk analysis.

Prevention and mitigation   The next step is an assessment of the initiatives that can reduce the likelihood that the individual events will arise and what the plan B might be if the event should arise. We have two fundamental strategies:

- Preventive measures for reducing the likelihood (requires resources, whether the event actually occurs or not).
- Plan B: mitigating measures to minimize the consequences (often only requires resources if the event actually occurs).

The choice of strategy depends on which quadrant the individual risk is placed in.

High likelihood, minor consequence
This type of event is a bit 'sneaky' because we don't normally worry about risks that have limited consequences. However, they have a high likelihood and therefore often occur.

The most important thing when dealing with this type of risk is to reduce the likelihood of the event occurring. This generally means incorporating extra activities into the project – extra testing, checks and reviews. It costs resources to reduce the likelihood and we will never know whether it was worth the extra expense.

High likelihood, serious consequence (high risk)
In a situation where the likelihood is high and the consequence is serious, then the risk is high. In such cases, it's not enough to prevent and reduce the likelihood. It may also be relevant to have a plan B if things go wrong.

It will often be appropriate to monitor how the likelihood develops over the course of the project so that plan B can be initiated at the right time. It's crucial that the plan indicates when the decision to implement plan B is to be made.

Low likelihood, serious consequence
In this situation, the project is monitored to determine if plan B needs to be implemented.

At a specified time, the decision is made whether to initiate plan B.

The decision point must be early enough to ensure that plan B can be carried out within the project's original timeframe.

Once, in an R&D project, there was uncertainty about whether it was possible to weld two very thin sheets together using a new method. It was therefore decided that the new method should be tested. If it worked, they would use it. If it didn't work, they would have to use the known technology. As a result, the testing period had to be moved forward, because plan B was based on being able to complete the project with the known welding technology.

Chapter 5. The Project Plan

Low likelihood, minor consequence (minimal risk)
In this situation, it isn't appropriate to initiate preventive measures before we see whether the project develops in a negative direction. The situation must therefore be monitored.

Both the preventive and the mitigating measures need to be specific enough that they can be incorporated into the milestone plan. After completing the risk analysis, the plan must be adjusted – otherwise the plan won't be more robust.

5.5.3. Risks in the various project types

Contracts and contractors

Engineering and construction projects
This project type entails a relatively low degree of uncertainty. The risks stem primarily from the quotation given – have all conditions been taken into account? Collaborative partners and sub-suppliers are also an important source of uncertainty. How reliable are they? What quality do they deliver? Etc.

During the course of the project, the physical surroundings, access conditions, weather and other natural conditions can cause surprises. (See the checklist in the Risk Analysis tool.)

Knowledge and method

Technology development and research projects
Risks are closely associated with knowledge and technology. Is the necessary knowledge available? Has the problem been properly defined? Has the best method been chosen?

There are often risks associated with the result. Can it even be done? Is the solution usable in all the areas that need it? If the solution is technically usable, is it also of commercial interest?

Customer needs and price

R&D projects
The biggest reason for most R&D project failures is that the product doesn't give the customer the benefit the customer is looking for. Have the customer's needs been correctly understood? Is the customer willing to pay the right price for the product? Is the buying segment large and attractive enough? Are the sales channels for this segment good enough? What are the competitors doing while the project is being carried out?

The other side of R&D projects is cost-effective production. Can the product be produced for the right price? Does the new technology work in the existing production apparatus? And so on.

IT and systems development projects
In this project type, the risks stem from, among other things, the quotation given – have all conditions been taken into account? Have the customer's wishes and needs been understood correctly? Changes in the customer's wishes and to the technology can cause big surprises. The new software to be used as the platform may still be suffering from teething troubles, etc.

This project type also tends to be plagued by resource problems and a lack of key personnel, who have found new jobs or are stuck in delayed projects elsewhere.

New technology and resources

Organizational change projects
Probably the biggest risk factor in this type of project is stakeholder resistance to change and their willingness and ability to enter into the new organization or workflows. Conflicting interests and necessary compromises that hollow out the 'optimal technical solution' are also major contributors to the uncertainty of an organizational change project's impact.

Another source of risk is the project participants' ability and time to implement the project. The participants are often project laymen who still need to attend to their regular jobs as well.

Stakeholders and other assignments

Policy development projects
Conflicting interests and necessary compromises can make it difficult to achieve usable results. This project type also sees conflict between being able to communicate clearly to foster motivation and keeping your cards close to the chest to ensure room for various compromises.

The project participants are often not active participants, but are involved to look after specific interests and to veto the project if necessary. There also tend to be problems with the participants' mandate and they may not be able to make decisions without informing their backers. Some participants may only be involved to ensure that the project is not implemented as planned.

Clear communication not possible

In this project type, risk analysis may present a special challenge. The greatest risk may not be that the project does not progress as planned, but that the project owner cannot use the results politically. It can be important for the project owner to be able to say, as the local government election approaches: 'We have appointed a taskforce to look into the matter.' However, it may be highly problematic if the project is completed before the election and the results become politicized!

The project plan isn't complete until the initiatives from the risk analysis have been incorporated

Use the risk analysis to create a robust project

In order for the risk analysis to have an impact as a management tool, it's important that:

- Initiatives for reducing the likelihood and consequences are incorporated into the milestone plan.
- The risk analysis is kept up to date, i.e. the project team works with it throughout the entire project, and not just in the beginning.
- The 10 greatest risks are discussed regularly with the project owner or steering committee.
- The risks are part of the project manager's follow-up – what is critical in the next month?
- Dates have been set for when the decision for the initiation of plan B must be made.

5.6. Reflections on planning

Think about your own project or a project you are involved in:
- How can quality be ensured in the milestone plan?
- Do the project participants agree on the plan? How could this acceptance be achieved?
- Can each individual see a correlation between the objective and their own efforts?
- How is the plan used for follow-up and management?
- How does the plan establish pace and intensity in the project?
- Do you know the critical path? And where are the greatest risks?

5.6. Reflections on planning

- What deliverables must be realized at this time?
- Has the project's uncertainty been reduced enough to progress to the next phase?
- What elements of this plan are critical for the next phase and the rest of the project?
- Is it still relevant to implement the project?
- Can you prioritize the 10 greatest risks?
- Does the project team agree on which risks are the greatest?
- What initiatives would you propose for reducing the likelihood of risks?
- What initiatives would you propose for reducing the consequences of risks?
- How are risks discussed with the project owner and steering committee?
- Are risks part of the project manager's follow-up? Does the project team discuss what is critical in the next month?

Organizing the project
– who can help me?

Surrounding yourself with people who can do the same thing you can is a waste of time

CHAPTER 6

Project organization

How can you organize your project to ensure the best conditions for success? And how should the entire project portfolio in your organization be organized? Organizations are constantly struggling with these questions and the challenges are many.

In this chapter, we will take a closer look at how to organize a project, while in Chapter 10 we will explore in more depth the organization and management of the entire project portfolio and the division into programs.

The challenges we often face in connection with project organization include:

- A lack of clarity about the distribution of powers and responsibilities in the various parts of the organization
- A lack of clarity about who the project owner/project sponsor is, who actually speaks on behalf of the project and who wants to see the results
- A lack of clarity among the members of the project team, steering committee and hearing committees about what is expected of them.

This chapter describes:

- How to organize a project that is helpful to the project rather than a hindrance.
- What powers and responsibilities come with the various roles in the project organization.

As a project manager, it's not enough to be good at the technical/specialist aspects of the project. You have to always bear in mind the organizational context of the project by ensuring

Challenges

Benefits

Focus

Chapter 6. Project organization

the right organization for the project. This is the focus of this chapter.

Tools Tool 6.1 Distribution of Responsibilities
Tool 6.2 Project Anchoring
Tool 6.3 The Resource Contract

6.1. Roles within the project organization

The foundation of the project's success is an organization that provides optimum support for each project. The organization should be designed to suit the individual project and will often need to be adjusted during the course of the project as the nature of the assignment changes. This makes project organization one of the most critical tasks in the project start-up phase. This is where you have to work hard to get the right people involved in the project at the right times.

Figure 6.1, below, shows the classic organizational diagram for projects. In short, it's about having:

- Someone who wants the results and can approve them, who can allocate the necessary resources (funding and/or

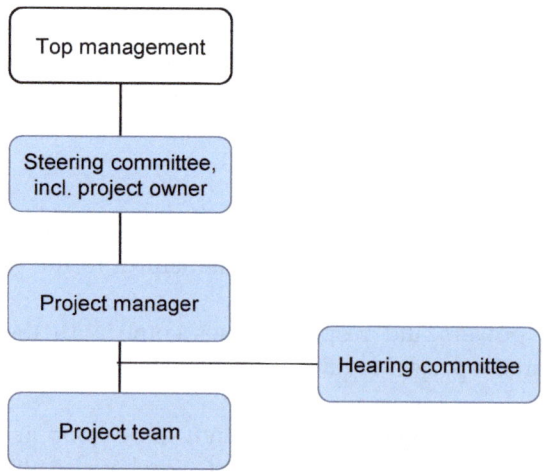

Figure 6.1. The roles and decision-making structure within the project organization.

staffing) and who has the authority to make decisions. This is the role of the project owner, possibly in collaboration with the steering committee.
- A person who leads and is responsible for daily operations, i.e., the project manager.
- People to carry out the work within the project – a well-qualified project team in possession of the necessary knowledge and skills.
- People who can contribute with knowledge, needs and ideas, i.e., one or more hearing committees.

In addition to these roles, there is the top management, and in political organizations, there is the political system. See more about these levels in Chapter 10.

This chapter describes the powers and responsibilities associated with these roles.

But why design a separate organization for each project? Isn't it overly bureaucratic and time-consuming when we already have a well-functioning line organization? It may seem a bit of a burden, but it is nonetheless vital to the success of the project, as the ordinary line management with its well-defined decision paths and management levels isn't designed for projects (Christensen 1994). The line organization is designed to perform operational tasks with a series of procedures that make it possible to perform them with great precision and efficiency. In contrast, projects are development tasks, which span departments and specializations. One example is a project to introduce a new IT system.

Why do we need a separate project organization?

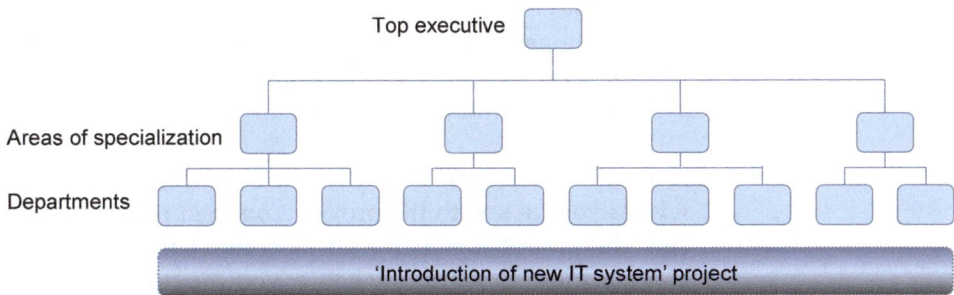

Figure 6.2. Projects span departments and decision-making structures.

Here, the IT department is responsible for allocating most of the resources to the project, but it isn't the IT department's project (if it seems like it is, then there is cause for concern about the future anchoring). The project cuts across departments, influencing all areas within the organization and requiring both funding and resources from many different areas. Consequently, it's necessary to design an organization based on the needs of this specific project.

When designing the organization of the individual project, it should:

- Enable decision-making on the right level
- Be able to allocate resources (funding and staffing) to the project
- Be highly qualified within the appropriate areas of specialization
- And especially: ensure the involvement of stakeholders, such as decision-makers and future users.

Projects are born, live and must die

According to Wenell, projects are born, live and must die – the faster, the better, regardless of whether it is a question of abandoning or completing the project (Wenell 2001). This, then, makes the project organization transitory. Its dissolution is planned ahead of time, a characteristic that differs significantly from the line organization, which is more long term and not continuously adapted to each task.

How should the roles be filled?

How the various roles are filled and the degree of awareness of the need for separate project organizations varies depending on the overall maturity level of the organization when it comes to projects.

Let's imagine three scenarios: You have been appointed project manager of a strategically important project and along with the appointment, you are given ...

A) ... a pat on the back from your head of department, who wishes you luck with the project. You then proceed to execute the project together with the project team – without giving further thought to whether you should report to an-

6.1. Roles within the project organization

yone outside the ordinary line organization or whether you have the right people on the team.

B) ... the names of the people on the steering committee and the project team.

C) ... the chance to compose a temporary project team, where you can hold a planning workshop for the project. When you have obtained an overview of the assignment, you have the opportunity – in collaboration with the project owner – to influence who is on the steering committee, whether there should be replacements on the project team and who should be on the hearing committees.

Which of these scenarios most closely resembles your reality as a project manager?

Obviously, scenario C is preferable, as it bases the design of the project organization on the nature of the project and the project manager seeks, via the project owner, to influence the composition of the steering committee and the project team.

In the following, we take a closer look at what characterizes the various roles in the project organization.

The project owner

It doesn't matter how amazing a project manager you are if you don't have the right project owner, which is someone who enquires about the project, is engaged and speaks on behalf of the project to the rest of the organization.

The project owner is often the person who commissions the project and is therefore also the one paying for it, i.e. allocating resources. For this reason, the project owner is also sometimes called the sponsor or commissioner.

This person should be a member of top management in order to have the authority to make decisions and the necessary control over the resources the project needs. Further, the project owner should ensure that the project has value for the organization as a whole and is in line with the firm's strategy.

The project owner is the project manager's closest ally and acts as sparring partner for the project manager in connection with the numerous day-to-day decisions that require quick responses. In many organizations, the project owner appoints the project manager. However, if the idea for the project comes from the 'bottom', that is, if it's the project manager's own idea, then the project manager may have to do a bit of searching for a project owner with the necessary resources and authority. There should be only one project owner.

> **The project owner**
> - Ensures that the project generates value for the organization a whole
> - Approves the contract (project description) and major changes to the project during the process
> - Has the overall decision-making power
> - Allocates resources to the project
> - Is chair of the steering committee
> - Serves as ambassador for the project throughout the entire organization
> - Acts as sparring partner for the project manager for the duration of the project

The steering committee

The fewer people there are to make the decisions about the project, the more flexible and simpler it can be. For this reason, it may be sufficient to 'just' have a project owner. However, there may be a need for broader anchoring of the project at the top management level, for example in projects that span several areas or organizations. In such cases, a steering committee should be appointed, with the project owner as chair. The project owner is always part of the steering committee.

It's important to keep the steering committee to a manageable size. The steering committee members should not be there for the sake of status or because 'the other managers are there'. As Wenell points out, you don't sit on a steering committee, you work in a steering committee (Wenell 2001). A good rule of thumb is to have a steering committee with as few members as possible and with representatives from as high up in the management as possible. The project manager should discuss appropriate steering committee members with the project owner based on the project's objective and stakeholder analysis. To determine whether a participant is suitable, you might ask: 'Do they have the authority to allocate the resources and make the decisions the project needs? And can they secure operationalization of the solution?'

The project manager uses the project owner – and the steering committee, if there is one – to approve the project contract, i.e. the project description. The project owner and steering committee should therefore also approve all major changes to the contract over the course of the project. All changes to the project triangle must be approved by the steering committee.

> **The steering committee members**
> - Ensure the resources for the project work
> - Make overall decisions about the project and any changes based on the project contract, i.e. the project description
> - Coordinate and anchor the project across the organization
> - Follow up on the progress of the project
> - At least one member should be responsible for the subsequent operationalization of the solution – ensuring the planned impact within the organization
>
> (Many of these responsibilities are the same for the project owner.)

The project manager

The project manager is responsible for supplying what has been agreed in the contract between the project owner/steering committee and the project manager/project team. Consequently, the project manager is responsible for daily operation of the project and for ensuring that the work gets done.

Because the work is carried out via the project team, the project manager's job is to delegate, motivate, follow-up, provide feedback and evaluate. Inexperienced project managers often make the mistake of thinking that they need to know and do everything themselves. They plan the entire project on their own and present it to the rest of the project team, saying it's 'just a proposal' and that they are open to other ideas. This may impress the team for a moment, but ultimately, the participants won't feel any sense of ownership of the project – which means the project manager will end up doing most of the work alone.

In many projects, the project manager tends to be the executor of many of the project tasks – and in some cases is the only executor of all the tasks. However, it is important for the individual project manager to consider whether that really is the best approach or whether things could be done differently with more success.

In addition to team management, the project manager's role includes dealing with the steering committee. This means liaising with the project owner and reporting to the rest of the steering committee, often combined with lobbying the individual steering committee members in-between the formal steering committee meetings. The project manager is also responsible for promoting the project and speaking on behalf of the project to other relevant stakeholders.

> **The project manager**
> - Is responsible for deliverables and success criteria realization
> - Heads the project through all phases and ensures proper handover to operations
> - Leads the project team by motivating, delegating, following up and providing feedback
> - Liaises with the project owner and reports to the steering committee
> - Manages the other stakeholders, promotes the project and speaks on behalf of the project

Hearing committees

Hearing committees, or reference groups as they are also called, serve three important functions:

- To involve stakeholders in the project, who are not actively working on the project
- To obtain stakeholder approval of the project results and process
- To gather knowledge and secure professional quality assurance of the project

The stakeholder analysis is used to identify who should be involved in the hearing committees. Typical members of hearing committees include end users, middle managers, liaison committee members, customers and experts. In projects executed within political organizations and in organizational change projects, hearing committees often play a crucial role as a way for the key stakeholders to voice their opinions and as a means of promoting ownership of the project.

Hearing committees – in contrast to steering committees – do not have decision-making competence on the project.

However, it would be wise to listen to their advice and opinions, as their approval of the project is often crucial to project implementation.

When appointing a hearing committee, it's important to avoid too many opposing stakeholders or hierarchical differences within the individual committees. It can be difficult to handle groups that are characterized by serious internal conflicts of interest. A good solution may be to divide the group into two or more smaller groups.

Another consideration is the number of hearing committee members. If there are too many committees or if the individual committees have too many members, you won't be able to achieve genuine involvement. This can do more harm than good. There's no point in hosting an information meeting for the hearing committee at the beginning of the project, and then they don't hear from you for three months.

Finally, the hearing committee isn't always a group. It may just be one person, such as a representative for an NGO, an employee from the department or an important customer. It's not always desirable to appoint a formal hearing committee. Sometimes, you just need input from one person during the process, without having formally informed them that they are a hearing committee.

> **The hearing committee members**
> - Approve the project's results and process
> - Contribute professional knowledge and communicate needs
> - Promote the interests of important project stakeholders
> - Serve as 'ambassadors' for the project within their area of the organization
> - Provide quality assurance & review

The project team

In simple terms, the project team comprises the people who will perform the work within the project. The whole point of creating a separate organization for the individual project is to make the assignment the center of attention. It is therefore vital that the participants are selected based on the competences needed to carry out the assignment, rather than designing the assignment based on which resources are currently available.

Chapter 6. Project organization

> **The project team members**
> - Possess the specialist knowledge and experience to execute the project's various tasks
> - Have the time needed to complete the tasks
> - Are responsible for planning their own work
> - Take a critical and constructive approach to tasks and planning
> - Are team players and are prepared to work together with the rest of the team to complete the assignment

Just as the project should be organized on an overall level with a steering committee and hearing committees, it's important to organize the project internally. This means breaking down the project into responsibilities and work streams and assigning people to each area. This internal project organization should be based on the objective breakdown structure, as illustrated in Figure 6.3.

When we look at the work streams that make up the project, it is generally clear which competences the project requires. In Chapter 5, the 'Happier Customers' project was

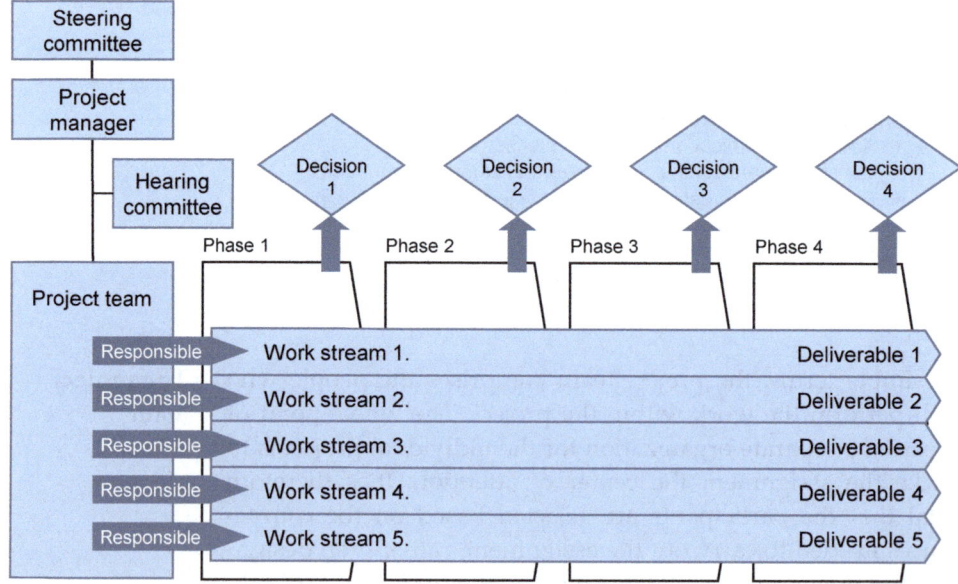

Figure 6.3. The internal project organization is based on the defined deliverables and work streams.

6.1. Roles within the project organization

broken down into work streams with a responsible person appointed to each work stream.

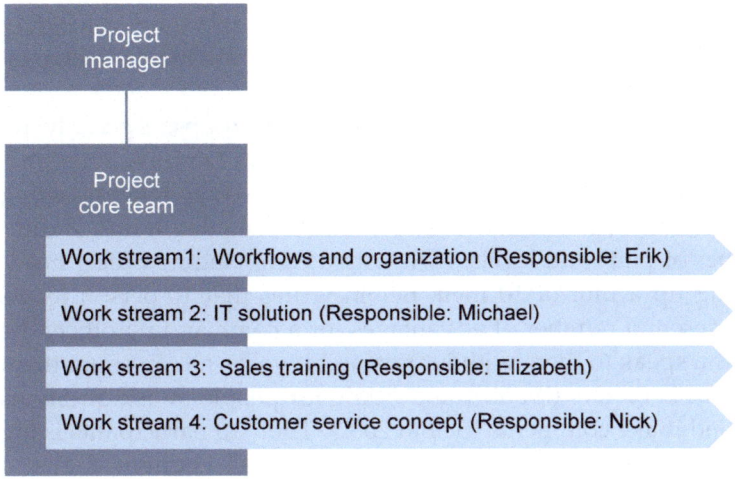

Figure 6.4. Project participants, each with responsibility for their own work stream.

In a project of this scale, the people responsible for each work stream will actually be sub-project managers with a project team under them. The project manager and the sub-project managers therefore represent a project core team, which meets often to coordinate across the work streams. Working with a core team and sub-project teams helps keep the project team to a manageable size. Having to bring together 12-15 people at every meeting would be extremely costly and result in very long and boring meetings.

We are often asked: What is the ideal team size? The answer is: it depends on the assignment.

Team size

However, as a general rule, a team of four to six members is a good size in many situations. According to management theorist Meredith Belbin, teams of four are particular effective if the team is expected to work under heavy pressure and to manage crises. In four-person teams, a family-like relationship develops, creating a high degree of engagement, intimacy and

219

tension, which isn't possible to achieve in larger teams. However, there is a risk that the intensity isn't all positive; hate and irritation can also develop. Slightly larger teams allow greater variation and give the individual participants more colleagues to identify with, which can help balance out the love-hate relationships.

Belbin's studies also involved larger groups, especially 10-person teams. Historically, 10 is a successful number for a unit. For example, the Roman army, considered the longest-lasting power organization in history, was broken down into a number of units and levels, each with a commanding officer heading up a unit of 10 men. Belbin writes that 10-person teams present a number of advantages for a commanding officer: he can speak to them without raising his voice, he can count them on his fingers (!) and there's time for people to ask questions and make comments (Belbin 2002). Thus, 10 participants is big enough to allow variation, but just small enough to give a sense of intimacy and team identity.

In larger groups, the individual can hide in the pack

However, project work differs from the Roman army in many ways. Teams of 10 have proven less effective when it comes to discussions, debates and decision-making. When 10 people all want to have their say, you get a listening time of 90% and a speaking time of 10% (provided you have a fair and very strict moderator). There is a significant risk that some may choose to drop out of the discussion altogether and that it will take too long to achieve a consensus. Furthermore, larger groups are subject to what social psychologists call social loafing, which is when a team member hides in the pack, avoiding responsibility in the hope that the others will pick up the slack.

For this reason, it is generally a good idea to divide the project team into a core team and a number of sub-project teams, as described above.

However, the best way to avoid creating project teams that are (too) large isn't always to break the project down into sub-projects. There may also be too many people on the project team who don't really do anything, for example in a well-intentioned attempt to involve as many as possible in the project. One clear sign is if you have project participants whose only contribution to the project is to attend certain meetings.

These people should preferably be on a hearing committee if they are deemed necessary to the success of the project. The project team should only comprise those people who have the professional competence needed for the project and who will carry out the project work. Sometimes a two-person project team, who can devote the majority of their time to the project over a specified period, is better than six people, who spend less time on the project.

The size of the team isn't the only thing that fluctuates depending on the project type. The composition of the team varies as well.

The team composition can change during the course of the project

Some project teams are close-knit groups that work together from start-up to completion. Other project teams change composition and size along the way, as the work form and content of the project changes.

As a project manager, it is therefore important to take stock at regular intervals and consider whether the size and composition of the team suits the needs of the tasks in the current phase of the project.

In Chapter 9, we will take a closer look at how to recruit the right people and what you need to pay special attention to.

Our society is based on a clear separation of powers into a legislative, an executive and a judiciary branch. This division can be compared to the division that should exist within every project organization. The steering committee corresponds to the legislative branch, while the project manager and team correspond to the executive branch. Finally, the hearing committee is the judiciary branch, as the hearing committee's 'verdict' on the content and quality of the project is key to the successful implementation of the project (albeit not in a legal sense).

A clear separation of powers

When designing the organization, it's important to clearly communicate to the individual groups what their responsibilities are so that everyone understands why they are part of the project and what they are expected to contribute.

In short, the steering committee makes the decisions and allocates the resources. The hearing committee expresses its opinions and/or shares its specialist knowledge. And the project team carries out the project work. These divisions between steering committee, hearing committee and project team should be very clearly defined. It is therefore not a good idea to have project participants on the project team who aren't actually doing any work. If they are important to the project, they should be placed on a hearing committee. It is also undesirable for hearing committees to think they have some sort of decision-making competence in the project. For example, it's not uncommon for a department or organizational unit to appoint a representative to follow the project, but not want them to be part of the steering committee. This should be avoided, as it muddies the waters when it comes to who actually makes decisions on behalf of the project. If a department or another powerful group makes overall decisions on behalf of the project, they should be part of the steering committee – where they will also be held accountable for the project's results and for allocating the necessary resources.

Are the participants acting out their roles 'correctly'?

It is one thing to have clearly defined roles and responsibilities of the steering committee, hearing committee and project team. How the individuals, as active participants in these groups, actually think and act is another thing altogether.

It's not possible to simply transform individuals into extras who act out their roles according to a script. They each have personal and professional interests and motives, which makes the project organization much less rational than it appears in the organizational chart. For example, there may be two top executives on the steering committee who are using the project as part of their internal power struggle. Meanwhile, there may be a member of the project team who thinks she should have been the project manager instead. And on the hearing committee, perhaps the industry representative and the trade union representative are vying to see who can achieve the most benefits for their members. Stakeholder management is about more than just clearly communicating everyone's responsibilities at the beginning of the project. The project manager needs to manage the stakeholders throughout the entire project, for instance at steering committee meetings by ensuring that the committee makes the decisions and allocates the resources without getting caught up in the technical details. Furthermore, the project manager needs to understand the political games that every project is part of and be able to navigate a politically charged environment.

Organization of the 'Happier Customers' project

The 'Happier Customers' project has a wide array of stakeholders, as the project team discovered during the stakeholder analysis phase. At some of the earliest meetings, the team worked with organizing these stakeholders in order to create the best possible conditions for the project.

Lisa has placed special emphasis on involving the individual departments, as she is concerned that the project will otherwise be construed as solely an IT and administration project. In an effort to achieve a broader sense of ownership in the other departments, she has therefore drawn up job notices for a number of project participant positions. She is actually looking for a large number of people, as each work stream is a larger project in its own right. The notices have been approved by top management, who agreed to help find appropriate participants for the positions. Most of the participants will initially allocate 50% of their time to the project. After completion of the first phase, the project participant needs will be reassessed.

The project team has also appointed a number of hearing committees, including one hearing committee for each specialist group. The project team expects to hold focus group interviews with the specialist groups in order to shed light on their needs and possible contributions.

There is also a hearing committee comprising key customers. The purpose of this committee is to draw on their experience with the firm's products and service, as well as to learn about their needs for new initiatives.

Lisa and the other project team members haven't had any influence on the steering committee's composition, as it was formed before the project team was selected. The steering committee comprises the Sales Director, who is Lisa's immediate superior, the Technical Director and the IT Director.

The steering committee's most important tasks are to secure support in all three functions, ensure the coherence of the overall strategy, allocate resources and make decisions regarding project start-up, progress and completion.

Finally, for each work stream, a number of external subcontractors to the project will be selected, especially in the area of IT.

6.2. Reflections on organizing the individual project

- Can the project owner and the steering committee communicate the purpose of initiating the project and the project's benefits to the most important stakeholders?
- Does the steering committee comprise people with overall decision-making competence? And do they have the necessary resources at their disposal?
- Does the steering committee include representatives from sufficiently high up within the organization?
- If the steering committee has participants who don't meet these requirements, what can you do to remove them from the steering committee?
- Does the project team comprise people who both possess the necessary competences and actually contribute to the project work?
- Is the size of the project team appropriate? Or should the project be divided up into a core team and a number of sub-project teams?
- Do the hearing committees comprise people whose opinions are vital to the execution and implementation of the project? And are all the relevant stakeholders sufficiently involved?
- Have clear and unambiguous lines of reporting been defined within the project, i.e., do the individual team and committee members understand their responsibilities?
- Have clear and unambiguous lines of reporting been defined in relation to the rest of the organization?
- Has the project organization been communicated to the relevant stakeholders?
- How will the organization be adjusted as the project develops?

The Project Manager as Captain

Be proactive – you're the captain

A captain doesn't pray for good weather –
she learns to sail

CHAPTER 7

The Project Manager as Captain

About active steering and follow-up

Everyone has heard about (and possibly even worked on) projects that have suffered serious delays and budget overruns. Or projects whose results were never used, perhaps because the world had changed and the project didn't adapt to the new conditions in the interim.

Many delays, interruptions and faulty deliverables in projects are the result of insufficient follow-up and poor steering, which is staying on course and ensuring that it is still correct after drawing up the project plan with the team.

Organizations have a tendency to underestimate the importance of follow-up and steering, which is often viewed as not very interesting and primarily a way for the project manager to call the participants' attention to her role as leader. This makes some project managers feel uncomfortable, especially if they are working in a culture where management is still associated with the hierarchy. Common objections by project managers to assuming the role of the person responsible for follow-up and steering include: 'My colleagues will think it's strange if I suddenly start monitoring the progress of their work.' And: 'It would seem unnatural if I suddenly started acting like I'm my colleagues' boss.'

Thus, the follow-up and steering process is about more than just useful tools and understanding the technical aspects. It is just as much a matter of establishing a culture in which it is legitimate for the project manager to follow up on the work carried out by the other participants in the project.

Challenges

Chapter 7. The Project Manager as Captain

Benefits This chapter answers the following questions:

- What should I focus on in my follow-up plan?
- Which overall dimensions should I bear in mind when steering my project?
- How can I conduct meetings to ensure they are of value to the project?

Focus Our primary focus will be on steering projects that are less strictly organized than traditional engineering and construction projects.

This chapter provides an introduction to the work that begins after drawing up the project plan in collaboration with the team. The project manager is responsible for following up on project participants and subcontractors to ensure deliverables, as well as for steering the project to ensure the continued relevancy of deliverables and that the project achieves its objective on time and on budget.

Finally, we provide some tips on how to conduct efficient meetings to ensure optimum use of everyone's time.

Tools Tool 7.1 Project Journals
Tool 7.2 Minutes of Meetings
Tool 7.3 Project Review

7.1. The project plan as a steering tool

Steering and follow-up

A captain doesn't pray for good weather – she learns to sail

Once the course has been set (the objectives defined) and the route has been charted (the milestone plan), then the ship can be safely steered to the right harbor. When we start out, we have little idea of what the journey will be like. We can't know whether a storm, fog or other difficulties will develop. We may have some notion about what we might meet along the way and we have, of course, taken the appropriate precautions.

We know where we want to go and what obstacles might lie in our path and we have estimated the supplies we will need to reach safe harbor.

Plans change, but that doesn't make planning superfluous

The project manager is the captain of the ship. Like the captain steering the ship, it's the project manager's responsibility to steer the project. And just as the weather affects the journey into unknown waters, there is an array of factors that influence the project and the plan. As Mintzberg once said: 'The real world keeps getting in the way of my plans' (Briner 1996). The painful fact is that no plan can survive the meeting with reality unscathed.

In such a turbulent environment, many project managers feel tempted to simply drop all planning and attempts at steering, arguing that: 'Making a plan is useless anyway. It's constantly changing, so we may as well get out there and start working, rather than wasting our time drawing up plans.'

But they couldn't be more wrong. A captain doesn't decide against setting a heading simply because she's crossing rough seas. Having a course to navigate by becomes even more important in a storm, for it shows us where we should be in relation to where we are at any given time. It also tells us what actions we need to take in order to get back on course and reach our destination.

The same applies to project management. We know the plan won't hold up and will need adjustment time and again throughout the course of the project, but that doesn't mean we can just drop all planning and steering. The dilemma of planning is that it's impossible to plan – but we have to anyway (Wenell 2001).

The foundation for steering and follow-up

The foundation for the project manager's steering and follow-up efforts is a clearly formulated objective and a sensible milestone plan. As previously pointed out, the project team needs to feel a sense of ownership of both the objective and the plan, which is primarily achieved by preparing the detailed objective definition and the plan in collaboration with the entire team.

Once the project plan is in place, it's important to be continuously aware of where we currently are in the process in relation to where we should be. This is the basic problem of project steering. Where are we in relation to what we had planned? We can't just blindly follow the plan, as it's often too general. We also need to steer according to the current conditions.

The purpose of management and follow-up

Steering and follow-up come after the planning process, serving the purpose of:

- Creating and maintaining an overview of the project's current status in relation to the plan and expectations.
- Ensuring early recognition of any deviations – and looking forward to spy 'potential detours' in the project.
- Actively taking action to influence the project's progress in the desired direction.
- Monitoring the project environment to ensure that the project is still feasible, i.e. that the project and its success criteria are still relevant and achievable.

We differentiate between steering and follow-up. Follow-up deals with the project management tasks aimed at ensuring deliverables at the agreed time and in the agreed quality in relation to the individual project participant or subcontractor. Steering is used in a wider sense and includes ensuring that the right course has been set for the project.

7.2. Follow-up in the project

Follow-up seeks to give us an idea of the current situation and enable us to assess what future action needs to be taken. Follow-up is not something that only takes place in crises, but should be a natural part of the project manager's management tasks throughout the project.

Follow-up ensures due diligence

It's vital that the project manager and the organization set up follow-up routines that focus on the essentials and reveal serious deviations in time to rectify them. It's easy to get bogged down by complicated administrative procedures for project follow-up. But the administrative procedures must not get out of hand and thereby take up a disproportionate amount of time, while negatively impacting the creativity of the project team.

We have seen projects where administrative routines were introduced that took up too much time in relation to the benefit.

Take for example an agency with a large number of ongoing projects. They decided to introduce a time registration system. The purpose was commendable: they wanted to obtain an overview of how people spent their time, which would be informative and help them draw up more realistic budgets. But the time registration system wasn't used with a view to the future. The employees felt it was used solely as a means of control by the management and because registering their time consumption was a relatively tedious process, they saw it as a waste of time. As a result, the time registration program was nicknamed 'Story of the Week' by the employees, because they eventually just registered the story they knew the management wanted to hear and not their actual time consumption. The follow-up system thus gave no genuine indication of the current status of the individual projects.

Administrative routines that are too detailed can drain the energy and motivation of even the most committed project managers and participants.

Is follow-up a matter of control and power or is it motivational and a way to display interest? This largely depends on the culture you work in. Consider the extremes. There is a higher likelihood of exerting control and power in the army. They can order the achievement of a milestone by March 1st and be relatively certain that it will happen. But what would happen in a volunteer organization, like charity collectors for the Red Cross or Greenpeace? Or in a research institution, like the authors contributing to an anthology? Can these people be expected to just follow orders? (If you don't do it, you won't be allowed to contribute to my anthology!?) No, because you don't have any formal authority and thereby options for sanctions, so some other type of follow-up is needed.

Is follow-up control or a display of interest?

For the vast majority of project managers, follow-up is not about control, but about developing the project participants' motivation and sense of responsibility for the project as a whole and for their own tasks in particular.

Chapter 7. The Project Manager as Captain

Make it okay to follow up

Many project managers find it difficult to assume the role of the person who follows up on the project participants. Follow-up calls attention to the manager's role in relation to the project employees – whom they may not think of as employees, but as colleagues. They are concerned that the other members of the team will feel the project manager is 'too much' and that she 'thinks she's better than everyone'.

In some cases, this concern can prove unfounded: As the project manager resists the role of leader, the project participants find it odd that nobody seems to be making any decisions, that the project meetings are disorganized and that everything seems open to debate. Project participants can quickly lose their sense of responsibility if they experience too often that others don't meet the agreed deadlines and that the project manager doesn't do anything to remedy the situation.

It may help to think about the kind of follow-up and management you would prefer if you were a project participant rather than the manager. When do you think a project manager's follow-up is 'too much'?

Agree on follow-up routines early in the project

At the initial meetings of the full project team, it's important to clearly explain that you consider follow up a central task for the project manager. Early in the project, the project manager needs to establish a consensus among the team members about the follow-up and steering routines to be used. This can be done by telling them what you intend to do and then asking for their input. At the beginning of the project, nobody is behind on their deliverables and so nobody is likely to feel the discussion is a direct reference to their own performance. And in the beginning, everybody is determined to keep the project on track, avoid delays and budget overruns, etc.

It's important to bear in mind that there are different degrees of follow-up depending on the individual's experience and the nature of the task. The type of follow-up needed to be motivating and to ensure progress can therefore also be a topic covered during the initial interview the project manager holds with the individual participants. There is good inspiration to be found in the theories on situation-based management, which propound the importance of adapting the management effort to the employee's experience and competence, as well as to the task in question. Furthermore, follow-up should also vary depending on whether the project is in the start-up phase, the completion phase, etc.

As you get to know your project participants better, you will also come to understand how optimistic or pessimistic they are when estimating how much time they need to complete a task. Wenell calls this the optimist-pessimist factor (Wenell 2001). When Amy assesses that she can complete the task in three weeks, it generally takes her only two, as she always adds extra time – just to be on the safe side. According to Wenell, this gives her a factor of 0.66. Tom, on the other hand, is a super-optimist, and when he says three weeks, it usually takes him at least four, which gives him a factor of 1.33. Once the project manager has time estimates from the project participants, she can multiply their estimate by their OP factor to achieve more realistic time estimates. The OP factor is by no means objective, and it loses its effectiveness if the employees know that their time estimates are being handled in this way. However, it can be a useful tool for the project manager to qualify estimated time consumption.

Once the expectations for follow-up and steering are in place at the beginning of the project, it's important that the project manager also shows an interest and maintains regular contact with every single project participant. Regular meetings aren't enough. The project manager must maintain a dialog with each participant outside the meetings as well. This is also true, even though the project team members are spread out geographically. There is nothing as demotivating as working on something and having nobody show any interest or ask you how it's going.

Use the plan
In addition to clarifying the expectations at the beginning of the project regarding how you, as the project manager, will conduct follow-up, it's also important to use the plan throughout the entire duration of the project. The plan should be the point of departure for every conversation about the status of the project. The plan and the milestones should be important!

The plan should be visible – hang it up! Mark every activity start-up and completion on the plan. Indicate both compliance and deviations (for example using the colors red, yellow and green). Call attention to milestones and make sure achieved results are visible.

According to motivational theory, achieved results are a valuable motivating factor. Show the project team that there is progress. The individual also needs an overview of where we are, what has been completed, what the next step is, etc. Take care not to hide the project plan on a computer and make sure to include it in all meetings.

Follow-up on and uphold the objectives

An important task is assessing whether the milestones that should have been achieved according to the plan actually have been. Is the result the expected deliverable? Does the result form a good enough basis for proceeding to the next step?

If the milestone hasn't been achieved, the project manager and the responsible project participant must decide how to proceed and get the job done. It is generally not a problem to assess whether a milestone meets expectations. However, disagreements do occur, e.g., 'we've delivered what we were supposed to' or 'this is not what we expected to receive'. An 'unachieved milestone' can easily be the result of inadequate reconciliation of expectations along the way. This is why it's important to assess whether the milestone can be used as a 'building block' in the further process. If it can, then there is no delay, even though some expectations have not necessarily been met.

It's also possible that objectively, the deliverable is exactly what was agreed, but in the meantime, greater insight has been obtained. This insight suggests that the milestone should be different in order to be able to use it in the further process. In such cases, there is a delay, even though the deliverable is exactly as agreed. The important thing is to have an eye for the final objective every time a milestone is assessed.

Milestones shouldn't be too far apart

To ensure that the follow-up process is as precise as possible, the milestones shouldn't be set too far apart. Experience shows that we don't 'discover' that we've fallen behind until the milestone draws nearer. For this reason, the work effort will often increase significantly leading up to the milestone deadline.

7.2. Follow-up in the project

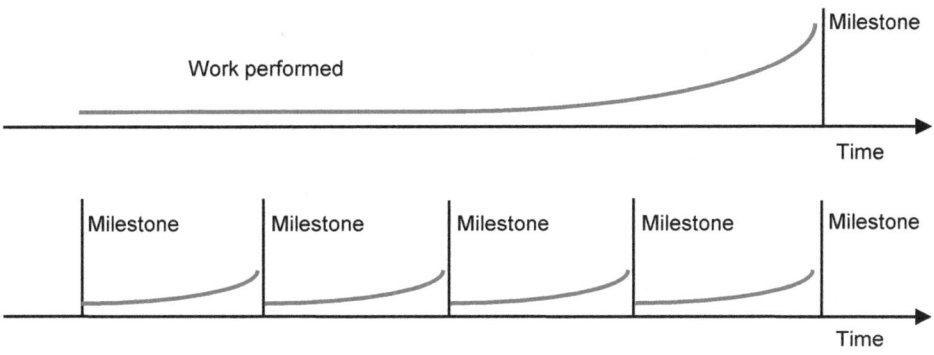

Figure 7.1. The precision of the follow-up process depends entirely on how far apart the milestones are.

It is therefore a good idea to break milestones down into sub-milestones to enable relevant follow-up. This also establishes a more even rhythm in the project work. The workload increases dramatically in the top curve, because for much of the time we aren't sure where we should be. Setting the milestones not too far apart also has a motivational effect, as it allows us to register our progress.

Learn from the process

If the milestone isn't good enough for the project to proceed as planned, then it's important to look back and assess the process leading up the situation that has arisen. What has gone well, and why did it go well? What do we need to hang on to in the future? What could have gone better, and what can we do differently in the future?

Follow-up is learning, too

Is the delay caused by specific actions that won't be repeated in the future? Or is it caused by conditions that will continue to exist in the project? Is the delay due to overly optimistic planning, inexperienced project participants, interruptions from the basic organization, etc.? If this is the case, will the delay continue to develop? It's possible that at this point, the delay is only one month, but it could develop into a delay of three months before the project is completed if the negative conditions aren't rectified.

235

Chapter 7. The Project Manager as Captain

While it is important to learn from the process, there is no guarantee that this is enough to rectify the situation at this point in time. If there is water in the boat, starting the bilge pumps isn't enough if the cause is a hole in the hull. However, if the water is caused by a passing storm with high seas, then starting the pumps is enough.

The plan-execute-review cycle

One way to promote learning is to incorporate reviews into the project. Reviews provide the project manager and team valuable information on the current project status, which can be used as a basis for making decisions about how to proceed (Briner 1996). All projects need to continuously gather knowledge. Cycles should be inserted into the project, where the participants not only plan and execute but also review the work performed.

Figure 7.2. The plan-execute-review cycle ensures that knowledge is collected and used with a view to the future of the project.

It's important to insert these review routines at regular intervals, such as every two weeks, to ensure that the project team continuously collects the experiences in the project, to keep the dialog going with the important stakeholders and, on this basis, to plan the upcoming project work. See also the section on feedback in Chapter 9.

The difficult part of the follow-up process isn't ascertaining delays, it's reacting to them. A lot of people are generally involved in drawing up a plan, which means that a lot of people can potentially see a delay, but few actually react – that is the manager's job!

However, it's not enough to just react to the actual delay; it's also necessary to react to the potential future delay, of which the current delay may just be a precursor. The reaction must be prompt, with immediate action being taken to bring the project back on track.

We tend to be far too patient and optimistic, e.g. 'we're sure to catch up later' or: 'let's wait and see. The next activities will probably be easier'. Even though everyone knows that there is never any extra time toward the end of projects, we are too reluctant to accept the consequences and take the necessary action. We know our plans tend to be overly optimistic – so why do we think that we'll have more time later in the project?

There are several reasons to take immediate action. For one thing, project plans are generally overly optimistic, so there is no time to waste. But a completely different reason is that everyone working on a project is under pressure from several sides. And so the individual tends to do the work that seems most urgent at the time and that he or she is being pressured to get done.

Look forward and accept the consequences

Take action at the first milestone delay

A good rule is to count on the project being delayed from the first milestone delay. Moving milestones has an impact on the end-objectives. This is why milestones shouldn't be allowed to slide, as it causes the project to slide.

It's a matter of getting the project participants to respect the milestones. We all know the type of person in an organization to whom it's best always to deliver on time. Just like we know the people who can always be counted on to call and ask for an extension. Nice, agreeable colleagues! But who do you deliver to first? By not reacting promptly to a delay, you will become one of those project managers people call to ask for an extension. However, take prompt action every single time and people will soon learn to get things done on time!

Establish a 'deliver on time' culture in the project

When a plan isn't adhered to, it's most likely because people don't consider it particularly important.

This is why you should avoid making too many changes to the plan, insist that the milestones be met and take action to put the project back on track. The sense of commitment and obligation to deliver declines when the plan is changed too often. The project participants who have worked all weekend to get something ready for the meeting on Monday learn a tough lesson when the meeting gets moved back a week, because there were others who weren't ready on time.

Making changes to the plan causes scheduling problems and brings out the 'good excuses'.

Everyone knows the fortunate situation when a plan has been changed: 'I was actually behind, but I've been saved by the change, and by the time I'm supposed to deliver I'll be on vacation.' It's a relief to be able to report to the project manager that because the plan has been changed, you can no longer deliver as she wants.

Even though the plan is 'wrong', a delayed project is still a problem. In some projects, an academic discussion can develop about whether the project was delayed because the plan was 'incorrectly' calculated or because the progress of the project was too slow – the subcontext being that if the plan is 'incorrectly calculated', then the project isn't 'really' delayed. The plan is 'just' wrong.

However, if the project is supposed to be completed by a specific time or has been calculated based on a specific payback period, it doesn't matter why the current stage isn't on schedule.

Plans are never completely 'right', but they are still the best indication of where we should be. An 'incorrectly calculated' plan can therefore still tell us we're delayed in relation to what we had expected. When we speak about the future, all we have is our expectations. For example, we will never finish developing knowledge; we can always find something we can improve. Consequently, it's important to put our activities into 'time boxes'. Two weeks have been allowed for this deliverable. Is the result good enough for us to proceed with the project? If yes, then we proceed, even though we could have done an even better job.

7.2. Follow-up in the project

The meeting plan should correlate with the milestone plan
In order to use the plan effectively, it's also important to establish a meeting plan that is correlated with the milestone plan. The series of meetings should be planned and the times reserved in the calendars of every project participant to ensure common meeting points.

It's important that the meeting plan correlates with the milestone plan. Meetings should take place immediately prior to critical points or just after important milestones to ensure a concrete point of departure for discussions at the meetings. A follow-up meeting about a milestone which should have been completed last week isn't as concrete as a meeting about the milestones that were completed two days ago. At meetings where the milestones should have been completed, it's easy to determine whether the milestone has been achieved.

The meeting plan might include:
- Project team meetings: Weekly and monthly project team meetings for, among other things, following up on the project's work streams and milestones.
- Steering committee meetings: Senior management-level follow-up. The meetings should be incorporated into the

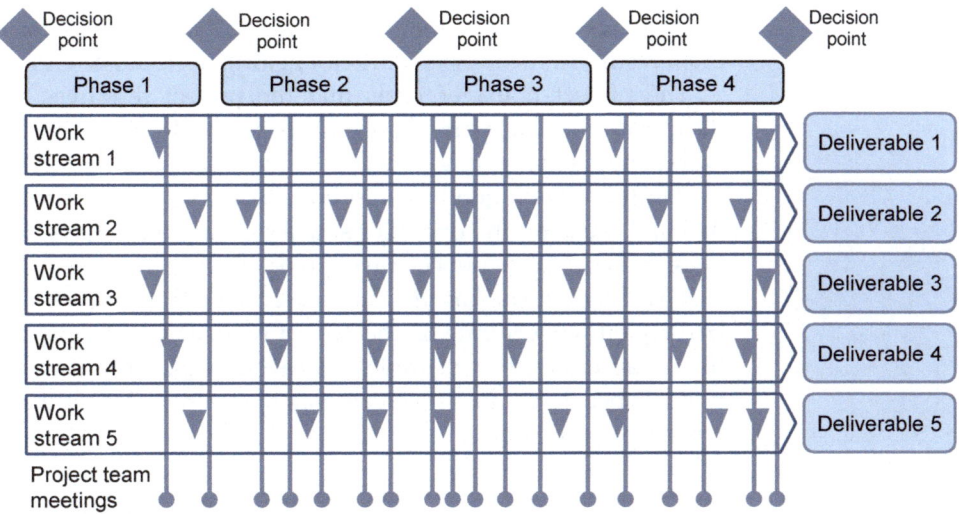

Figure 7.3. The meeting plan should be correlated with the milestone plan.

plan and take place, as a minimum, at the phase transitions. Some of the meetings may be defined by the organization's project model.
- Management reporting: Status updates, i.e. regular reporting on the current status of the project in selected areas, such as finances, time and quality. This type of reporting is used in portfolio management.
- Other project meetings: Follow-up on hearing committees, subcontractors and others.

It's important that the project has a good rhythm. For example, it can be a good idea to hold work stream meetings on specific days of the week or every other week. The work can be planned in such a way that new results must always have been achieved before the next meeting, before next Friday, and so on. This ensures a dynamic project and makes it possible to take quick action at the slightest sign that things are veering off course.

Think in terms of short lead times rather than capacity levelling

Pace and intensity

The plan should also be used to set the pace and intensity of the project work. Figure 7.4 shows a typical workweek for a project participant. The workweek is dictated by the operational environment, and the project work will often be carried out whenever there's time. However, this type of work form often results in the project work not getting done at all.

The project manager finds that the project resources are disappearing. The participants have set aside time for the work, but it's not getting done.

It is therefore a good idea to introduce a dedicated project day and focus on the operational tasks on the other days. For large projects, more project days can be added per week.

This work form has the advantage of letting the project participants concentrate on the project work as well as making follow-up easier. For example, it's easier to plan the completion of specific results if participants spend two days a week working on the project.

7.2. Follow-up in the project

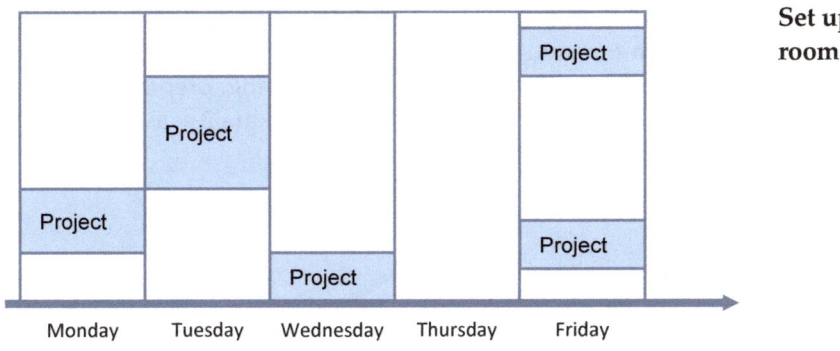

Figure 7.4. The operational environment dictates when during the week the project work can be carried out – often there just isn't time for it!

Set up a project room

With dedicated project days, it's also easier to have the team sit together during the hours they are to work on the project. Make sure there is a project room available where the participants can work on the dedicated days. The project days can be planned ahead of time and booked in the project participants' calendars.

When using dedicated project days, it's a good idea to think in terms of workshops or seminar days. (This is also a good idea when not working with dedicated project days.)

Use workshops

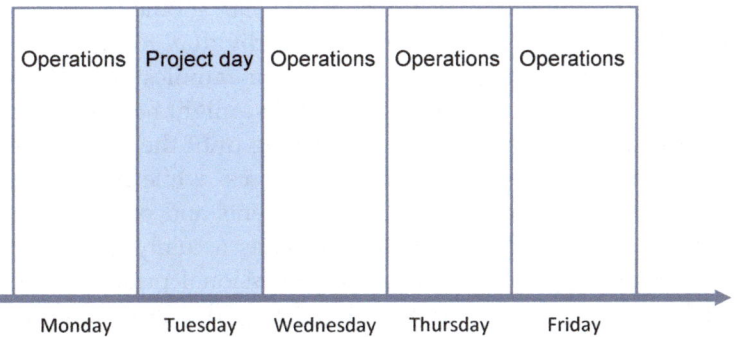

Figure 7.5. Work with dedicated project days, such as one or two days a week.

241

Over the course of the project, there will be activities that benefit from the entire team, or part of the team, devoting two or three days to them. These include planning, preparing reports, conclusions of analyses, evaluations, quality assurance, reviews, presentations, etc.

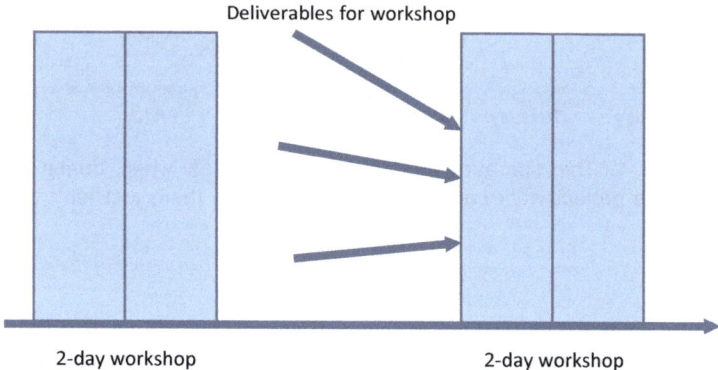

Figure 7.6. Use workshops as an intensive work form and have the project participants deliver to the project team – not to the project manager.

The use of workshops has many advantages. First, it makes it easy to book the day in calendars. Once everyone has entered the day in their calendars, that time is no long available for operational tasks. If the workshop is to end with a specific result, it makes follow-up work easier. For instance, the conclusion of a questionnaire survey analysis should have been found. It also makes it easier for the individual to plan his or her working time. They can say to their families: 'On Thursday, we have to finish the conclusion, so I might be home late.'

Second, it's possible to keep working until the job is done. This makes it easier to manage resources, while minimizing the tendency toward eternal improvements and perfectionism among some participants. Many projects actually grow from the inside out – the participants' professional pride can be a major issue when it comes to meeting deadlines on time (timeboxing).

A third advantage of workshops is that deliverables can be defined for the workshop to ensure that the individual project participants do their preliminary work prior to the workshop. This means that the participants deliver to the entire team at the workshop rather than just to the project manager.

Delivery to a workshop where six other project participants have set aside two calendar days to work with 'my' material comes with a powerful sense of obligation.

However, the sense of obligation is not as strong if the task has to be done by Thursday because the project manager will likely ask about it at the next project meeting.

In short, workshops ensure that the participants enter the activities in their calendars and feel a stronger sense of obligation, while also making follow-up easier.

As described above, the project manager's follow-up responsibilities are a combination of:

- Making it legitimate to assume the role
- Designing the plan so that it can serve as a basis for follow-up
- Organizing the meeting structure and work form to make follow-up possible and to encourage the individual project participants to assume responsibility for the agreements they enter into

7.3. Steering the project

The project manager steers the project to ensure that it's still on the right course. That is, to check that the objective is still relevant and to bring the project successfully to completion in accordance with the agreements that have been entered into with the steering committee.

Steering at project start-up

Traditionally, steering is concentrated in the three corners of the project triangle: that the agreed quality is delivered (the deliverables) and that the project is on time and on budget (the resources).

Steering quality, time and resources

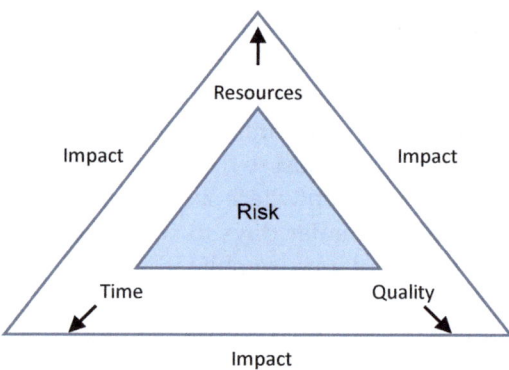

Figure 7.7. Steering traditionally centers on the deliverables, time and resources. But steering should also have an eye for the project risks and the impact, as these two dimensions are affected by any changes to the dimensions of time, quality or resources.

Steering risk and impact, too

There are two other dimensions the project manager needs to steer as well. One is risk, i.e. considering and communicating the degree of risk you are prepared to accept in the project.

The second is the project impact, i.e. the success criteria that represent achievement of the project purpose. Moving the corners of the inner triangle affects the impact. For example, the payback time is extended if the project costs increase, or the newly developed product might lose market shares if delivery is delayed.

Part of the project planning process is defining the success criteria for the project and determining which deliverables are needed to achieve the desired impact. As a project manager, you can't deliver impact, but you can decide on the timing, quality (deliverables) and resource consumption that will make it possible to achieve the success criteria.

When carrying out projects, there's a tendency to lose sight of the success criteria and focus solely on the deliverables. But if the environment changes, you risk ending up with a completed project that nobody needs and that will most certainly not be remembered as a success, even though it contains the deliverables in the agreed quality, was delivered on time and stayed within budget.

Let's look at an example. A technology company starts development of a computer game with the aim of securing the company 30 percent of the market for this game genre within two years. The project proceeds as planned and they manage to launch the game at the agreed time, in the agreed quality and on budget. An apparent success, if it wasn't for the fact that the competition had in the meantime introduced a new technology that removed all customer demand for this type of computer game. Another example is the Concorde jet, which was a technological marvel, but rising oil prices and growing environmental focus resulted in the production of only 11 aircraft.

The project manager must look forward to the expected end-result and what follows after that. Will the project deliverables still have the impact you are looking for? And is that impact still what you want? This means maintaining a dialog with both the end-users and the project owner, as well as being aware of anything else going on that might influence the project. A project manager can't rely on excuses like, 'But that was what the project owner asked for – so I thought I'd better do it.' In the end, you will rarely be evaluated on whether you met the deliverables stated in the original plan, but on whether the end-result was good and the desired impact was achieved. As a project manager, you are responsible for keeping tabs on whether the project is still relevant and whether continuing with the project is in the firm's business interests. You can't just promise deliverables; you also have to fulfill the success criteria.

Focus on the expected end-result

This can cause serious dilemmas for the project manager, as you may, at some point, be forced to shut down a project you have worked very hard on.

Project steering is based on a good plan and contract (also called the project description or mandate) that is manageable, clear and specifies the five dimensions of project steering.

When carrying out the project, you want to create *with a given certainty* (risk) a *specific impact* (possible effect) by delivering a *specified quality* at a given *time* and within the allocated *resource framework*.

The project contract forms the basis for the steering process

Depending on whether the customer is external or internal, projects generally differ as to how detailed the binding project contract is.

If the project owner is an external customer, these contracts are always a high priority, as they represent a legally binding agreement specifying what the customer is to receive, when and how. This would be the case, for instance, with a contractor commissioned to build a new institution for a local authority or an ad agency hired to carry out a marketing campaign for a client.

If the project is internal, for instance creating a new HR development program for your firm, there is an unfortunate tendency not to draw up a detailed contract/project description, or it is of such a general nature that it can't be used for the purpose of steering the project, because it doesn't specify risks, impact, quality, time or resources. As we will see later in the chapter on portfolio management, it's crucial that project manager draws up a detailed contract – regardless of whether the customer is external or internal. That contract doesn't just establish a sense of obligation in the project team and the customer; it also enables the project manager to negotiate with the project owner (the customer) when there are changes to the project. For instance, if they want to expand the project 'just a little'. In such situations, the project manager must negotiate with the project owner for more resources, more time or anything else that affects the five dimensions of project steering.

Changes to the contract mean changes to the plan Changes to the contract are unavoidable and necessary. As mentioned in the introduction to this chapter, no plan can survive the meeting with reality unscathed. During the course of the project, you face wishes or demands for change from the end-users and the project owner, just as the project team will undoubtedly discover a number of places where it would be advisable to change a deliverable in relation to the original plan.

Changes to the contract result in changes to the project plan, which is why the plan must not be so rigid that it can't tolerate relevant and necessary changes. (At the same time, you want to avoid constantly changing the plan, as this causes scheduling problems and 'good excuses' for late deliverables from the other project participants.)

When there are relevant and necessary changes, it's important to always use the plan actively in the project steering process, rather than just changing the deliverables and milestones without incorporating the changes in the plan. First, this is a fast way to undermine the plan (why look at the plan if it's not up to date?). This makes it difficult for people, especially loosely affiliated participants, to figure out what to base their work on. Second, you may one day need to be able to document which changes have been decided, by whom and when. Therefore: When changes are made to the deliverables, they should be included in the plan and communicated to the relevant parties.

Informed changes

For this purpose, it's a good idea to maintain a project logbook (decision log), where all major decisions about the deliverables and process are entered. Significant changes should be communicated to the relevant parties, often the project team and project owner, but in some cases also other stakeholders. Further, it's also a good idea to agree on a procedure for decision-making within the project team and with the steering committee to avoid everyone making changes independent of each other.

Decisions should be entered in the project log

The following is an example of a page from a project log:

Date	Change	Approved by	Responsible for implementation

Figure 7.8. Project log (decisions long) for registering changes to the project.

Specific measures for project steering

Looking back on the five dimensions for project steering – risk, impact, quality, time and resources – what specific project steering measures do you have at your disposal? Below is a description of the five steering levers you would normally adjust. The challenge is assessing when and in which situations it is most effective to pull on each lever. The five levers are:

Resources

In case of problems or changes to the project, you can add more resources in the form of extra staff or more funding for purchasing external assistance. However, it is also a good idea to consider whether the problem truly is resource-dependent, or whether it may be caused by other factors. For instance, might replacements be made on the project team to bring in more experienced people or people with other competences relevant to the current changes or problems? And what effect would it have on the overall team performance? Does it mean carrying out the storming phase again? And how should that process be managed? See Figure 9.1.

Approach

Instead of pushing back the deadline for the project, it may be possible to win time and save resources, as well as improve quality, by looking at how the work is planned. By reconsidering the work plan and milestone plan, it is often possible to streamline the approach. Potential changes include working more concurrently, conducting a pilot project or changing the order of the activities.

Level of ambition

The third steering lever the project manager has at her disposal is the level of ambition. Is there any excess fat that can be trimmed? Is everything 'need to have' (business critical) or are there perhaps some 'nice to have' elements that might be dropped without seriously affecting the project's impact? Changes should, of course, be agreed upon with the relevant parties, especially the project owner. In projects focusing on knowledge development, it is particularly important to understand that you will never be done. There is always room for improvement – that's how it's been since the Stone Age!

7.3. Steering the project

It is also a good idea to reconsider the project's work process, i.e. how you work (in contrast to the approach, i.e. which sub-objectives and activities are planned and in what order). For example, would you work more intensively and effectively if the project group could sit together in a dedicated project room? Could the project participants sit together in pairs or divide the work up?

Can decision paths be streamlined, for instance by planning more frequent meetings with the project owner? Are people spending time on tasks that aren't really important?

Work process

How great a risk are you willing to accept in this project? This is an important discussion in the project team and, especially, with the project owner. The project manager must clearly communicate the risks in the project for the situation in question. The project manager needs the project owner to say whether these calculated risks are acceptable. It's important to bear in mind that adjusting the other four levers often automatically changes the project risks.

Risk acceptance

Figure 7.9. At the top of the control panel, we see the five project steering dimensions: quality, time, resources, impact and risk. At the bottom are the five levers the project manager can adjust to influence the results.

Perhaps it's possible to save time if you are willing to accept a slightly higher risk. For instance, can the project proceed even though everything hasn't been fully tested?

In summary, the project manager needs to make sure the five steering dimensions are specified in the project contract – and that the contract is changed every time adjustments are made to these dimensions. In addition, you also need to be aware of the five levers you can pull to steer the project, and evaluate from time to time what might help the project to successfully reach its objective.

The Earned Value method

Follow-up on results, resources and finances

When assessing the progress of the project, another challenge is being able to not only compare the project costs incurred with the project budget, but also with the expected results, i.e. determining the actual value of the work that has been performed.

There are several methods available for this purpose, including milestone follow-up, trend curves and calculating the rate of progress of the project.

The following is an introduction to using the Earned Value method as a tool to shed light on the value created by the work performed. There are several versions of the method and it goes by many names, including S-curve follow-up.

With the Earned Value method, you can calculate the value of the work performed to obtain a true indication of the project costs incurred that can be directly compared to the work actually performed during the project. The value of the work performed is defined as the budgeted costs associated with the completion of the milestone in question.

The simplest way to carry out this follow-up is to draw up a list of the milestones in their order of completion. Next to each milestone, enter the costs and resource consumption, for instance in person days. This makes it possible to draw up a budget and later follow-up on the costs per milestone. It will also be possible to set up the expected accumulated costs as a function of the milestone achieved.

The strength of the Earned Value method is the graphic presentation of the project progress.

7.3. Steering the project

Milestone	Date	Accumulated budget (BCWS)	Accumulated consumption (ACWP)
Workflows mapped	January 15th	4 person weeks	5 person week
Change approved	March 5th	1 person week	1 person week
New workflow designed	March 25th	3 person week	5 person week
New workflows described	May 15th	8 person week	

Figure 7.10. Milestone plan indicating milestones, deadlines and budgeted resource consumption (BCWS = Budgeted Cost of Work Scheduled).
The column on the right can be used to indicate the current consumption per milestone (ACWP = Actual Cost of Work Performed).

It is possible to draw a diagram showing how the earned value increases over time. The figure 7.11 is an example of this type of diagram, including the key concepts and correlations:

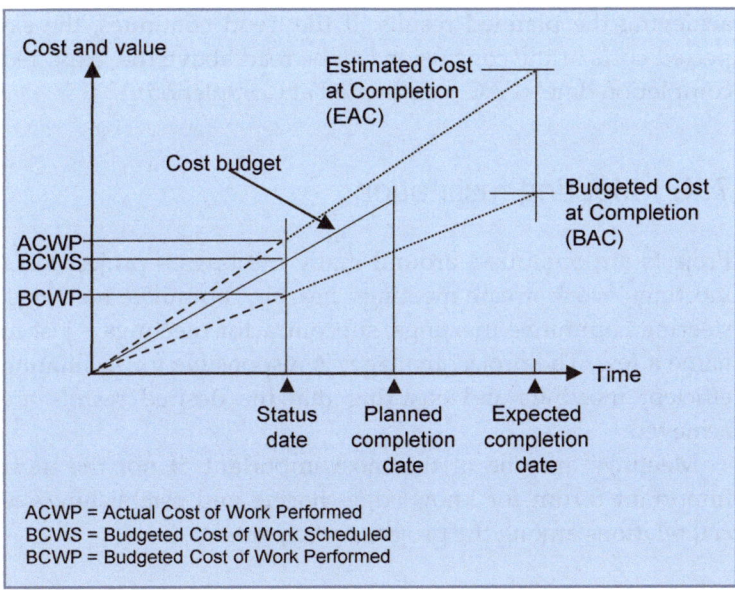

ACWP = Actual Cost of Work Performed
BCWS = Budgeted Cost of Work Scheduled
BCWP = Budgeted Cost of Work Performed

Figure 7.11. Earned Value diagram showing the costs and value as a function of time in the milestone plan.
The solid line in the diagram in the figure shows the planned earned value over time, called the 'cost budget'.

251

The method is characterized by very clear curves showing the actual costs of the work performed and the planned costs, which either move farther and farther apart or run parallel. If they are parallel, we have had a temporary problem and we have to work to catch up. If the curves move away from each other, there are more persistent problems; thus, the delay and the budget overrun will be greater and greater.

If the project follows the plan, then the two curves will merge.

This follow-up technique is an expression of Hastings' thoughts on looking back to learn from the process and looking forward to assess what this knowledge means for the rest of the project. We can address any issues and take action based on this picture. The BCWP curve indicates our experience of where we are on the 'start date'. If this curve is extended up to the budgeted costs we have used, we can read on the time axis when the project can be expected to be completed, if we don't make an extra effort (BAC = Budgeted Cost at Completion).

The ACWP curve is our experience of the cost so far of achieving the planned results. If the trend continues, the expected costs at the conclusion can be read above the 'expected completion date' (EAC = Estimated at Completion).

7.4. Meeting facilitation

Projects are organized around many meetings – project team meetings, work stream meetings, hearing committee meetings, steering committee meetings, subcontractor meetings – just to name a few. The project manager is responsible for facilitating efficient meetings and ensuring that the desired results are achieved.

Meetings are one of the most important, if not the most important forum for knowledge-sharing and establishing social relations among the project participants.

When it comes to meetings, a typical reaction is: 'Oh no, not another meeting. We're meeting our lives away.'

In our experience, this animosity toward meetings stems from too many meetings that are too long and poorly conducted. A typical meeting might look like this: 10-15 minutes after the agreed start time, just about everyone has arrived and after an additional 10 minutes, everyone's done eating the bagels and ready to start. The project manager passes around the agenda for the meeting and presents his/her proposals for the upcoming work. After a 5 to 10-minute monolog by the project manager, most of the people in the room have vacant looks on their faces, are doodling to keep themselves awake or are thinking about what they could be doing instead of sitting here wasting their time. The first item on the agenda becomes a lengthy discussion and ends up taking 80 percent of the time allotted for the meeting, which means they have to rush through the remaining five items. Everyone leaves the meeting feeling somewhat irritable about having wasted their time, but nobody openly questions the meeting form.

Too many, too long and poorly conducted meetings

There is a better way! Meetings are where you, as the project manager, really have a chance to distinguish yourself by making improvements. The following are a few tips on what the project manager should do to optimize meeting efficiency within the project. First, we look at what the meeting facilitator should do before, during and after the meeting. Then, we will explain the various meeting types. Finally, we will take a closer look at the steering committee meeting.

Holding streamlined meetings that leave people with a sense of time well-spent requires an effort before, during and after the meeting. The project manager is responsible for ensuring that the time the team spends together is well-spent, but she may also delegate tasks pertaining to the meeting.

An active effort to optimize meeting efficiency

Before the meeting
Consider:

- Is the meeting really necessary?
- Who needs to be at the meeting? Invite only them. Break a long meeting with many items on the agenda up into short

meetings with the participation of only the relevant people. This will help you avoid having too many people waiting impatiently for 'their' item on the agenda.
- Send out a detailed agenda well in advance of the meeting, specifying the purpose of the meeting and the deliverables.
- Take contact with people before the meeting if necessary! The chances of influencing others are generally greater before meetings.

During the meeting
- Start the meeting on time! That way, you avoid wasting the time of those who arrived on time and 'teach' the others to come on time.
- Make the agenda visible – using a flip-chart or white board.
- Remember to specify the timeframe. Indicate the times on the agenda – this ensures that you won't have to rush through the last items and makes it possible to cut through less relevant discussions.
- Specify the purpose of the meeting, what exactly needs to be achieved by the end of the meeting and what the various participants' roles are. For instance, 'I have invited you here today to hear your creative ideas' or 'you must decide what needs to be done in this case'.
- Facilitate dialog rather than doing most of the talking yourself. Make sure to get everyone involved. Listen and ask for the participants' contributions.
- It's the meeting facilitator's responsibility to ask clarifying questions, sum up the discussion and present conclusions at the end of each item. Remember to check that everyone is in acceptance or agreement.

After the meeting
- Draw up a minutes of decisions – this is an important tool for lobbying and may be the project manager's only documentation of what has been agreed.
- Follow-up on what has been agreed and continue lobbying the relevant people.

First and foremost, the project manager should carefully consider whether each meeting is really necessary. To call in several people for a meeting, there must be a reason for their physical presence. When the project manager does most of the talking, that's a sure sign the meeting will be considered a waste of time.

Consider whether the meeting is necessary

The meeting frequency depends on the nature of the project. The more complex the project is and the more resources, activities and parallel dependent work streams there are to coordinate, the greater the need for meetings within the project team and the work streams.

Even though you should carefully consider the necessity of each meeting, it's still important to include fixed project team meetings in the project plan from the outset to ensure the times are booked in the project participants' calendars. If a meeting should turn out not to be necessary, it's easy to cancel. The point is, it's easier to cancel a meeting than to call in eight busy people for ad hoc meetings. (Convening meetings ad hoc usually results in the meetings taking place at 7:00-8:00 am or 5:00-7:00 pm – to the irritation of everyone.)

Always remember to set fixed meetings in the project team

Joint meetings in the project team are important for the following reasons:

- The meetings underpin knowledge-sharing and increase the overall quality of the project
- The meetings involve the team members in discussions and decisions, thus promoting a stronger sense of ownership and engagement in the implementation of the decisions
- Efficient meetings promote team identity and a sense of being a cohesive unit
- Meetings offer a chance to celebrate successes together and to evaluate results and processes

Various meeting types

We often hold meetings without communicating to the participants or even fully understanding the type and purpose of the meeting. When the purpose and what the participants are expected to contribute aren't clear from the outset, it creates confusion about the meeting. For example: a project manager

Facilitation based on meeting type

convenes a meeting with the hearing committee where he expects them to contribute ideas on how the project can best be implemented within their organization. But instead of receiving a steady flow of ideas, he meets a wall of silence. Not because of resistance to the project, but because the hearing committee members were only expecting to receive information from the project manager and weren't prepared to make an active contribution.

The first step to ensuring optimum meeting efficiency is therefore to clearly communicate what type of meeting you are convening. We differentiate between four meeting types based on the overall purpose of the meeting (see more about the meeting types in the toolbox).

Meeting type	Purpose	Examples
Involvement meeting	Create enthusiasm, motivation, interest, unity and acceptance	Project kick-off Information meetings
Idea generation meeting	Work together to come up with as many ideas as possible	Brainstorming Product/concept development meetings
Troubleshooting meeting	To find solution(s) to a given problem	Crisis meetings Planning meetings
Decision-making meetings	To make decisions based on previously issued/presented material	Steering committee meetings Follow-up meetings

Figure 7.12. The four meeting types have different purposes and should therefore be facilitated differently.

Meetings should be prepared for and facilitated differently depending on their type. There is a tendency to mix more than one meeting type, for instance combining troubleshooting and decision-making in one meeting. However, it's a good idea to break this type of meeting up into two, because it allows you to invite the right people, state the purpose and clarify what the participants are expected to contribute.

Involvement meetings

The involvement meeting is also called an information or orientation meeting. However, those names are rather misleading, as what we really want to achieve with this type of the meeting is for people to become interested and involved in the project. It is therefore important to strongly emphasize a meeting form that promotes dialog and active participation, partly in your own communication and partly in the meeting process.

The most important thing for this meeting type is to limit the target group. Who should attend the meeting and what are the interests or concerns of this target group?

What do we want this group to do? What messages do we want to send to this group?

With regard to communication, for instance at the project kick-off for firm employees, you need to clearly present the vision of the project and be honest about the cost of change. An overly enthusiastic speech rarely comes off as trustworthy. At the involvement meeting, you need to consider whether it's possible to address the specific needs of the participants. If the target group is too broad, the desired impact may not be achieved. It is therefore a good idea to divide the participants up and hold smaller, more targeted meetings based on the stakeholders' needs, wishes and concerns. (See more on the chapter on communication.)

Nothing kills an involvement meeting like a long presentation followed by questions from the floor. This type of meeting is not likely to boost involvement at all! If you want people to walk away from the meeting with a sense that it was relevant and engaging, you need to plan a meeting process that promotes involvement.

A couple of simple tricks are to break the presentation up into smaller blocks and to allow the participants to process what has just been said in small groups or by chatting with the person next to them. Activate the small groups by asking questions like: Why don't you talk among yourselves about what you found most interesting? What are you wondering about? What does it mean for your workday? And so on.

Activate people at the orientation meeting

You can bring energy to the meeting by alternating between smaller groups, presentations and plenum discussions. The options for staging are countless.

Creativity in the project

The idea generation meeting

Creativity in projects is often overlooked. However, being able to develop new ideas and see new perspectives is vital to the entire project in order to expand the range of possible solutions, both at project start-up and during the process. The quality and output of the idea generation meeting depend to a great extent on the group of participants and on how the process is facilitated. When selecting participants for this type of meeting, it's important to think unconventionally. The participants should preferably represent different backgrounds and perspectives, as well as possess an openness to thinking outside the box and playing with crazy ideas.

Creativity requires a framework. It is therefore important to be very clear about the meeting process, for instance to specify which phases have room for wild and unconventional thinking and which phases require concrete ideas.

Finally, it's important to give creativity and idea generation time. It's interesting that in most organizations it's fully acceptable to spend two hours on a meeting to analyze a problem, while spending two hours generating ideas and new thinking is often considered a 'foolish waste of time'.

There are a wide range of creative techniques you can freely use to stage an idea generation meeting.

Brainstorming

Brainstorming is an excellent tool – as long as it's done correctly! Brainstorming is useful for generating a large volume of ideas. It doesn't necessarily produce creative depth, but it does establish a good foundation for further creative work. The word brainstorming is often used about generating a list of three to five ideas. But that's not brainstorming. When brainstorming, it's important to follow the rules about differentiating idea generation from the assessment of the ideas, to devote enough time to the process (as a rule of thumb, you want to generate 50-100 ideas before stopping the process) and to think outside the box in order to generate unusual ideas.

Another technique is Edward de Bono's thinking hats. He broke the creative process down into phases, each symbolized by a colored hat. The white hat indicates that the participants are dealing with facts on the topic, the green hat signals that they are generating a lot of unconventional and even outlandish ideas, and the black hat is for critical and evaluative thinking. The strength of De Bono's concept, which has become widely popular all over the world, is how the meeting participants move in parallel throughout the creative process. This makes it possible to avoid the classic situation where one person comes up with crazy ideas that are immediately shot down by another person, while a third analyzes facts and demands more information before you can proceed.

de Bono's thinking hats

The troubleshooting meeting
This type of meeting is very common in project work. The premise is basically: We have a problem. How can we solve it?

These types of meetings are often relatively streamlined, because there is a concrete result that must be achieved. However, confusion can develop if you haven't defined and achieved consensus about the problem. In such cases, an inordinate amount of time can be spent talking at cross-purposes, arguing for solutions others consider utter nonsense, etc. It is therefore vital that you always start the meeting by clearly defining the problem and the result you want achieved by the end of the meeting, and securing the participants' acceptance. It's a good idea to appoint a facilitator to be responsible for this task as well as for ensuring that the meeting moves smoothly in the right direction, that you don't get bogged down by details and that conflicts don't keep you from achieving a result.

The meeting facilitator should also make sure to secure the involvement and acceptance of the participants during the process. This is especially important if the prospective solution depends on all the participants being in agreement about and working together to realize the solution. Examples include, if the problem is insufficient support from an important stakeholder group or if the pace needs to be changed over the next two months to achieve an important milestone.

The decision-making meeting

An efficient decision-making meeting requires that the participants have the competence to make decisions. It's no use having representatives present who have to go back and ask for 'permission', as that detracts from the project manager's ability to maintain a dialog with the actual decision-makers.

Before a decision-making meeting, a short, precise decision paper with recommendations should be sent out to ensure that everyone understands what decisions they are expected to make at the meeting. If material is not sent out prior to the meeting, then the meeting should begin with a clear outline of what decisions are to be made and on what basis.

The meeting must be carefully conducted. This is done by following a clear agenda, which must be visible during the entire meeting. Write it on a flip-chart, whiteboard, etc. so you can refer to it during the meeting and cut off discussions that aren't relevant. One of the most common reasons decision-making meetings derail is because the discussion of the project get bogged down by details, especially if the participants have in-depth specialist knowledge of the project's technology or method.

Make sure everyone is included in the process; ask for agreement and obtain partial acceptance where necessary. Enter the decision in the minutes, as later you may need to be able to document a new course or decision in the project.

The steering committee meeting

The project manager must, in particular, master the steering committee meeting, as this is where the important overall decisions about the project are made. Here, we will take a closer look at how to prepare for a steering committee meeting and how the project manager or the project owner should facilitate it.

First and foremost, it's vital that you, as the project manager, participate in the steering committee meeting! Unfortunately, it's quite common for project managers not to participate in steering committee meetings, but that doesn't make it any less wrong. Especially in public-sector organizations, the office manager will often present the project to the steering committee on behalf of the project manager if the committee comprises members from senior manager. But that is not how it should be! The project manager must do the presentation herself, as she is the one who knows exactly what is going on in the project and who has to implement the steering committee's decisions.

Preparation is the key to a successful steering committee meeting. It is especially important to secure the support of the project owner and make him or her your ally at the meeting. This means maintaining a dialog with the project owner prior to the meeting and ensuring that you don't present anything at the meeting that comes as a surprise to the project owner. In some cases it is also wise to have clarified items bilaterally with other members of the steering committee.

In addition to lobbying prior to the steering committee meeting, preparation for the meeting also includes gaining an understanding of who the steering committee is as a target group, i.e.:

- Their individual wishes and interests (What's in it for them?)
- Their concerns (What are they particularly concerned about?)
- The appropriate language (i.e. What arguments should you use?)

If the steering committee comprises senior management, they are often concerned about the benefit for the firm as a whole, which might include improved image, increased earnings, visibility in relation to the market or the minister, etc. Streamlining and savings are often also hot topics. Then there are the more personal objectives, which aren't always explicitly stated. If the CEO has a favorite focus area or pet peeve, it may help to incorporate this into the argumentation.

When facilitating a steering committee meeting, it's good to remember the following:

- Either the project manager or the project owner is the meeting facilitator!
- Communicate clearly to the steering committee which decisions they are expected to consider – draw up an agenda.

- Be aware of what the steering committee is expected to agree or partially agree to during the meeting.
- Involve and clarify questions of doubt along the way.
- Steer the steering committee – avoid going into detail and keep your focus.
- Make sure the agenda is visible using a flip-chart, white board or similar.

7.5. Reflections on project follow-up and steering

- Are your project plan and follow-up process designed so that you can follow-up before reaching a milestone?
- How far apart are the milestones in your project?
- What is the meeting frequency in your project?
- Has a budget been set per milestone to enable financial follow-up?
- How do you conduct the ongoing reconciliation of expectations with the stakeholders with regard to the success criteria?
- Do the stakeholders understand the limits of the project? What is NOT included in the scope of the project?
- What meeting types are used in your project?
- How are changes agreed upon and managed?
- Do you have the resources you expected?
- How might you secure the steering committee's acceptance of the project risk?
- What is stopping you from using more intensive work forms in your project?
- How might you use workshops in your project?

Communication and Change
Urgency, vision and involvement

If your project is secret, nobody will be aware of it

CHAPTER 8

Communication and change

You can't 'not communicate'; the project's surroundings will always view the project in some light or other! It is therefore important to provide relevant communication to the right stakeholders at the right time in order to control how people see the project. — **Challenges**

Many projects live an isolated life, where their existence is unknown to others. This makes sense for some projects – for example a takeover by a competing company, downsizing or the development of a new product to be released before a competitor's product.

But such projects are the exception. For most projects, the chances of success increase significantly with targeted and strategic communication to the key stakeholders from the very beginning of the project.

Chapter 8 introduces the most common project communication errors and offers tips on how to achieve effective project communication. — **Benefits**

This chapter provides insight into:
- Working with targeted and strategic communication within the project
- Establishing a project 'brand'
- Promoting change with communication

This chapter focuses on communication outward from the project, i.e. to internal and external stakeholders. — **Focus**

Chapter 8. Communication and change

Figure 8.1. Communication outward from the project targets both internal and external stakeholders. Inspired by Briner et al. 1996.

Communication downward to the project team is covered in Chapter 9 on the project manager as the team leader, while communication upward to the project owner is covered in Chapter 7 on the project manager as captain.

Tools Tool 8.1   The Communication Plan
Tool 8.2   Resistance to Change Mapping

8.1. Projects often suffer when it comes to communication

Projects are a disruptive element in many organizations: They take resources away from the line. The outcome is generally uncertain. The purpose and deliverables often change along the way due to outside influence on the project. They result in both major and minor changes to the organization or its customers. These are but a few of the challenges that come with project work.

The driving forces of change
Change always means that someone must alter their behavior. There are two primary driving forces that get people to change something about their behavior. Either we are forced to change due to circumstances, or we change because we have spotted a better opportunity.

Thus, we operate with two key concepts within change management: the *burning platform* and the *vision for change*.

The burning platform means that we can see the urgency of changing our behavior, because the ground is burning under our feet. Meanwhile, the vision is an image of a desirable future – a place where the grass is greener than where we're currently standing. Communicating these messages to the organization is an important task.

It is vital that everyone within the organization can see the burning platform and the vision, accept them and feel comfortable with the path to be following from the current situation to the uncertain future that lies ahead. Consequently, organizational change projects often include two extra work streams: one work stream to establish an understanding of the situation now and in the future and one work stream to establish an understanding of the path for reaching this new future.

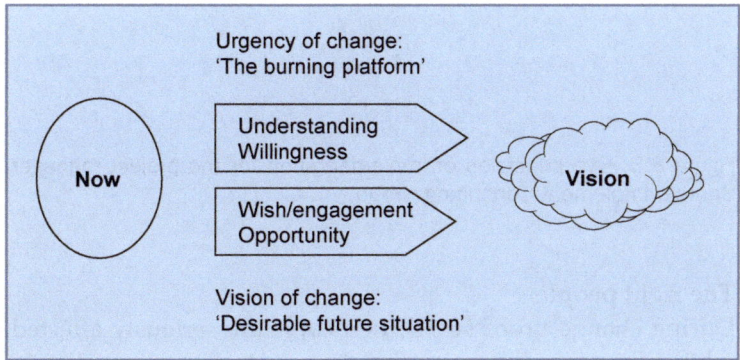

Figure 8.2. The driving forces of change.

The key activities are communication, further education and staff training.

However, it isn't enough for the employees to just understand the situation, they also need to accept that they are on a journey of change and they need to perceive the vision as attractive. This can only be achieved by actively involving the employees in parts of the project, which requires communication and dialog.

Five principles for the project manager seeking to achieve change
At the Implement Consulting Group, we have 450 consultants working on a wide array of organizational change projects. Over the years, we have developed five principles for working as a project manager on such projects.

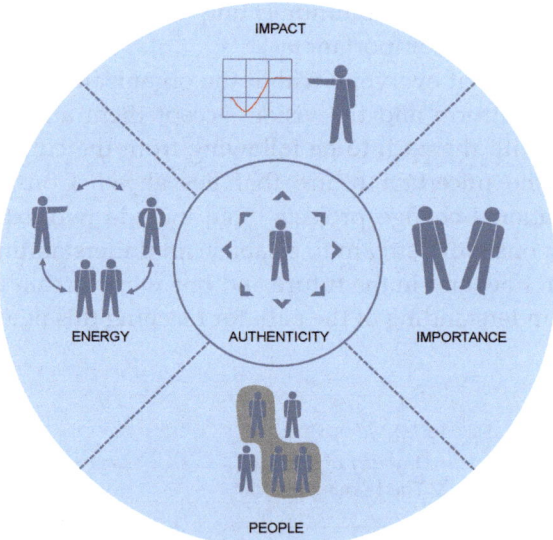

Figure 8.3. Five principles of implementation for the project manager. Source: Implement Consulting Group.

The right people
During change processes, some people are seriously affected, while others hardly notice the change at all. You need to be

able to define the target groups most affected by the change and determine how to help these people during the process.

There is often a specific group of people who can facilitate the change process. The project manager therefore needs to identify and establish an active dialog between the 'right' people early in the process and facilitate that dialog in a professional manner. According to Ralph Stacey, change is achieved in the dialog between people.

Urgency and action
To help the employees to take action and change their behavior, they need to see the urgency of change and the importance of reaching the new situation. This is John P. Kotter's first principle: 'We need to establish a sense of the urgency for change', i.e. the burning platform.

In other situations, it may be necessary to take action first or initiate a pilot project to help skeptics see the urgency. For instance, improvements carried out in one department can make other departments think: 'We want to work that way, too'.

The project manager therefore needs to challenge the urgency of change and provide time for reflection, doubt and opinion-shaping. Remember, we work with change of perception and behavioral change.

Atmosphere and timing
An important tool is to establish the right atmosphere at the right time. Leaders often think that they just need to generate enthusiasm, but equally important is creating an atmosphere that promotes awareness, curiosity, reflection and a sense of team spirit.

The project manager needs to 'feel the organization' and adapt the process accordingly, consciously planning and staging the atmosphere. It's important to consider the atmosphere before the content. The atmosphere is often established by means of communication. In this capacity, the project manager acts as an agent of change, in the words of Ralph Stacey.

Timing is everything. There are times when something that may otherwise seem impossible can actually be done. It's a matter of jumping in at the right time, even if the plan says that it's not supposed to be done until the next quarter.

Impact

Change is about impact. If there is no impact, then there is no change. In contrast to engineering and construction projects, where the focus is on the deliverable, the focus of organizational change projects is on the impact. This means that the deliverables are continuously changed to achieve the desired impact (see section 10.6).

In order for this to work, the project manager needs to provide the employees and the project team with the necessary business insight. Success criteria need to be defined for both the business and the people aspects of the project. The project manager is responsible for both measuring and following up on the impact. Kotter speaks of the necessity of achieving perceptible success quickly.

Authenticity

In organizational change projects, the project manager will be under tremendous pressure from various stakeholders looking out for their own interests. The slightest hint of favoritism within the group can cause serious problems for the project manager. For this reason, the project manager needs to maintain a high level of integrity and be attentive and respectful at every level of the organization.

The project manager must react on her gut instincts – humbly and providing honest feedback, both professionally and personally. It's important that everyone knows where the project manager stands, and that you express your own qualified opinion and stand by it. The project manager must act to gain people's trust.

Tactical execution of the implementation phase

In order to properly take into account the right people, the atmosphere and the timing during implementation, you need to carefully consider the implementation plan. Is it wise to implement the change in one fail swoop or should you do it one department at a time and assess the results before moving on to the next? Perhaps it's better to divide the overall change

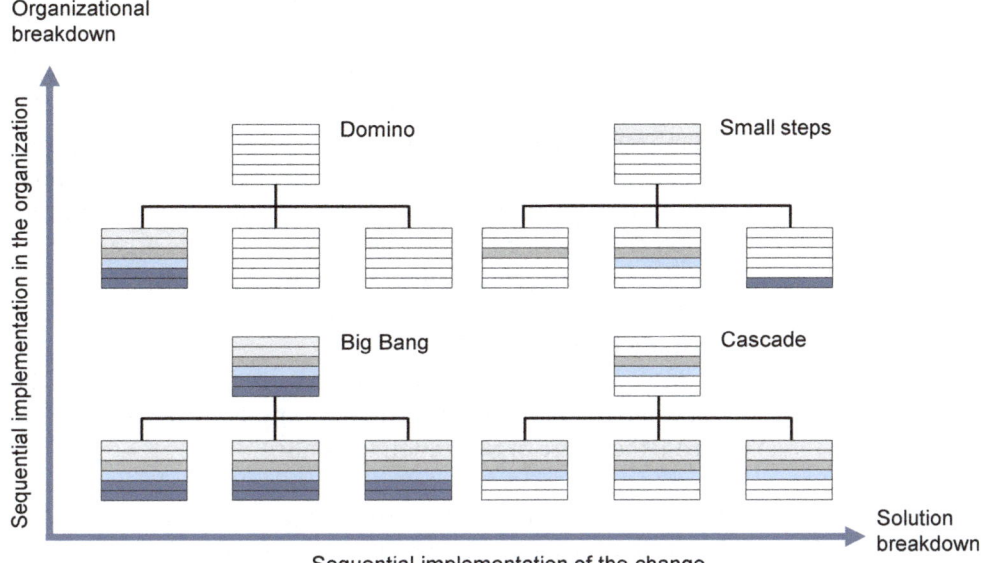

Figure 8.4. Tactical execution of the implementation phase.

up into smaller changes, which are then implemented simultaneously across the organization?

The project manager needs to carefully consider how the change should actually be implemented and at what pace.

The challenge of a Big Bang change implementation is that the task becomes extremely complex. You need to quickly establish uniform qualifications across large parts of the organization. In this connection, you should expect a reduction in efficiency for three to four months, while follow-up and behavioral change represent a daunting task.

Can we handle the communication needs of such a big project?

Domino implementation
With a domino rollout in the organization, the entire change is implemented in one department at a time. This makes it possible to carry out a pilot project before proceeding to the next department. This also allows other departments to learn from

the experiences gained during the pilot project and gives you a chance to communicate the impact achieved.

The challenge of this method is that it is very time-consuming and entails a large number of start-ups. Parts of the organization may grow impatient. The impact of the changes can also vary from department to department, which can result in disappointments. The timing of training and communication efforts can be problematic, as the various organizational units are at different stages of the change process.

Cascade implementation
In cascade implementation, the task is pared down so that only part of the overall change is implemented step-by-step across the entire organization (globally).

Small steps, local step-by-step change
The primary challenge with this type of implementation is that it is extremely time-consuming (introduction at every step) and can result in some fatigue among the recipients and the project team members. Another problem is that methods and departments are continually being adjusted, which leads to a feeling of constant change. Finally, it can be difficult to achieve a sense of team spirit and an acceptance of the overall result.

Another version of this strategy is step-by-step change that takes place locally. Here, the change process is broken down into steps and implemented across the organization sequentially.

The challenge is that it is extremely time-consuming and the path is uncharted.

The impact of the individual part-implementations will also be relatively unpredictable, as the same part-implementations won't be carried out in the same order throughout the organization. In the long term, it will be difficult to secure the support of management for improvisations.

This implementation strategy also makes it difficult to communicate the project purpose and well-defined deliverables to the entire organization.

Project management is largely a matter of communication

To steer a project to safe harbor, the project manager needs to provide relevant communication to the project stakeholders, which makes project management largely a matter of communication. Tag along with a project manager at work and you will find that she spends most of her time talking!

How often has a project manager thought: 'I haven't gotten anything done today, because I had to deal with three stakeholders who disagree, explain to a middle manager that we need his employees on the project, resolve a conflict between two project participants and explain to a third that his work doesn't live up to the quality expectations'? But this is the project manager's job in a nutshell – what else should she be doing? In reality, the project manager in this case achieved consensus on the expectations and thereby approval of some deliverables. She also assured quality by securing the necessary resources and ensuring the project participants the peace they need to work. And all of this was achieved solely by means of dialog.

In one of his many books on project management, Peter Drucker writes that the ability to communicate may be the most important skill a successful leader can possess (Drucker 1952).

Unfortunately, the majority of projects neglect relevant communication to the key stakeholders, despite the fact that most project managers have personal experience with how inadequate communication can have a backlash and hinder the success of the project. For example, stakeholders may misunderstand the purpose of the project or simply forget the project even exists. Or important stakeholders may start to resist at the time of handover to operations.

A study of organizational change projects in government authorities, agencies and service institutions in five European countries asked employees:

'What do you think management can do to motivate employees to view change as an opportunity rather than a threat?' The answers were clear:

65% said better communication
24% said involvement in the decision-making process
8% said education/training
2% said higher pay
Source: Hagemann 1993.

Neglecting communication and involvement reduces the chances of motivating and achieving acceptance of the change. The amount of energy needed to communicate to the stakeholders depends on the nature of the project. If the project's success is contingent on stakeholders changing their behavior and/or providing their acceptance, then it makes sense to devote a good deal of energy to communication. The examples are many:

- The introduction of a new IT system, where success also depends on how the users receive it and integrate it in their workdays.
- The renovation of a school, where success is also assessed based on how the users have experienced the actual change process and how satisfied they are with the result.
- A basis for decision-making in a political organization, where several political parties must be consulted during the process.

Some projects consist of pure 'desk work' – analyzing and drawing conclusions before anyone is expected to give their approval or do something other than what they usually do as a result of the project. In such projects, it is possible to 'take a communicative shortcut'. Chapter 4 gives an idea of how much time you should expect to devote to stakeholder management in the six project types. In simplified terms, you can say that in the project types where stakeholder management plays a crucial role, communication plays a similarly crucial role.

8.2. Common mistakes in project communication – if there is any communication at all

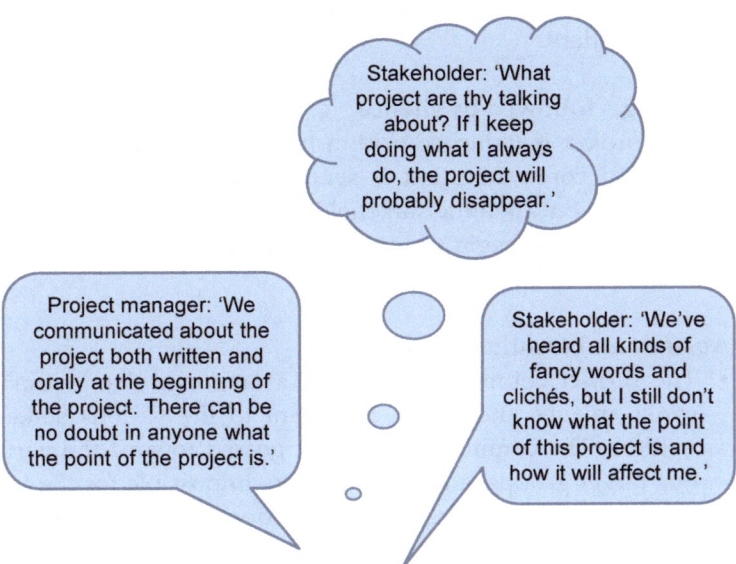

Figure 8.5. Views on the quality of the project communication tend to differ depending on who you ask.

Let's face it, communication is a buzzword. It's something every leader and project manager knows they ought to practice. And it's something everyone involved in the project would say there is too little of. However, you don't necessarily want to communicate more. We are inundated with information every single day – broadcast emails, CC emails, intranet news, newsletters, etc. The amount of information we have to deal with on an everyday basis has never been greater and most of us are kept plenty busy sorting through it all.

Instead, the trick is to send out relevant and targeted communication to the right people at the right times. The following are a few ideas on how to go about this, but first we will take a closer look at the most common mistakes made in project communication.

Silence!
- Why is this project necessary? What will happen? And how does it affect me? Project managers forget surprisingly often to answer these three basic questions for the project stakeholders.

Big Bang – followed by silence
- The project is launched with a huge fanfare and relevant, targeted communication is sent out to the project stakeholders – but then the stakeholders hear nothing for a long time and they begin to wonder whether the project is still active.

Abstract and unsuitable language
- The project communication uses a language that doesn't evoke images and seems irrelevant to the various stakeholders. The communication isn't geared toward the various target groups, and it is therefore impossible for the individual to find the answer to 'How does it affect me?'

Forgetting that dialog is a two-way street
- The communication is only one-way. The project neglects valuable feedback from the stakeholders and thereby risks losing their support, because they feel they aren't being heard.

Actions speak louder than words
- Concurrently with the start-up of a cost-cutting project, the project team spends endless hours in meetings and the CEO replaces an older company car with a brand new Mercedes. When there is no correlation between what you say and what you do, it's easy to lose credibility and support.

The wrong messenger
- What is said is often less important than who says it. It does make a difference whether it is the youngest sales rep or the CEO who speaks out in support of the project and is responsible for following through on it.

Many of the above mistakes aren't the result of ignorance or incompetence. They arise because allocating time for analyzing the communication needs and the subsequent communication tasks isn't a high enough priority. At the beginning of the project, there is a backlog of general planning and analysis tasks, and there is a natural tendency (in both individuals and the corporate culture) to want to 'just get started on the work'.

Communication isn't made a priority

However, considering the difficulties and resistance that many projects run into due to inadequate communication, the question is whether you can afford not to devote time to communication!

In the following, we will take a closer look at three aspects of effective project communication.

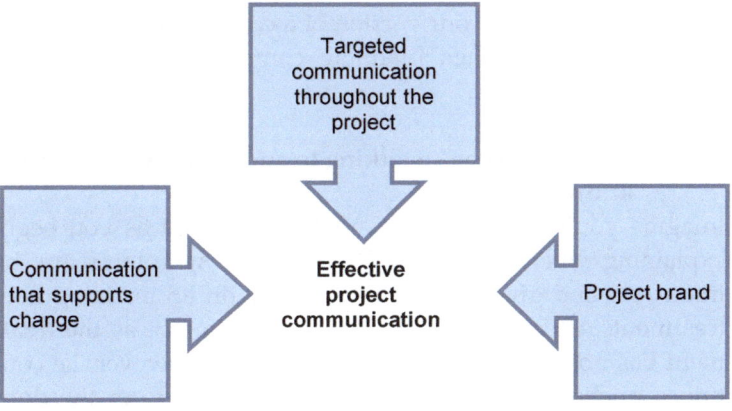

Figure 8.6. Three aspects of effective project communication.

8.3. Targeted communication throughout the entire project

It's important to consider project communication in the earliest planning phase. According to Kotter, you can't motivate people emotionally or intellectually without a high degree of credible communication (Kotter 1997).

Communication to external and internal stakeholders is often only made a priority in connection with a start-up meeting and the obligatory announcements on the intranet or in the staff magazine. This gives everyone a chance to read about the project. But honestly: How often do you read – and form an opinion about – such articles? Every single day, we are flooded with information. Mindless mass communication is therefore rarely enough when you need stakeholders to take a stance – preferably a positive one – on a project. Instead, you need to carefully consider who to target with your information as well as when and how to communicate it.

Section 8.3 is about how to target project communication so it hits home in the individual stakeholder groups. We will present a model for stakeholder communication that helps equip the sender to understand the recipient's expectations and language use.

We also introduce our version of a communication plan for use by the team when planning communication at project start-up.

8.3.1. Know who you're talking to and what they need to know

Imagine you're at a doctor's appointment. Just as you begin explaining where it hurts and what your symptoms are, he interrupts and gives you a long lecture on an amazing new treatment. After a while, you try to cut him off, as the treatment has no relevance for your symptoms. However, he continues unabated and finally gently pushes you out the door with a brochure in your hand containing information on the new treatment. In the waiting room, you see three other patients – all holding the same brochure.

Do you leave with a feeling that you have received the right treatment? Do you feel that your doctor has a genuine knowledge of what's wrong with you? Hardly.

As grotesque as this situation sounds, this is how a great deal of project communication takes place. We forget to think about who we are communicating to and what their needs are.

Think about the target group
In other words, there was not enough consideration for the fact that different stakeholder groups have different communication needs. As the sender, we tend to mistakenly focus only on what we personally think is interesting and important

8.3. Targeted communication throughout the entire project

in our communication. Like the doctor, there is only one treatment, regardless of the patient's symptoms. As a consequence, the communication misses its mark, coming nowhere near the people we are trying to communicate with.

The target group is the group of stakeholders at whom the communication is aimed – and the goal is to hit a bull's eye rather than fire at random. The chance of hitting anyone by 'communicating to everyone' is very small.

Avoid firing at random

The target groups will often be the same as the stakeholders (both individuals and groups) identified by the stakeholder analysis, where you determine who has an influence on and is necessary for project execution, plus how to manage them.

When considering your target groups, you should also include an assessment of what type of discourse to utilize for each group. The discourse is the code (or language) and values that the target group considers important in relation to the topic in question. If you're communicating with senior management, the discourse will most likely focus on the project's earnings, quality and risks. If you're communicating with shop stewards, their primary interest will probably be working conditions. And if your target group is an environmental organization, for example, the discourse might be about sustainability. Thus, the same project needs to be communicated in many different ways, depending on the target group and their discourse.

The right discourse

An example is how the HR department communicates with senior management. Within human resources, there is a long tradition of discourse about human values, keeping the people in focus, professional and personal development, etc. This kind of 'soft' discourse often doesn't have the same impact in the firm's executive hallways. Progressive HR departments are therefore increasingly using a more financial and bottom line-oriented discourse in their dialogue with upper management. For instance, arguments for implementing a competence development project for the hourly employees might include how it would help the firm retain employees longer, which would save X number of dollars for the firm every year on recruitment, training, etc.

The communication with the hourly employees would, of course, follow a different discourse. Rather than using an argument like savings for the firm to sell the idea of a competence development project, you might focus on the prospects of professional and personal development for the individual and the sense that as an often overlooked staff group, hourly workers are important to the firm, since management is willing to invest time and money in their training.

Does telling a different story and using different arguments for different people mean that you're lying or twisting the truth about the project? Certainly not. The messages communicated to the different target groups should be in line with each other, but the discourse, and thus the messages themselves, should be targeted to the people you are speaking to.

Avoid specialist jargon and consultant terminology

In some cases, you need to communicate with larger target groups that don't use the same discourse. For instance, you may need to draw up a brochure, video or speech targeting not only the 'the man on the factory floor' but also lawyers, economists, IT staff, etc. In such situations, it is especially important to avoid wrapping the communication up in technical lingo, professional jargon, consultant terminology and smart acronyms. Instead, you should express the message clearly and concisely. If you're a lawyer and communicating only to lawyers, then it's appropriate to use the specialist language. However, as soon as you have to communicate to other professional groups or across departments/firms, etc., the language you use needs to be simple and direct.

A model for stakeholder communication

It can be helpful to outline the most important guidelines for communicating with important stakeholders. This can be done by clarifying:

- What the 'trade-off' is, i.e. what we (the project) want from the stakeholders and what the stakeholders want from the project.
- The most effective discourse, i.e. what 'language' and which arguments are appropriate when communicating with this stakeholder.

- Which issue is the stakeholder's primary interest, i.e. the aspect of the project the stakeholder is most interested it.

Here's an example:
The HR department in a large firm wants to initiate a competence development project for the firms' 150 administrative employees. Some of the program will take the form of overnight courses and some will be via e-learning.

The project team has drawn up the following overview, which seeks to provide guidelines for their communication with the most important stakeholders.

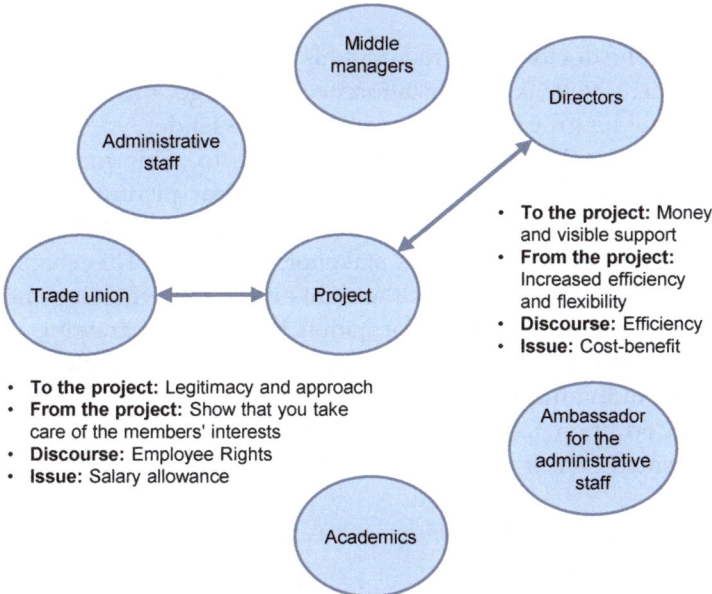

Figure 8.7. A model for stakeholder communication, specifying the trade-off, discourse and most important issues for each stakeholder.

The project team has defined the trade-off, discourse and key issues for some of the most important stakeholders. For example, the project wants the trade union to legitimize and approve the approach, while the union is looking after the interests of its members. The discourse that the communication should follow ought to focus on the future role of the union

Chapter 8. Communication and change

members and pay levels within the agency. The biggest issues in the communication are thus whether the competence boost justifies a pay supplement and whether they will be paid for the extra time spent on the residential courses.

Another example is communication with senior management. Here, the project team is looking for visible support and funding to carry out the project, while the senior management wants increased efficiency and greater flexibility from the administrative staff. The discourse should thus focus on increased service and streamlining workflows. The biggest issue in the communication is whether it is worthwhile to spend money on competence development for administrative staff.

The benefits of using this model for stakeholder communication

Just as the doctor needs to target his treatment to the individual patient, your communication needs to target the individual stakeholder group. This means that, as the sender, you need to determine who you are communicating to. This model for stakeholder communication provides a clear picture of what you should focus on in the communication in order to capture the attention of the various stakeholder groups. This enables the project team to prepare the right arguments when it comes to negotiating, holding information meetings or drawing up written material. It also lets the project team assess which topics the individual stakeholders should be involved in.

In addition to the model for stakeholder communication presented here, it may also be relevant to consider:

- What do the stakeholders already know (via formal and informal channels)?
- What are their biggest doubts about the project? And what are they most excited about?
- Which stories and rumors that are already going around about the project do you need to bear in mind in your communication?

If the target group consists of a few people, you should enter into dialog with them (perhaps do something so revolutionary as to simply ask them!). If the target group is larger, sometimes taking a random sample and posing questions to a few people in the group is enough. A target group can also be very large, spread out geographically and have a need for more valid knowledge. In such cases, you might hold focus groups, send out questionnaires, etc. to map the stakeholders' knowledge and attitudes.

8.3.2. The communication plan

By preparing a communication plan, you can integrate communication in the project. The communication plan should be drawn up at the beginning of the project, for instance in connection with the stakeholder and risk analyses. The purpose is to:

Prepare a communication plan at project start-up

- Stop or minimize resistance to the project
- Create and promote awareness of the project among relevant stakeholders

A good communication plan should consider the following six elements:

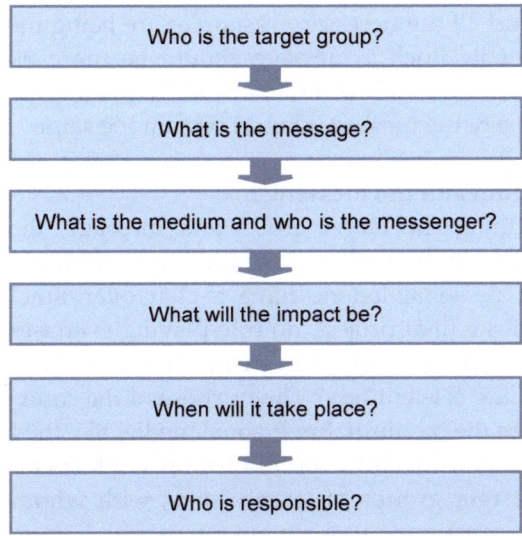

Figure 8.8. The six elements of the communication plan (see also the toolbox).

The six elements are presented in more detail below.

Chapter 8. Communication and change

What is the message for the target group?

The target group and message

Based on the stakeholder and risk analysis, you should identify the most important target groups for the project communication, i.e. who should be communicated to and what they perceive as the advantages and disadvantages of the project. The identification of target groups can be supplemented by the model for stakeholder communication to provide you with a clear picture of the stakeholder.

Then, the message needs to be formulated. The message of the communication should be well-considered. You need to be able to express in a single sentence:

- What is the aha-experience this communication should give the target group? What is the point?

In the communication plan, the formulation of the message shouldn't necessarily be finalized. For instance, a message may be that 'management considers this project to be very important and all the necessary resources are being mobilized to implement it.' Such a message should be more elegant and engaging in the final formulation of the communication, but the essence of the message should remain the same.

The medium and the messenger

After defining the target group and message, the medium needs to be identified: Should you organize kick-off meetings, send out personal letters, have a chat over lunch, display models of the final project, do role-playing exercises, facilitate discussions or café meetings, create alternative screen images or something else entirely? The purpose of the communication determines the medium. Impersonal media, like the intranet or brochures, work well for providing basic information – especially to larger groups of stakeholders, with whom it can be very time-consuming to maintain a personal dialog. However, getting stakeholders to actually change their behavior requires personal dialog and involvement. The messenger is important – who signs the email or initiates the dialog?

The impact

Many projects fail in their communication because they haven't considered what impact the communication should have. What exactly do you want the stakeholders to do differently as a result of your communication?

Awareness, opinion and behavior

- Should they acquire new knowledge?
- Should they change their opinion?
- Should they change their behavior?

Changing opinions and behavior requires a greater effort than being informative. These three items are not simply three steps of a process, with new knowledge automatically leading to a change of opinion, which again results in altered behavior. Just look at the many public campaigns to get people to change their diets or quit smoking. We all know smoking is unhealthy and that too much unhealthy food and not enough exercise causes obesity. A lot of people do consider smoking

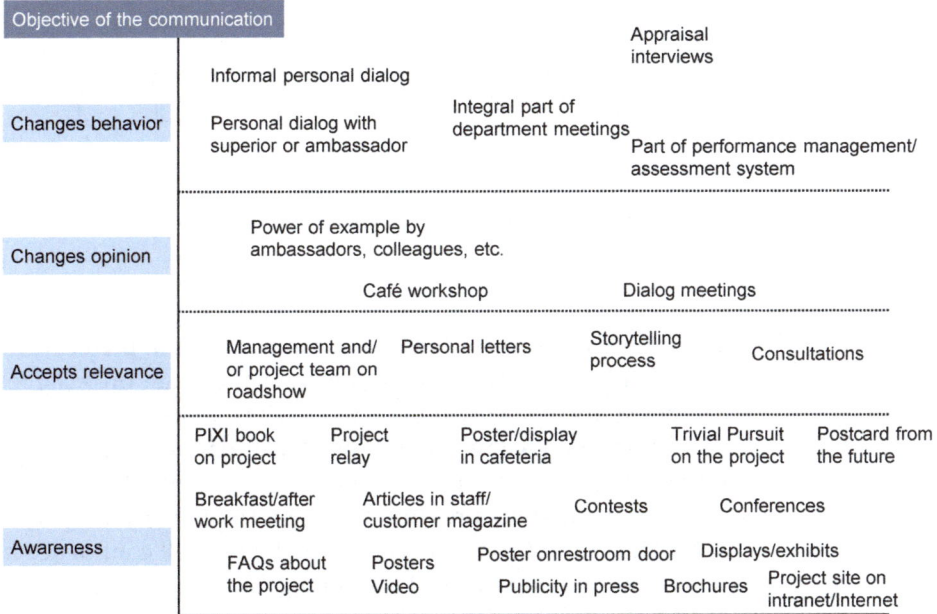

Figure 8.9. Examples of communication activities suitable for creating awareness, communicating relevance, influencing opinions and changing behavior.

unhealthy and try to eat right and get enough exercise. But being aware of an issue and having an opinion about it is not the same as changing your behavior in that area. The same holds true in projects.

The desired impact of the communication among the target group must be clearly stated in the plan and will often serve as a criterion for the success of the communication.

The list of possible activities is endless. Figure 8.9 is a small selection for your inspiration.

Timing

The timing of the communication is crucial. In large projects, communication should therefore be a separate work stream marked with milestones and phase transitions throughout the entire duration of the project, often continuing into the hand-over and operational phases.

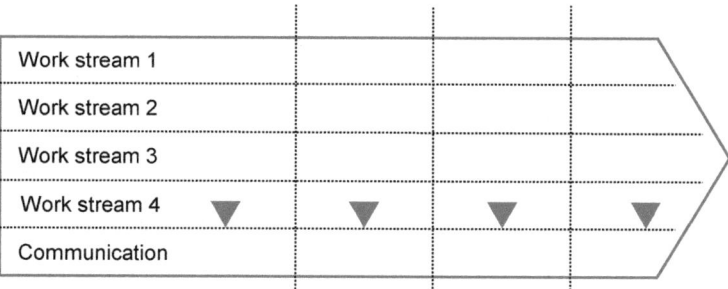

Figure 8.10. Communication should be a separate work stream in the project plan.

The timing of the communication can be difficult; projects are, by definition, uncertain. In organizational change projects, for example a merger of two departments or a cost-cutting round, you often don't know exactly what will happen. Good communication is also knowing when to say you don't know something but will provide more information by a specific date. This type of communication can help instill confidence in the process when you can't give any guarantees about the end result.

Responsibility
Finally, the sixth element in good communication is appointing someone to be responsible for the work stream or for the individual milestones. This tells the team who is responsible for the communication and makes it possible to set clear deadline. If the project requires a lot of written or visual communication, it may be a good idea to bring someone from the communication department onto the project team.

Responsibility for communication

With this type of plan in your hands – and with sound project management with milestone follow-up – you are well on your way to achieving successful project communication.

The complete Communication Plan tool can be found in the toolbox, while selected elements are covered in more detail below.

8.4. Project branding

As the project manager, you need to ensure your project has a clear profile and status within the organization. You need to 'brand' your project. Branding is traditionally associated with products, like Coca-Cola as a brand (i.e. trademark) of soda and Levis as a brand of jeans. Today, branding has taken on a broader meaning and many firms spend impressive sums on corporate branding. Corporate branding deals with how companies express who they are and what they represent in relation to their stakeholders. It's about identifying the characteristics that make the firm unique for use in public relations. The brand is recognizable by the consumers and the employees, allowing them to form an opinion about the firm's unique values (Holten Larsen 1998). In short, it's about creating positive expectations of the firm among the stakeholders. For firms, a strong brand makes it easier to:

The project needs a clear profile

- Capture and retain attractive customers, thereby making it easier to sell your products/services – often at a higher price than competitors with much weaker brands.
- Attract qualified employees and managers.
- Boost current employees' pride in their firm.

- Improve the likelihood of positive publicity in the press.
- Develop a 'resistance' to scandal.

Why brand your project?

Branding isn't just relevant for firms, it's also useful for large-scale projects. A clear project brand is important for:

- Securing support in the line organization.
- Positioning the project in the struggle against other projects for staffing, funding and the attention of senior management.
- Attracting competent employees to the project. The project manager needs the project to seem interesting, with an aura of exciting challenges and of future success.
- Motivating the project team and creating an identity and sense of pride about being part of the project. You need to be able to communicate the 'meaning' of the project. Not really knowing or having any interest in the project you spend most of your time on can be quite demotivating.

A clear project brand is especially relevant for organizational change projects. The expectations of the project influence the stakeholders' openness to change. The stakeholders are more willing to change if they feel certain the project will actually be carried out and be a success. However, if they or their colleagues or leaders display any reluctance ('Let's wait and see if anything actually happens') or skepticism ('They'll never succeed with such a dramatic change'), then it can be extremely difficult to convince the stakeholders to embrace the change wholeheartedly.

The project manager should be the 'stage director' and make sure to brand the project, i.e. focus on the positive pictures, views, experiences and expectations that the various stakeholders associate with the project. Everyone has their own view of the project; you need to make sure that everyone views the project the way you want them to. That is branding.

Credible branding starts from the inside

Before considering specific ways to brand your project, it's important to understand what makes a brand credible.

For a brand to be credible, there must be consistency between the project's or the firm's external image – what is known in rhetoric as the ethos – and the internal culture and strategic visions.

This can be illustrated as follows:

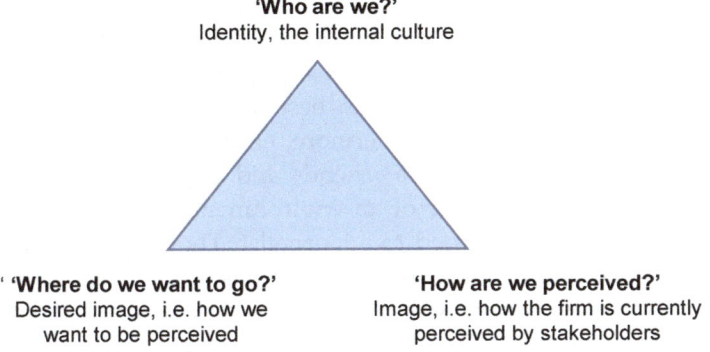

Figure 8.11. Credibility requires consistency between what you say, what you do and how you are perceived. Inspired by Petersen 2002.

The desired image is expressed in the management's strategy: How do you want to be perceived? Taking that as your point of departure, a number of initiatives can be launched: advertisements, profile brochures, website, conferences, etc. In order for the communication to be credible, i.e. to actually achieve successful branding, there must be consistency between what you say and what you do. For example, you can't base a brand on inadequate products or unethical actions.

An example of a Danish firm that has taken a targeted approach to branding is the food ingredients firm Danisco, which was once known for producing sugar, frozen potatoes and methylated spirits. Since 1999, they have streamlined their business by means of, among other things, divestment of their alcohol factories and a number of other subsidiaries. Today, their primary focus is on food ingredients. In 2011, Danisco was acquired by DuPont. It is a tribute to the strength of the brand that it's activities are still carried out under the Danisco name. Danisco's clear strategy is to be a modern, innovative firm. Thus, they seek to brand themselves as a modern and innovative firm as embodied in their slogan 'First you add knowledge'.

The brand is credible because the stakeholders can see a direct correlation between what Danisco says and what Danisco does/is. This applies to all stakeholders, from employees and managers, to investors, journalists and ordinary consumers. In branding, the employees represent a very important stakeholder group, as they can best determine whether you are/do what you say. Furthermore, employees communicate outside the firm, talking to friends and acquaintances. They may even be a member of an environmental organization, a political party or married to a journalist. The image they present in more informal communication has a significant impact on how other stakeholders perceive the firm's formal communication. One way Danisco sought to promote understanding of the new brand was by having all 8,000 employees complete an e-learning program, which explained the background of the brand.

Far too many projects live a quiet life – and then die

As the example shows, branding processes are often extremely comprehensive. Few projects need such a large-scale branding process. However, there is a need for credible branding (or to use a more low-key term, *profiling*) of the project. Far too many projects live a quiet life – with the result that they die or fail because they didn't garner the necessary support and confidence.

Projects need to brand themselves and fight for attention in an over-communicated organization and an over-communicated society. Some projects need both internal and external branding. This includes megaprojects, like the building of a large bridge, a new subway line or an airport. But projects of a smaller scale can also benefit from working consciously with the perceptions of external stakeholders. This is especially true of projects that are dependent on political support or the support of the citizens/public-sector.

As mentioned, internal branding within the organization is relevant for large-scale projects, especially projects involving a degree of change, such as a new HR policy, a new IT system or moving to new headquarters.

What concrete actions can you, as the project manager, take if you want to work with branding your project?

You can start with the credibility triangle and ask:

'Who are we?' Why has this particular project been launched? What is our identity? Much of this is included in the project's purpose, but should be supplemented by dialog within the project team. If many project participants are involved, you might select a few and conduct interviews.

'How are we perceived?' This is about listening and asking questions. What rumors are going around among the stakeholders about the project? What are their expectations?

'Where do we want to go?' How do we want to be perceived? What should the stakeholders say about the project? This focusing process should be carried out by the core project team and in dialog with the steering committee and/or project owner.

A simple way to initiate the project profiling process is to have a recognizable project name and logo. You should also tell an engaging story about the project.

Projects tend to have names that are too anonymous and meaningless – or simply have no name at all. The project name should be easy to remember and should signify the impact the project seeks to have. Which sounds better?

A memorable project name

'Revision of quality manuals with a view to optimizing quality assurance procedures'

or

'Quality that moves us forward'?

Or how about:

'Analysis of workflows aimed at customer service'

vs.

'The Happier Customers Project'.

The next time you're in the cafeteria and someone asks you what your project is about, you should be able to explain what you're doing in just a few words – to make it easier for the other person to remember it. Why bother explaining it, if your recipient can't remember what you've said?

We legitimize with our minds, but act with our hearts

In addition to giving the project a recognizable name and logo, you should also tell an engaging story that can be communicated to the project's various stakeholders. Engaging stories that people can identify with are an effective supplement to the facts and endless PowerPoint slideshows that rationally and logically argue in favor of the project.

Stories speak to both the mind and the heart, thereby covering all three types of appeal dictated by classical rhetoric. Fafner refers to the importance of winning the recipient's good will (through ethos), arguing convincingly for truth (through logos) and evoking emotions (through pathos) (Fafner 1995).

Rolf Jensen's main thesis in his book *The Dream Society* (Jensen 1999) is that we as consumers act based on our emotional needs. Consumers buy with their hearts – not their minds. For this reason, the majority of branding is achieved by appealing to our emotions and dreams. In the context of project work, this means an increased focus on the project's vision and on making the project attractive so that an engaged stakeholder will feel inclined to 'borrow' the identity, in much the same way consumers do when buying a specific brand.

The strength of stories lies in their ability to:
- Sell your messages better.
- Bring the project's purpose and deliverables to life, making them relevant to the stakeholders.
- Combine facts and emotions about the project. When we accept something new or change our behavior, we don't do so based solely on rational arguments. We are also guided by our emotions. Does this project seem like a good idea? Do I like this idea? Can I see myself reflected in what they're talking about?

However, few firms systematically use storytelling as a communication tool, because we are generally trained to argue rationally for our points of view and we're afraid that it will be misconstrued as 'trivial' if we involve emotions and personal commitment.

According to David Snowden, who has conducted research in storytelling for many years, one of the most important reasons for communicating in stories is that it's a simple way to present complex and abstract thoughts and make them easier to remember. We often overcomplicate simple ideas, according to Snowden, who also criticizes consultants and managers at management courses for wrapping up their story in buzzwords and fancy expressions (Snowden 1999).

Tell an engaging story

There are a wide range of templates for developing a good story and for choosing which players to include in the story to make it interesting. The following are a few useful rules of thumb:

- Keep the language stimulating. Use metaphors and imagery.
- Get all the details right. This increases the credibility of the story.
- Make sure the point/message is clear.
- Having a hero and a villain in the story, as well as a prize worth fighting for, adds intensity (just like in fairytales, where the prince has to vanquish the dragon in order to get the princess and the keys to the kingdom).
- It can be a good idea to use the actant model and give the 'story' a villain, a victim, a hero and a helper.

If the story seeks to promote understanding of the project among a broad stakeholder group, you should include the following four questions in the structure of the story and/or the other project communication:

1. **The burning platform:** Why is change urgent?
2. **The vision:** Where are we going?
3. **The path to get there:** How and when will it take place?
4. **Personal consequences,** i.e. everyone affected by the project – especially those who are involuntarily affected – needs to know: How do the changes affect me/my department/my team? What will I have to do differently than I do today?

Structure the story based on four central questions:

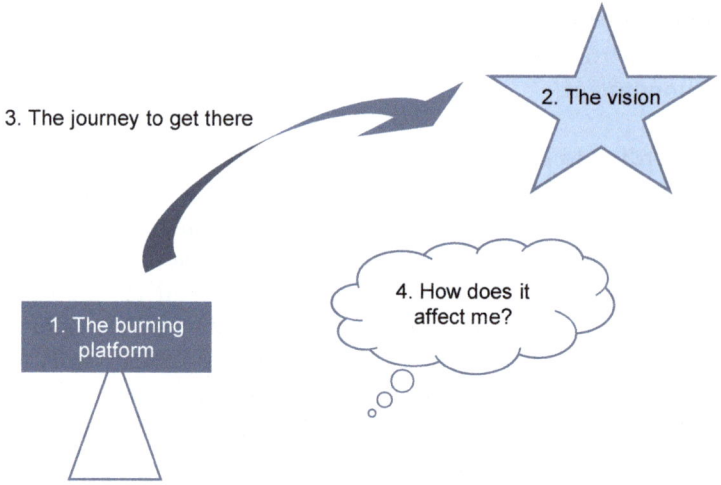

Figure 8.12. Template for structuring the story about the project.

The burning platform is made up of the arguments for the inadequacies of the current situation. Why is it necessary to implement the project? If the stakeholders can't see the urgency, you will have trouble convincing them to 'buy' the project.

For example: a medium-sized Danish bank wanted to launch a new strategy and, subsequently, a series of projects. They formulated the burning platform: 'We need to concentrate more on the areas where we make money and on how we can do an even better job. Otherwise we risk being acquired by one of the aggressive Swedish banks currently looking to enter the Danish market.'

The vision is the image of the desired future. The vision should be attractive and should motivate as well as coordinate our actions for achieving the objective. The vision should also signify the level of ambition for the change.

Going back to the bank example, they produced a video to present the vision. In the video, we see what it would be like to be an employee and customer at the bank in four years' time, after the implementation of the strategy.

The path to get there: Once a stakeholder understands the urgency of implementing the project and what the outcome should be (not in terms of deliverables, but in terms of value and vision), they need more specific information about how we get from A to B. As Daryl Conner points out, change is a process of moving from something known to something unknown. In the course of this process, we develop new attitudes, opinions and behavior, which makes it possible to achieve the vision. However, the process can also produce a fair amount of uncertainty, conflict and stress, for we always want to maintain control, according to Conner (Conner 1993). Thus, the communication should also tell us how. Here, you may pick and choose among the deliverables – just make sure to adapt the degree of detail to the target group. You should always consider whether it is something they need to know or whether it is in some way 'obligatory' information.

How does it affect me? This level isn't necessarily something the project manager/team or project owner should – or can – communicate. Often, the individual department manager or team leader is best equipped to conduct this dialog with the individual employee or employee group. But even though the project manager is not the one carrying out the communication at this level, she still bears the full responsibility.

Storytelling doesn't necessarily have to be long stories about every detail of the project. It can also be used in a more traditional manner to spice up an article and capture people's attention. For instance, you can begin with a personal experience to illustrate why the project is so important. Or you can lighten up a list of dry facts and figures about the project by also sharing colleagues' and customers' reactions to it. What the customers think is a strong argument, especially for senior management.

Storytelling can be an effective tool for branding the project, as long as it is used with respect. It is also important to strike a balance between creating positive expectations of the project and avoiding a declaration of victory before the battle has been won. Just as we pointed out in connection with corporate branding, it's important to maintain consistency between what you say and what you do in storytelling.

Are there rumors about the project? Another important aspect is the stories or rumors that are already going around about the project. For example, a Danish ministry set out to merge all of its agencies, councils and boards into a single organization. The aim was to create a strong identity for the organization and ensure the same procedures and high degree of quality throughout the entire organization. As a result, employees and managers would be able to move around freely within the organization – regardless of whether they were employed in a department, a council or some other part of the organization. However, the many different employees and managers were not given enough information about why, when and how. As a result, they started calling it 'the lowest common denominator' project, as rumor spread that the organization was to be unified according to the lowest common denominator in order to centralize power. All future information communicated by the project team and management was thus interpreted based on this story. The moral of the story is: if you don't consciously assign the roles in your story, the employees may end up adopting the role of 'victim' and thinking of the project as the 'villain'.

8.5. Communication that supports change

Resistance should be predicted and managed Organizational change projects tend to meet resistance; and we often hear that there are always certain people or groups who will be resistant to change. However, in our experience, this generalization is unfounded. People or groups are not by definition resistant to change, but they can be resistant to this particular change or the way the change is being implemented and communicated.

Resisters can be difficult to convince – often because they believe they are doing what's right for the firm, their department or their team. Think about a situation where you decided to oppose something: Seen from your point of view, your resistance was, of course, based on rational arguments and common sense. And yet, when others resist your project, is your initial reaction that they lack the will to change?

On the basic principles of change, Daryl Conner (Conner 1993) writes:

8.5. Communication that supports change

- All change has a cost
- But not changing also has a cost
- We only change if it costs less than not changing

Individually or in groups, we all subconsciously weigh the advantages and disadvantages associated with accepting – or not accepting – this change. And we only choose to change if we see more advantages than disadvantages to accepting it.

Arguments for or against change are rarely rational. Perhaps we don't like the project manager, or we think we'll lose prestige within the organization if we agree with those launching the idea. Maybe we feel insecure about the new situation. There are an infinite number of factors that influence how we handle every single change we're confronted with.

As an individual, you receive all kinds of recommendations to change your daily routines. Not just in relation to changes in the workplace as a result of projects, but also messages from authorities encouraging us to quit smoking, cut back on salt, eat five portions of fruit and vegetables a day, sort our trash, etc. According to sociologist Henrik Dahl (Dahl 1997), the sender of such messages often problematizes something that the recipient did not previously view as a problem. This means that behind the many innocent suggestions lies a colossal challenge. What we're actually asking you is: Have you considered changing your entire lifestyle?

Have you considered changing your entire lifestyle?

Changing habits requires energy and disrupts our lives. In such situations, simply providing information and arguments has no effect, as you are just sending a message that threatens too great a disruption to the recipients' world and their view of things, at worst resulting in their complete rejection of the message. Festinger, in his theory on cognitive and emotive dissonance from the mid-1950s, demonstrated that the recipient either rejects a message she completely disagrees with or attempts to find arguments that enable her to rationalize her current behavior despite the new message. For example, in response to the message 'Smoking harms your fetus', a person might think, 'But my mom smoked 20 cigarettes a day while pregnant with me and I turned out just fine.'

As a project manager, it is important to be aware that suggestions of even relatively minor changes to the stakeholders' behavior may meet resistance. Thinking of change as a fence to be climbed over (it actually takes both courage and energy to change), you will often see three groups:

- Enthusiasts: They hear about the fence challenge and immediately run right up to it and climb over without thinking twice.
- Resisters: This group stands in front of the fence, looks at it from all angles, discusses the pros and cons and finally agrees that it's a bad fence – the materials are poor quality, the construction is not optimal, it looks like similar fences that didn't last, etc.
- Doubters: This group sits up on top of the fence, uncertain about whether they want to jump down on the other side or climb back to the side they came from. They are waiting to see which group 'wins'. Will it be the resisters or the enthusiasts who ultimately experience the most advantages and fewest disadvantages? They base their choice of side on what appears to be the safest decision in the long run.

Figure 8.13. Three approaches to change: Enthusiasts, Resisters and Doubters.

Resistance has many faces and appears in many degrees – both out in the open and hidden from view. An example of open resistance is protest/crisis meetings among the staff about the 'moving' project's new proposal for open-plan offices (where 98 percent of the plan has been decided by the CEO and can't be changed). Open resistance can also take the form of complaints from the managers about the fact that the new quality assurance manual drawn up by the 'Quality' project has no basis in reality, but instead makes life more difficult for everyone.

Open and hidden resistance

Hidden resistance often represents a greater danger to the project than open resistance, in part because it isn't always detected (especially if you have forgotten why you have two ears and only one mouth) and in part because dealing with it is much more difficult. Resistance will often be hidden from the project manager and senior management if the stakeholder feels that pointing out any problems, voicing criticism, etc. wouldn't make any difference anyway. This is often seen in firms where the culture is characterized by mistrust and fear.

Hidden resistance is generally discovered late in a project or after the project has been completed and the operational phase has begun. For example, a new filing system that nobody uses even though everyone had the opportunity during the project to share feedback with the project team, read information on the intranet and participate in a large information meeting held in the cafeteria.

Bring the resisters out of hiding
Daryl Conner (Conner 1993) points out that people who are successful at implementing change are able to get stakeholders to express their resistance. They bring the resisters out of hiding. This has several advantages. First, it lets you enter into dialog with them on how you might rectify what they consider problematic. Second, it often defuses some of the tension when the resister feels listened to by management or the project team (and by her other colleagues, to whom she is also in opposition).

Some ways you can get stakeholders to express any resistance they may feel include:
- Involve them in the project organization, for instance as a hearing committee. However, take care to avoid hearing committees where all the resisters are gathered together and the project team is shot down no matter what they propose.
- Maintain direct contact, where the project team/project manager actively seeks out the resister(s). An informal chat often has a stronger impact than a formal meeting.
- Hold meetings where you encourage the expression of constructive criticism, for example by means of resistance to change mapping (see below and the toolbox).
- Participate in online forums where people can ask questions and express their opinions – possibly anonymously.

What's most important – and most difficult – is establishing a culture around the project, demonstrating in words and action that feedback is welcome and taken seriously. However, this doesn't mean that the project blows in whatever direction criticism takes it this week. It's important that you make clear what is open for discussion and what isn't.

Resistance to change mapping

Change requires someone to change their behavior. The question is who?

Resistance to change mapping is a concrete tool serving two functions:

- It helps shed light on resistance and doubt.
- It makes clear what the cost of change is. All change has a cost. The question is who will have to pay.

Because this tool requires dialog and a facilitator, it is suitable for use at meetings with people who feel held hostage by the project.

In resistance to change mapping, the people affected by the change and the project team/management work together to list the advantages and disadvantages of the situation as it is today and as it will be in the future after completion of the project.

People who speak out in favor of the project (management, the project team) often only focus on all that doesn't work in

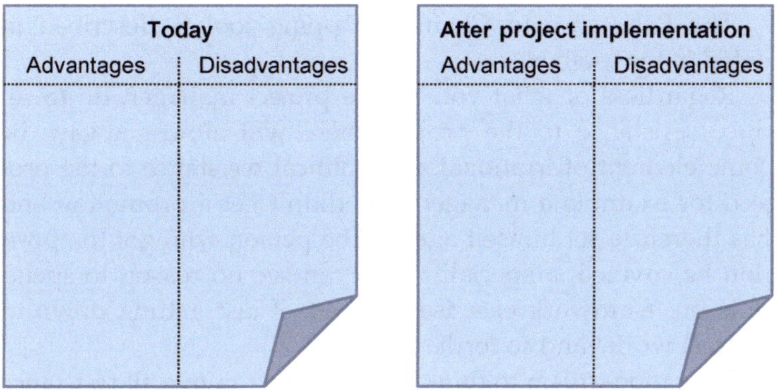

8.5. Communication that supports change

Today	
Advantages	Disadvantages

After project implementation	
Advantages	Disadvantages

Figure 8.14 Resistance to change mapping clarifies the cost of change.

today's situation, i.e. the burning platform, and all the positive aspects of the future situation, i.e. the vision. In contrast, the people affected by the change will often see the advantages of the current situation (you know the system, have established routines with colleagues, etc.) and the disadvantages of the future situation (extra time for training in the system, teething troubles in the system, new routines, high development costs, etc.). The people affected by the change will feel that they are losing the advantages they already have and gaining the disadvantages they perceive in the future system. This tends to make them blind to the disadvantages of the current system and the vision of the future system.

The purpose of this exercise is to let everyone air their frustration so that it doesn't fester and come out in other situations, such as in the cafeteria and the copying room. Another purpose is to clarify the cost of the change and assess whether something can/should be done to reduce this cost. Resistance to change mapping often gives rise to new initiatives to alleviate some of the negative aspects of the change, for instance training activities, team building activities, etc.

What matters is that people feel their feedback is being heard and taken seriously by management and the project team. This requires a willingness to listen – without constantly defending your own solution or trivializing the concerns of those affected by the change.

Chapter 8. Communication and change

The Resistance to Change Mapping tool is described in detail in the toolbox.

Regardless of what you, as the project manager, do to reduce resistance to the project, there will almost always be some element of irrational and political resistance to the project, for example a manager who didn't get a promotion and has therefore set himself against the person who got the position he coveted, a specialist who can see no reason to spend time on 'teamwork exercises instead of just getting down to the real work,' and so forth.

It's a pipe-dream to think that you can remove all resistance – just as conducting a risk analysis can't eliminate all risks. But with the right communication and involvement, you can reduce or remove a significant share of the resistance and thereby boost the project's chances of success.

You have an obligation to equip those who speak on behalf of the project

Who besides you speaks on behalf of the project? When carrying out organizational change projects that affect the entire organization, it's important to think about the line organization and communication. According to Kotter (Kotter 1997), a common trait of all successful major change projects is project communication that doesn't just comprise detached, isolated elements, but is part of everyday activities, with managers, middlemanagers and senior managers looking at their daily activities through the lens of the new vision. You want managers and staff to have your project at the front of their minds, to remember it and talk about it as they do their work on a daily basis.

The line management

Good change communication takes place both centrally and locally

Top management should spearhead the project – provided it is a project of a certain nature and importance. When the project is launched, top management should visible display their unequivocal support for the project. Even more importantly, they should have the project top of mind and incorporate it into their other communication in many different forums. Top management should be provided with the metaphors, images and stories to help them communicate their visions and objectives with the project to the stakeholders. But having top management communicate about the project isn't enough. In organizational change projects, 80 percent of top management's communication should be aimed at middle management to get them involved and take ownership of the change process.

You need to use a so-called central/local strategy (Petersen 2002). This strategy combines 'central' communication (mass communication) with 'local' communication (face-to-face communication within the individual department/team). The following are examples of central and local communication (Petersen 2002):

Central	Local
Staff magazine	Department meetings
Meeting of entire organization with senior management	Seminars
	Employee interviews
Intranet	
Brochures	

Figure 8.15. The central/local strategy emphasizes the importance of combining mass communication with personal communication in the local environment (Petersen 2002).

Centrally within the firm, management communicates the burning platform and vision and establishes confidence in the result. At the same time, you can hang up flyers in the cafeteria, while in the staff magazine and on the intranet you can read about the project and the change process that is taking place. But this central communication needs to be combined with local efforts. Employees want to hear important messages from their immediate superiors, i.e. the middle managers and front-end managers. They have daily contact with the people who will be implementing the change process and are the only ones who can answer the question: 'How does it affect me?'

The middle and front-end managers are the ones who will ensure the changes actually take place. They need to be equipped to translate top management's messages about the project so that they are meaningful to their employees. Helle Petersen points out that 'pass-the-buck communication' is very common among firms: 'Yes, but I did inform my staff about the new project'. Pass-the-buck communication is inspired by soccer, where players simply pass the ball back and forth without really doing anything with it and without focusing on the goal. Obviously, this type of play doesn't result in a high goal count.

Instead, you need to be creative with the ball, dribble, assess the positions of the other players, and think a few moves ahead.

The same is often seen in line communication, according to Helle Petersen. Many managers simply pass top management's messages about the project on without 'translating' them and putting them into a meaningful context for the individual employee. We have to cut costs, we should have the best customer service and similar messages from senior management need to be translated. As a manager, you need to enter into a dialog with your employees about what it means for their department and for them as employees. Managers don't mean any harm; it's just that they haven't necessarily been given training in this type of communication. As the project manager, it is your responsibility to equip managers for this dialog, as it is a huge advantage if they can speak on behalf of the project. There are many ways to go about this. For instance, you can draw up a list of Frequently Asked Questions (FAQ) with relevant answers. Or you can design a concept for dialog meetings, providing the managers with guidelines on how to hold meetings about the project, possibly accompanied by material on the project, suggested issues that might be discussed with the staff, etc.

It is vital that the middle managers feel comfortable with the messages. Otherwise they won't be convincing when they pass the messages on to their employees. Petersen points out that middle managers need to be informed well in advance of changes being widely communicated and that they should be informed openly and in detail (Petersen 2002).

Ambassadors in the informal organization – or externally
In many projects, it will also be relevant to find ambassadors for the project in the informal organization. Who has something to say about the project? And how can you get them to speak out in support of the project?

Traditionally, there are three types of communication strategies (Windahl 1992):

- The linear model, where communication is a one-way process.
- Feedback loops, where the sender needs to know the recipient's reaction to the message so that the message can be modified if necessary.
- Network communication theory, which claims that messages are understood better through dialog within the target group rather than as direct communication.

In line with the third approach, the project manager can seek inspiration in experiences from the public health sector, which has worked for many years with communication aimed at changing attitudes and behavior, such as anti-smoking campaigns, HIV/AIDS campaigns, etc.

Research clearly shows that mass communication is an expensive and relatively ineffective way to change attitudes and behavior. In contrast, network communication has proven highly effective. Network communication builds on the understanding that when we choose to change our behavior, it isn't because we saw an ad or read a brochure, but because we are influenced by people we are close to and whom we trust or look up to.

An example is the HIV/AIDS campaigns carried out in Denmark in the late 1990s. The Danish public health authorities changed tactics from past television ads, where celebrities – politicians, actors and others – advocated using condoms, to instead using sharp segmentation to reveal the primary target groups. They included soldiers stationed in Croatia and Bosnia, long-haul truck drivers crossing international borders, and people stationed in Africa. These specific groups were targeted, and 'ambassadors' (also called change agents) were identified in their networks to communicate the message. For example, it wasn't the Board of Health, but the union representatives for the truck drivers who discussed safe sex. This also overcame the significant risk of shutting down all dialog with the truck drivers by sending out brochures explaining the dangers of picking up prostitutes on their trips abroad, as it was usually their wives or girlfriends who opened the mail at home!

Using ambassadors in your communication efforts requires:
- Identification of the right ambassadors and, especially, ensuring that they garner the necessary respect from the target group.
- The sender being able to let go of the message and trust the change agents to translate it into something meaningful to the target group. You should be open to dialog with these ambassadors on how best to communicate the message.

When applying these experiences to organizational change projects, you need to identify ambassadors who are close to the individual target groups. Perhaps the shop stewards? The team leaders? The super users? You also need a strategy for what they will get out of the process. What makes it attractive for an ambassador to speak on behalf of the project? In this regard, it's often a good idea to think in terms of prestige, knowledge, the experience of leading the way, improving the lives of their colleagues, etc. But again, this requires solid project branding. Few people are willing to use their position to speak out on behalf of a project if they think it will be a flop.

Hopefully, the above has brought home the importance of thinking in terms of both formal communication, i.e. mass communication and line management communication, and informal communication, i.e. rumors, storytelling and ambassadors and the importance of making room for expressing criticism.

The formal information channels should be drowned out by the informal

Helle Petersen (Petersen 2002) studied how employees learn what is going on in their firm and found that:

- 10% is obtained from formal information channels
- 90% is obtained from networks and unofficial 'chats' with the boss

This illustrates the importance of not limiting your communication efforts to the formal channels, such as the CEO's speech and articles in the staff magazine and on the intranet. Your communication efforts should include both formal and informal communication, written as well as spoken. It is also important to establish a framework for communication. For instance, concepts for dialog meetings across the firm, organizing consultations, making the project a fixed item on the agenda of the monthly management meetings, etc.

Further, the project team needs to be available and have their feelers out to sense what is going on in the informal organization. What are people saying about the project? Who is on board? Who is against it? And who is on the fence? A wide network is invaluable in this regard. Here, you can also initiate more organized activities, such as focus groups, questionnaire surveys, etc.

According to Jesper Højberg, the perspective from which we view the organization influences the kind of communication we tend to prioritize. One perspective you can take of the organization is the structured perspective as illustrated by the organization chart, or organogram. (For other perspectives on the organization, see for example Gareth Morgan: *Images of Organization*, Sage Publication 1997.)

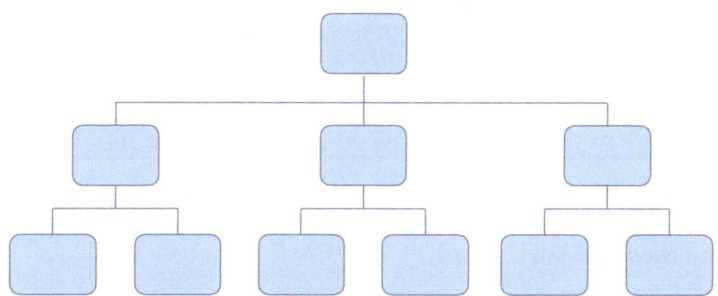

Figure 8.16. If the organization is viewed as a structure, for instance as illustrated by the organogram, then the communication paths are clearly and efficiently laid out.

Here, there is a clearly defined hierarchy, a strict chain of command and one truth (namely that originating from the top of the hierarchy). This is the formal communication that moves from the top down and is repeated at each level. When the organization is viewed from this perspective, the chain of command appears manageable and efficient. From this perspective, top-down communication is suitable. This includes both mass communication – in the staff magazine, on the intranet and via brochures – and line communication, where each level efficiently repeats the messages issued from the top.

But as Helle Petersen's findings show, only 10 percent of employees' knowledge about what's going on in the firm stems from this type of communication. The remaining 90 percent comes from networks and informal 'chats' with the boss. In connection with planning your communication efforts, it is therefore useful to combine the structured perspective with a process perspective.

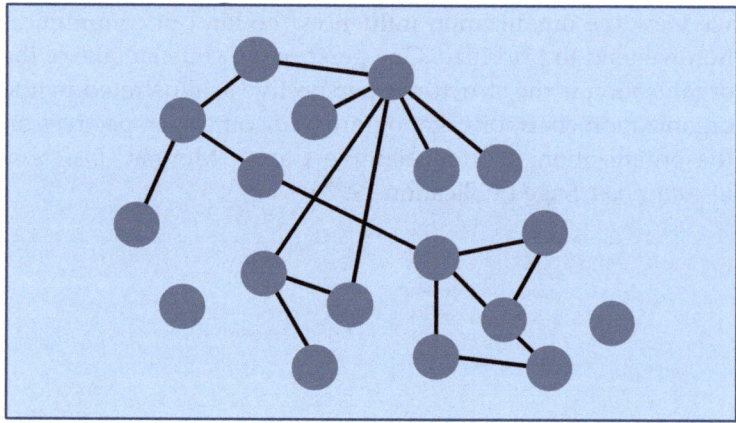

Figure 8.17. If the organization is viewed from a process perspective, the many informal communication paths that criss-cross the organization become clear.

The process perspective reveals the volume of informal communication that criss-crosses the organization. Here, it is not the top-down communication that makes people and events meaningful. Instead, we create meaning via the stories, anecdotes, jokes and rumors about what went well and, especially, what went wrong. With the process perspective, you need to let go of the idea that the project team or management has a monopoly on the 'truth' about the project. Truth is a construction of social reality – unless we are speaking of cold, hard facts, of course. The truth comes to light when opposing interpretations are discussed and negotiated within the organization and the team. Some interpretations are rejected, others are accepted; stances are viewed as meaningful or pointless, true or false, reasonable or unreasonable, etc. This awareness is crucial in connection with projects, as projects live via the stories that are told about them within the organization, and the truths that arise about them.

Backup your words with action
The 'Innovation' project was a large-scale undertaking. Over a period of two years, an international consulting engineering firm sought to aim focus at creating a more innovative culture. They organized creativity courses, exchanged ideas at meetings across departments and countries and funded study trips and courses. The vision for the project was also repeatedly communicated and made very clear by top management. After the first year, they took status and discovered that the progress was too slow in relation to the effort that had been put into the project. The project team and management were disappointed. 'We need to figure out why,' said the project manager. After a number of interviews with managers and employees on all levels of the firm, the reason was clear. An obvious, yet overlooked, reason: the firm's reward system didn't support innovation. For example:

'I can't hear what you're saying, because your actions are speaking louder'

- Salaries were set based on how much the person invoiced and sold, not based on what ideas and products the person contributed.
- Promotions were awarded to 'the safe bets'; recruitment was also based on 'safe bets', i.e. people who resembled those who were already successful in the firm.
- The employee appraisal interviews did not focus on professional development and creativity.

When systems within the organization pull in the wrong direction, it undermines the project. The same also applies when the project team or management/project owner act against the interests of the project. In the same innovation project, many of those interviewed stated that they were afraid to conform to the messages of creativity, as they could see that the safe solutions and stable efforts were rewarded on a daily basis. The firm had a strong 'zero errors culture', with a tendency to view errors as personal failures and where it was unacceptable to make too many errors. Obviously, this did not promote a desire to test wild, new ideas that broke with the standard.

In order to let actions speak louder than words, the project manager and project owner need to maintain an overview and insight. If you're wearing blinders that only let you see your own objective formulation and plan, then you run the risk of overlooking the context within which the project exists. You need to notice any leaders or role models who are acting against the interests of the project. Are there systems that work against the project? Are there other ongoing projects that have an influence on this project? A firm like the biotech company Novozymes measures any inconsistencies between word and deed by means of a process called a say-do gap analysis, where the employees assess the individual manager based on whether they do as they say and promise they will.

It's important to bear in mind the symbolism used within the firm. If the objective of a project is to move employees from smaller offices to large open-plan offices, then the location of the CEO's desk has strong symbolic value. For example, in a large government organization, the managing director led the way in just such a change process, making his floor the first to remove the walls of the smaller office partitions, including the walls to his own elegant office. He then sat – just like everyone else – in the open-plan office. He did, however, have a conference room at his disposal so he could speak privately with employees and managers when the situation called for it.

Who the members of the project team and the project owner are also has a great deal of symbolic value. The project team can comprise the dregs of the firm or people who command respect. The latter would thus signal that 'this project must be important, since they have put these people on the team.'

Employees and managers tend to be influenced more by what they see others do than by what they hear them say at social gatherings or in interviews in the staff magazine.

Communication in the Happier Customers project

The project manager, Lisa, is concerned. On her visits to the departments in various European countries, she has been met with questions and ironic comments. 'Oh, you're still here.' And: 'We thought the Happy Customers project was dead.' The Happier Customers project seems very far removed and verging on non-existent in most people's minds. Neither staff nor management in the various subsidiaries appear to have any interest in it, she realizes with concern.

Lisa decides there is a critical need to increase awareness of the project. This is especially important, as they will soon be implementing the new IT system and workflows in the first three departments, where a great many people will be directly affected by the new modes of cooperation and workflows resulting from the project.

One week later, Lisa convenes a meeting with the four sub-project managers and the communication representative attached to the project. As per Lisa's instructions, the communication representative has already carried out a mini-study to shed light on the degree of awareness of the project. From working with the subsidiaries, they know that questionnaires are too slow and focus groups are too difficult to establish, as the staff is already extremely busy. The communication representative therefore chose simply to visit some subsidiaries and ask the employees and managers she met in the halls and at lunch what they knew about the Happier Customers project.

At the meeting, the communication representative presents her findings, which show that awareness of the project is extremely low among all staff groups. Those who knew about the project had heard about it from colleagues attached to the project or who work in the department where the pilot project is being conducted. The information about the project available on the intranet has hardly been used and it doesn't look much better for the staff magazine, which includes a regular 'Update on the Happier Customers project'.

The team agrees to intensify the process of spreading the message about the project, i.e. promoting the project more to all staff groups.

They already have an idea of how they are perceived. So now they discuss how they should promote the project to increase awareness and instill confidence that the Happier Customers project will produce results and be successful. They decide to focus primarily on the three departments that are to begin implementing the IT system and workflows in two months' time.

The participants start by breaking the staff of the three departments down into target groups. They then complete the communication plan so that the communication representative can use it as a basis to continue her communication efforts after the meeting. Some of the most important target groups are the managers and middle managers in the three departments, as they are responsible for a successful implementation process. Another important target group comprises sales representatives and technical staff who provide support in the customer service and quotation process. They are the 'psychological hostages' in the project and many of their routines will need to be changed as a result of the project. The plan is for these groups to receive training in the IT system and the new customer service concept in the month prior to implementation of the workflows and IT system. It is crucial that these groups have a positive attitude about the project so that they prioritize participation in the training. The communication plan for these groups therefore appears as follows:

At the meeting, the team comes up with the following proposals for measures to promote the project:

- Large posters to be posted in the cafeteria and staff rooms illustrating the project
- Bulletin boards with monthly news from the project
- Management information from the CEO and Director of Sales to the individual professional groups – to be communicated at the weekly meetings
- Information at the departments' monthly staff meetings for all staff groups, where the staff of the pilot department share their experiences with Happier Customers and Lisa presents the plan for implementation within the individual departments.

Who	What	Where	What impact	When	Responsible
Managers and middle managers	The new workflows and IT are ready for rollout and will soon be implemented in your department. You are responsible for ensuring a smooth implementation process	Meetings with project manager, supplemented by written info, including roll-out plan	Assume ownership + feel well-equipped to give 'Happier Customers' your full support in your daily activities	Personal meetings with project managers – no later than 2.5 mos. prior to launch in the individual departments	Liza + sub-project managers
Sales and technical staff	'Happier Customers' is ready for rollout and will make daily life simpler	See list below	Generate goodwill toward this work form and prioritize training in the IT system	To be fleshed out in relation of the individual activities	Communication representative is responsible for materials – Lisa is responsible for meetings

Figure 8.18. Example of measures to promote the Happier Customers project.

- Follow a sales rep and technician working in the pilot department by video or in writing. They are to be followed week by week and talk about what is difficult and irritating and what is positive about the new work form.

The high-energy meeting concludes after a few hours. Lisa rounds off by saying that they have made significant strides in the right direction for improving communication to the departments. They agree to meet again in a week. During the week, the communication representative will draw up a more concrete communication plan and develop proposals for the other target groups they have identified.

8.6. Reflections on project communication

Consider how the communication efforts of your own project are progressing:

- Has a communication plan been drawn up?

- Has the communication plan been converted into a work stream with milestones and delegation of responsibilities?
- Does the project team have a good idea of who the most important target groups are and what they think about the project?
- Have the burning platform and vision been presented to the most important target groups and can they remember them?
- Does the project have a memorable name that conveys what the project is about?
- Does the project have a brand among relevant stakeholders?
- Have senior management, managers and ambassadors been equipped to speak on behalf of the project?
- Is there a forum where it's okay to express resistance?

Leading the Team
Diversity gives strength

Who is manning the bridge?
Leadership is achieving results through
– and with the help of – other people

CHAPTER 9

Leading the Team

The project manager is a leader. She is responsible for getting the project implemented by drawing on the project team's potential – not by doing the work herself.

However, projects often focus solely on the professional challenges, with the project manager selected solely for her specialist knowledge in the area. As such, there is also a tendency for the specialist to end up doing the majority of the work, which can make the other project team members feel there is no real need for their contribution since the specialist always knows better.

The larger, more cross-organizational and interdisciplinary – and thus more complex – projects become, the more important it is to prioritize leadership in project management. The project manager doesn't necessarily have to possess the most specialist knowledge on the project. What matters is the ability to see the potential of the project team members and to ensure the best possible conditions for their work. This means that, as a project manager, you need to master many of the management disciplines used in line management, such as motivating the team, conflict resolution and coaching the project team members to perform their best.

Thus, instead of being the only hard-working player on the field, the project manager needs to be a player coach to achieve a motivated and effective team.

Chapter 9 provides answers to the following questions:
- How do I establish the team?
- What development phases will the team pass through?
- How do I motivate the project team members and keep them motivated?

Challenges

Benefits

- How do I incorporate feedback into my day-to-day project management?
- How do I coach instead of issuing orders and rules?
- How do I deal with conflicts on the team?

Focus The focus of this chapter is on the project manager as the team leader, especially at project and team start-up, as this is where the foundation for the project work is laid.

Tools and methods will be introduced for a number of the 'softer' project management disciplines, such as conflict management, coaching, team motivation and team development. The methods are presented in separate sections, but when they work well in practice, they won't seem like separate methods, but like 'practicing leadership'. The methods should therefore be applied in conjunction with the other tools presented in the preceding chapters. For instance, drawing up the objective breakdown structure in collaboration with the team is also a good way to motivate the team, while having all project participants prepare milestone plans for their respective areas of responsibility in the project enables them to see the mutual dependencies across work streams, increasing the likelihood of on-time delivery and preventing conflicts about missing deliverables.

This chapter is particularly relevant for project managers with genuine leadership responsibilities, i.e. with several working project employees attached to the project over an extended period of time.

Tools
Tool 9.1   Project Team Recruitment
Tool 9.2   The Team Constitution
Tool 9.3   Evaluation and Feedback
Tool 9.4   Planning Workshop

9.1. From management to leadership

An administrator, not a leader The meeting takes place at 6:30 pm in a dark building after most people have gone home. There are major problems with the project's main deliverable. The project owner, an experienced manager in the production division, has brought Implement Consulting Group in to see if we can help get the project back on track. The project has a budget of around $9 million and has been ongoing for 2.5 years. Also in attendance are the project manager, a quiet young man of about 30, and an older manager from another department. The latter was assigned to the project within the last week as a kind of extra resource, explains the project owner.

After the meeting, we make an observation: We have spent an hour and a half listening to the project owner and the newly attached manager list the problems and concerns they have about the primary subcontractor. The project manager didn't say a word, even though she has been working on the project for more than two years and should be the one who possesses the most knowledge about the status of the project.

At every meeting we have attended, the project manager has remained passive and reserved. She has drawn up the right plans, but it seems clear that she lacks both clout and respect within her own organization and in relation to the subcontractor, which is one of many causes of the problems with the main deliverable.

Unfortunately, this is not an uncommon situation. In project management, administration is not leadership.

There may be many reasons why the project manager doesn't assert herself as a leader:

- The internal roles within the organization may not be clearly defined. For instance, the project owner may interfere in the daily work and thereby undermine the respect of the project manager.
- There may be resistance within the organization to assuming the role of leader – either because 'you shouldn't think you're better than your colleagues' or because leadership is a commitment requiring that you don't back down from taking responsibility. This is an especially common attitude in public-sector organizations, where project managers are often called 'coordinators' and similar titles in an effort to play down the fact that the project manager role also includes leadership responsibilities.

- In this case, an inexperienced project manager has been appointed, who lacks the necessary clout – both within the organization and in relation to external stakeholders.

Even among project managers with responsibility for strategically vital projects, we often see that they have very little to no previous project management experience – or even management experience. Mette Amtoft (Amtoft 2000) writes that many organizations use projects as incubators or sometimes as 'testing grounds' for specific types of employees. These employees have a combination of high-powered drive and unrealistically high expectations of their own capabilities. Projects can often be so challenging, so uncertain and loaded with so many obstacles that it may actually take just this type of personality to even dare such an undertaking.

Project managers can be like bumble bees: they fly, even though they shouldn't be able to

Sometimes, things go really well – like the bumble bee that can fly, even though all logic says it shouldn't be able to.

Other times things go wrong, with terrible consequences for the project, the organization and, not least, the project manager, who may come out battered and bruised at the other end.

In the following, we will take a closer look at what characterizes the role of the project manager as team leader.

The challenge of a good leader is to stay two steps ahead while keeping to the background

The world of sports understands the powerful influence a coach can have on a team's performance. If a team performs badly in the big leagues, the coach will often be fired and bringing in a new coach can completely transform a team. Of course, the star players are also vital to the success or failure of the team. But it is the coach who comes up with the strategies, composes the team, knows how to put the potential of the individual players to best use and understands how to motivate each player and the entire team. The project manager – like a good leader – must be able to:

- Stay two steps ahead while keeping to the background.

This requires both self-confidence and faith in the project team members to delegate and distribute responsibility.

This also means that, as a project manager, you don't necessarily have to be a specialist in the project's focus areas. Take, for example, a project to get overweight children to exercise more. A chief physician in children's nutrition and exercise possesses unique knowledge in the field. However, there is no guarantee that a great specialist will make an equally great team leader. The specialist may have a preference for the technical aspects of the project and forget all about the stakeholders or she may be so focused on her own ideas that she ignores ideas from the rest of the team. There is a lot to be said for project managers not being technical specialists, but instead experts in leading specialists and other project employees in the area in question.

For the project manager, the leadership role differs in some areas from being a leader in the line organization, as project managers don't have 'stars on their shoulders'. You are outside the hierarchy of the line organization and have no formal authority, which places extra demands on your abilities to negotiate, motivate, troubleshoot and resolve conflicts. You need to keep your eye on the objective but avoid blinders, as you need good visibility to all sides to see any potential threats to – or benefits for – the project.

A leader without stars on her shoulders

The project manager can't hide. You have to be willing to live an exposed life, as you are never better than your most recent performance. The project manager is directly responsible for achieving the project's objectives and thereby for its success or failure.

Because you're operating outside the normal hierarchy, there are generally no rules for how you should act as a project manager. This means a great deal of freedom, but it can also cause doubts about what is expected of you. Most of the top executives we meet tell us that they want their project managers to push the boundaries for what is permitted within the organization. They expect their project managers to have the guts and will to change 'business as usual', to stick out their necks and to challenge the management.

The project manager should challenge 'business as usual' within the organization

However, when we discuss this in our project manager training sessions, we often hear: 'That's not what management wants from us.' One course participant explained how he tried to get permission to hold a two-day planning workshop, but the project owner rejected the idea, saying that it would be better if they just got started on the work instead of 'sitting in a circle and chatting for two days'. What can you learn from this? First off, this is what the boss is supposed to say. She is challenging the project manager to find out how necessary the workshop is, how well thought out it is and whether it is something she really wants to do. As a project manager, you shouldn't give in, but rather take up the discussion and don't let go of important ideas. You need to be able to argue your case.

Despite all of these challenges, the role of project manager also comes with many positive aspects. Few other jobs have such a clearly defined objective and direction, come with so much responsibility and present so many opportunities for professional and personal challenges.

In the following, we take a closer look at leadership in the role of project manager. Leadership isn't about drawing up budgets, preparing plans and other administrative tasks. Leadership deals with the side of the project manager job that focuses on leading other people, both the project team and the other stakeholders. Leadership takes place when you have 'confrontation time', i.e. when you, as the project manager, interact with the team or the other stakeholders. Here, we will concentrate on team leadership and introduce some of the most important elements you, as the project manager, may need to actively deal with when you make the leap from management to leadership.

9.2. Forming the project team

Project start-up is a crucial time for the project manager

Establishing the project team and getting them started lays the foundation for the project. The start-up phase is therefore a crucial time for the project manager, as a great many of the problems that might turn up later in the project can be traced back to a bad project start-up. The project manager should therefore focus on:

9.2. Forming the project team

- Recruiting the right people to the project
- Creating a close-knit team, both socially and professionally

These two leadership challenges will be the focus of this section.

9.2.1. Recruiting the right people to the project

Many project managers tell us that they don't have any influence on who gets appointed to their project team and that the project participants are sometimes appointed even though they have neither the time nor the desire to participate.

Fighting to get the right people on your team

This is discouraging, as the composition of the team and how and when the members come on board are critical to the success of the project. Consequently:

- The project manager must seek to influence which people are part of the team. Assembling the right team is one of the most important leadership activities.

The project manager shouldn't quietly accept the 'dregs of the firm' on her team. After all, she will be evaluated on the success of the project. It takes assertiveness and perseverance for the project manager to get her will, as well as the courage to be unpopular. It is rarely easy, as you must present arguments in favor of your own project and against the competencies and skills of your own colleagues to the superiors who are attempting to man the project team for you. This also applies when senior management disagrees internally about which employees to allocate to the project and you, as the project manager, know that two of the employees are being considered, not because they are the best people for the job, but because their departments can best live without them. If you don't think they're right for the job, you need to make this clear to management now, not later. If the project gets off track, claiming that you weren't assigned the right people just isn't a credible excuse. In other words, you need to act fast when – or, if possible, before – the project is launched.

Chapter 9. Leading the Team

The project manager should be selected first

In order to have an influence on the composition of the project team, the project manager obviously needs to be selected first. It is the project manager's responsibility to make this happen. And if you experience the opposite, i.e. if the team and the project manager are appointed simultaneously, you must explain to the project owner that it is a bad idea and make sure that you can influence who gets appointed to the project team.

If you already have an idea about who you want on the team, then you have some lobby work ahead of you. As the project manager, you need to sell the idea of the project to the people you want on the team and to their respective bosses.

Composing the team in collaboration with line management

However, the dilemma is often that the project manager doesn't know who the best minds are out in the various departments in the line organization.

In such cases, the project manager needs to collaborate with the relevant line managers to find the right people for the project. The project manager, together with the project owner, should, based on their preliminary impressions and/or analyses of the assignment, also draw up a list of the profiles they need, possibly with job descriptions. It's important to consider:

- Which professional qualifications are needed on the project?
- Which personal skills and abilities are needed?
- Which personality types can solve the assignment – and how do they fit together as a team?

These job descriptions can be used in the discussion with the line management to help them with the initial assessment of who from their department might be suitable for the job.

Job exchange for projects

An in-house job exchange for projects is another approach used by a growing number of organizations. This is where project positions, which employees can apply for, can be posted. The advantage is that it expands the base of potential project employees, so that you don't always draw on the same old guard and run the risk of burnout.

Even though you have recruited the right specialists to a team – based on their professional profiles at least – this doesn't guarantee you a perfect team. An effective, well-functioning project team isn't just a product of the professional expertise of the team members, i.e. qualifications like education, experience, courses, etc., but also of their personal skills, abilities and personalities, i.e. what they each bring to the teamwork.

Specialist expertise isn't everything!

Take, for example, Kimberly, who always contributes lots of good ideas and loves to turn things on their head – even when the deadline is only a week away. Or David, who is a guarantee against jumping to conclusions, because he always points out the need for more information and detailed analysis. Or Bob, who contributes to a positive atmosphere on the team and calls attention to any problems among the members or if someone is stressed, etc.

Each person contributes to the team with specific preferences and competences. It is important that the project manager has the opportunity to take these differences into consideration and not just recruit participants based on who is available or their specialist qualifications.

The project manager should always conduct individual 'job interviews' with the potential project participants, regardless of whether they are being recruited externally, in-house via a job exchange, recommended by line management or selected by the project manager, herself. There are three reasons for this:

Conducting 'job interviews'

First, it ensures that you get project participants you can work with and who have the right attitude toward the project. Can the candidate be flexible if the project requires overtime up to deadlines? Does the candidate have empathy and is she a good listener, if the project requires a good deal of contact with difficult stakeholders? A personal interview gives you the opportunity to meet the candidate and assess whether she supplements the rest of the team and is suitable for the assignment.

Second, job interviews help clarify expectations. The project manager is responsible for discussing the expectations she has of the project participant/project team, just as it gives the project participant an opportunity to express her expectations regarding the project work and the project manager. The project participant has the right to know why she has been selected for this project. Reconciling expectations can also help prevent misunderstandings and conflicts when the project gets started, as you have already discussed your mutual expectations.

Third, the interview should give the project manager a clear idea of why the project participant wants to participate in the project. What about this particular project drives and motivates the participant? Is it a break from everyday responsibilities? A special professional challenge? The prospect of working with specific people? Or something else entirely?

Drawing up resource agreements   The final element you need to be aware of in connection with recruiting project participants is drawing up a resource agreement with every single team member and their superiors. The resource agreement stipulates how much time the individual participant is expected to spend on the project over a specified period of time and, especially, which sub-deliverables that person is responsible for.

For example: Debby is a member of the 'Boost Our Earnings Project' and is assigned to the project for 30 percent of her time from February 1 to June 1 in the current year. During this period, she is expected to contribute the following deliverables: ...'

The resource agreement is primarily a clarification of expectations between the project manager, on the one hand, and the project participant and her daily manager, on the other. The agreement also protects the individual project participant, as it specifies to the individual's manager how much time the project participant will have to take off from her daily responsibilities. If the participant usually works 100 percent of the time on operational tasks and is allocated to the project for 30 percent of the time, then the project participant and her manager will need to find someone else to attend to the remaining 30 percent of her ordinary operational responsibilities.

Resource agreements are also very useful for the project manager as documentation of what was agreed at the beginning of the project if problems should develop with retaining project resources.

When recruiting the project participants, the project manager has thus:

- Been appointed before the rest of the team has been formed
- Identified the project participants in collaboration with line management
- Conducted job interviews
- Drawn up resource agreements

These four measures will help your project get off to a good start and lay a solid foundation for the future work.

And in the not-so-perfect world?

Unfortunately, the world is far from perfect, and we often get appointed as project managers to projects that are already started, half-way completed or need to be restarted. There can be a good deal of history and many decisions may have already been made.

If the world isn't perfect, the project manager needs to restart the project and do what should have been done in the beginning:

- Assess what each team member contributes based on professional qualifications and roles on the team, compensating for any deficiencies or overlaps.
- Conduct 'job interviews' with the individual project participants and reconcile expectations.
- Draw up resource agreements.
- Bring the team together and work on (re)planning the project plan, OBS and various other analyses.

9.2.2. Creating a close-knit team

Now you have assembled the right team, or at least reconciled expectations with your team.

However, a newly formed team is rarely a close-knit group or high-performance team from the outset. The next step in the establishment phase, then, is for the project manager to get the group to feel and work like a team. To do this, the project manager needs to consider how the team develops and which activities can be initiated to bring everyone closer together. Therefore, in the following we will take a closer look at:

- The team development process
- Various team building activities

The team development process

When we think about how teams develop, most people have probably experienced the awkward, overly polite atmosphere that develops when you bring a team together for the first time, regardless of whether it's at work, in private or in a learning context. Many have probably also experienced the major disagreements that can develop on a team: For example, what do you do about a participant who is freewheeling and not doing his fair share of the work? Should everyone be asked for their input on everything, or is it okay that one team member is more dominant? Luckily, most have also experienced how great working in a team can be. Like when everyone pitches in and you successfully meet a tight deadline, when a difficult victory has been achieved against all odds, etc.

A good deal of research has been conducted on group dynamics and how cooperation within a group and the sense of being a team changes over time. It is a good idea for the project manager to be acquainted with this field of knowledge as it will equip you to:

- Better understand your team's reactions
- Adapt your management style to the situation
- Establish an effective team fairly quickly

The following model for group development is inspired by Lenéer Axelson. We use it here, as it provides a good framework for the concrete team-building activities for promoting team spirit, which we will present later in the chapter.

According to Lenéer Axelson, groups pass through five phases.

The phases describe what happens in the relations between the team participants and their perception of being part of the team. The phases are, of course, an over-simplification and some of the nuances are lost. However, the model still provides a useful and manageable framework for assessing and working with the development of your team.

9.2. Forming the project team

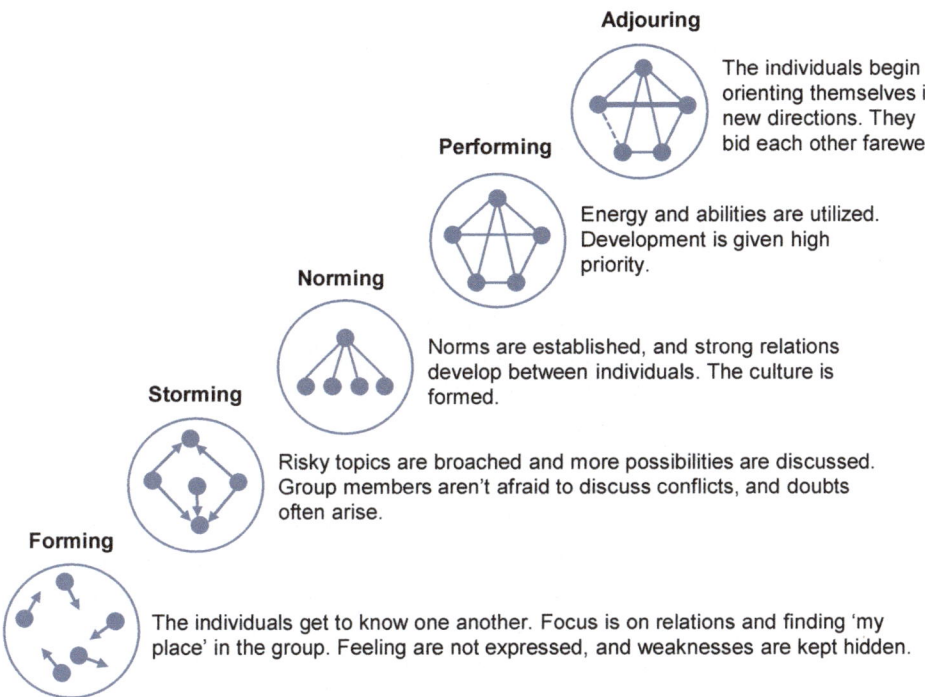

Figure 9.1. The phases of group development. Source: Lenéer Axelson 1995.

As a project manager, you want a high-performance team from Day 1, that is you want them to be in the performing phase. However, according to Lenéer Axelson, the performing phase can't be achieved by focusing solely on the work tasks from Day 1. It's simply not possible to skip the preceding phases, although they can be shortened and simplified significantly by exercising careful project management. Let's take a closer look at the five phases.

Forming – the team meets

Forming

The early days with a new team are a kind of honeymoon period. We seek to show ourselves to best advantage, communication is polite – verging on the superficial – and we are hesitant, appeasing and avoid calling attention to differences of opinion and conflicts. Our primary focus is on being accepted by the others and attaining social status within the team.

We assess which individuals or alliances we will lean toward and interpret what the project manager, in particular, does and says as an expression of the kind of project manager she is. The participants will often view the team as perfect, but will also wonder about the objective.

What does this mean for the management of the project?
The team's need for visible support is strong, and the project manager's efforts in the forming phase will be crucial for how the team members work together. The project manager is the nucleus of the communication in this phase, as she possesses the most knowledge about the project at the current time. The project manager must therefore communicate clearly and share her knowledge so that the project participants can learn enough about the project and their future tasks to enable them to work independently with the project and communicate with the other team members without constantly having to consult the project manager. In addition to communication, the project manager should also focus on involving the team in the planning of the many elements of the project. If you don't do this, you run the risk of the participants not assuming ownership of the project, but instead feeling less committed to the work that needs to be done.

In the forming phase, the project manager also has a need to establish herself in the role of project manager. You should be conscious of how you 'present' yourself, for instance at the earliest team meetings.

Concrete activities
A clearly defined framework, team building and planning that promotes involvement are the keywords for the activities the project manager should employ in the forming phase.

A well-defined framework can be established by the project owner and possibly also other members of top management or customers, clearly explaining to the team their needs for the project. One way is to invite the project owner and a customer to share their expectations. A well-defined framework also means that the project manager takes responsibility for chairing meetings, planning a set schedule for team meetings, clearly communicating about requirements, project deadlines, etc.

In this phase, the project manager might also consider whether the project team should have a dedicated project office/space to allow the team members to sit together. The aim is to increase the opportunities for close communication within the team and reduce the risk of interruptions from the participants' own departments.

The purpose of team building activities is to bring the individual members of the team closer together and establish a good basis for the future work and cooperation. In the next section, we will outline concrete activities, such as team member introductions, clarifying team members' expectations and concerns, and drawing up a set of common ground rules for the team. Conducting these activities in the forming phase may help make the storming phase seem less overwhelming, as many of the issues that can otherwise develop into actual conflicts have already been discussed.

Planning that promotes involvement is the final activity type the project manager should initiate in the forming phase. In this context, the most important activity is the project planning workshop, as this is where work on the project starts and you can begin 'building' the team, as they work together and participate in various concrete team-building activities. At the planning workshop, the project manager should focus on leading the process by ensuring that everyone contributes to the discussion and is heard as the plans for the project are gradually drawn up.

Storming – power struggles   **Storming**

After the honeymoon, a storm of conflicts and power struggles begins to brew. Life is not necessarily as rosy as it first seemed. Critical decisions have to be made within the team, and people's differences are more conspicuous, For example in discussions about which method to use or about how much each team member should contribute. The project manager's role is often challenged, and there are struggles for status in the hierarchy: Who makes the decisions here? While these conflicts are necessary to help the team establish its own order and culture, this phase can be both shortened and made less overwhelming by working consciously with the elements in the forming phase.

For instance, by holding a planning workshop, discussing cooperation within the team, laying down ground rules, etc.

What does this mean for the management of the project?
In the storming phase, it's imperative that the project manager position herself as the team's only leader. The challenge for the project manager is to create a forum where discussions and conflicts within the group can be dealt with, but without the team floundering in the storming phase for too long. The participants expect the project manager to set out the guidelines for the team and act as 'culture bearer' for the behavior of the entire team. In this phase, the project manager should assess which conflicts to become involved in – and when – to avoid destructive conflicts within the team.

Concrete activities
In the storming phase, the project manager should pay attention to the conflicts. Later in this chapter, we will cover conflict management. Several of the activities mentioned under the forming phase can also be used here, such as laying down ground rules, if you haven't already done so.

It is a good idea to add 'team cooperation' to the team meeting agenda. This is a good place for the team to informally evaluate the process to date and adjust the future process, if needed.

The project manager can also arrange more informal ways to bring the project team members together, such as a team dinner, site visits, bowling or other events that aim to help the participants get to know each other and, hopefully, understand each other better.

Norming

Norming – creating the team norms
The outcome of the storming phase should be that the team has established 'our way of doing things', i.e. their set of norms. These are rarely written agreements, but unwritten rules for what is to be done, is expected and is permitted on this team. The team's set of norms is an important part of the evolving team identity. Norms are necessary to avoid the cooperation ending in chaos.

Lenéer Axelson is talking about how the social peer pressure chokes individuality like a noose (Lenéer Axelson 1998). In other words, as individuals we are forced to change slightly in order to fit in and function well as a group.

In this phase we also see a budding (informal) hierarchy, where there is consensus about who plays which role. This may be the result of conflicts or discussions in the storming phase. The formal organization within the project will often also contribute to defining the various roles within the team, such as the appointment of sub-project managers/delegation of responsibility for work streams.

Establishing common norms instills a sense of calm and renewed hope within the team. Furthermore, the norms make it possible to handle conflicts and opposition more effectively and allow a higher degree of focus on the content of the tasks, whereas the focus in the early development phases was on the people and relations.

What does this mean for the management of the project?
While the participant was previously guided by the project manager, the type of leadership the team needs changes significantly at the end of the norming phase: The project manager is no longer the nucleus, as the responsibilities and objective are now clearly defined. Further, frameworks and relations have been established across the team, as well as norms and routines for how to perform tasks and cooperate. This means that the manager is no longer the center of everything. Instead, you provide coaching, delegate and establish the conditions that give the participants the space and opportunity to thrive.

Concrete activities
The project manager coaches the participants and conducts the necessary steering and follow-up to give them the freedom and responsibility to solve their own tasks. Provided you have done the preliminary work in the forming phase well, this will help things in the norming phase to go both faster and smoother, so that you can quickly move on to the performing phase.

Performing **Performing – the team goes into action**
The team is now fairly well established in terms of norms and the power hierarchy, and can now focus its full attention on the assignment. Each participant keeps the project objective in view and works effectively toward it. However, there is no guarantee that the team will remain in this productive phase. You must make sure to include opportunities to maintain and develop the social elements of the team throughout the curation of the project.

What does this mean for the management of the project?
In this phase, the need for management is more about coaching than steering. The project manager is responsible for keeping the team's motivation up, showing an interest in their work and following up. This is done primarily via the daily contact and at the regular project meetings, but also by celebrating milestones and other victories during the process with the team. See more about this in the toolbox and in the next section.

Major changes to the team or the project will often cause the team to 'regress' back to an earlier stage. This generally happens if: new participants are added or old participants leave the team; the project follows a new course, for instance if the pace is increased; or there is extra pressure from senior management or other important stakeholders.

Concrete activities
In case of major changes, the project manager must carefully monitor whether the team's development falls back to a previous phase and whether it is necessary to initiate activities to quickly get the team back up to the performing phase again. For instance, if a new team member has been added, you can devote some time to a team welcome, including a presentation and an overview of what has been done so far. This can also be a good opportunity to check the plan for the near future and bring the new team member up to speed. If the pace of the entire project needs to be increased, for instance because the product needs to get to market two months earlier than originally expected, you can organize a re-planning workshop

where you adjust the project plan and the project description to meet the new requirements.

Adjourning
Adjourning is the final phase of the group development process. When the project is nearing completion, the project participants are mentally – and often also literally – already working on new assignments and new projects. There may be a degree of burnout and uncertainty in relation to the project's results, i.e. anxiety about how the project will be received: Will it be a success or a failure?

Further, the participants may be sad that the team is breaking up or concerned about what will happen to them (can my boss and colleagues still use me?). This applies particularly to those who have been attached 100 percent to the project for an extended period of time.

What does this mean for the management of the project?
In the adjourning phase, the project manager needs to assume a more steering and visible role to ensure the project reaches completion.

Concrete activities
Follow-up should be stricter, with milestones closer together, and the project manager should generally keep focus on maintaining the team's enthusiasm and motivation all the way to the end.

The project manager should also have the team evaluate the teamwork as well as the project's results, preferably in collaboration with the steering committee of customers. It is the project manager's responsibility to remember everyone when the champagne bottles are popped, and to share the honor for the work.

Finally, it is important to give everyone within the project the opportunity to say good-bye, possibly with a banquet or similar.

Lenéer Axelson's model, with the forming-storming-norming-performing-adjourning phases, is just one way to view a team's development process. It doesn't really matter whether you, as the project manager, use this or another approach, as long as you are aware that project teams pass through various development phases, which require different approaches to management from the project manager. Furthermore, the development can also be influenced to a large extent by a conscious effort on behalf of the project manager. For instance, it is a good idea to bring the team closer together quickly, to avoid getting caught up in an unproductive forming phase or a storming phase filled with conflict.

Team building activities In the following, we present various team-building activities that you, as the project manager, can use in the process of establishing your team. These activities can, for the most part, be integrated with the various planning elements in project start-up, as teams are primarily established by getting them to work together.

Incorporating team-building activities into the project seeks to quickly establish a good and effective project team and ultimately improve the team's results and prevent unnecessary conflicts and problems.

Considerations before initiating team-building activities Before initiating team-building activities, the project manager should consider the needs of the particular project and team. For example, Karen, an agency head of section and project manager for a team of five, needs to draw up a rule simplification proposal in a complex field of law. The project participants know each other from various contexts, and the deadline for the project is very short. Karen therefore considers whether it is even necessary to spend time establishing the team or whether they can 'get started' right off.

Karen decides to organize her considerations and lists the points that can help her decide how much and what kind of team building she will use. Karen considers:

- How well do the participants know each other?
- Are there any potential problems among the participants that might affect cooperation?
- How motivated are the participants?
- How closely does the team need to work?

Karen concludes that she needs to be careful, as three of the participants don't seem particularly enthusiastic and are very busy with work in their respective sections. Her concern is that they will try to get away with working as little as possible on the project. The project also requires that the participants work closely, especially in the first and last phases of the project. Based on this, Karen concludes that she can avoid conflicts and missing deliverables later in the project by spending some time on team establishment.

Specifically, she decides to integrate team building activities with the other professional activities at the start of the project. It is especially important that she hold a planning workshop where everyone is involved in defining the objective and milestone plan, as well as in preparing the plan for their own work. At the planning workshop, the team also discusses their expectations of the cooperation and lays down five ground rules for how they should behave in relation to each other and to the project. Additionally, she sets each employee to estimate the time they will need for their own tasks in the project to ensure that this corresponds to the official resource agreements. Finally, she introduces an item on the agenda for the weekly team meeting called 'Team work and cooperation: learning and reflection', where the team can discuss any problems with cooperation and rectify them before they have a negative impact on the team or the project.

Karen's project management is an example of the relatively simple measures a project manager can initiate to ensure an effective team. Devoting time and resources to the social aspects from the outset will increase the likelihood of achieving fantastic performance in the long term. However, if you skip this step and proceed directly to the project work without discussing the work form, expectations and project participants' own objectives for the project, you risk conflict, lack of motivation and the participants not assuming ownership of the project.

Examples of activities include:

- Project participant introductions
- Reconciliation of expectations
- The Team Constitution

Below, we briefly explain the purpose of each of these activities.

Project participant introductions

The first meeting is crucial for the participants' expectations of what life will be like working on this project and team, and is thus an important event that requires careful planning by the project manager. At the first meeting, the participants' primary focus will be on establishing relations to the people on the team: Who are the others? What are their attitudes about the project? How does the project manager assume her role? How committed does she seem to the project? And what is her attitude toward the rest of the team?

Introductions often consist of each person simply stating their name, position and age – or they're skipped entirely if the participants already know each other. The point of spending more time on introducing the project participants to each other is to:

- Reveal the resources available on the team
- Reveal the strengths and weaknesses of the team in relation to the project

The introductions should therefore focus on the specific qualifications and interests of the participants in relation to this particular project. In addition to clarifying each participant's professional contribution to the team, the introductions should also shed light on the personal contributions to the team.

The project manager can supplement the introductions with background info explaining why this particular person has been selected for the team.

Once everyone has gained an overview of the team's resources, strengths and weaknesses, you have a good basis for discussing whether they are suited for the assignment or whether changes should be made to the team.

Reconciliation of expectations

Mutual expectations have been discussed by the project manager and each participant at the preliminary individual interviews. However, it's also important to discuss expectations and concerns with the entire team. The point of this is to:

- Allow people to voice any concerns that might have a negative impact on motivation and progress within the project so that you can begin clearing as many obstacles from the path as possible in the initial phase.
- Motivate the project participants by helping them focus on what they can achieve personally by participating in the project, e.g. competence boost, influence, profiling within the organization, networking.
- Establish an open and honest atmosphere on the team.

It is important that the project manager has thought about her own expectations and concerns beforehand and about how to communicate them to the team.

Team Constitution

The purpose of laying down ground rules within the team is to discuss and reach a consensus on how cooperation within the team should work. Laying down ground rules in the forming phase means that the rules are already set out for how to handle conflicts and disagreements before they arise. This can significantly reduce the number and severity of conflicts. Furthermore, it's much easier to establish the rules in a pleasant start-up phase rather than in the storming phase, where conflicts and misunderstandings can make it difficult to get the work done.

The good thing about working with ground rules is that regardless of whether any conflicts actually develop, the ground rules become part of the team's ongoing evaluation of their own work.

If conflicts arise in the future, it's a good idea to have the ground rules to refer to. The project manager will always be able to ask whether the conflict has arisen because a ground rule has not been followed or because the project needs another ground rule. Or whether the agreed rules are relevant.

9.3. Motivation and feedback

9.3.1. A motivated team

A motivated project team increases the chances of success

Motivation is a key factor in project work and one of the project manager's most important jobs is to motivate the project participants. A motivated project team performs better, ensures higher quality solutions, has higher morale and considerably increases the project's likelihood of success.

With a demotivated project team, on the other hand, you have an increased risk of conflicts, stress, budget overruns and missed deadlines. All things considered, it is extremely difficult to achieve success with a demotivated team (unless the project manager completely takes over and does everything herself, which is contrary to the point of project work and project leadership).

This section therefore presents some concrete things the project manager can do to motivate the team, as well as factors in the environment around the project that either hinder or boost motivation.

Motivation is a state of mind

One definition of motivation is a state of mind, an inner energy that helps the individual to – voluntarily – make an extra effort to achieve both personal and project goals (Verma 1995).

A motivated person is someone who wants to make an extra effort, possibly in the form of overtime, but also in terms of the energy and passion they bring to their work. There is personal satisfaction associated with the work and a sense of pleasure in contrast to the tasks that are only done out of a sense of duty. Motivation is contagious.

It should be possible to achieve personal goals

Thus, to feel motivated, the participants need to feel there is something in the project worth achieving – that their personal goals are somehow in alignment with the project objective. Personal goals can include many things, such as:

- The cause itself – I am interested in improving conditions for patients, customers, etc.
- Power goals – I want to have an influence on the solution.

- Status goals – I want to increase my visibility within the organization and land more interesting assignments as a result of this one.

Money is not normally considered a decisive motivational factor. However, bonuses, pay raises and the like should not be ignored when the project manager sets out to establish the motivational framework of the project.

Motivation has been the subject of a great deal of research. The Hawthorne studies were among the first. They were conducted at the Western Electric Company factory near Chicago at the end of the 1920s. The researchers studied how a variety of physical factors, such as lighting, temperature and sound, influenced workers' performance. They found it odd that no matter what they did (turned down the heat, turned up the heat, dimmed the lights, made the lights brighter, etc.), it appeared to have a positive effect on workers' performance. They concluded that it wasn't the physical conditions alone, but the researchers' interest in the individual's work that had a positive effect on performance. These findings are entirely in line with later studies, as well as with everyday experience, which shows that interest and feedback from others (especially a person's superior) motivate people to make an extra effort.

On the basis of various theories of motivation (Verma 1995), the following presents a collection of concrete measures you, as the project manager, can initiate to motivate your team. It is worth noting that many of these measures are intended for implementation in the project start-up phase. Consequently, due consideration should be shown to planning and prioritization at the start of the project.

Measures that motivate

Plan the project with your team!

Examples:
- Hold a planning workshop!
- Don't have the solutions ready beforehand, but be open to contributions by the team. Otherwise, it is just pseudo-involvement that doesn't promote ownership within the team.

Plan the project with your team

Chapter 9. Leading the Team

- Involve the team in the process when making changes to the project and communicate the reason for the changes, e.g. to comply with the wishes of the steering committee, time pressure, etc.

Attach rewards to good performance	**Attach rewards to good performance – anything you measure and reward will get done.** Examples: - Negotiate rewards for the project team with the project owner and assess which rewards best motivate the individual participants based on the preliminary interviews. - Assess what should be measured and rewarded: meeting deadlines, staying on budget, quality, innovation, learning, or something else entirely. Bear in mind that this entails the formulation of deliverables and milestones as SMART objectives. - Assess whether the rewards should be collective or individual. Note that individual rewards can have a negative effect on the sense of team spirit.
Protect the project team from outside interruptions	**Protect the project team from outside disruptions – take up the fight on behalf of your team.** Examples: - Draw up resource agreements so the participants' superiors are aware of how much time the participant is expected to allocate to the project. - Establish a project room for the team, where they can work on the project together without interruptions. - Defend the project's resources. If you, as the project manager, relinquish resources without a fight, this says that the project isn't very important and that the project participants are dispensable.
Praise the project team to relevant stakeholders	**Praise the project team to relevant stakeholders** Examples: - Make the project and the team visible, for instance in articles and interviews in the staff magazine, on the intranet, at management meetings, etc.

- Call the performance of individual team members to the attention of their daily manager in an informal chat.
- Assume responsibility for and defend the project participants. In connection with late deliverables, it is bad form to tell the steering committee that it was Steve's fault they couldn't deliver on time. The project is the project manager's responsibility, and criticizing participants in public is counter-productive.

Show interest in the individual team member's performance and express how important they are for the project as a whole.

Show interest in every team member

Examples:
- Ask interested questions about the individual's tasks – and not just when the deadline is in peril.
- Provide qualified feedback on daily work.
- Make sure the milestone plan, with work streams and dependencies between the work streams, is clear so everyone understands that their own area is an integral part of the entire project.

Show you trust your team, delegate responsibility to the individual members and hold them accountable

Delegate responsibility

Examples:
- Make sure the plan clearly shows who is responsible for what and that the individual has contributed to the plan.
- Avoid taking over participants' tasks when pressure mounts. It may save the day in the short term, but it takes responsibility away from the individual.
- Make sure to delegate responsibility for both the process and the result. As long as the deliverable is completed on time, the individual should have the flexibility to plan the process as they see fit.

Share team victories with the participants

Share the victories with the project participants

Examples:
- Celebrate the achievement of milestones. Cake, champagne or a bonus – it doesn't matter. According to Christensen

and Kreiner (Christensen 1996): 'Share the project's successes with the participants. Chances are you'll have to rely on each other again.'
- Pamper your team – being part of the project should be a special experience. Organize a halfway party, completion party, etc. Remember to invite all the participants – also the ones who were only involved in the early phases.
- Remember to share all positive mention of the project with the participants.

Show commitment | **Show commitment in both word and deed**
Examples:

- Highlight the importance of the project and make sure the objectives are clear. As Daniel Goleman says: 'Leadership is not domination, but the art of persuading people to work toward a common goal' (Goleman 2000).
- Only take on tasks you know you can complete. It's hard to insist that others meet their deadlines if you don't meet your own – regardless of how valid your excuse is.
- Management's commitment and attention also needs to be secured throughout the project and made visible to the team. Invite the project owner, the CEO or others to selected meetings with the project team and let senior management communicate their current expectations of the project.

As you can see, there are a wide range of things you, as the project manager, can do to boost your team's motivation. However, boosting motivation is rarely a separate activity or item on the agenda. It is something the project manager needs to integrate into the other project activities, like the planning workshop and team meetings. Section 9.2 on forming the project team and the following sections on feedback and coaching are therefore also important aspects of motivating your team.

9.3.2. Feedback

Feedback is one of the most important factors for establishing and boosting team motivation. In this section, we will take a closer look at how to give good feedback when working in projects.

9.3. Motivation and feedback

In 2001, Oxford Research asked employees at 98 Danish firms about their satisfaction with their firm as a workplace. Surprisingly, McDonald's in Denmark was ranked the third best workplace in this survey. The findings showed that it wasn't the content of the job at McDonald's that earned such a high satisfaction rate, but the fact that the employees feel respected and seen, that they have influence on their workplace, that the management trusts the employees and that there is an open, honest, caring and friendly atmosphere between employees and management. Among other things, McDonald's works with continuous and systematic daily feedback, which all employees receive from their immediate superior.

As a project manager, it is worth noting that feedback, trust and having an influence on one's own work are extremely important for employee satisfaction. If we look at what people identify as having the strongest impact on their motivation, they say praise and critical feedback, in that order. Receiving no feedback whatsoever is directly demotivating. Unlike McDonald's, as a project manager you are in the privileged position of being able to offer relatively interesting job content to your project team members.

Not only does feedback motivate the individual participant, it is also the key to ensuring the quality of the project deliverables. Via feedback, we provide each other with the necessary information to continue working in the same way, while a lack of feedback makes it more difficult for the individual to assess what the project manager, the rest of the team and the other stakeholders think of their work and what is expected of them. **Feedback increases product quality**

We all need feedback on where we are effective and where we are less effective, where we are successful and where we have failed – that is, both praise and constructive criticism. **We all need both praise and constructive criticism**

In most firms, feedback is generally inadequate – there is either too little of it or it's just not useful. If we comment on another's performance, we often just say 'It was good' or 'It wasn't good enough'. That kind of feedback does not promote learning! According to Goleman, providing feedback as a generalized claim or personal attack is extremely destructive for the workplace climate (and unfortunately quite common). For

Chapter 9. Leading the Team

example, 'You really botched this one' or 'You apparently had no idea what you were supposed to do' (Goleman 1995).

Defense mechanisms in response to bad feedback

There are many defense mechanisms in response to bad feedback:

- Going on the defensive (No, you're wrong. What I meant was ...)
- Making excuses (I was really busy, so I didn't have time ...)
- Avoiding responsibility (It's Tom you should be talking to ...)
- Reacting with silence and avoiding future contact with the person in question

One reason we might resist giving feedback is that we put ourselves on the line by telling others what we really think. If the feedback isn't worded properly, there is a risk of retaliation. So what is good feedback?

Good feedback is descriptive and non-judgmental

First and foremost, good feedback is descriptive rather than judgmental. I describe what I see, hear and experience as well as what it does to me. In this way, I give the recipient of my feedback the freedom to use the information anyway they like. I avoid using expressions of assessment, judgment or personal attacks on the person's character, as they only increase the recipient's need to defend themselves.

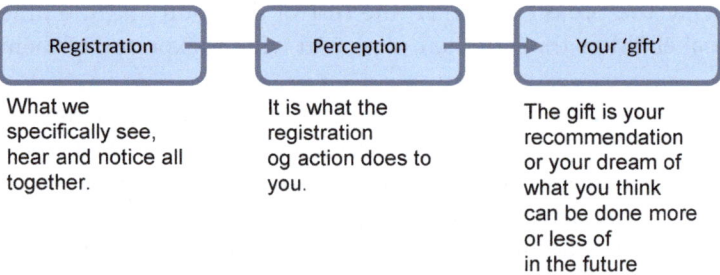

Registration	Perception	Your 'gift'
What we specifically see, hear and notice all together.	It is what the registration og action does to you.	The gift is your recommendation or your dream of what you think can be done more or less of in the future

Do not make an interpretation of your registration and perception. Because you don't know and your will loose the listener.

Figure 9.2. Good feedback describes what you observe, what effect it has on you and possibly suggests a solution. It does not contain any kind of personal judgment.

9.3. Motivation and feedback

An example of inappropriate, judgmental feedback is:
'You're just a lazy bum, who's never on time.'
An example of useful, descriptive feedback is:
'You were 20 minutes late for the team meeting today and half an hour late on Monday. I can see that this has a negative effect on the rest of the team's discipline and sitting around waiting for four people makes me feel ridiculous. Please come on time from now on.'

You may find the following formula helpful:

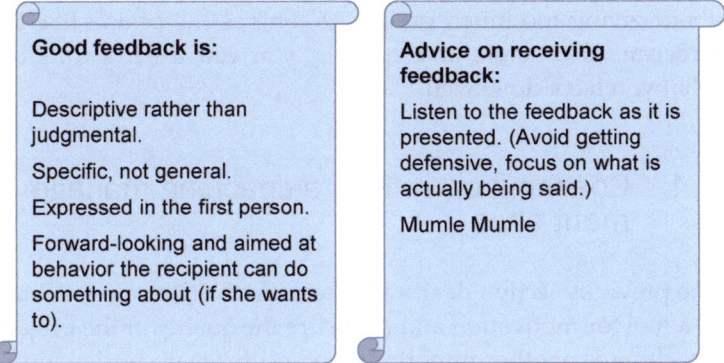

Good feedback is:

Descriptive rather than judgmental.
Specific, not general.
Expressed in the first person.
Forward-looking and aimed at behavior the recipient can do something about (if she wants to).

Figure 9.3.

Advice on receiving feedback:

Listen to the feedback as it is presented. (Avoid getting defensive, focus on what is actually being said.)
Mumle Mumle

Figure 9.4.

Figure 9.3 shows what good feedback is, while Figure 9.4 provides good advice on how to receive feedback in a way that strengthens the giver's desire to provide feedback again and encourages more detailed feedback to make it as useful as possible.

Feedback is indispensable – both for the motivation of the team and for the quality of the project. Consequently, it is important that you, as the project manager, take responsibility for establishing a good feedback culture within the project team – not just criticism, but appreciation and praise as well. Constructive feedback should always be forward looking, i.e. it should help the person understand how to react in future situations. In this way, feedback becomes feed-forward.

Projects can benefit greatly from including feedback at regular intervals as an agenda item at team meetings. Of course, this does not mean that you can skip the daily feedback. But by

Feedback as an item on the project meeting agenda

formalizing and planning the feedback, it's possible to make adjustments along the way before things get off track, be it team cooperation, stakeholder contact, professional content, etc.

Many project managers on our courses are rather skeptical of the importance of praising one another. Typical responses include, 'That's not how we do things where I work', 'You learn from making mistakes, not receiving compliments' or: 'We can't go around patting each other on the back all day'.

The response to this is simple: There is no need to worry about giving too much praise. As long as the praise, like the criticism, is concrete and specific, you can learn a lot from what you have done well.

9.4. Coaching or, rather, a coaching management style

The project manager as coach

The previous section dealt with team motivation and feedback as a tool for motivation and to ensure the quality of the project. Coaching is another important method for team leadership. If we compare the two approaches, we find that feedback is a response to something that has been done (although it should preferably have an element of feed-forward as well), while coaching is broader and more forward looking.

Coaching characterizes both a type of discourse and a management style

Coaching is used here in reference to both:

- Coaching sessions, which take place between the project manager (the coach) and the coachee (generally a project team member or a subcontractor) for the purpose of solving a problem.
- A coaching management style in which the fundamental principles of coaching are used in an everyday context. Consequently, coaching is not just a technique and a type of discourse, but rather a leadership method and a way of interacting with others.

Coaching is the opposite of an authoritarian and rule-governed management style. Coaching helps the project manager release the employee's potential instead of simply dictating how they should do things. The thinking is that there are a lot of untapped resources in employees that don't come to light with authoritarian and bureaucratic management styles. The coaching management style and the coaching session are relevant for project managers (as well as most other modern leaders) because they rarely have the formal authority (or interest) to issue orders, but rather practice management by motivating and influencing employees and other stakeholders in the project. Further, you will often play the role of project manager to employees who possess greater specialist knowledge in certain areas than you do. Consequently, you can't act as an expert in all professional solutions.

Coaching can be used in many project management contexts, such as for motivating the team, team-building, reconciliation of expectations with the project owner, project participants and stakeholders, and so forth. Coaching is also useful in delegation, planning and follow-up, as well as troubleshooting.

Ways to use coaching

In this section, we describe what coaching is and how the project manager can use it to best effect. We also provide suggestions on how to practice it.

The concept of coach comes from the sports world, and there is a wealth of literature on the subject, as well as countless athletes who have established themselves as professional coaches in the business community.

Inspiration from the sports world

If you look at top performing athletes and businesspeople, you will find a combination of mental attitude, technique/knowledge and method/experience. Mental attitude, in particular, is considered by both top athletes and business leaders to be extremely important, and this is where coaching as a tool comes in.

One of the first people to write about coaching was Timothy Gallwey, Harvard professor and tennis expert. He wrote *The Inner Game of Tennis* in 1974, in which he pointed out the concept of inner resistance, i.e. the mental aspect of athletic performance, and argued that the individual player's thoughts about her own capabilities and performance represent a greater and stronger opponent than the person on the other side of the net. The coach's job is therefore not just to provide tips on

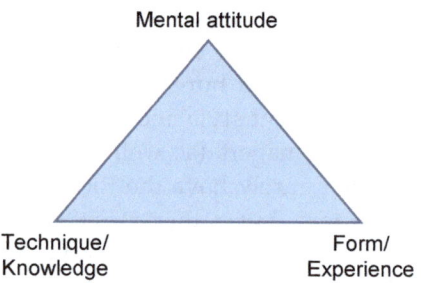

Figure 9.5. Mental attitude is the key to top performance.

technique and evaluate the player's form, but to help the player reduce or completely remove this inner resistance in order to improve the player's performance on the court.

A definition of coaching

In the business world, the term coaching is widely used. Our definition of coaching is:

> 'Coaching is unlocking someone's a person's potential in order to maximize their own performance. It is helping them learn rather than teaching them.'

Source: Whitmore 1998

In other words, coaching is a method in which one person helps another person, by means of dialog, to develop new ideas, creating new opportunities for action and thereby achieving better results. By coaching another person, we help sharpen her awareness of the topic in question. The coach assists this process, not by telling the person what she is doing right or wrong, but by asking questions that focus the person's attention and help her come up with the answers herself. The coach is not the expert who gives answers and good advice, but provides coaching by asking questions and concentrating on enabling the other to find the answers on her own. When it comes to giving good advice, coaching has the advantage of aiding memory, instilling a sense of ownership and highlighting personal potential.

When coaching in project management, you are not the expert on the content – regardless of whether it is professional difficulties, such as with the implementation of an IT system, or problems working with a colleague or stakeholder. Instead, you are the expert in establishing the framework for reflection and a dialog that can help the coachee move forward.

Coaching requires mutual trust and respect between the coach and the coachee. You need to earn the right to act as coach for your project team members, who are often your colleagues and hierarchical equals, or perhaps even superiors. Further, as a coach, you need to possess a degree of empathy and openness to ideas that differs from your own and put aside any desire to act as though you know everything.

The coachee, on the other hand, needs to want and have the will to learn and to reflect on her own actions.

Coaching requires mutual trust and respect

An important premise for coaching is appreciation, i.e. making sure that the coachee feels appreciated and respected. Appreciation promotes development and facilitates learning. Any negative assessment by the coach will be transformed by the coachee into defensiveness in an effort to maintain a positive self-image.

Appreciation is sometimes confused with praise. Coaching that only takes the form of praise will have no effect at all. Appreciation is when the coachee feels listened to and taken seriously.

Here's an example:

The coachee says that she is finding it difficult to perform at the same standard as the rest of the team.

Here, the praising coach would say: 'I don't agree. I think the quality of your work is fine,' which basically sweeps the coachee's experience off the table as a figment of her imagination. The appreciative coach, on the other hand, might say: 'Try to be more specific about which situations have made you feel that way and how it affected your work.' This takes the coachee's experience seriously and together you explore where the experience stems from and the effect it has.

Appreciation forms the foundation for change

Another premise and task of coaching is to create an appropriate interruption, that is, the coach uses questions and statements to challenge the coachee's ideas and actions – taking

An appropriate interruption

care not to criticize them. This balancing act can be difficult, but the interruption is necessary to illicit change in the coachee and ensure that you are not just confirming the person's view of the problem. An interruption may be questioning how a coachee usually does something or an attitude they usually have.

Here are a couple of examples:

'Have you considered what would happen if you didn't take responsibility?'

'Do you know that they do this? Or is this something you hope they do?'

Interruptions promote reflection and challenge the obvious. However, the interruptions must be appropriate. You should take care not to knock the coachee's feet out from under her with questions that are too interruptive, but rather use them gradually until the coachee is ready to come to her own realizations.

Is there time for coaching? When project managers and leaders are first introduced to coaching, a common response is that coaching is right, effective and useful ... but it takes too long, and will never be something they use on a daily basis.

'It is faster to tell John what he should do instead of helping him figure it out for himself by asking questions. Besides, telling him what he should do ensures that I get what I want,' argued one project manager.

It is true that, in some cases, a leader does need to be able to issue clear instructions. If there is a fire, the leader should not coach John on how to put out the fire, but order him to immediately use the fire extinguisher. However, most tasks in projects are more complex than that.

Furthermore, issuing orders instead of coaching will not necessarily save time in the long run. Managers who issue orders have to spend time on control, looking over the shoulders of their employees and answering detailed questions from their employees. And they don't feel certain that their employees will act in accordance with what was agreed (or rather: with the manager's orders).

Time spent on coaching is an investment. By responding to the coaching questions, employees who have been coached focus their attention on the critical aspects of the task and on their own potential, and are thus able to work more independently and responsibly. At the same time, the employee's answers give the manager in-depth insight into the employee's thoughts, making it possible to determine how much follow-up is needed along the way to ensure a positive outcome. A coaching management style results in more motivated employees, higher quality and development of the individual employee's potential.

Questions are the coach's tool

The trick with coaching is to ask good questions. The coach's most important job is to ask questions that 'interrupt' and promote reflection in the coachee. The coach doesn't ask questions to learn something, but to help the coachee learn something.

*[sidenote: **Questions produce reflection**]*

The coach needs to resist the urge to give advice for the simple reason that we can rarely use other people's good advice. While you may think you have been in a similar situation as the person speaking, it is highly unlikely that the same solution can be applied in both cases.

Similarly, the coach should also refrain from making statements about 'absolute truths' ('The fact of the matter is...' or: 'X has always been difficult. You can't change other people.') Statements about truths and expert advice have a tendency to shut down the dialog instead of opening it up and raising new questions.

As mentioned above, coaching can be both structured and unstructured. Structured coaching is the coaching session, i.e. a planned interview where the purpose and roles are agreed. For instance, I, as an employee, might ask my boss or colleague to coach me on a specific problem I've been struggling with. Unstructured coaching is informal, and the employee or colleague often doesn't even realize she has been coached. They just see that you are leading, which is a sign that you are achieving success with your coaching management style.

In both types of coaching, questions are the most important tools the coach has at her disposal.

Chapter 9. Leading the Team

The various steps of the coaching session

Now we will take a closer look at the coaching session, as many of the principles used in the coaching management style are most clearly visible here.

To begin a coaching session, you need to establish a psychological contract between the coach and the coachee. The agreement covers confidentiality and the length of the session, just as it is the coach's responsibility to clarify her own role (not to provide answers, but to ask questions – unless the coachee has other needs).

The next steps in the coaching session deal with:

- **GOALS**: What do you want?
- **REALITY**: What is happening?
- **OPTIONS**: What might you do?
- **DECISIONS**: What will you do?

However, it is important to emphasize that coaching is not a fixed interview or a specific set of pre-defined questions. Coaching is first and foremost a dialog; the trick to good coaching is to let the conversation flow and let the coachee decide which aspects are important to explore. You could say the coach and the coachee have to 'find their way together'.

The objective of the session

The purpose of the first step is to agree on what the outcome of the session should be and how to incorporate it into a possible long-term goal.

Preliminary questions include:
- What do you want to get out of this session?
- What is the most important issue to gain a better understanding of in the time we have at our disposal today?
- How far do you expect to progress during our session? And in how much detail?

Normally, the coachee can't be very concrete about results, as the reason for the coaching is often some sort of uncertainty or confusion. For example, you may agree that the objective is for A to throw out some ideas about the project in order to gain a better understanding of which ideas are tenable going forward in the project. Or to give B inspiration as to how she can avoid frequent misunderstandings with E. Or that C has some ideas on how she can boost her strengths as a leader.

The next step in coaching is to ask questions about the reality (or realities). Based on the agreed objective, the coach asks detailed questions about the issue. This is done to clarify the issue for both the coach and the coachee and as a kind of reality check of the coachee's point of view. This is done by, among other things, exploring who is otherwise involved and what their relationship is to the issue. **Reality**

Examples of questions include:
- When did you become aware of the issue?
- What have you done so far to address it?
- What effect have your actions had so far?
- Who else is aware of the issue?
- How do you think they would describe it?
- Who is most concerned about the situation?
- On a scale from 1 to 10, how good do you think the proposed solution is?

The purpose of the questions during this step is to shed light on the issue from several angles so that it unfolds in all its complexity.

The third step is to explore the coachee's options in relation the issue in question. The purpose of this step is to get the coachee to look forward and come up with ideas on how she might handle the current challenge. The questions explore the coachee's options and sets up what-if hypotheses, i.e. replacing the given conditions by saying, for example, 'What if you had 26 hours in the day? How would you spend those two extra hours?' Or: 'What if your project owner loved the idea? How would that affect your future management of the project?' During this step, it is important not to steer toward the right solution, but to come up with several possible options. **Options**

Examples of questions include:
- Make a list of all your options – big and small, crazy and off-the-wall.

- What are the pros and cons of the individual options?
- What is the wildest thing you could do?
- Which solutions seem most attractive to you?
- If you were the project owner, what advice would you give yourself right now?
- If anything were possible, what's the first thing you would want to do?

Decisions The last step is to draw up a specific agreement about what the coachee decides to do. Draw up an action plan to ensure that what you have discussed is actually realized. It's vital that the agreement is realistic – successful baby steps are preferable to incomplete giant leaps, which just give the coachee a guilty conscience.

Examples of questions include:
- We have talked about three options – which one do you think is best?
- What is the first step you will take?
- What steps do you need to have taken within two weeks in order to be satisfied?
- Will that action lead to the achievement of your goal?
- What obstacles might you meet along the way?
- On a scale from 1 to 10, what is the likelihood that you will get it done? What can you do to increase that likelihood?
- Should we arrange a meeting to follow-up on what happens?

Learning takes time Coaching is very simple, in theory. It's a matter of asking sharp, appreciative questions that cause the coachee to reflect and makes her aware of her own potential. In practice, however, it is difficult and takes time to learn. The only way to get good at it is to practice. Luckily it can be practiced in a variety of situations. For example, instead of giving a quick answer, ask two or three sharp questions. You can also practice the techniques in smaller groups with everyone taking turns coaching each other, for instance if you have a project manager network in your organization or if you're a member of an external network. However, as with many leadership disciplines, it is like learning to play the violin. It's not enough to read about it, you have to practice, practice, practice – and it sounds terrible in the beginning.

9.5. Conflict management

Projects are conflict magnets. It is the nature of projects to attract conflicts, as they are, by definition, major assignments involving a degree of development as well as uncertainty about the objective and means, and even have their own organizations that span the traditional structure of the organization.

Conflict is an unavoidable part of project work

Within the project team, it seems inevitable that conflicts will develop when people from different disciplines, organizational areas and with different experiences, expectations and ambition levels have to work together to make decisions and achieve the project objectives, as well as their own personal goals – often with tight deadlines hanging over everyone's heads and operational tasks waiting in the wings to be dealt with.

Conflicts within the project team

On the project team, we generally see conflicts about authority, resources, quality, time and cooperation.

As mentioned in connection with the development process of teams, after the norming phase (e initial polite phase) the team will move on to the storming phase, where conflicts are likely to develop. As the project manager, if you are observant of the team's development, you can avoid or mitigate a variety of unproductive conflicts within the team. However, downward in relation to the project team isn't the only source of a potential risk of conflict. There is also a basis for conflict looking upward, outward and inward.

Looking upward at the project owner, steering committee and top manager, we often see conflicts about the definition of objectives, struggles for resources (funding, staffing), deadlines, the attention and priorities of top management in relation to the other projects, as well as power struggles about who decides what about the project.

Conflicts looking upward

Conflicts looking outward	Looking outward at the other stakeholders, there are conflicts with 'psychological hostages' who are being forced to accept changes they have not asked for, as well as various groups seeking to influence the project to their own advantage.
Inner conflicts	Inner conflicts are the project manager's conflicts in relation to the project, which may have something to do with the manager's personal values, morals and ethics being in conflict with those of the project or organization. Or there may be role-related conflicts about work-life balance, personal ambitions for the project and outside demands of the project, just to name a few.

The ability to handle conflicts in a competent manner is a core competence in project management, and a large share of the project manager's energy is devoted to resolving these issues and managing conflicts. |
| Proper groundwork can avoid many conflicts within the team | Many conflicts within the project team can be 'defused' beforehand with good team building and project team establishment. At the planning workshop, the project tasks can be distributed so as to minimize a number of conflicts (such as who gets the interesting tasks and who has to do the boring stuff). Agreements on role distribution can prevent a number of power conflicts (such as whether expert A or the project manager is responsible for contact with a specific stakeholder). It is also possible to prevent or minimize future conflicts by discussing expectations and laying down ground rules for the team. |
| ... and with stakeholders | Similarly, both the stakeholder analysis and the risk analysis help shed light on which activities the project team should initiate in order to minimize the risk of destructive conflicts with stakeholders. However, not all conflicts can and must be prevented, so it can be useful to look at various theories on conflict. |

9.5.1. Theories on conflict

There are a number of theories on conflict. One of the first dates back to the early 1900s, but still exists today. It claims that conflict is bad and has a negative impact on the surroundings, and so the leader (project manager) must prevent conflicts or tone them down so that they don't build up.

Another theory stemming from the 1940s doesn't consider whether conflict in itself is good or bad, but simply concludes that it is unavoidable and can have either a negative or a positive impact. Consequently, it is not the project manager's responsibility to stop conflicts, but rather to manage them in a competent manner.

The earliest theories view conflict as something to be avoided or toned down

According to more recent theory, conflict is necessary to promote innovation, progress and change. The project manager's job, therefore, is not to simply accept conflict, but to also create a breeding ground for a certain conflict potential. Verma writes (Verma 1995):

More recent theory views conflict as a catalyst for innovation and change

'A project with no conflict whatsoever has little incentive for innovation, creativity or change because its participants are comfortable with the status quo and they are not concerned about improving their performance.'

Based on the latter theory, an organization's or project's level of performance and level of conflict can be illustrated as follows:

Based on these theories, as well as on practical experience with projects, it is possible to conclude that:

- Conflict is an unavoidable – yet necessary – part of project work.
- Conflict in itself is neither positive nor negative. Depending on how the project manager and team deal with conflicts, they can either have positive or negative effects and can thus be either constructive or destructive.

Chapter 9. Leading the Team

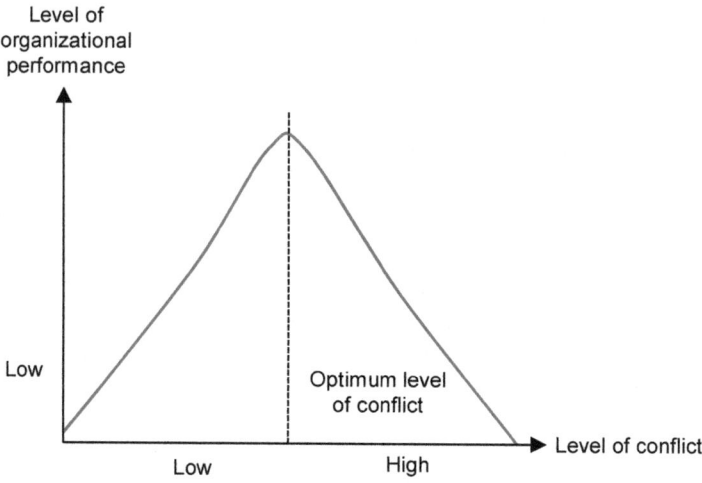

Figure 9.6. A certain level of conflict is needed to promote innovation, progress and change within an organization or project. A conflict level that is either too low or two high will have a negative impact on performance.

The project manager must ensure an optimum level of conflict – and have the ability to handle conflict in a competent manner

This means the project manager should help establish a project culture that permits a certain level of conflict, as this helps promote development and change. This can be done by:

- Ensuring breadth and diversity on the project team, both professionally and personally. This can also be carried out during the project process by bringing new people into play.
- Promoting the forming of new and more points of view rather than consensus or truths.
- Creating a forum for discussing decisions and solutions – both within the team and with stakeholders – and listening to arguments both for and against (see the Resistance to change mapping tool).
- Pushing the limits for 'what is permitted' and 'business as usual' within the organization and the project.
- Incorporating the Devil's advocate, for instance as an item on meeting agendas and in evaluations.

When assessing the level of conflict in the project, the manager might consider:

- Is she surrounded by yes-men?
- Are the project participants afraid or reluctant to admit uncertainty and different points of view to the project manager and the rest of the team?
- Is there too much focus on making sure no one gets offended or feels slighted?
- Is there more focus on being well-liked than on speaking your mind and broaching unpopular discussions?

While the project manager creates a forum for conflicts, she should also deal with destructive conflicts at an early stage before they get out of hand and damage the project. There is a significant risk of destructive conflicts escalating if they aren't dealt with quickly. What started out as a professional disagreement between two project team members can escalate to the point where the other participants feel forced to 'choose sides' and the conflict can grow to involve more than the original source of the disagreement. Further escalation of the conflict can involve attacks of a more personal nature, such as slander and difficulties cooperating, possibly even open confrontation, where one party seeks to ensure the other party loses face in public.

Destructive conflicts must be dealt with early

Conflicts that escalate can obviously have a damaging effect on the project, such as by demotivating the team, delaying the project and causing budget overruns, while extended periods of unresolved conflict can result in key employees quitting their jobs or withdrawing from the project.

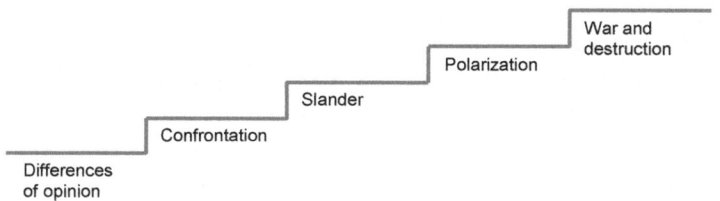

Figure 9.7. Illustration of how conflicts can escalate from ordinary differences of opinion to all-out war and destruction. Although the latter is rare in project work!

In the following, we will take a closer look at how the project manager can deal with conflict in a competent manner.

9.5.2. Resolving conflicts
Being able to handle conflicts means:

Registering the conflict

1. Identify that there is a conflict
There is a big difference in our level of awareness when we are personally involved in a conflict and when people around us are in conflict with each other. As project manager, you need to be able to identify conflicts before they steamroll you or others. A good indicator that something is developing into a conflict is when people begin avoiding contact with each other, e.g. postponing phone calls and meetings or avoiding each other at work. Conflicts are often first perceived with the gut, rather than the mind.

Analyzing the conflict

2. Analyze conflicts to determine whether to get involved
After identifying a conflict, the next step is to analyze: What type of conflict is it? Who is involved? And is it a conflict the project manager should get involved in? As a project manager, you may find it useful to draw up a list – a 'conflict portfolio' if you will – at regular intervals. These are the conflicts the project manager is in contact with. The purpose is to determine which conflicts require your active involvement. The project manager shouldn't waste her energy on every little disagreement on the team or on every conflict she gets drawn into, but should choose her battles with care.

Choose the right 'tool' before taking action

3. Taking action
If a conflict requires the active involvement of the project manager, it is important to use the right tool to resolve the conflict. There are various types of interviews for this purpose. We present a small selection below. You can also take measures in relation to the more formal elements of the project, such as subcontractor agreements and the steering committee mandate. FYI: Conflicts cannot be resolved by email! You have to pluck up the courage and 'grab the bull by the horns'.

Analyzing the conflict

There are four types of conflict:

Conflicts of interest This conflict type involves opposing wishes or demands. The question is: What needs should be satisfied – yours or mine? Conflicts of interest can often be resolved by means of negotiation and compromise.	
Misunderstandings Here the question is: Why do you do what you do? This type of conflict can be about a lack of tolerance for differences or misunderstandings – assumptions that the other person has bad intentions because they behave in a way that seems to make no sense. Misunderstandings can often be resolved by people spending time together. For example, have the team sit together in the same project room.	
Power struggles This theme is as old as day: 'Who makes the decisions here?' With this type of conflict, the project manager needs to take the reins and show the team who's boss. It may be necessary to go over a person's head and have someone higher up in the organization put them in their place.	
Conflicts of value/opinion These types of conflicts are more deeply rooted than conflicts of interest and misunderstandings. The core of the conflict is: What goal should we strive for? What means should we use to achieve that goal? In conflicts of value, the parties will disagree on how the various tasks should be prioritized and/or what needs to be done in order to achieve a specific goal. The focus is on values, such as quality, diligence and work-life balance. Within the project, it is often not an option to change the fundamental values of the participants. A good solution can be to lay down a set of ground rules.	

Figure 9.8. Four types of conflict

Four types of conflict: conflicts of interest, power struggles, misunderstandings and conflicts of value

Clarifying the type of conflict you are dealing with provides a better basis for handling the conflict, as there are a variety of methods for dealing with the different conflicts. Power struggles, for instance, are often dealt with as though they were conflicts of interest, by attempting to negotiate and distribute resources and responsibilities, taking everyone involved into due consideration. However, if it is a genuine power struggle, then the problem is not about resources and responsibilities, but about who is the boss.

This misconception is often seen in projects involving moving to new premises. Conflicts about who gets which office – or even more problematic: who sits where in open-plan environments – can rarely be resolved by means of rational distribution of resources and rights. They are more often about power (How many windows do you have? What floor is your office on? How close is your office to the CEO?, etc.) and privileges that people don't want to give up.

In power struggles that have become deadlocked, it is often necessary to bring in someone from higher up in the organization with more power to decide on the issue at hand.

There are no simple solutions to conflicts of value/opinions. They require dialog and time to allow understanding and respect for each other's actions, values and opinions to develop gradually.

Few conflicts have just one cause

Once you have determined the type of conflict you're dealing with, the next step is to analyze the cause. Few conflicts have just one cause. And yet, we still use a linear line of thinking when dealing with conflicts. We look for the cause and for someone to blame for the problem. Here's an example: A member of your project team, Kurt, has again fallen behind on his project work, and Kurt's deliverable affects the project's other deliverables. You confront him with the problem, and he says that he is under a lot of pressure from his own department. You therefore speak to his boss and arrange to have his departmental workload reduced over the next few weeks, so that he can prioritize the project.

9.5. Conflict management

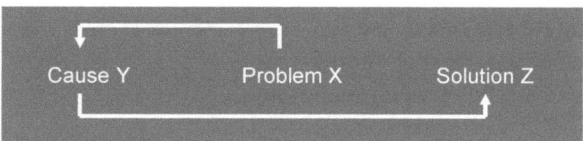

Figure 9.9. We often stick to a linear analysis: once we have found the cause of problem X, we also know what the solution is.

But conflicts are often more complex than can be perceived using the linear cause-effect model. After two weeks, Kurt has still only delivered half-hearted contributions to the team, and the frustration of the other team members is building up. The project manager and Kurt therefore work together to analyze the conflict using circular conflict analysis. They start by looking at who is involved in the conflict and whether they have gotten caught in a vicious circle. This produces the following picture:

Circular conflict analysis lets you see the conflict from different angles

In addition to Kurt being pressured by his department manager, it turns out that his manager has an old conflict with the owner of this particular project and therefore does not actively support Kurt's participation in this project. Furthermore, Kurt feels the project manager assigns only uninteresting and less important tasks to him, and so Kurt puts even less energy into solving them – which again causes the project manager to assign him uninteresting and unimportant tasks. And so on.

With circular conflict analysis, an issue is understood by examining its context. Every action has an effect on and is affected by countless aspects. Circular conflict analysis is about involving different perspectives and viewing the problem from different angles. The purpose is to understand the context and take a holistic approach in order to see that the conflict can be resolved at several stages and on more than one level. It is also about exploring how you may be part of the conflict. In the above example, Kurt's role in the conflict gradually becomes less significant.

The following questions can guide you in the circular analysis of a conflict:

Investigate the facts/case
- What is the conflict about?
- How long has it been going on?
- Who did what and when?
- Why is it important that you deal with this conflict at this particular point in time?

Find out how the involved parties view the issue
- Who else is affected by the conflict?
- What would person A, B and C, respectively, say about the conflict?
- How are relations between the other parties in the case?
- What have the other involved parties done in the case? And what effect has this had on the other parties/the conflict?
- When is the conflict least noticeable – and why?
- Who have you spoken to about this case?

Circular analysis is neither better nor more correct than linear analysis. However, circular analysis is useful when linear analysis has been unsuccessful or when the complexity of the problems requires several angles.

Taking action
The conflict has now been identified, analyzed and you have decided whether to get involved. If the conflict requires the project manager's active involvement, you have several 'tools' at your disposal. Which tool to use depends on the type of conflict and the stage the conflict is at. The earlier you begin to deal with a conflict, the greater the chances of success.

Conflicts sometimes require structural changes

Many conflicts require structural changes. According to Verma (Verma 1995), certain structural aspects of projects can be contributory factors in conflicts, even though the project participants each behave reasonably. And that is where you need to take action. There may be **inexpedient procedures**, such as approval or purchasing procedures (Does the project manager have to go to her own superior before she can contact the project owner? Does the supplier have to be contacted via other channels than the project team itself?, etc.). There may be **unclear authority and roles** (Does the project manager have any real opportunity to make even minor decisions without having to 'ask permission' of the project owner? Does the hearing committee think they have a mandate to make decisions about the project?, etc.).

Getting involved in a conflict will, in the vast majority of cases, entail entering into dialog with the party/parties involved in the conflict. Below, we introduce three different tools for dialog in conflicts, i.e. different types of conflict resolution interviews.

Three tools for dialog in conflicts

1. The solution interview
2. The difficult message (the clear-cut message)
3. Mediation

Experience shows that the majority of the conflicts the project manager becomes involved in will require a solution interview. The two other types – the difficult message and mediation – are not used as often. For this reason, we will only give brief introductions to the difficult message and mediation.

When is the solution interview used?

The solution interview is used when you are involved in the conflict and you want to work together to find a lasting solution. The coaching question technique is very useful in most solution interviews, as you will see below.

The solution interview is used when you are part of the conflict and want to achieve a win-win solution

Start the interview by establishing a common frame of reference and explaining the purpose of the interview.

For example: 'Pamela, I want to start by telling you how very satisfied I am with the work you are doing on the project. You should know that your expertise is crucial to the quality of the solutions. However, I feel your comments and body language during team meetings are undermining my authority as the project manager of the rest of the team. I think we should work together to come up with a way to improve our cooperation in the best interests of the project.'

When conducting a solution interview, you also need to give the other person the opportunity to express how they experience the situation. You then work together to draw up a joint agreement, often including a follow-up interview to evaluate together whether the solution has had the desired effect.

Cooperation is key here, as the goal is to achieve a win-win situation and avoid one party coming up with a solution (which will generally be to their own personal benefit) and then presenting it to the other party/parties as a foregone conclusion. This creates a loser and a winner, which is not conducive to a productive working environment. Sustainable solutions are found when the parties working together agree that there is a problem and that they will each assume responsibility for resolving it.

The solution interview only works as long as the conflict is not so deadlocked that it prevents the parties from conducting a constructive conversation. If the situation is that serious, you will need to find a neutral person to act as mediator (see mediation below). Furthermore, you must also feel confident that the other parties in the conflict are actually willing to resolve the conflict – that they are willing to play ball. If you discover during the process that they are either passing the buck or being defensive, i.e. agreeing to resolve the conflict but not doing anything to change the situation, then you must re-think the strategy. This might bring you to the difficult message, which is an option if you have given up on getting the person involved in finding a solution.

The difficult message is used when you alone decide the result

When to use the difficult message

The difficult message differs from the solution interview in that the outcome is not a joint decision, but decided by the project manager beforehand. It is often used in conflicts that are at a later stage than those where the solution interview can be used. For example, the message may be that a person is being dismissed from the project or a subcontractor is being terminated. Or the message may be telling two employees that they will have to share the same focus area on the project in the future. The aim is to communicate a message in the most appropriate manner.

The difficult message requires careful preparation by the project manager; the facts of the case must be in place and the introduction must be prepared with great care. It is essential to get to the point quickly and to give well-founded reasons for your decision.

If Pamela still obstructs the project manager despite repeated solution interviews and the project manager assesses that they are not getting anywhere, the next interview might be as follows:

'Pamela, we have now had three meetings and made agreements to improve our dialog. This has not changed the situation, as I still find that you are not keeping up your end of the agreement. I have therefore decided that you will no longer be part of this project. I am pleased with the work you have done, but, unfortunately, I cannot ignore our conflict and your attitude toward me is having a negative effect on the atmosphere of the entire team.'

Here, you must give the other person the opportunity to tell you how she feels about the decision. Despite any objections or emotional outbursts, it is crucial in the difficult message to uphold your decision. You are also responsible for limiting the damage, for instance by offering assistance, compensation and looking forward.

When to use mediation

Mediation, or the intervention interview, is used when you are not part of the conflict, but act as intermediary between the parties, for example between two members of the project team. The mediator must remain neutral in order to help establish a framework that enables the parties to find a tenable solution on their own.

Mediation is when you act as an intermediary between the parties in a conflict

The mediator should clearly explain her role. She is responsible for helping the parties listen to each other's versions of the conflict. Together, the parties then draw up a common problem formulation and a series of possible solutions. Finally, they choose one solution, which they put into an agreement. The mediator needs to make sure to give both parties equal influence on the solution to the conflict.

Conducting good conflict resolution interviews takes practice. Most people feel they have to 'pluck up the courage' to conduct them, as they can be quite emotional and the fate of the project can be at stake.

Team leader of the *Happier Customers* project

Training in the new workflows and the IT system in the first three departments is set to begin in just one month. This means that everyone on the project is working double-time. Lisa is putting the final touches on the agenda for a project team meeting to take place tomorrow afternoon. Tomorrow, Lisa has extended the usual bi-weekly meeting from two hours to four hours, followed by a team dinner – for several reasons. First, Michael, who is responsible for the new IT solution work stream, has unfortunately found a new job. Lisa has therefore – after a long struggle with the steering committee – been permitted to hire Christopher for the duration of the project. He will now take over responsibility for the IT workflow. Lisa has held a number of meetings with him to bring him up to speed on the project. She has also coached him on how he can ensure progress in the team's work over the next few critical months and win the respect of the team as quickly as possible. The other employees in the IT work stream met Christopher last week, but tomorrow he will be introduced to the entire team.

Another reason to expand the meeting is that there has been some friction within the team – especially between the IT staff and those responsible for the IT training program for the staff.

Finally, there is a need to optimize the team's cooperation over the next few months, as Lisa is concerned about the delay of several critical milestones.

Lisa has drawn up the following agenda for the meeting:
1. Welcome to Christopher and the participants' presentations of themselves and their areas of responsibility within the project
2. Planning the work to be done over the next few months: A critical look at the milestone plan with a view to risks, mitigating actions and deadlines
3. Evaluation of the cooperation on the team: Does the team follow its own ground rules for cooperation? Are they still relevant or do they need adjusting?
4. Team dinner

Lisa has based this agenda on the following considerations:

It is important that Christopher is properly introduced to the rest of the project team and that the other participants are given the opportunity to tell him what they are currently working on. In addition to giving Christopher information, this can also help boost understanding among those participants who are not up to date on what everyone is doing.

The next item is about boosting the pace of the project. This item serves several functions:

In preparation for this item, Lisa has asked those responsible for each work stream to take a critical look at their milestone plans. She has emphasized that this should be done in cooperation with the relevant project team members. In one month's time, the training program is to commence in the first three departments, which means that all delays need to be overcome. Lisa has asked them to assess the risks and draw up a new milestone plan for the next few months. At the meeting, they will review the three work streams' milestone plans to determine the dependencies across the work streams. Lisa is convinced that this exercise will help improve the dialog between the IT staff and the training staff, as it provides good insight into their respective areas. The exercise also gives Christopher a good overview of the project as a whole.

For the meeting, Lisa has prepared the milestone plan for the communication and project management work stream. She spends a good deal of time managing the many stakeholders who have opinions about and requirements and wishes for the project. To optimize the work over the next few months, she has also secured a common project room so that all the participants can sit together instead of working from their own offices in the various departments. This will make communication among the participants easier. This will also speed up the decision-making process, give everyone a good idea of what the others are doing and give Lisa the opportunity to follow-up on and coach the individual participants. She has already checked with each team member to find out what they think about the idea. At the meeting tomorrow she will tell them that she has found a space they can use.

Another good piece of news is that she has managed to secure a bonus for the entire team, provided that they meet the agreed deadline for the commencement of training.

The team is now in the performing phase. Lisa is aware that the need for leadership has changed from the preceding phases, where her tasks primarily involved steering. For example, the participants now seem to have less need for her to steer and coordinate the individual activities, as they are relatively autonomous. Instead, there is a significant need to boost the motivation and energy levels of the busy participants and for more of a coaching management style in her day-do-day interaction with the team. Lisa is also conscious of the fact that adding a new member to the team may at some point cause the team to fall back into the forming phase, followed by the storming and norming phases, as they will need to find a new hierarchy and new modes of interaction among the participants.

Item three, on cooperation on the team, is a discussion of the ground rules that the team laid down at the start of the project. Lisa wants to discuss whether the ground rules are being followed and, thus, what works and what doesn't in the cooperation. She also wants to know if the rules need to be revised based on the practical experiences of the team.

9.6. Reflections on team leadership

How does the team perceive your leadership?

- Have you recruited the right participants for the project?
- Do the participants feel that they have been handpicked for the project?
- Do the project participants know what you expect of them and do you know what they expect of you as a manager and of the project as a whole?
- Which development phase is your team currently in, and what, in particular, will you focus on as a leader in this phase?
- Is your group a close-knit, effective team? Which team-building activities (professional and social) will you initiate to promote or maintain this development?

- Have you held a planning workshop with the involvement of all the participants?
- Is the team motivated? What will you do to boost/maintain their motivation?
- Do the individual participants feel they receive sufficient and useful feedback from you on their day-to-day performance?
- Is the level of conflict in the project optimal? If not: What can be done to optimize or minimize it?
- Are you, as the project manager, dealing with the relevant conflicts within the project?
- Do the participants feel they each receive the coaching and support they need?

Project Governance Management of multiple projects

Someone has to launch the ships and lead the entire fleet

It is only an armada as long as the ships are sailing in the same direction

CHAPTER 10

Project Governance Management of multiple projects

Projects used to be one-off assignments, but in many organizations and firms, projects have become part of daily life and critical for survival and efficiency. The assignments are growing more varied and mounting pressure on organizations to develop and adapt is resulting in more and more resources being allocated to project assignments.

This leads to more projects, more project types, more project managers and more project resources. The process of managing this portfolio of projects in a way that optimizes efficiency and minimizes resource consumption has subsequently developed into a senior management task. Management of the organization's development, i.e. of the projects, needs to be just as efficient and targeted as in the line management. This overriding management task is often called 'project governance'.

Chapter 10 describes the demands and challenges associated with project governance and management of the entire project portfolio.

This chapter provides insight into:
- Establishing a correlation between strategy and projects
- Prioritization of projects and resources
- Controlling the total project volume
- Breaking down the portfolio into programs and projects
- Organization of the portfolio management process
- Developing the organization toward Project Excellence

Challenges

Benefits

- Key concepts within project governance
- Using impact measurement in projects and programs

Focus The focus of this chapter is on establishing project governance in practice.

How do you break down the entire project portfolio into various project types? And what does this mean for the choice of project processes and methods?

How do you give the project portfolio strategic focus to ensure coherence between the individual project and the overall strategy?

The focus will be on tools to help you prioritize projects within the portfolio and strike a balance between risk, urgency and resource allocation.

We also explain how to establish project governance in a way that ensures a correlation between the project committee, steering committees, program managers, project managers and any project director or senior responsible owner. Further, we describe how the project management office (PMO) can continuously develop the organization's project management competences and how impact measurements are conducted in projects and programs.

Finally, we consider how an organization can be developed from its current level of project maturity toward Project Excellence, including the work streams involved in this process.

Tools
Tool 10.1   Project List
Tool 10.2   Portfolio Overview
Tool 10.3   Project KPIs
Tool 10.4   Health Check or Risk Level Check
Tool 10.5   Strategic Fit of Project
Tool 10.6   Project Auditing
Tool 10.7   Project Management Models, Project Models
Tool 10.8   Project Descriptions, Project Contract
Tool 10.9   Idea Description

10.1. Project governance

Project governance – but why?
In many organizations and firms, projects are carried out in overwhelming numbers. Some are cross-organizational; others are conducted in one or two departments. The projects report to the people who initiated them, such as a department head, office manager or director. Some projects are so comprehensive that they report to a steering committee.

Projects are launched throughout the organization; project teams are formed and steering committees hold meeting after meeting. The projects draw on the same resources and the employees are given the same assignments by their boss and three project managers. But who coordinates it all? Who has the bird's eye view of the projects that have been initiated? Who prioritizes resource deployment among the various projects?

Generally, far too many projects are launched simultaneously and without proper coordination. As a result, the projects lack focus and the resources aren't used to optimum effect. The projects take much too long, there are overlaps between the projects and there are far too many re-prioritizations along the way.

Four steering levers in project governance
The four steering levers most senior managers install in their organization when they introduce project governance are:

- A general overview of the project portfolio
- Well-defined roles and distribution of responsibility
- Transparent and solid basis for decision-making
- Common language in the form of a common project model and methodology

Before going into detail on the four steering levers, here are some key definitions pertaining to portfolio management (Table 10.1):

Chapter 10. Project Governance. Management of multiple projects

Key definitions	
Dictionary definitions	
Governance: Act of governing, manner of governing, method or system of governing, controle, power. **Governor:** Person who is the governing head of a province or colony. The governing body of an institution. Regulator in a machine, automatically controlling speed or the intake of gas, steam etc.	**Project Governance** The overall steering and management of an organization's development efforts. From strategy breakdown, programs and projects to measurable impact in a changed organization. Maintaining an overview and steering of the portfolio, transparent decision-making structure, well-defined roles and responsibilities, common language and methodology within the project organization.
Portfolio A folder containing documents; a collection of securities. An insurance company's range of policy types. A minister or commissioner has an area of responsibility – a portfolio. In French, portefeuille, is a wallet or letter bag. Portfolio theory is the analysis of the consequences for an investor of investing in many different securities.	**The portfolio** All projects and programs. The portfolio is the complete collection of projects and programs that have been approved for execution. The projects don't have to be initiated, but they do have to be approved to be part of the portfolio. The portfolio is a snapshot of the approved projects at any given time. The portfolio has no completion date. When projects are completed, new projects in the portfolio are initiated. There doesn't have to be any direct connection or dependency between the projects in a portfolio.
Program In Greek, *programma*, is a public declaration or agenda. A program or a plan for how something is to proceed, for instance a party or performance. To be with the program is to be on the agenda. A program is the collection of ideas and objectives for a political party or movement. A specific radio wave length is a program. It can also be a musical program comprising a selection of musical numbers. The program is the overview of transmissions.	**Program** Projects with a common purpose A program is a group of projects, which together create the desired impact of the program. The projects are often of the same type, or they underpin a common strategy or a specific and clearly defined purpose. There is a correlation between the projects in the form of dependencies and deadlines, but the program can still be executed even though one of the projects isn't completed or its content changes. The program has a deadline and is headed by the program manager, who focuses on the impact – the purpose.
Project In dictionary definitions, to project means to devise or plan. It can also be a major undertaking. To project an image on the wall. The words projectile, projector and projection are all members of the same family. It is the process of projecting an image, an idea, a material onto a new place – from the mind or a sheet of paper onto reality – and altering reality toward the focal point.	**Project** The large dimensioned assignment. A project is a large, one-off, development-oriented assignment that can't be executed naturally by an operational unit. The projects are often interdisciplinary and cross-organizational assignments with a high degree of uncertainty. Projects are dimensioned in terms of deliverables, resource consumption and deadline. There is a defined minimum size for when an assignment is a project. The project is headed by a project manager, who focuses on delivering the agreed 'product' deliverables.

Table 10.1 Key definitions pertaining to portfolio management.

10.1. Project governance

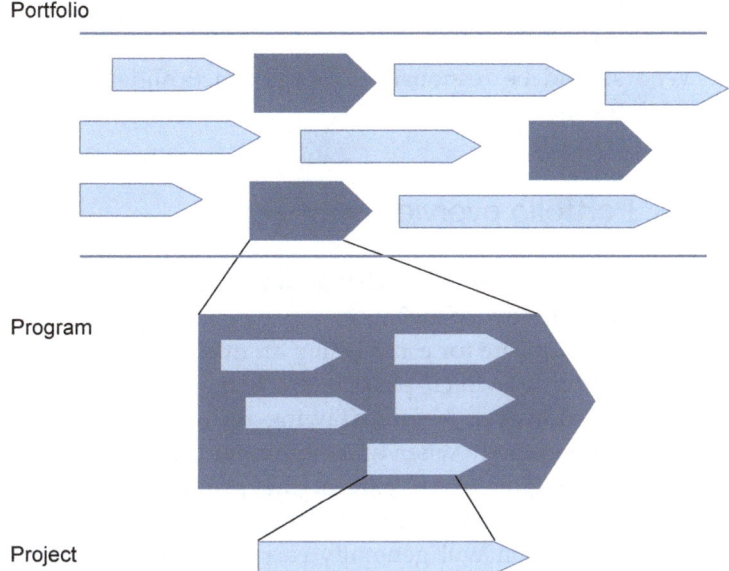

Figure. 10.1 Overview of correlations between the project portfolio (every project and program), programs (clusters of projects with the same purpose) and the individual project.

Project governance deals with prioritizing projects to ensure that the resources are deployed to the projects that underpin the firm's or the organization's strategy. It also deals with obtaining an overview to enable management to follow the progress and thereby create value in the entire project portfolio. Finally, it seeks to ensure that the available resources match the workload.

Project governance is a necessity when the project volume increases

When an organization sets out to work with project governance, there are several considerations to bear in mind:

- What types of projects should be carried out and how should a suitable project process be described for these projects?
- How can the projects be prioritized to ensure a correlation between the strategy and the projects?
- How should the project management of the types of projects the firm carries out be organized?

- How do we conduct follow-up to ensure the progress of the entire portfolio?
- Who should be responsible for the practicalities of maintaining it all?

10.2 Portfolio overview

10.2.1. Project definition – what assignments are part of the portfolio overview?

The first prerequisite for establishing an overview is that there is an inventory of which projects are being executed – i.e. a project list. However, before drawing up a project list, you need to define exactly when an assignment is a project. When should an assignment be part of the project portfolio and when does it belong in the line management?

An organization will generally carry out several different types of projects. It is a good idea to group them by project type, or gather them into programs (projects with a common purpose).

Definition of project types

Which project types make up the complete project portfolio?
The project types carried out by the organization need to be defined. The breakdown into project type should be based on the common characteristics of the projects, for example:

- Size and complexity
- Benefit, political and strategic importance
- Management reference person, competence requirements and draw on resources
- Risk and time pressure

The firm
When breaking down project types in a private-sector firm, the categories might include:

- IT and organizational change projects at group level
- Organizational change projects at firm level
- R&D projects

- Competence development projects
- Marketing and market development projects

In the product development function, projects might be broken down as follows:

- Technology development projects (long-term projects with high uncertainty)
- Development of new products
- Maintenance and revision of existing products (short-term projects with low uncertainty)

In a construction company, ad agency or consulting firm, where the projects are the firm's products, the breakdown might be as follows:

- Customer type (public/private, industry, etc.)
- Product type (residential building, commercial building, etc.)
- Internal organizational change projects
- Internal IT projects

Local government
In a local authority, region or ministry, the categories might be:

- Organizational changes (cross-organizational)
- Straightforward IT projects
- Development of new services (average degree of uncertainty)
- Political development and proposals (high degree of uncertainty and time pressure)
- International projects (EU projects with international partners)

Organizational change projects might be broken down into projects involving the entire local authority and projects only involving a single administration.

The breakdown into project types is a key prerequisite, as it makes it possible to define the person each project should report to (management reference person). Is it at group level or firm level? Is it the head of the local authority, administration or the individual office?

The first step in obtaining an overview is therefore to draw up a project list – see Tool 10.1. The project list shows each project with the following data: project number, project title, initials of project manager, initials of project owner, budget, deadline, etc. The idea is to describe up to 25 projects on a single standard page.

To achieve a more detailed overview, it is common to work with two snapshots/project lists.

10.2.2. Project pipeline

One snapshot should show the complete pipeline and all planned projects. This overview is needed in order to plan how many projects can be carried out simultaneously. This is

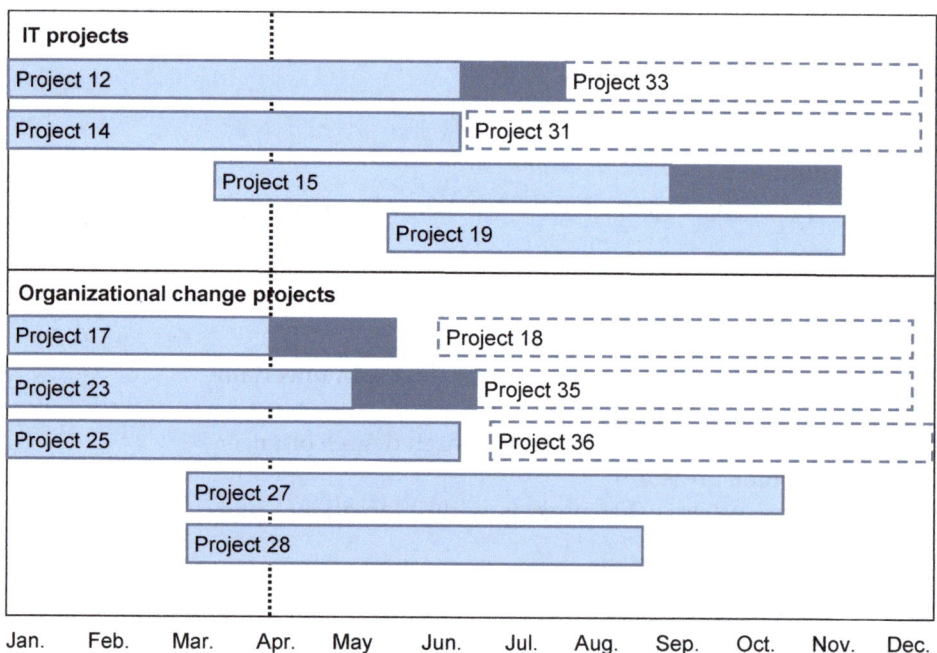

Figure 10.2. The scheduling dependencies, indicating anticipated delays. Each project is listed with its planned lead times and deadlines. The dark blue markings indicate the prognosis for late delivery.

often a matter of resource allocation. How many resources has the management allocated to development assignments?

This overview provides a clear picture of the order in which the projects should be executed. It also gives a good idea of which subsequent projects might be affected by a possible delay, thus giving management a good sense of how to prioritize – as launching every project at the same time just isn't an option.

10.2.3. Following up on progress

Having an idea of how the projects should be executed is one thing; obtaining an overview of the actual status of the portfolio is another thing altogether.

Before deciding which type of overview is most appropriate for your current situation, it's important to clarify the following:

- What decisions need to be made based on the overview?
- What conditions should the overview call attention to?
- What data are needed to render these conditions visible?

A good deal of data and background info is often gathered that isn't actually used to make the decisions in question. The senior management, for instance, needs to select projects in a balanced manner based on strategic importance, benefits and risks.

If the aim of the overview is to underpin the portfolio management of engineering and construction projects, the problem isn't that the projects need to be carried out, but rather the draw on resources, the degree of risk and the progress, as a contract has been concluded with the client.

There are many methods available for following up on progress. However, one simple and flexible method is a project list with 'traffic lights' indicating the status of the projects.

This will enable management to gain an overview of 30 to 40 projects and examine in more detail the red-lighted projects.

This overview can be constructed in levels. It might be an overview of a program, or it might be a summary of the portfolio management's general overview. It can be broken down by project type, if you want to follow up on the progress of, say, all the IT projects. However, it is important that the over-

Chapter 10. Project Governance. Management of multiple projects

Planned				Prognosis		Time	Resources	Risk
Project	Value	Resources	Deadline	Resources	Deadline			
001	0.5 mil.	18 FTE	04	19 FTE	05	●	◐	○
002	0.5 mil.	14 FTE	05	14 FTE	05	◐	◐	○
003	2 mil.	36 FTE	04	38 FTE	06	●	●	●
004	3 mil.	40 FTE	06	40 FTE	06	◐	○	●
005	2 mil.	18 FTE	08	18 FTE	08	◐	◐	○
006	5 mil.	60 FTE	08	64 FTE	09	○	●	●
007	3 mil.	36 FTE	10	38 FTE	10	◐	◐	●
Total	16 mil.	222 FTE	10	231 FTE	10			

Figure 10.3. In principle, a project list consists of traffic lights for the crucial parameters: deadline compliance, resources and risks. Green (gray in this figure) indicates that there are no problems, yellow (white in the figure) that problems are brewing and red (black in the figure) that there are serious problems.

view shows the total resource consumption allocated to the portfolio or program.

This overview is an important tool, not only because it indicates status, but because it provides a prognosis as well. Perhaps a project is currently on schedule and within budget, but there may have been delays, which will lead to further delays? This is important information to include. A traffic signal showing whether the risk level has increased or decreased is an important indicator for management.

The project may be delayed now, but catch-up is still possible, which would mean the prognosis remains unchanged.

Please note that the first four columns in Figure 10.3 are master data from the project descriptions. The project managers only need to report the data in the last five columns in order for management to obtain this overview (the prognosis and traffic lights).

10.3 Well-defined roles and distribution of responsibility

10.3.1. Project-oriented organization

As long as the project volume is small and the share of the total resources allocated to projects is negligible, the individual projects can be carried out within the line organization. However, as soon as the project volume increases, the volume of resources allocated to projects will grow, making it irresponsible not to control and lead this resource consumption.

In this situation, portfolio management will become a necessity and it will need organizing. The project organization utilizes a different organizational form and other building blocks than those used in the line organization, as illustrated in Figure 10.4.

Organize by assignment: operations, project and programs

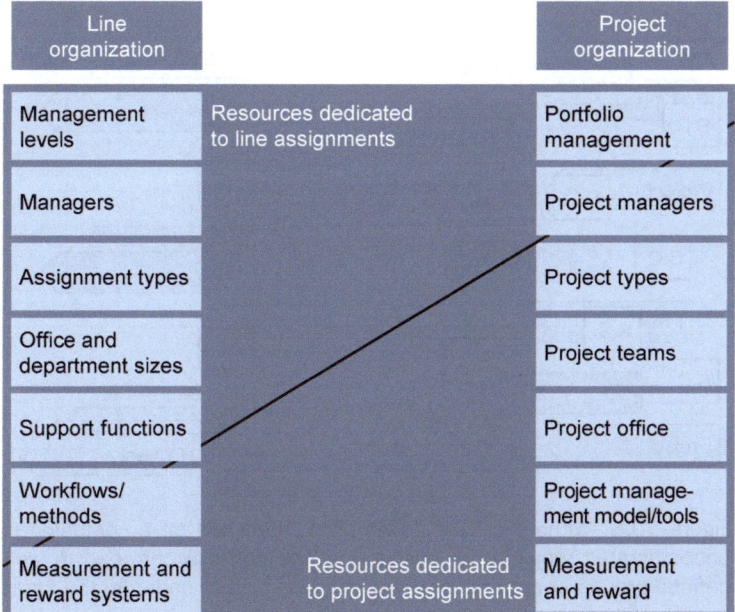

Figure 10.4. In the line organization, on the left, the majority of the resources are dedicated to operational tasks. The organization is therefore built up in a traditional hierarchy comprising the well-known elements of the line organization. In the project organization, on the right, the majority of the resources are allocated to projects, requiring an organization based on the building blocks of the project organization.

Chapter 10. Project Governance. Management of multiple projects

In the line organization, the type of task determines the breakdown of the organizational structure into departments and offices. In the project organization, the project types and programs determine how the projects should be grouped.

In the line organization, there are several management levels, with senior managers, departmental managers and section heads. In the project organization, the levels are the portfolio management, the program management, the steering committee and the project manager.

Without careful structuring of the project organization, the projects will be carried out in a confusion of steering committees, project teams and project managers with no proper coordination.

Define project types and group them into clusters

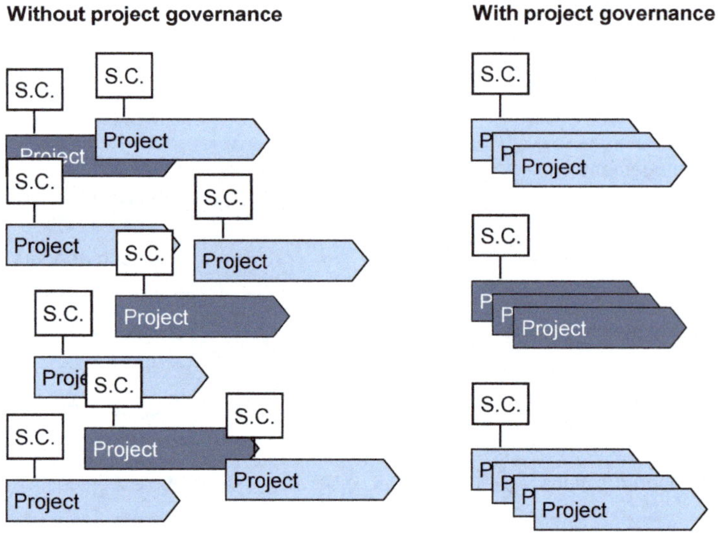

Figure 10.5. Without project governance, there will be a confusion of uncoordinated projects. An overview of the portfolio can lead to well-defined groups of projects of the same type or that underpin the same purpose (programs).

The line organization has support functions within finance and human resource development, for example. In the project organization, the support function is the PMO, which is tasked with maintaining the project processes and collecting the basic data for the portfolio management.

The line organization has procedures, workflows, budgets and accounting systems. The corresponding elements in the project organization are the project management model, plan, budget and toolbox.

The line organization's measurement systems primarily focus on reducing errors and on what is achieved per time unit or resource. The reward system follows the hierarchy. In the project organization, the focus is on measuring progress and lead times. However, the reward system is unfortunately still very hierarchical, even though it ought to be linked to the project results.

The organization of the entire project portfolio has the following structure:

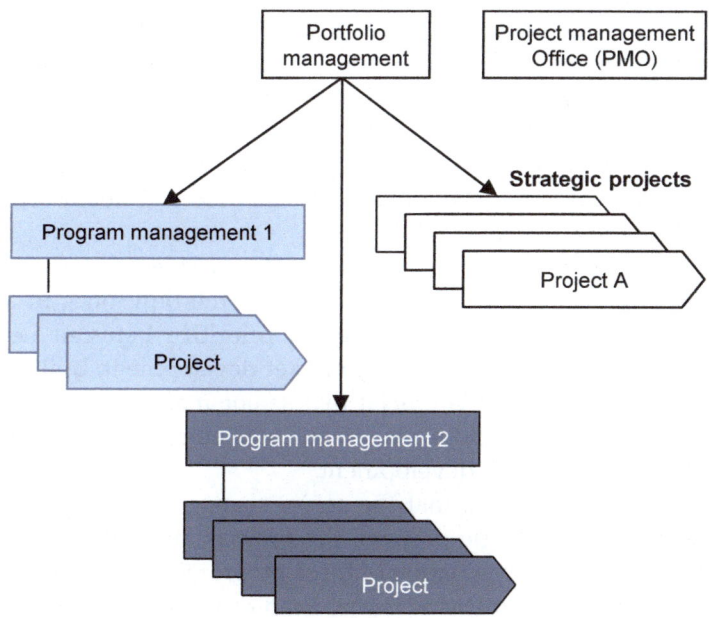

Figure 10.6. Structure of the portfolio management, program management and PMO.

Someone needs to be responsible for managing the complete volume of projects. Within the individual project, there are two distinct roles. The assignment is often commissioned by a steering committee or project owner. This is the 'in-house' customer, who consequently needs to be able to allocate the resources and make the overriding decisions. The project manager and the project team are the executing party undertaking responsibility for completion of the assignment.

Portfolio management entails a good deal of coordination across the projects. It is therefore necessary to either insert a layer to carry out this coordination or group the projects together under common steering committees.

10.3.2. The portfolio management

The entire portfolio

The portfolio is the complete collection of projects and programs that have been approved for execution. The projects don't have to be initiated, but they do have to be approved to be part of the portfolio. The portfolio is a snapshot of all approved projects at any given time. When projects are completed, new projects are initiated in the portfolio. There doesn't have to be any direct connection or dependency between the projects in a portfolio. The projects can have very different management references and draw on many different staff groups and resources.

The overall portfolio management is carried out by the senior management. They are generally the only ones in an organization with the authority to prioritize between new product development projects, market development, building new factories, etc. It is crucial that senior management is involved in the portfolio management, as it entails management of the organization's development.

In order to ensure that the senior management maintains focus on the strategic projects, the projects are gathered into programs. The coordination of these programs is then delegated so that the senior management can concentrate on the important strategic projects.

The portfolio management has three primary tasks:
- Compose the portfolio – prioritize the projects
- Plan the project pipeline – how many projects need to be carried out simultaneously? Which should be carried out first?
- Follow-up on the project portfolio

10.3.3. Program board and senior responsible manager (the program owner)

The programs in the portfolio

A program is a group of projects and ad hoc assignments, which together produce the desired impact of the program. The projects may be of the same type, or they may underpin a common strategy or a specific and clearly defined purpose. There is coherence among the projects in the form of dependencies and deadlines, but the program can still be executed even though one of the projects isn't completed or its content changes. Every project in a program shares the same management reference – the program management or program manager.

The structure of the program management depends on the size of the projects. Smaller projects may report to one shared steering committee (program board), while it is sometimes better for larger projects to have their own steering committee.

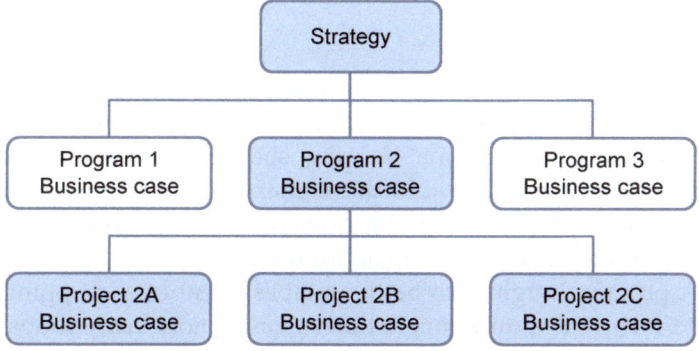

Figure 10.7. The correlation between the overall strategy, the programs and the individual projects. The combined impact of the projects should produce the desired impact of the program.

The individual project's business case is part of the overall business case for the program. You can also say that the individual project's purpose and sub-purposes make up the building blocks of the overall strategy.

Examples of programs:

New product development projects, which are broken down into product families or product lines. The purpose of this type of program is to maintain and develop one product line. All projects with this purpose are coordinated by the program manager. Within product development, this might be a product manager.

Organizational changes, e.g. in connection with the merger of two firms or the amalgamation of two municipalities. In this context, a program might consist of all the IT projects that need to be carried out in order to establish a new joint system. In the merger of two firms, a program might consist of all the projects the two firms carry out in order to harmonize the services targeting a specific market segment.

A firm looking to reduce lead times in production might establish a program consisting of an IT project, an organizational change project and an engineering project to design new production equipment.

In the construction sector, a typical program might be the development of urban districts, for instance of a run-down harbor area with a marina, housing, shopping center, restaurants and fitness facilities. In this context, how the individual construction projects are to be carried out is not completely fixed, but there is an overall plan for the area.

A program might also be the establishment of a shopping center, where it is uncertain in the beginning how many shops, restaurants and cinemas there will be.

The program management's tasks
Once the program has been defined, it is broken down into projects, which also need to be defined. During this process, the project management has two primary tasks:

10.3 Well-defined roles and distribution of responsibility

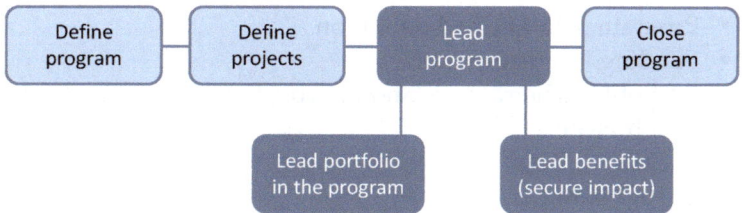

Figure 10.8. The life cycle of program management.

- Management of the portfolio of projects in the program, including coordination and resource allocation, and ensuring the right deliverables in the right quality.
- Ensuring that the anticipated impact is achieved. This element is a vital part of program management, as it is not something the individual project managers can carry out.

In an organizational change program, the project delivers new workflows, IT systems and a new organizational plan, but the program management (particularly the business change manager) ultimately ensures implementation. It is the program management's job to bring everything together.

This means that the program management is closer to the projects than the overall portfolio management. Portfolio management is often conducted by senior management, which is also responsible for operations. Program management is often carried out by a project director who is highly skilled in working with projects.

The tools for program management and portfolio management are often the same, but in program management, it may be necessary to closely monitor milestones in the individual projects using an overview of key milestones that have dependencies with other projects within the program.

Organization of the program
The program organization often includes the following roles and areas of responsibility:

Sponsoring group (senior management)
- Provision of the organizational context for the program
- Strategic direction and objectives

393

- Program mandate and definition
- Funding for the program
- End-of-tranche reviews and approval of progression to the next tranche

Program board
- Definition of acceptable risk profile and risk thresholds for the program
- Ensuring that the program delivers within the agreed framework/boundaries
- Maintenance and realization of the blueprint, i.e. the description of the program's ultimate objectives
- Ensuring operational stability and effectiveness throughout the program life cycle

Senior responsible owner (program owner)
- Creating and communicating the vision for the program
- Establishing the program governance
- Ensuring that the program delivers a coherent capability, achieves its strategic outcomes and realizes its benefits

Program manager
- Planning and designing the program
- Daily management of the program
- Development of the program governance framework
- Managing and mitigating any risks

Business change manager(s)
- Responsible for specific business area or site
- Senior-level manager responsible for operations after 'go live'
- Defining the benefits
- Defining the future operating state of the business area they represent
- Assessing progress toward realization of the benefits
- Performance monitoring, benefits tracking
- Responsible for achieving the planned benefits

10.3 Well-defined roles and distribution of responsibility

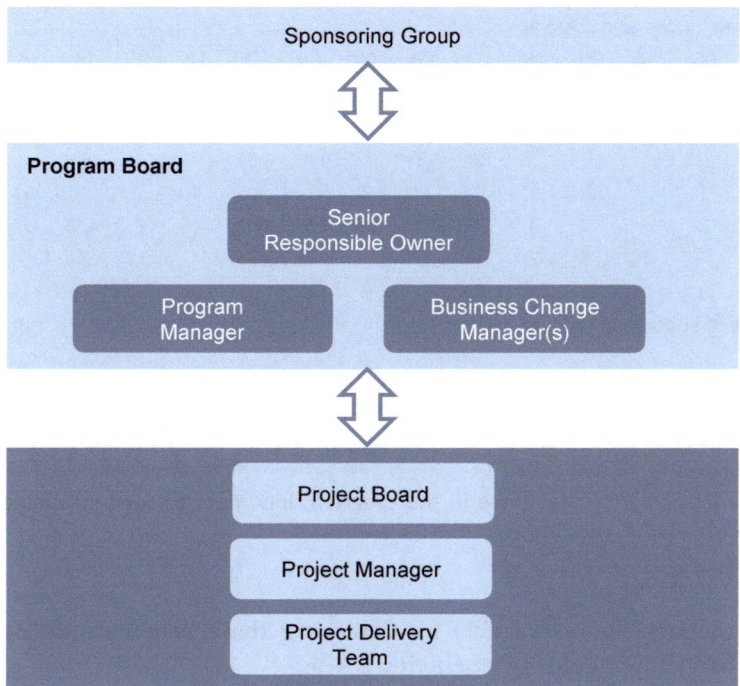

Figure 10.9. Program organization inspired by MSP (Managing Successful Programs, TSO).

To secure the planned benefits (success criteria), these benefits are monitored during the course of each project and after completion.

In the following overview, the top half shows in which weeks the various projects must deliver various milestones (the milestones are numbered).

The bottom half shows how the value is calculated on a weekly basis by measuring the various success criteria – SC 1, SC 2 and SC3. Some projects deliver SC 1, others SC 2 and so forth.

One issue with program management is that the benefits or success criteria can't be measured until the individual project has been completed. It is therefore important that the program is broken down into tranches, which end in a well-defined state or set of deliverables and part-delivery of the overall blueprint. When these deliverables have been achieved, the first benefits can be collected. The program's business change

	Calendar week no. and milestone														
	01	02	03	04	05	06	07	08	09	10	11	12	13	14	15
Project 1		1	2	3	4	5		6				7		8	
Project 2	1		2	3			4			5					
Project 3					1		2	3		4	5			6	
Project 4				1		2			3			4			5
Project 5		1	2			3	4			5			6		
Project 6				1		2		3			4			5	
Project 7	1	2	3	4	5		6		7	8		9			
	Total value of success criteria														
SC 1															
SC 2															
SC 3															
Value															

Figure 10.10. Overview of project milestones in the program, incl. possibility of indicating the value of the realized benefits (success criteria).

manager is responsible for achieving these benefits and for carrying out effective benefit tracking.

10.3.4. Steering committees or program manager

For large, complex projects, the program management may take the form of a steering committee for each project. However, the program manager is responsible for the 'daily' contact with the project manager.

The projects in the programs

10.3.5. Project managers

Just as the individual project can be broken down into work streams, a program can be broken down into projects, with each project headed by a project manager. In the 1990s, it wasn't uncommon for the project manager's responsibilities to be expanded as projects grew larger. However, with the growing use of program management we see today, programs are more often broken down into several smaller projects with more coordination by the program manager.

If the organization has experienced project managers, the project volume can be reduced by increasing the project size, with the project manager taking on a larger share of the coordination responsibilities. If the organization doesn't have ex-

10.3 Well-defined roles and distribution of responsibility

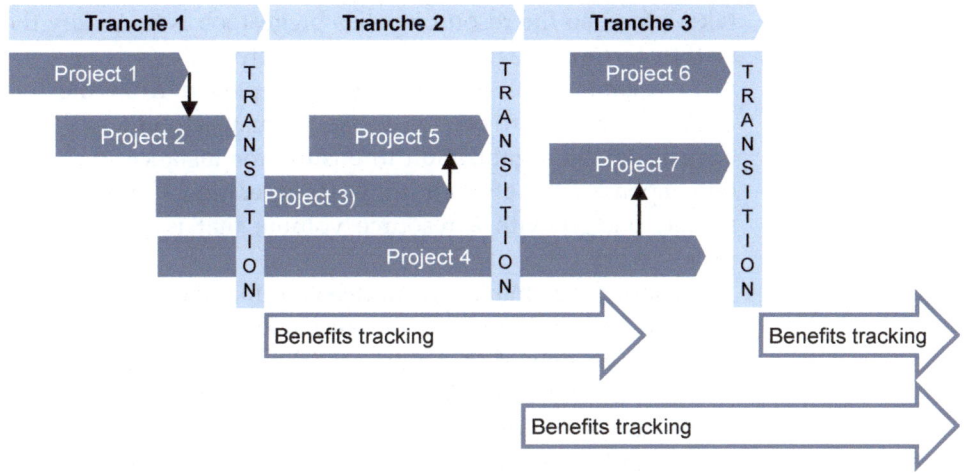

Figure 10.11. Program with seven projects, three tranches and benefit realization (inspired by MSP, TSO).

perienced project managers on staff, the program can be broken down into smaller projects, in which case the program management would take on a larger share of the management responsibilities.

Program management is often conducted at middle management level. A change in the organization toward a greater focus on projects will therefore not simply shift power away from the middle managers toward the project managers. The middle management team will actually be assigned new responsibilities.

10.3.6. Resources

Resource allocation

One of the biggest challenges is allocating resources to the projects. Projects are uncertain, so it can be difficult to predict the resource consumption. However, even in the situations where there are good project estimates, we often find that resource consumption in the line organization isn't quite as well known and predictable as originally thought.

There are basically two paths you can follow. In organizations with an extremely high volume of projects, various resource pools can be established, for example in an R&D department. This is where the bulk of the activity in the projects takes place, so the resource pool's biggest job is to qualify the staff to perform the tasks needed in the projects.

In organizations where staff are deployed from the line organization to project assignments, management needs to dimension the organization to ensure, for instance, that staff only spend 70% of their time on operational duties. You should budget with a resource volume that is available for project work.

In both cases, management needs to maintain an overview of the project volume and the associated resource consumption. This is one of the primary arguments for introducing portfolio management. If every project is included on the project list and every project uses the Project KPIs tool (Tool 10.3), then it will be possible to calculate the resource consumption for every single project.

Regardless of whether you use resource pools or bring project participants in from the line organization, it's a good idea to draw up a resource agreement for each project participant. The resource agreement concluded between the project manager and the project participants is basically a 'mini-project triangle' for the individual's efforts in the project, setting out which deliverables the participant is expected to contribute, when they are expected to be delivered and the expected resource deployment.

The sum of the resource contracts provides the employee with an overview of her project load/resource input, while giving her superior in her department an idea of the department's project load. This also provides the project manager with an overview of the project's resource allocation.

10.3.7. Project management office (PMO) – lubricating the 'project machine'

The PMO is the organizational unit responsible for putting project management on the agenda. All firms have a finance department, IT department or HR department, but who is responsible for ensuring the efficient use of the project model? One prerequisite for portfolio management is a standardized project process with tools and the collection of correct data – who is responsible for all of this?

The PMO is not a large unit. In organizations with 500-600 project employees, there are generally 1.5 to 2 people in the PMO. In some organizations, the office is headed by an experienced project manager and a secretary. The project manager is seconded to the PMO for a year, after which time another experienced project manager takes her place.

In other organizations, the PMO is the responsibility of the project director – the project managers' boss. The project managers report to the project director and are seconded to the projects. This type of organization is often seen in development functions or organizations where projects are the primary service.

The project management office (PMO) is responsible for the following:

Provision of services to portfolio management and program management
- Maintenance and organization of the portfolio process (owner of the process), including development and implementation of tools
- Provision of services to project committees and program management
  Development of decision-making analyses and overviews
  Updating the project list and portfolio overview
- Establishing and maintaining measurement systems

Provision of services to the projects
- Supporting project managers in connection with kick-off seminars
- Serving as a facilitator at workshops
- Preparing project management overviews
- Coaching project managers

Maintenance and development of the project process
- Maintenance and development of the project process (owner of the process)
- Maintenance of project manuals
- Provision of relevant IT support to projects
- Development and maintenance of templates

- Development and administration of project portal
- Maintenance of project management toolbox

Development of project competence
- Planning the systematic training of project managers and managers
- Career development for project managers
- Experience exchange between project managers
- Project audits
- Benchmarking of projects and programs
- Knowledge-sharing about project management disciplines

Data collection
- Collection and organization of project data
- Development of resource overviews
- Development and collection of time logs
- Collection of project costs defrayed
- Risk ranking for the individual projects
- Calculation of projects' value to date
- Project's business case

10.3.8. Summary of distribution of responsibilities and assignments within the project organization

A summary of the elements in the project portfolio is presented in Figure 10.10. This list is not exhaustive and is meant solely as a guide. There is no hard and fast rule stipulating that the resource consumption in a portfolio must be measured in person years, while in programs it must be measured in person months. However, this does give an indication of the scope of the assignment. If the resource consumption isn't to be measured in person years, then it isn't necessary to introduce one level for portfolio management and one level for program management with underlying projects.

Distribution of tasks and responsibilities

	Element in portfolio management			
Descriptive element	Portfolio	Program	Project	Ad hoc assignment
Content	All projects that are bigger than the minimum limit plus programs	Projects and ad hoc assignments of the same type or that underpin a common purpose	Work streams, milestones and activities	Activities
Person responsible	Primary top management	Primarily management at function level	Project manager	Person responsible for assignment
Responsibility	Prioritization. Resource allocation. Balanced portfolio.	Secure program's impact. Responsible for business case.	Secure deliverables on time and on budget	Deliverable on time
Management model	Project management model	Project management model and project model	Project model and milestone plan	Assignment description
Objective management	Correlation between strategic objective and project purpose.	Correlation between strategic objective and project deliverables	Project purpose, deliverables and success criteria with deadlines	Deliverable and deadline
Measuring progress	Measurement at phase level	Measurement of phases and primary milestones	Measurement of milestones	Measurement of sub-deliverables
Resource allocation	Different person types by person-years	Persons often stated in person-months	Named persons stated in person-months	Few named persons stated in person-months
Deadline	Infinite	Finite, fixed deadline. Ends in the future.	Fixed deadline in years and months	Fixed deadline in months and weeks
Correlations	Underpins common strategy. Dependencies on purpose level.	Dependencies between strategic objective and project deliverables	Dependencies between work streams, milestones and deadlines	

Figure 10.12. Comparison of responsibilities and tasks in the project portfolio as a whole.

10.4 Solid basis for decision-making – prioritizing projects

10.4.1. Management decisions should be made in an established meeting structure

One of the most important control mechanisms for management of the project organization is making the overall decisions.

It is therefore necessary to define which meeting forums should be part of the project organization, as well as who should participate in the various meetings and which decisions should be made.

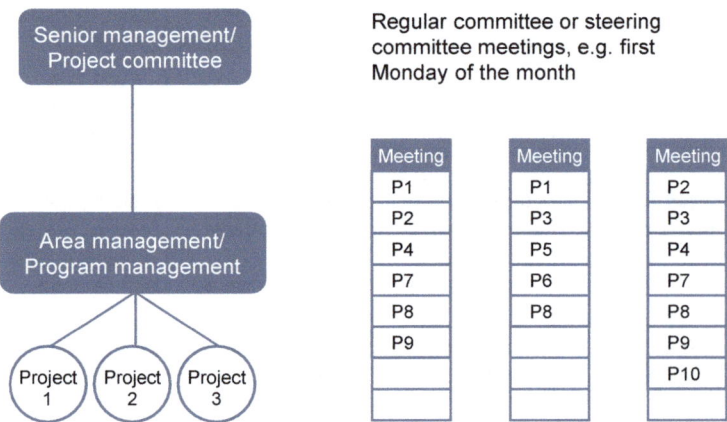

Figure 10.13. Establishing a fixed meeting structure with regular meetings of the management team, for example every other Monday. This is where the projects can have an audience with the management. It is important that this meeting structure is flexible. For example, in the progress overview in Figure 10.3, the rule might be that management will only summon red-lighted projects or those projects where the project manager has requested a meeting.

Decisions are only made in accordance with a written decision-making analysis, in which the project manager has presented the project team's opinion and recommendations.

For decisions requiring prioritization between several projects, the PMO should draw up an overview and recommendation.

10.4.2. Correlation with the strategy

The meeting structure and the basis for decision-making should underpin the correlation with the organization's strategy or overall policy. The annual strategy process in the firm or organization usually produces action plans, which are again broken down into plans for the functions and departments. But this is not the way to implement changes. A strategy and other changes can only be executed as a portfolio of change projects.

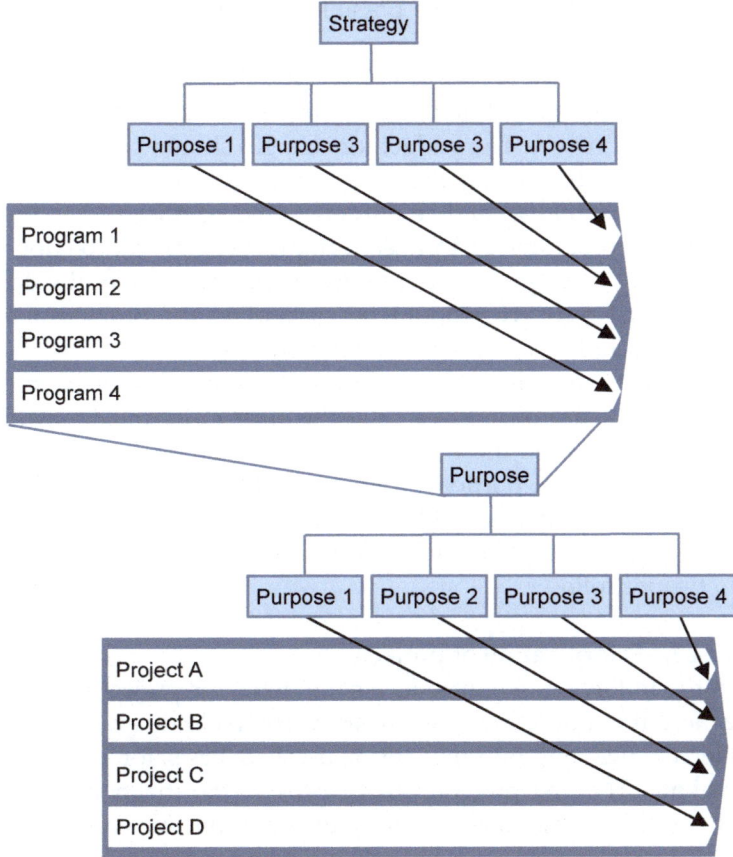

Figure 10.14. The strategy (the overall purpose) can be broken down into project programs by asking 'how'. These can again be broken down into projects by asking, 'How do we carry out program 4?' By initiating projects A, B, C and D. Project A can then be broken down further into work streams, like a Chinese box (see the OBS tool).

A hierarchy can be established for the project portfolio, just like the objective breakdown structure (OBS) in Chapter 3.

Also just like the OBS hierarchy, we can climb the project portfolio by asking 'why'. Why are we carrying out project C? To achieve the purpose of program 4. Why has program 4 been initiated? Because it underpins the strategy.

In practice, very few actually draw up a hierarchy for the project portfolio, but the mindset and principle are quite useful. If the sum of the projects doesn't indicate a high likelihood that the strategy will be realized, then projects are missing. Similarly, it should also be possible to explain why a specific project has been initiated.

Many strategy processes fail because the budget for implementation is spread out among the organization's departments and offices. The budget for changes should be placed in the organizational unit that implements the changes, i.e. the project. The budget and resources should be allocated to the portfolio, programs and projects. In practice, this can be done by having management decide that a specific share of the departments' resources should be earmarked for projects and may therefore not be used for operational tasks.

In many firms and organizations, this type of strategy process takes place once a year. But this doesn't harmonize with the dynamic life of these organizations. It should be possible to adjust the project portfolio at any time if the need or a project idea arises. And it should be possible to immediately make new projects a higher priority in relation to the other projects in the portfolio.

10.4.3. Prioritization of projects

In the following, we introduce some tools for project prioritization. It is important that decisions are made in a recognizable manner and informed by a detailed basis for decision-making. The first prerequisite for project prioritization is that all relevant projects are actually included on the project list! This may seem obvious, but when we and our 450 colleagues visit firms and organizations all over, we see that more than 80 percent do not have a list of their ongoing projects (as of spring 2015).

10.4 Solid basis for decision-making – prioritizing projects

It is a good idea for the project list to contain information on project status, budget, duration and risk.

Project list

Project	Project manager	Status	Budget	Urgency (strategic fit)	Risk ranking
Project 1	JRO	Phase 2	USD 200,000	4	8
Project 2	MLN	Phase 5	USD 1,200,000	3	2
Project 3	HAR	Phase 3	USD 500,000	5	5
Project 4	KK	Phase 1	USD 400,000	5	10
Project 5	OSA	Phase 2	USD 2,300,000	3	10
Project 6	HR	Phase 4	USD 2,600,000	1	5

Figure 10.15. The project list is updated on a regular basis by having the project managers report their status and risk ranking. The program management then updates the urgency, e.g. in connection with program management meetings.

The risk ranking is assessed by the project team and the project manager based on a project risk analysis or health check. The urgency is assessed by the steering committee or program management based on specified criteria (strategic fit). These criteria vary greatly from project type to project type.

Criteria for urgency of R&D development projects include:
- The new product meets legislative requirements
- Resolves safety issue
- Product is unique on the market
- Expected market share within one year (often only months for consumer electronics)
- Resolves quality issue
- Short ROI
- High contribution margin
- Increases customer satisfaction

Criteria for urgency of organizational change projects include:
- Resolves environmental issue
- Cuts costs
- Results in shorter lead time

- Reduces errors
- Improves employee satisfaction
- Increases accuracy

Criteria for urgency of projects within a political organization include:
- There is political demand
- Quickly improves conditions for members/citizens
- Places members/citizens in a better situation in the long term
- Positions our organization in relation to members/citizens
- Cuts costs internally

Criteria for urgency of customer projects include:
- Project is a good reference
- Project gives access to additional sales
- Revenue
- High contribution margin
- Possibility of developing own service in collaboration with customer

Figure 10.16 is an illustration of a portfolio overview featuring the information from the project. This type of overview, which is a classic way to illustrate the current state of affairs and the projects' placement in the portfolio, is typically drawn up by the PMO.

The size of the circles indicates the budget/resource consumption of the project in question. Light blue = on schedule, dark blue = delayed. (For other ways to illustrate the portfolio, see the Portfolio Overview tool.)

The portfolio overview is a dynamic tool that can quickly be adjusted when circumstances change. New projects are often introduced in the left-hand corner, as they generally have a high level of uncertainty at start-up. This uncertainty should, however, falls over the course of the project (otherwise, this should catch the attention of the portfolio management).

For example, sudden changes in the political or market situation can result in project 2 increasing in urgency and rising to the top of the overview. In contrast, new legislation or action by a competitor might render project 3 irrelevant.

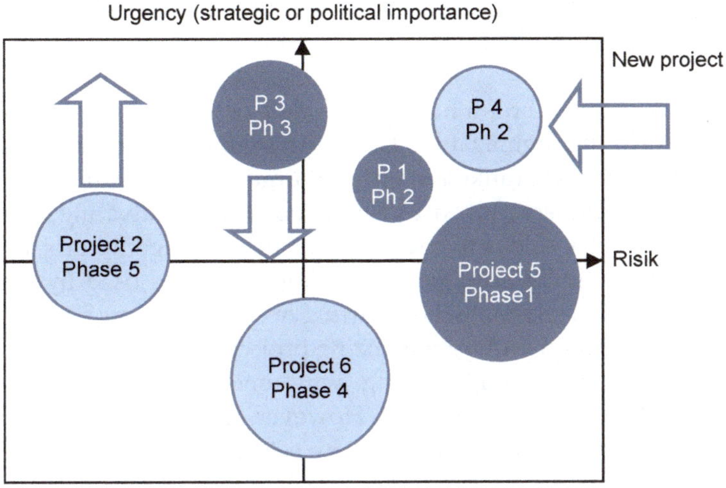

10.4 Solid basis for decision-making – prioritizing projects

Figure 10.16. Portfolio overview of six projects. Projects 3, 1 and 4 have the highest strategic or political importance. Projects 1, 4 and 5 have the highest risk levels.

The urgency scale is defined based on criteria that have been specified beforehand. The observant reader may have already noticed that these criteria bear a close resemblance to the typical success criteria for the project type in question. This is another advantage of grouping projects into programs. The success criteria will generally be of the same nature for all the projects in the program.

With a bit of structuring, it will thus be possible to select common success criteria on a scale. For example in new product development projects: 'Contribution margin one year after release'. This is a success criterion for the individual project, but it can also be used as a scale for how urgent the project is. Finally, the contribution margins can be summed up to give a total value for the portfolio (see the Project KPIs tool).

In some portfolios and programs, urgency is determined by dependencies. In large-scale IT projects and R&D projects, technological platforms may also need to be defined and tested before other sub-systems can be tested. Thus, it may be necessary to supplement or replace the overview with a series of timelines showing the order in which the projects need to be executed (Figure 10.2).

Use urgency with care You need to be careful how the urgency of projects is communicated to the organization. Some firms simply draw up a list of all the projects ranked in order of urgency. However, working on the project ranked 28 isn't particularly motivating! It is therefore a good idea to communicate that all ongoing projects are important. The urgency scale should only be used by the portfolio management when starting or stopping a project.

In connection with reprioritizing projects, the criteria can be helpful when communicating why one project has been stopped and another initiated. However, it is again important to communicate that all ongoing projects are important.

10.4.4. Strategic considerations – value and balance

There are traditionally four key strategic considerations:

- Value – does the portfolio comprise the projects that generate the most value?
- Strategic fit – are there enough projects to execute the strategy?
- Balance – how great is the total risk in relation to the potential?
- Investment – how high is the total resource consumption needed to complete the portfolio?

Value

One starting point is for the portfolio to be composed of the projects that generate the most value with the available resources. In this case, value might be the future contribution margin, largest market share, highest recognizability or greatest political value.

In project portfolios consisting of new product development projects or cost-cutting projects, it isn't possible to calculate an actual total value for the portfolio using success criteria. Instead, you need to use something like the Project KPIs tool.

Strategic fit

Another approach is the strategic or political 'fit'. Here, the aim is to compose the portfolio so as to best underpin the strategy. This may not be the portfolio that generates the greatest value in the here and now, but in the long term it looks best from a strategic point of view. Perhaps there should be a combination of projects that produce quick results and strategic projects with a long-term impact.

An important consideration is whether the portfolio is large enough to achieve the strategic or political objectives. Are there enough projects to secure organizational change? Are there any projects that don't underpin the strategy and should consequently be stopped?

Balance

Normally, management prefers to balance value with risk or value in relation to short and long-term objectives. However, it is not enough for the portfolio to have a high value if all the projects have a high risk level or are very resource demanding.

In a private-sector firm, management will often compose the project portfolio to ensure a combination of projects with high and low risk. Important projects can be very high risk, thus it is important to consider how many high-risk projects should be executed simultaneously. In some political organizations, the risk axis isn't as relevant as the ratio of short and long term. The risk axis can then be replaced by an axis that breaks the projects down into short and long term.

The portfolio management's job is to prioritize this balancing of the highest impact of the projects in the here and now, the long-term impacts and the portfolio's risk.

In the portfolio in Figure 10.16, projects 2, 4 and 6 – the least important projects – use most of the resources. While this may be caused by the nature of the projects, it is definitely worth considering whether the resources are being deployed to the right projects, i.e. to the projects that have the greatest political and strategic impact. For example, the important project 4 is delayed, so perhaps resources can be brought in from the less important project 6.

Few, but fast projects

Another consideration for the portfolio management is the prioritization of the ongoing project volume. Figure 10.17 illustrates two ways to organize the project portfolio.

The portfolio depicted at the top comprises a great deal of projects, resulting in long lead times. Furthermore, there are many coordination issues, as the same employees are working on several different projects at once. Finally, eight project managers are needed, which means that either some project managers have to head up several projects or inexperienced project managers will have to be used.

The risk level in the top portfolio is high, as quite a long time passes from investment to benefit achievement. Due to the long project timeframe, a large number of changes have to be made along the way to adapt to an ever-changing world. At worst, the project may become obsolete.

Project by time unit

Figure 10.17. Focused portfolio with few projects and short lead times. In both cases, eight projects are carried out within the same timeframe.

The **traditional portfolio** contains:
- Many ongoing projects
- Long lead times
- Major coordination issues
- High capital tie-up before result
- High total risk
- Need for many project managers
- Staff work on several projects

The **focused portfolio** contains:
- Few ongoing projects
- Short lead times
- The freeing up of resources
- Lower capital tie-up and faster results
- Need for few project managers
- Possibility for staff to be dedicated to just one project

In the focused portfolio, the coordination issue has been reduced significantly. It is possible to put the four best project managers on the assignments, while working on these projects is fun, as everyone can quickly see the results of their work instead of constantly feeling guilty.

So why aren't projects carried out as in the latter portfolio? Possibly because nobody knows how many ongoing projects there actually are! Or perhaps there is no prioritization! This is the portfolio management's most important job – prioritization! Who else is going to do it? There is no strategy if the organization doesn't say NO to anything!

10.5. Common language – project model, methodology and KPIs

10.5.1. Project process and methods

The definitions of project types form the foundation for a description of the project approach. The various project types may have different requirements, but it is still a good idea to have one overriding, generic project management model that everyone is expected to follow.

Find the common characteristics: process, management reference person and resources

It can then be supplemented by a project model for the individual project types.

The various project approaches may differ in terms of their requirements for:

- Project start-up, primary milestones in the projects and project completion
- Decision points/phases
- Work streams
- Reporting requirements
- Resource allocation and budgeting
- Steering committee composition

Once the projects are defined by type, it is possible to describe the approach.

There are several reasons why it is a good idea to operate with a common project management model and common methodology:

- The projects need to be comparable for management to be able to monitor the progress of the portfolio.
- A common language within the organization is important so that everyone knows what is meant by project, objective, design phase, risk analysis, etc.
- With uniform templates for documentation, the project managers don't have to re-invent sliced bread and management can read the plan without exclaiming: 'They've never seen it like this before!'
- Understanding the methodology boosts the quality of projects. Projects are uncertain, but that doesn't mean the approach and methodology have to be.
- Cross-departmental and cross-divisional participation is easier when everyone is uses the same model and tools.
- Project managers can concentrate on managing the project instead of teaching the participants how to use the project work form.

A generic project process, called a project management model, consists of a number of pre-defined phases that each project must pass through. Between the phases are the decision

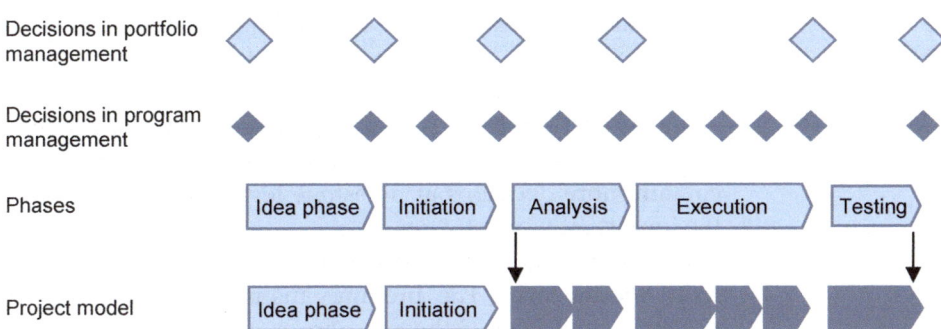

Figure 10.18. The project management model describes the phases every project passes through, while the project model describes a specific project type in more detail. In practice, the correlation is not as strictly defined, but it is a good principle to bear in mind when designing the project management model and project model.

points. It also defines the result that should be achieved after the completion of each phase.

The project management model describes how every project looks, from the point of view of the portfolio management. The model is a prerequisite for portfolio management. However, the individual project will also find project management models useful, even if the firm hasn't introduced systematic portfolio management.

Within the overall model, there may be variations among the different project types. This often causes a bit of terminological confusion. It is therefore a good idea to define two levels of project processes.

1. The project management model is a generic model for management and steering of all projects within the portfolio. This model comprises the project phases, a description of the decision points where the portfolio management is involved and a description of the key results in each phase. It also contains an overview of the project management tools that are to be used in all projects, such as the milestone plan template. **Project management model**

2. The project model is specific for the individual project type. The overall phases are the same as in the project management **Project model**

model. However, when we go into more detail with analysis, implementation and testing, there will often be differences in the content of these phases, depending on whether we are dealing with, say, a new product development project, an IT project or an organizational change project. Consequently, it is characterized by the area of specialization that is the focus of the project. The project model will be more detailed and will contain more decisions at milestone level, as well as defining the important work streams.

The portfolio management steers at the project management model level. The program management steers at the project model level if the program comprises projects of the same type. However, some programs comprise several project types that underpin the same purpose, in which case the program management can steer with the help of the project management model.

LFA The Logical Framework Approach (LFA), which is used in EU projects, is an example of a project management model containing seven standard phases: identification, feasibility study, project design, detailed planning, monitoring, project review and evaluation. The project phase transitions are described using a matrix containing information on objectives and indicators for these objectives. The necessary activities and resource input are also described, as well as a continuous assessment of external factors that may affect the project. LFA focuses on describing the project objective in terms of the sub-objectives of a program objective. This is because the approach was developed for aid projects and programs, like USAID, the UN and the OECD.

PRINCE2 PRINCE2, used especially for IT projects, is another example of a project management model. Its point of departure is the management processes in the project and describing how the project management should be organized. It comprises only two phases: project start-up and project initiation. The implementation phase can vary depending on the project type. For this reason, PRINCE2 describes how to manage a phase and how to carry out a phase transition. The number of sub-phases that make up the 'implementation phase' depends on the individual project. PRINCE2 also describes how to plan project evaluation.

The following is an example from a new product development process.

This project model could easily be one of the project types under the general project management model featured in Figure 10.18. The idea phase is the same. It is followed by project initiation and the establishment of a project team. Here, the overall analysis phase is broken down into analysis and planning, while the overall implementation phase is broken down into design and product maturation. In the R&D department, the testing phase is called test production.

Phase	Decision	Results
1. Idea phase	Idea approved	Idea description Business idea
2. Idea phase	Project proposal approved	Business case Concept described Technology assessed Market assessment
3. Planning	Project contract approved	Specification Success criteria Milestone plan Project organization Budget
4. Design	Design approved	Design of prototype ready Production principle ready Production equipment designed Marketing plan ready
5. Product maturation	Ready for test production	Prototype complete Technical testing compete Production equipment ready Procedural instructions ready
6. Test production	Released for sale	0-series production complete Technical documentation adjusted Production documentation adjusted Marketing material ready

Figure 10.19. Project model describing the process for an R&D project in a typical production company. The model consists of six phases, the important management decisions and the results that should be achieved after each phase.

The project model describes the project in general terms. For instance, the product maturation phase should always result in a prototype. This will always be the case, regardless of the apparatus being developed. Even a minor adjustment to an existing product results in an adjustment of the prototype.

If a minor adjustment doesn't result in changes to the production apparatus, then the 'production equipment ready' result is annulled, as it already exists. The standard milestone plans can be part of the project model in a similar way. In large-scale projects, all milestones must be included, while in smaller projects, some milestones can be dropped (see the Project Management Model tool). The model can also include a requirement that there always be the following work streams in R&D projects (the principle of concurrent engineering):

- The product
- Production preparation
- Introduction to market and service
- Purchasing and logistics

It is important that the project model is flexible so that it doesn't feel like a straitjacket and cause unnecessary bureaucracy. It is therefore a good idea to include the freedom to drop areas where the requirements of the model aren't essential. Other requirements, on the other hand, may be obligatory, such as milestones or tools, which must always be used.

Another approach is to organize the model in such a way that the decision regarding which milestones and results can be left out in the subsequent phase is made in, say, phase 2. The project model also includes a toolbox, like the toolbox that accompanies this book. It will often indicate which tools are required in the different phases.

There are also many different project models for IT projects, such as the RUP model and ASAP methodology.

10.5.2. Measuring impact in the portfolio

Galileo's words have never been more relevant.

His work triggered a scientific revolution, as he was the first to make experiments quantitative. So Einstein had good reason to call Galileo the 'the father of modern science'.

> **Measure what is measurable, and make measurable what is not so.**

Quantitative measurements have also entered the world of management in the form of key figures and key performance indicators (KPIs). In the finance sector, the Dupont pyramid created a system of key figures, while the Balanced Scorecard model expands the indicators to also include customers, processes and employees.

In project work, it has always been good form to ensure that deliverables and success criteria are measurable. There is just one problem – the success criteria can't be measured until the project has been completed and transitioned into the operational phase.

In this section, we take a closer look at the concept of measuring impact during and after the project process. In a perfect world, we would aim for the impact and then adjust the deliverables in the project to achieve the desired impact. However, in practice, the deliverables are fixed entities in the projects. Normally, the project agreement comprises the corners of the project triangle: 'deliverables, time and resources'.

To illustrate the principle of management with the help of impact measurements, we will use a case story from a real estate agency.

CASE

An international real estate agency with branches in 10 cities wants to introduce an IT-based case administration and filing system. They don't want to focus solely on the IT deliverable, but to also emphasize maximizing the impact of the investment.

The real estate agency's expectations are that the IT system will result in shorter case administration times, fewer errors, better knowledge-sharing among staff and better, more flexible, customer service. At the same time, they expect to be able to reduce their resource consumption on case administration and reallocate the newly freed up resources to improve customer assistance for both sellers and buyers.

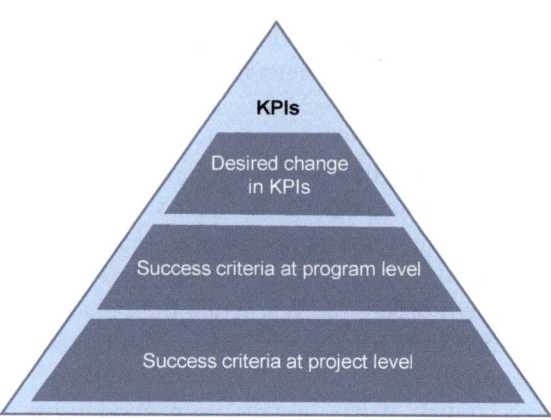

Figure 10.20. Illustration of the breakdown from strategic objective to the desired changes to selected KPIs – from changes to the KPIs to success criteria at program or project level.

The idea is for all incoming mail and documents to be scanned and then delivered electronically to the case administrators. Once the documents are in the filing system, everyone will be able to access them. Communication with sellers and buyers can take place on paper or by email as needed.

The real estate agency understands that this transition will result in changes to workflows, work tasks and the organization. They also realize that it will require some training for the employees and that some employee groups will actually need to have their skills completely upgraded.

Management by impact begins with the strategic objectives!

Which strategic objectives should the project or project portfolio help realize? The overall strategic objective should be broken down and correlated with the KPIs realized by the organization today. What is the value of the current KPIs and what change is desired?

Our real estate agency measures, among other things, the KPIs in Figure 10.21 and is looking to improve the key indicators in the following areas:

KPIs at organizational level	Current value	Desired value
Sales staff/case administrators	273	350
Case administration time	2 hours	1,5 hours
Hours/case	25 hours	15 hours
Customer satisfaction sellers	4.1	4.6
Customer satisfaction buyers	4.2	4.6

Figure 10.21. Current and desired KPIs in the real estate agency.

10.5. Common language – project model, methodology and KPIs

Breaking down the objectives in programs

Based on the desired changes, the following programs might be established:

- Program for boosting productivity by changing the relationship between sales staff and case administrators.
- Program for developing employee job satisfaction.
- Program for reducing lead times and improving customer satisfaction with case administration.

Success criteria at program level	Value one year later
Must reduce case administration time to:	1.5 hours
Must reduce hours spent per case to:	15 hours
Must increase customer satisfaction sellers to:	4.6
Must increase customer satisfaction buyers to:	4.6

Figure 10.22. The success criteria for one of the programs.

The program contains several projects, one of which is the case administration system, which is broken down into a joint project at the main office and individual projects at the branch offices.

It has been assessed that the case administration system ought to result in shorter case administration times, some error reduction, promotion of knowledge-sharing among staff and making customer service more flexible. The following success criteria are thus defined:

Success criteria at project level	Value one year later
1. Case administration time must be reduced to	1.5 hours
2. Avg. hours spent per case must be reduced to	15 hours
3. Errors in cases must be reduced to	5%
4. Knowledge-sharing via look-ups in other cases in	10 % of cases
5. First case administrator can close case in	90 % of cases
6. Case can be dealt with online outside opening hours in	10 % of cases

Figure 10.23. The projects' success criteria.

Success criteria 1 and 2 are the desired impacts, which are directly related to the program's success criteria and the real estate agency's KPIs.

Success criteria 3-6 are related to the sub-purposes and the impact that can be expected once the individual deliverables are establis-

419

hed. Consequently, these success criteria can be measured at an earlier stage in the project and will thus be able to give an indication of which deliverables need to be adjusted.

For instance, errors in case administration might be tested during the course of the project, making it possible to immediately adjust the workflows and staff training accordingly. Achievement of success criteria 3-6 is a prerequisite for achieving success criteria 1-2.

10.5.3. Measuring impact during the project process

It is important to establish a measurement system that correlates the project's work streams with the desired impact. A detailed OBS will reveal which deliverables have a relatively strong influence on the various success criteria.

For example, new workflows will have a direct impact on case administration lead times and resource consumption.

The training of staff will affect the number of corrections and errors.

> **Example from the case**
>
> In the IT-based case administration system project, corrections and errors need to be reduced. Achieving this requires staff training and boosting competences. The staff have already taken the first step, having participated in the training and expressed satisfaction.
>
> The **first measurement** might be their reaction to the course, seminars and proposals (Is there acceptance?), e.g. via course evaluation and employee satisfaction surveys. While satisfaction with the training program won't result in fewer errors, it is the first prerequisite for moving the staff in that direction.
>
> The **next measurement** might be whether they have learned anything – is the learning in place? Measure whether the employees have understood the messages, heard the information, are acquainted with the new principles, e.g. via an exam, test, survey, recognizability analysis, or similar.
>
> If the work stream deals with technology, the measurement might focus on whether the technical solution is in place.
>
> The **third measurement** is whether the employees have changed their behavior. Learning simply isn't enough. It is therefore a good idea to measure whether the project has resulted in changes in behavior and workflows, e.g. by means of auditing, 360-degree evaluations, satisfaction surveys, opinion surveys, etc.

Decision-making meeting

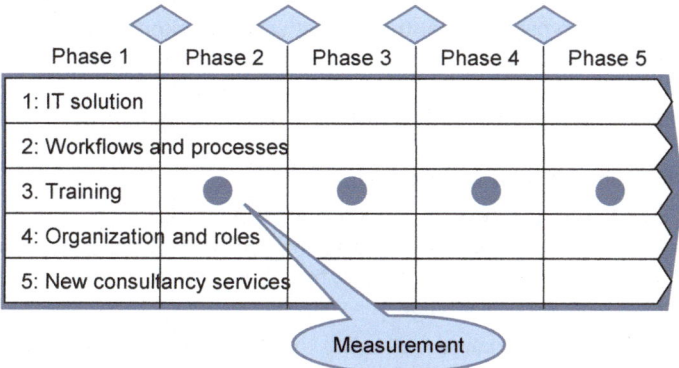

Figure 10.24. Measurements in the training work stream during the project period. The measurements should be planned so that the results are available prior to important decision-making meetings, enabling the adjustment of subsequent deliverables.

Another option is to measure changes in the technical performance (now that all the cases are available at the individual's workstation).

The **fourth measurement** is the business-related impact after the employees have learned something new and changed their behavior, for example fewer corrections and errors.

Prognosis for the success criteria

Another method is to assess how realistic the success criteria are at different levels during the course of the project. As we know, we learn more and more as the project progresses.

Objective (1)	After phase 1 (2)	After phase 2 (3)	After phase 3 (4)	After phase 4 (5)
Case administration time reduced to 1.5 hours	1.5 hours	1.6 hours	1.6 hours	1.8 hours
Avg. hours spent per case. 15 hours	15 hours	15 hours	15 hours	15 hours
Errors in case must be reduced to %	5 %	5 %	8 %	8 %

Figure 10.25. This is a description of three of the project success criteria. Column 1 shows the original success criteria. Column 2 shows the prognosis for the success criteria after phase 1, and so forth.

The point is to assess after each phase how you expect the success criteria to be fulfilled and then take the necessary action and adjust the project so that the original success criteria can be achieved! As we can see in Figure 10.23, the lead time appears to hold, but there are serious problems with achieving improvements in resource consumption and reducing the number of corrections.

Measuring impact in programs

The program manager is responsible for ensuring that the program as a whole achieves the expected impact, while the project managers are responsible for ensuring that their individual projects realize the planned deliverables.

Using programs makes it possible to adjust and vary the deliverables to achieve the desired impact. Within the program, projects can be closed or initiated to secure the planned impact.

Going back to the real estate agency case, we find there is a program for reducing lead times and improving customer satisfaction with case administration and customer assistance. The implemen-

		Success criteria					
Department	Total	1	2	3	4	5	6
Copenhagen							
London							
Paris							
Berlin							
Amsterdam							
Prague							
New York							
Stockholm							
Oslo							
Rome							
Total							

Figure 10.26. The impact of follow-up at program level over 10 projects in different departments. The success criteria are: 1. Case administration time must be reduced. 2. Avg. time spent per case must be reduced. 3. Errors in cases must be reduced. 4. Knowledge-sharing via look-ups in other cases. 5. First case administrator can close case. 6. Case can be dealt with online outside opening hours. (White corresponds to green light – no problems. Light blue corresponds to yellow light – attention point. Dark blue corresponds to red light – danger.)

tation of the IT-based case administration system comes in under this program.

If the measurements show that the employees haven't learned anything after completing the two-day courses, then the program management can launch a competence development project to address this issue. Figure 10.26 shows the program management's overview of the projects in the 10 branch offices.

According to the overview, there are problems with achieving the desired impact in Prague and Rome, while Copenhagen, Berlin and Amsterdam are on the watch list. There are especially problems with three specific success criteria regarding resource consumption and corrections in case administration (success criteria 2, 4 and 5). It is a good idea to assess the success criteria regularly, as the knowledge base grows.

10.5.4. Definition of measuring points – approach

When establishing a measuring system for the project, the following approach is recommended:

Define the project's OBS hierarchy

The project's OBS hierarchy needs to be drawn up. It is important to find correlations between the overall strategic objectives and the project's purpose. The project's purpose should be broken down into sub-purposes and deliverables so that the project can be organized into work streams.

Plan the project

Define the project's work streams based on the deliverables. Define milestones for the individual work streams. Remember to incorporate measurement into the plan when designing the project in the beginning.

Establish a measurement system

The measurement system is designed as a hierarchy corresponding to the OBS. At the top of this hierarchy is the firm's overall KPIs. Below them come the impacts of the project, which are derived directly from these KPIs.

The success criteria are often the changes to the KPIs that the project is to produce (the impact of the project).

It is also relevant to measure impact before the project is completed in order to adjust the deliverables during the course of the project. It is better to aim at closer targets, hit them and then replace them with new targets than to never hit the overall targets far off in the distance. Measurements should be conducted often and the results communicated quickly in order to render visible the correlation between the effort and the results.

Start early
Insist that the measurement system be established early in the project period. Define impact measurement by means of direct correlation with the success criteria. Spend the necessary time on establishing the measurement system – including the practical aspects.

Measure on several levels
It's important to measure on several levels to ensure traceability and coherence between effort and impact. If measurements are only conducted close to the deliverables, you lose focus on the overall impact. If measurements are only conducted on an overall level, it is impossible to take mitigating action during the project period and difficult to see the impact of the sub-activities.

Organize the process
If the measurement process isn't organized, the measurements will not be visible.
 It's important to define who does what and when.

Keep it simple
Measurement systems have a tendency to grow in scope, especially the task of compiling data, which can become unmanageable and extremely elaborate.

Communicate the measurements
If you don't communicate the measurements, rumors can quickly spread and interest in delivering data can drop. The measurement results should be visible and should be included in the official overviews.

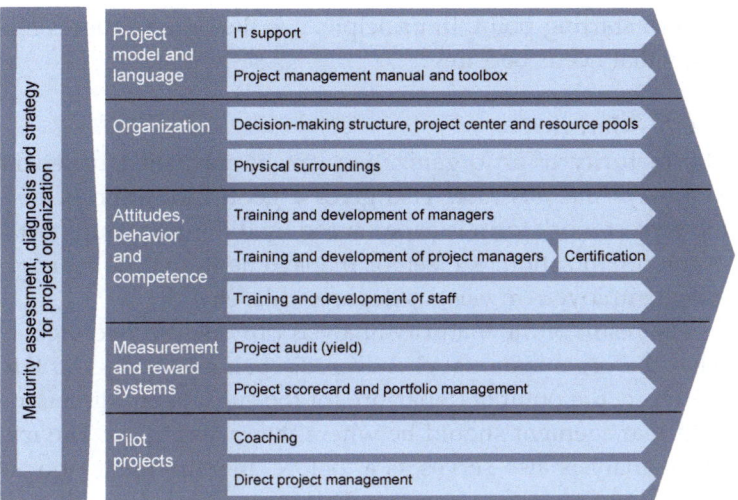

Figure 10.27. The Project Excellence model is used to introduce the project work form. The model covers the following focus areas: maturity, project management model and language, organization, competence, behavior and attitudes, objective management and auditing and pilot projects. This model has been developed by Implement Consulting Group.

10.6. Development of the organization toward Project Excellence

10.6.1. On the path toward Project Excellence – approaching LEAN project management

Many organizations are working toward a more project-oriented approach. Our workdays now include participating in organizational development projects, with the aim of increasing the organization's maturity when it comes to working with projects – to develop the organization toward Project Excellence.

We use the concept of 'Project Excellence' as a model for the implementation of this type of organizational change project. The model ensures that all important elements are addressed in the process of creating a project-oriented organization.

When developing the organization, it is important to take the organization's maturity in terms of the project work form as your starting point. In principle, it is the organization's maturity that needs boosting.

10.6.2. Maturity

Where do we start?
The maturity of an organization can be measured using the Maturity Analysis tool. This gives a good indication of how the project work form is experienced by different groups within the organization, e.g. senior management, middle management, employees in various departments, etc.

The result of the maturity analysis provides an overview of what the organizational change project should focus on. Furthermore, the point of departure for the subsequent discussion with management should be where they want to go. The maturity analysis also serves as a 'before' measurement prior to initiation of the change project. This measurement can then be repeated after the project has been completed. It can be carried out at regular intervals as well, for example every other year.

It is important to understand that the maturity analysis can't be used as an 'objective' measurement of the current state of affairs, as it is an expression of the subjective experiences of different employees. However, a discussion within the organization about why individuals experience the situation the way they do can be very fruitful at the beginning of an organizational change project.

In the Project Excellence organizational change project, the design of the assignment is based on a combination of the maturity analysis and management's wishes. The project is broken down into the model's work streams, as illustrated in Figure 10.27.

10.6.3. The project management model and language

Common work form
An important work stream in this process is establishing a common understanding within the organization with regard to project work. The organization must operate within the same conceptual framework.

It is therefore necessary to develop a project management model that is underpinned by relevant tools and methods. In the past, this would have taken the form of a project manual and toolbox. Today, it is designed as a project portal where you can 'click' your way to the project management model

10.6. Development of the organization toward Project Excellence

and 'link' to the various process descriptions and tools, which are available as electronic templates.

IT support is another major area. The project portal isn't the only place where support is needed; there is also the whole process of collecting project data, time registration and financial data. We need to figure out how data can be transferred from the projects to the financial management system and vice-versa, how project-relevant information can be extracted from the financial management system. And so forth.

Any use of electronic project management tools, such as MS Project, Primavera, Arthemis, Timeline, Timelog, etc., also needs to be defined. What is relevant for use? And is it possible to transfer the data to other systems?

10.6.4. Organization of the project work form

The organization needs to change so that it can handle project assignments. This includes establishment of a decision-making structure for portfolio management. Who should be part of the senior portfolio management? Which programs should there be?

Who does what?

You need to decide whether the project managers are to be brought in from the departments on an ad hoc basis or whether to establish a project manager team that reports to a project director. Where do the project participants come from? Should the departmental structure be retained? Or should the departments be dismantled and replaced by resource pools?

These decisions depend on the volume of the project assignments in relation to the operational tasks, i.e. how far to the right the organization has moved in Figure 10.4. The physical conditions need to be adjusted, depending on the organizational solution. A project-oriented organization requires more conference rooms and the staff in the various project teams need to be able to move around if they are to work together in the same space (as a project team should).

The PMO needs to be established and staffed. The PMO is the 'line organization' that will carry on the Project Excellence process once the project is complete and the consultants have gone home.

10.6.5. Competence, behavior and attitudes

How do we go about it?

Training and development of the project managers is an important work stream, as they are the ones who will follow through on the projects. This generally entails extended training programs related to the projects being carried out. The training is often combined with personal coaching, allowing the project managers to put theory into practice.

Part of the training is management training aimed at changing the individual's behavior. This type of training is characterized by less complex theory and a greater focus on exercises and practice – just like learning to play the guitar. It's not something you learn by reading a book. A growing number of project managers conclude this training with an internationally recognized certification program, either via the American Project Management Institute (PMI) or the European program, the International Project Management Association (IPMA) or PRINCE2.

Project managers need to know how to lead a project, but it is just as important that managers and management can function in their roles as steering committee members and program managers. And this entails providing training and competence development to the manager team.

The middle management team, in particular, tends to be skeptical of the introduction of the project work form, because it delegates power to the project managers. Power is shifted from the departments over to the projects – that's the whole purpose!

Many middle managers don't realize, however, that this change will create exciting new assignments for them, for instance in program management and on steering committees. Finally, it's important that the individual employee be given training in the project management model and the tools. The aim is to establish a common language, but that can't be achieved if this 'language' is only spoken by the project managers.

10.6.6. Pilot projects

We had better test to see if it works!

Once the project management model and tools have been defined, one or more pilot projects can be conducted before rolling out the work form to the entire organization. It is good form to reduce uncertainty in projects by conducting tests early in the project process – this also applies to organizational change projects. In connection with the implementation of pilot projects, coaching project managers, program managers and steering committee members is an important activity, as everyone is in a learning process. The project management methods and organization can also be tested in a single program before rolling out the work form to all the programs in the organization.

10.6.7. Management by objectives and auditing

Once the project management model and processes have been implemented, the PMO can conduct audits of the projects, program management and steering committees. In its simplest form, this auditing can consist of checking whether procedures are being followed. Has a plan been prepared according to agreement? Has a risk analysis been conducted? And so on. In combination with forward-looking coaching, this audit process establishes a well-defined method within the organization.

We measure the impact

What is excellent today may be mediocre tomorrow. It is therefore important to measure the project organization's performance. It is a good idea to benchmark the projects and programs, as well as conduct comparisons with other sectors and organizations.

Thus, measurement in projects and portfolio management is a vital activity. The initial aim is to determine whether the Project Excellence process achieved the expected results, but it is also to achieve lasting excellence. The measurements can be compiled in a project scorecard.

10.6.8. Make the project organization lean – LEAN project management

All organizations face increasing demands for efficient operations and constant change. Many organizations have therefore worked systematically to make their production and administration more 'lean'. Similarly, much has been done to increase organizations' adaptability by developing the project work form.

Some organizations have adopted a conscious strategy to free up resources from the line organization with the help of LEAN principles in order to use them in project work and thereby secure the long-term development of the organization.

Many organizations even advertise how many resources they devote to development. However, the value of the development function is not determined by the amount of resources consumed by the projects, but by the results actually achieved.

The time has now come to think in terms of LEAN project execution.

LEAN comprises five fundamental principles, which, when applied to the project work form, have the following content:

1. Identify customer value
In project work, this is done by means of focusing on important value-generating deliverables in the projects and a very precise definition of the project objective based on the customers' needs.

To make the project organization LEAN, it is also important on portfolio level to execute extremely consistent prioritization of the projects to be carried out – the few, but key projects that generate value and underpin the organization's strategy.

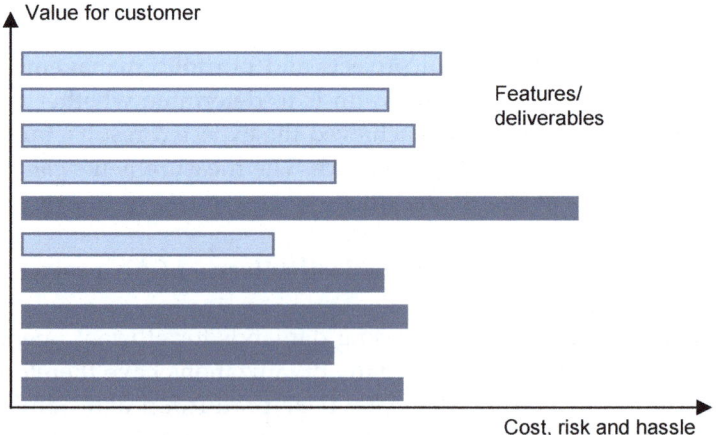

Figure 10.28. Project specifications should be focused on that which gives the customers value. This is achieved by devoting resources in the earliest phases of the project to customer and stakeholder analysis (front loading the project).

When working with projects, customer value is secured by focusing on impact measurement within the projects.

A focused portfolio, as illustrated in Figure 10.17, should be established and the project descriptions should be simple so that you only deliver exactly what the customers and stakeholders consider most important.

Remember, there is no correlation between the value the customer gains from the deliverables and the hassle the deliverables cause during the project. Product properties that generate little value can cause a good deal of hassle.

Implement a consistent prioritization of what should be included in the project. The black deliverables will have to wait until the next project. The 'perfect' solution is often not the optimal business case.

2. Create value streams
Projects can be broken down into value streams (work streams) that form a concrete starting point for the project's objective.

The projects are front loaded, i.e. a good deal of resources are consumed in the beginning to plan the entire project, not just the product.

Visual planning is used with the involvement of key stakeholders and focusing on value-generating main deliverables. See Figures 5.11-5.13 in Chapter 5.

3. Create flow without stops
Flow is created in projects by introducing takt and rhythm in the project portfolio. This is done by means of a very strict prioritization of the projects so that only a few projects are executed simultaneously – in return, they have short lead times.

Working with few projects with fixed handover days enables consistent staffing, preferably with employees allocated full time to the projects and using the best project managers.

Fixed deadlines ensure management focus. Establish several portfolios with different paces. Define smaller projects and use program management for coordination.

Fixed deadlines require detailed planning in the beginning of the project.

Chapter 10. Project Governance. Management of multiple projects

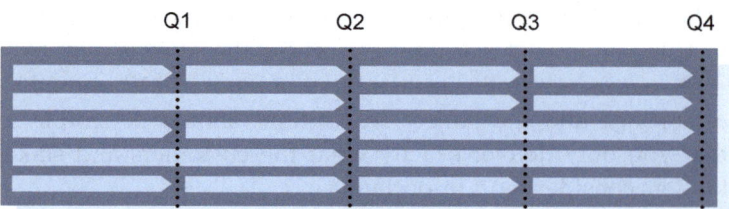

Figure 10.29. Create takt and rhythm in the project portfolio with fixed deadlines. Work with short lead times of three and six months. Establish several portfolios with different paces.

4. Introduce new guiding principles
One of the most important new guiding principles is the introduction of takt and rhythm in the project portfolio. For this to work, however, there must be takt in the output of the projects, which requires timeboxing as a guiding principle.

Add resources to the project when tasks are delayed. Only use employees who are allocated full time to project work. Establish the team. Measure whether the team achieves the milestones and whether management has allocated the necessary resources.

5. Do kaizen every week and work in sprints
Conduct a visual planning process within the project team once a week. The weekly re-planning provides a shared over-

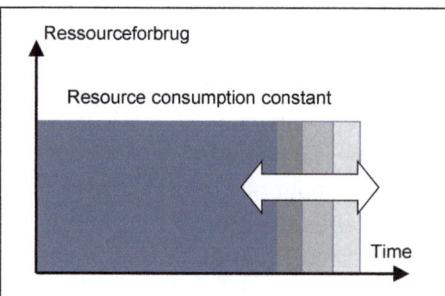
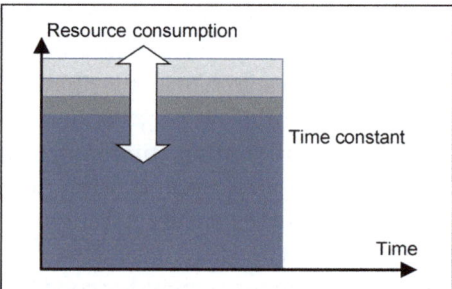

Figure10.30. Use timeboxing – the exam principle. The task should be carried out within the set timeframe. Sometimes the outcome will be average; other times it will be outstanding. However, the assignment must always be completed with 'passed'. To focus on output, visual plans are used, which are prepared by the project team.

view, instills a sense of obligation and enables process adjustments (project kaizen).

During these weekly workshops, the process and results should be evaluated and all necessary adjustments to performance should be made. Continuous follow-up is also carried out on milestones, resource deployment and impact.
- Measure the milestone production – have we achieved the milestones according to plan for the period? This is the project manager's and project team's responsibility.

- Measure the resource deployment – have we received resources according to plan for the period? This is management's responsibility.
- Continuous impact review – what is our assessment of the progress on the success criteria? See Figures 10.25 and 10.26.

Ten good initiatives
We have worked with these five LEAN principles in project work for many years. Based on this experience, we have defined 10 operational commandments for LEAN project management. These 10 commandments describe the initiatives that we believe are needed to achieve LEAN project management.

The 10 commandments for LEAN project management
1. Establish a focused portfolio
2. Create takt and rhythm in the portfolio
3. Assign only full-time allocated employees to projects
4. Focus the project scope – only do what is required
5. Use timeboxing and short lead times (sprints)
6. Front loading – deploy a great deal of resources at project start-up
7. Use visual planning
8. Measure milestone production and resource deployment
9. Conduct regular impact reviews
10. Use project kaizen

10.7. Reflections on project governance and the project work form

Think about your own organization or a project you are involved in:

- What is the correlation between your project and the organization's strategy or policy?
- What might a project model for your project look like – what phases would it comprise?
- Is your project part of a program? And what are the dependencies?
- Are parallel projects carried out that could be part of the same program as your project? What would be the advantages of this?
- Which project methods and tools are lacking in your daily project management?
- Is it possible to work in cross-organizational teams? And who does the team report to?
- Do you have an agreement with your superior regarding the amount of time you are expected to devote to the project?
- Does everyone who works on the project have a 'resource agreement' – a formal agreement on resource consumption?
- How often are projects shut down in your organization?
- Who prioritizes the projects? And who do you think would be best for the job?
- How are projects in your organization evaluated?
- Which services would you like a project management office to provide to your project?
- Which criteria can be used to prioritize the type of projects you work on? What makes your project important to the organization?
- Which types of projects are carried out in your organization?
- What do you think a maturity analysis of your organization would show?

- If a health check were conducted of your project, what do you think it would reveal?
- If you wanted to improve your organization's ability to execute projects, which work streams in the Project Excellence model would it be most important to take action on?

Bibliography

International

Beck, Kent (2000): Extreme Programming Explained. Embrace Change. Addison-Wesley.
Belbin, R. Meredith (1981): management Teams: Why They Succeed or Fail. Butterworth & Heinemann.
Briner, Wendy, Colin Hastings og Michael Geddes (1996): Project Leadership. Grower.
Buttrick, Robert (1997): The Project Workout. A toolkit for reaping the rewards from all your business projects. Pitmann Publishing.
Conner, Daryl R. (1993): Managing at the Speed of Change. Villard Books.
Cooper, R. G., S. J. Edgett og E. J. Kleinschmidt (2001): Portfolio Management for New Products. McMaster University.
Cooper, Robert G. (1993): Winning at New Products. Accelerating the Process from Idea to Launch. Second Edition. Addison Wesley.
Covey, Stephen R. (1990): The 7 Habits of Highly Effective People. Published by Fireside Books, New York.
Delong, Thomas J., Gabarro, John J. & Lees, Robert J., (2007): When Professionals Have to Lead. Harvard Business School Press.
Flyvbjerg, Bent m.fl. (2003): Megaproject and Risk. Cambridge University Press.
Goleman, Daniel (2000): Working with Emotional Intelligence. Bantam.
Grundy, Tony & Brown, Laura (2004): Strategic Project Management – Creating Organizational Breakthroughs. Thomson.
Hagemann, Gisela (1993): Die Hohe Schule der Motivation. Verlag Moderne Industrie.
Harvard Business Essentials, (2004) Managing Projects Large and Small. Harvard Business School Press.
Haugland, Cato, Tore Gjøs, Steinar Hagen, Aage Ronningen, Knut Samset, Eli Sletten, Inger Stoll og Anne Strand (1990): The Logical Framework Approach (LFA). Handbook for Objectives-Oriented Planning. Second Edition. NORAD – Norwegian Agency for Development Cooperation.
IPMA, (2009): Competencies in Project management, National Competence Baseline for Scandinavia. IPMA.
Kotter, John P. (1997): Leading Change. Havard Business School Press.
Kotter, John P. (2008): A Sense of Urgency. Havard Business Press.

Kræmmer, Michael & Divert, Henriette, (2009) Change & Effect. Implement Press.

Loehr, Jim & Schwartz, (2005), The Power og Full Engagement. The Free Press.

Nordström, Kjell A. & Ridderstråle, Jonas, (2007): Funky Business Forever – woe to Enjoy Capitalism. Book House Publishing Sweden AB.

Olsson, John Ryding (1996): Manual on market research and analysis. TASIC Services DG IA. European Commission.

Pinto, Jeffrey K. (1996): Power and Politics in Project Management. Project Management Institute PMI, USA.

PMBOK Guide, (2001): A Guide to the Project Management Body of Knowledge. PMI.

Sarpathy, Tridibesh, (2013): A Guide to the Scrum Body of Knowledge (Sbok Guide). Scrumstudy.

Shaw, Patricia (2002): Changing Conversations in Organizations – A Complexity Approach to Change. Taylor & Francis Ltd.

Snowden, David, (1999): Story telling: an old skill in a new context. Business Information Review 16(1) March 1999.

Stark Jr, George & M. Hout, Thomas, (1990) Competing Against Time. The Free Press.

Stacey, Ralph. (2010): Strategic Management and Organisational Dynamics – The challenge and Complexity. Pearson Education Limited.

Sull, Donald Normann, (2009): The Upside of Turbulence. Harper Collins Publishers.

TSO, (2011) MSP: Managing Successful Programmes.

TSO, (2007) MOR: Management of risk: Guidance for Practitioners.

TSO, (2009) Managing Successful Projects with PRINCE2. TSO.

Turner, J. Rodney (1993): The Handbook of Project Management. McGraw Hill.

Turner, J. Rodney, Kristoffer V. Grude og Lynn Thurloway (1996): The Project Manager as Change Agent. Leadership, influence and negotiation. McGraw-Hill Publishing Company.

Verma, Vijay K. (1995): Human Ressource Skills for the Project Manager. Public Management Institute, Inc.

Wheelwright, S. C. og K. B. Clark (1992): Revolutionising Product Development. The Free Press.

Windahl, Sven m.fl. (1992): Using Communication Theory. An introduction to Planned Communication. Sage Publications.

Scandinavian

Andersen, Erling S., Kristoffer V. Grude og Tor Haug (2004): Målrettet Prosjektstyring. NKI Forlaget. (Norsk).
Andersen, Ole Steen (2000): At gøre en forskel. Professionel forandringsledelse. Børsens Forlag A/S.
Andersen, Ole Steen, Niels Ahrengot og John Ryding Olsen (2002): Aktiv Projektledelse. Mål. Milepæle. Mennesker. Børsen Bøger.
Belbin, R. Meredith (1982). Belbin. Ledelsesgrupper. Betingelser for succes eller fiasko. Børsens Forlag A/S.
Bendixen, Jan og Ole Steen Andersen (1995): Forandringsledelse. Kommunikation, adfærd og samarbejde. Børsen Bøger.
Blaabjerg, Aksel og Poul Erik Graversen (1988): Det irrationelle element. Mennesket i organisationen. Forlaget Kaalbye.
Bono, Edward de (1993): Tænk kreativt. Engagement, humor og perception. Børsen Bøger.
Børsens ledelseshåndbog: Projektledelse. Børsen Forum A/S 2000. Redaktion Implement Consulting Group P/S.
Christensen, Søren og Kristian Kreiner (1996): Projektledelse i løst koblede systemer – ledelse og læring i en ufuldkommen verden. Jurist- og Økonomforbundets Forlag.
Collins, Jim (2002): Good to Great. Børsens Forlag A/S.
Conger, Jay A. (2000): Overbevis dem! Lademann.
Covey, Stephen (2003): 7 gode vaner. Schultz.
Dahl, Henrik (1993): Har du overvejet at ændre hele dit liv? Studier i den uopfordrede henvendelses teori og praksis. Artikel i Sociologi nr. 1, 4. årgang.
Dahl, Henrik (1997): Hvis din nabo var en bil. Akademisk Forlag.
Dalsgaard, Lone og Jan Bendix (1996): Netværksorganisering. Etablering og ledelse af netværk som ny organisationsform. Børsen Bøger.
Evan-Jones, John (1997): Præsentationsteknik. Få gennemslagskraft som taler. Børsens Forlag A/S.
Goleman, Daniel (2000): Følelsernes intelligens. Borgen.
Hein, Lars og Mogens Myrup Andreasen (1985): Integreret Produktudvikling. Jernets Arbejdsgiverforening.
Hein-Sørensen, Tune (2000): Den kompetente virksomhed. Børsens Forlag A/S.
Jensen, Rolf (1999): The Dream Society: Hvordan det kommende skift fra facts til følelser vil påvirke erhvervslivet og vor hverdag. Jyllands-Postens Erhvervsbøger.
Kirkegaard, Lars, John Ryding Olsson og Peter Aagaard Nielsen (1996): Produktudvikling. Med Bang & Olufsen som eksempel. Børsen Bøger.
Koch, Jørgen (2001): Projektstyring med Project 2000. IDG Danmark A/S.

Kotter, John P. (1997): I spidsen for forandringer. Industriens Forlag.
Kotter, John P. (2001): Hvorfor forandringer mislykkes. Børsens Projektledelseshåndbog.
Larsen, Mogens Holten og Majken Schultz (1998): Den udtryksfulde virksomhed. Bergsøe 4 A/S.
Lennéer-Axelson, Barbro og Ingela Thyelfors (1998): Om konflikter – hjemme og på arbejdet. Hans Reitzels Forlag.
Lennéer-Axelson, Barbro og Ingela Thyelfors (1993): Arbejdsgruppens psykologi. Hans Reitzels Forlag.
Levine, Harvey A. (2001): Behov for et projektkontor. Børsens projektledelseshåndbog.
Lichtenberg, Steen (1990): Projektplanlægning – i en foranderlig verden. Polyteknisk Forlag.
Mikkelsen, Gunni F. H. (1999): Styring af teambuilding. Sådan opnår virksomheden resultatrige erfaringer med teambuilding. Børsens Forlag A/S.
Mikkelsen, Hans og Jens O. Riis (1996): Grundbog i projektledelse. Forlaget Promet.
Olsson, John Ryding (1998): Projektlederens værktøjskasse. Implement Consulting Group P/S.
Payne, John og Shirley Payne (2000): Giv slip – Lær at uddelegere ansvar. Lademann. (Dansk oversættelse af Hanne Jul-Rasmussen).
Petersen, Helle (2002): Forandringskommunikation. Samfundslitteratur.
Rees, David, Rodney Turner og Mahen Tampoe (2001): Projektlederen som forandringsagent – leder eller chef. I Børsens projektledelseshåndbog.
Sehested, Claus & Sonnenberg, Henrik, (2009): Lean Innovation. Børsens Forlag.
Unt, Iwar (1998): Forhandlingsteknik. Børsens Forlag A/S. (Bearbejdning og dansk oversættelse af Keld Jensen).
Vinje, Poul Staal (1997): Projektledelse af systemudvikling. Ingeniøren I Bøger.
Voxted, Søren m.fl. (2003): Viden og Forandring. Gyldendal.
Wenell, Torbjörn (2001): Wenell om projekt. Uppsala Publishing House AB.
Whitmore, John (1998): Coaching på jobbet. Peter Asschenfeldts nye forlag.

Index

A

Acceptance 89, 97, 112, 151
Accumulated costs 250
Action lists 68
Activities 152, 153, 156, 158, 163
Actual Cost of Work Performed 251
Actual delay 237
Ad hoc meetings 255
Ad hoc tasks 51
Adjourning phase 335
Agent of change 269
Agile project management 42
Allocate resources 212
Ambassadors 304
Analysis phase 160
Appreciation 351
Appreciative questions 356
Approach 248
Attitudes 338
Authenticity 270
Authority 321
Awareness 285, 311

B

Balance 409
Balanced Scorecard 417
Behavior 135, 285, 295, 297, 420
Behavioral change 269
Benefits 261, 385, 394, 395
Benefits tracking 394
Big Bang 271
Blueprint 394, 395
Brainstorming 258
Branding 290, 295
Budgeted Cost of Work Performed 251
Budgeted Cost of Work Scheduled 251
Bureaucracy 27
Burning platform 71, 267, 269, 293, 303
Business case 94, 199, 392
Business change manager 393, 394
Business insight 270

C

Career development 400
Cascade implementation 272
Certification program 428
Change 301
Change agents 305
Change communication 302
Change process 303
Changes to the contract 246
Changing behavior 71, 420
Changing the plan 246
Clarifying questions 254
Clear profile 287
Clear-cut message 367
Close-knit team 323
Coaching 317, 344, 348, 354
Coaching question 367
Collaboration 228
Collaborative partners 70
Commitment 97, 112, 238
Common language 379, 411, 412, 428
Communication 71, 136, 150, 257, 265, 269, 271, 273, 274, 275, 281, 302, 304, 311, 331
Communication needs 277, 278
Communication plan 278, 283
Competences 122, 325

441

Completion phase 233
Complexity 119
Concept development 64
Concept testing 65
Concurrent engineering 416
Conduct meetings 228
Conference rooms 427
Conflict management 318, 332, 357
Conflicts 332, 337, 339, 357, 366
Conflicts of interest 363
Conflicts of value/opinion 363
Conflicts that escalate 361
Contracts 60, 93, 99, 245
Coordination 150, 255, 379
Coordinators 319
Costs 250
Costs per milestone 250
CPM: Critical Path Method 30
Creative objective-setting 103, 104
Creative techniques 258
Credibility 121, 276
Crisis seminar 172
Criteria for urgency 405, 406
Critical path 151, 163, 178
Cultivate relations 122
Culture 331
Culture bearer 332
Customer collaboration 66
Customer satisfaction 126
Customer value 430
Customers' needs 430

D
De Bono's thinking hats 259
Deadline 93, 113, 158
Decision 385
Decision log 247
Decision paper 260
Decision point 64, 152, 413
Decision-making 150, 212, 402, 427

Decision-making meeting 161, 256, 260
Decision-making process 274
Decisions 161, 214
Dedicated project days 241
Delayed 199
Delegate 158, 343
Deliver on time culture 237
Deliverables 89, 91, 92, 95, 98, 102, 109, 119, 152, 155, 417
Demographic data 135
Departments 211
Dependencies 152, 158
Design phase 160
Desired changes 419
Desired image 289
Desired impact 270, 417, 419
Development phases 336
Dialog 233, 245, 261, 354
Difficult message 368
Discourse 279
Disruption 297
Distribution of responsibility 379
Domino implementation 271
Dupont pyramid 417

E
Earned Value method 250
Education 274
Emotional needs 292
Empathy 325
Energy 340
Engaging stories 292
Engineering and construction projects 58, 59
Enthusiasts 298
Establishing relations 338
Estimating 152, 190, 252
Ethos 292
Expectations 125, 291, 326, 338
Extreme programming 37

F
Facilitate dialog 254

Index

Facilitator *300*
Feedback *300, 318, 340, 343, 344, 345, 346, 347*
Feedback culture *347*
Feedback loops *305*
Few projects *410, 431*
Fire at random *279*
Flow without stops *431*
Focus groups *223, 307, 311*
Focused portfolio *410, 411, 431, 433*
Follow up *151, 157, 158, 227, 228, 230, 232, 234, 235, 239, 240, 250, 334, 335, 382, 385, 391*
Forming phase *330*
Frequently Asked Questions (FAQ) *304*
Front loading *431, 433*
Full-time allocated *433*
Future delay *237*

G

Gantt chart *157*
Gate models *64*
GO, WAIT, STOP *180*
GO/NO GO decision *64*
Goodwill *122*
Ground rules *332, 339*
Group dynamics *31, 328*
Group work *104*

H

Health check *405*
Hearing committees *74, 76, 211, 216, 221, 222, 300*
Hidden resistance *299*
High-performance team *329*
Hypothesis *69*

I

Idea generation meeting *256, 258*
Impact *91, 92, 102, 245, 270, 393*
Impact measurement *378, 417, 424*
Impact reviews *433*
Implementation *393*
Implementation phase *161*
Influence *118, 128, 171, 185, 266, 323, 345*
Information *278*
Information meeting *217*
Integrity *270*
Intensity *240*
Interdisciplinary *53*
International Project Management Association *428*
Intimacy *122*
Investment *408*
Involvement *257, 268, 302, 330*
Involvement meetings *256, 257*
IPMA *428*
Issue lists *181*
IT and systems development projects *58, 65*
Iterative process *66*

J

Job interviews *325*
Joint agreement *367*
Journey of change *268*

K

Key milestones *70, 393*
Kick-off meeting *171*
Kick-off seminar *104*
Knowledge-sharing *252*

L

Lead times *34, 410*
Leader *317, 320*
Leadership *83, 147, 317, 319, 321, 322, 340, 344, 348*
LEAN *430*

443

LEAN project
    management *45, 425, 429,*
    433
Learning *97, 236*
Learning organization *37*
Learning process *66, 429*
Legitimacy *137*
Level of ambition *248*
Likelihood *196*
Likely guess *191*
Lobbying *97, 216, 254, 261*
Logical Framework Approach
    (LFA) *414*
Logistics *60*
Logos *292*
Long term *110*
Long-term development *430*
Long-term objectives *409*
Look back *98*
Looking outward *126*
Looking upward *93, 125*

M
Manage resources *242*
Management reporting *240*
Management style *328, 349*
Management tasks *230*
Managing stakeholders *117*
Mandate *203*
Master project plan *166*
Matrix organization *28*
Maturity *426*
Maturity analysis *426*
Mean value *191, 192*
Measureable *112*
Measuring impact *420, 422*
Measuring progress *389*
Measuring system *423*
Mediation *367, 369*
Medium term *110*
Meeting *253, 254*
Meeting facilitation *252*
Meeting forums *402*
Meeting frequency *255*
Meeting plan *239*
Meeting structure *402*

Meeting types *255*
Megascale project *62*
Mental attitude *349*
Message *284*
Message needs *284*
Messenger *284*
Metaphors *293*
Middle managers *78*
Milestone plan *229*
Milestone production *433*
Milestones *152, 155, 156, 158,*
    233
Minimize resistance *283*
Minutes of decisions *254*
Misunderstandings *363*
Mitigation *200*
Monitoring *230*
Motivating factor *234*
Motivating objective *96*
Motivation *95, 317, 334, 335,*
    339, 340, 344, 408
Multiple *377*
Multi-trade consortia *60*

N
Natural uncertainties *185*
Needs assessment *31, 64, 65*
Negotiate *190*
Network communication *305*
Networking *120*
Norming phase *333*
Norms *60, 333*

O
Objective *89, 92, 229*
Objective breakdown
    structure *89, 152*
Objective-setting *98, 99, 102*
Obligation *238, 243*
OBS: Objective Breakdown
    Structure *103, 105, 152, 423*
Open resistance *299*
Opinions *295*
Opinion-shaping *269*
Optimistic guess *191*
Organization *209, 212*

Organizational change 267
Organizational change
    projects 58, 70
Organizational diagram 210
Organizing 153, 158
Output 152

P
Pace 240
Pace change 171
Participant introductions 338
Passion 340
Pathos 292
Payback time 244
Perfectionism 242
Performing phase 334
Personal consequences 293
Personal dialog 284
Personal plan 167
Personal skills 325
Personal values 358
PERT: Program Evaluation
    and Review Technique 30
Pessimistic guess 191
Phase plan 166
Phase start-up 172
Phase transition 161
Phases 152, 159
Pilot project 269, 428
Plan 149, 233, 245
Plan B 201
Planning 148, 149
Planning workshop 168, 170,
    331, 337, 341, 358
Planning Workshop 168
PMO 398
Policy development
    projects 58, 73
Political 'fit' 409
Political flair 74
Political process 71
Portfolio management 83,
    246, 377, 385, 387, 388, 390,
    398, 399, 408, 413, 414, 427
Portfolio overview 382, 399,
    406

Post-its 104, 139
Power 209, 428
Power hierarchy 334
Power struggles 222, 331,
    357, 363
Praise 342, 348
Pre-defined phases 412
Preferences 325
Prevention 200
PRINCE2 414, 428
Prioritization 82, 431
Prioritization of projects 377,
    391, 402, 404, 408
Prioritizes resource 379
Problem-dependent
    activities 188
Procedure-dependent
    activities 188
Process descriptions 427
Process-dependent
    activities 187, 189
Product manager 392
Professional development 96
Professional expertise 325
Profiling 290
Prognosis 386
Program board 391, 394
Program governance 394
Program management 83,
    388, 392, 395, 399, 428
Program manager 378, 391,
    394
Program organization 393
Program owner 391, 394
Programs 377, 381
Progress 234
Project audits 400
Project brand 265, 288
Project branding 287, 306
Project budget 250
Project core team 219
Project costs 244
Project culture 360
Project department 78
Project description 246
Project director 393, 399

Project end *110*
Project estimates *397*
Project Excellence *377, 425, 429*
Project governance *377, 378, 379*
Project list *382, 384, 399, 405*
Project log *196, 247*
Project Management Institute (PMI) *428*
Project management model *389, 412, 413, 426, 429*
Project management office (PMO) *378, 398*
Project manager *213, 216, 219, 330, 336, 378, 388, 396*
Project manuals *399*
Project model *379, 398, 412, 413, 415*
Project name *291*
Project organization *209, 210, 213, 218, 387*
Project owner *98, 209, 213, 214, 216*
Project pipeline *391*
Project portal *427*
Project portfolio *81, 82, 377, 379, 381, 404*
Project process *381, 389, 399*
Project progress *250*
Project risks *249*
Project room *241, 342*
Project scope *433*
Project scorecard *429*
Project sponsor *209*
Project start-up *258*
Project status *236*
Project team *209, 217, 219, 222, 325*
Project triangle *93, 215*
Project types *57, 59, 378, 382, 388*
Project volume *377, 387, 398, 410*
Project work *51*

Project-oriented organization *81, 83, 425*
Promote awareness *283*
Prototype *64*
Public relations *287*
Purpose *89, 91, 95, 98, 102, 103, 110, 119*

Q
Quality *151*
Quantitative measurements *417*

R
R&D projects *58, 63, 415*
Rate of progress *250*
Realistic *89, 112*
Realistic objective *96*
Recommendations *402*
Recruiting *323*
Reference groups *74, 76, 216*
Reflection *351, 352*
Regulations *60*
Relations *120, 121*
Reliability *122*
Reporting requirements *412*
Research and technology development projects *58, 69*
Resistance to change mapping *300*
Resistant to change *296, 298, 299, 300*
Resource agreements *326, 337, 342, 398*
Resource allocation *190, 378, 397*
Resource consumption *386, 387*
Resource contracts *167*
Resource deployment *433*
Resource pools *397*
Resource-dependent activities *187, 189*
Resources *58, 214, 248*
Respect *319, 351*

446

Responsibility *96, 153, 171, 209, 211*
Re-start *171*
Results paths *153*
Reviews *70, 236, 394*
Rewards *342*
Right people *275*
Right resources *57*
Risk acceptance *249*
Risk analysis *152, 195, 196, 197, 283, 358*
Risk level *386*
Risk ranking *198, 405*
Risks *202, 385*
Roles *211, 379*
Rule-based management *27*
Rumors *296*

S

Sales concept *65*
Satisfaction surveys *420*
Scope *126, 170*
Scrum *42*
S-curve *250*
Segmentation *64, 132, 134*
Senior management *390*
Senior responsible manager *391*
Senior responsible owner *394*
Separation of powers *221*
Short lead times *240, 410, 431*
Short meetings *254*
Show interest *343*
Situation-based management *232*
Six types of projects *49, 58*
Small talk *121*
SMART *111*
SMART objective *89*
Social relations *252*
Solution interview *367, 368*
Specializations *211*
Sponsoring group *393*
Spread *191, 192*
Sprints *432*
Staff training *268*

Stage gate *64, 179*
Stage gate models *179*
Stakeholder analysis *118, 127, 130, 295, 358*
Stakeholder group *282*
Stakeholder identification *117*
Stakeholder management *74, 120*
Stakeholder prioritization *117*
Stakeholder segmentation *134, 136*
Stakeholders *58, 71, 117, 121, 123, 212, 265, 270, 273, 280, 288, 299*
Standardization *28*
Start-up meeting *278*
Start-up phase *233, 322*
Start-up seminar *171*
Steering *227, 228, 230, 243, 247*
Steering committee *83, 98, 161, 214, 215, 216, 222, 388, 428*
Steering committee meetings *239, 260*
Steering quality, time and resources *243*
Steering risk and impact *244*
Steering routines *232*
Step-by-step change *272*
Stories *296*
Storming phase *332, 357*
Storytelling *292, 295, 306*
Strategic communication *265*
Strategic fit *408, 409*
Strategic focus *378*
Strategic importance *382, 385*
Strategic objectives *418*
Strategic projects *390*
Strategy *149, 377, 381, 392, 403, 404*
Strategy processes *404*
Structured design *32*
Subcontractors *228*

447

Sub-project managers 219
Success criteria 89, 91, 98, 102, 110, 119, 395, 407, 417, 419, 421
Successive calculation 178, 193, 194, 195
Successive planning 32
Superusers 69
Support 276
Surroundings 58
Survey 420

T
Takt and rhythm 431, 432, 433
Target group 269, 279, 284, 306, 312
Target group segmentation 65
Targeted communication 275, 277
Task management 56
Tasks and projects 50
Team building 97, 171, 328, 330, 331, 336, 337, 358
Team composition 221
Team Constitution 318, 337, 339
Team development 328
Team meetings 157, 239, 255
Team member 326
Team size 219
Team spirit 328
Team welcome 334
Teamwork 325
Technology development 64
Temporary organization 55
Test 420
Testing schedule 69
Three-point estimation 178, 191
Time-bound 112, 113

Timeboxing 238, 242, 432, 433
Timeframe 158
Timing 286
Toolbox 389
Traffic lights 385
Training 69, 71, 274
Training program 420
Trend curves 250
Troubleshooting meeting 172, 256, 259
Trust 122, 171, 345, 351
Type of conflict 362
Types of projects 381

U
Uncertainty 53, 184, 190, 194
Uniform templates 412
Urgency 267, 294, 295
Urgency of change 269
Urgency scale 407

V
Value 408
Value streams 431
Value-based management 37
Vision 91, 292, 294
Vision for change 267
Visual planning 431, 432, 433

W
Waterfall charts 66
WBS: Work Breakdown Structure 103, 153
Win-win philosophy 122
Win-win situation 368
Work process 249
Work streams 83, 152, 153, 155, 159, 218, 431
Working plans 166
Work-life balance 125
Workload 124
Workshops 167, 171, 241